BASE
NATION

BASE NATION

HOW U.S. MILITARY BASES ABROAD HARM AMERICA AND THE WORLD

DAVID VINE

FOREWORD BY SIMON WINCHESTER

Skyhorse Publishing

First Skyhorse Publishing edition 2017

Foreword © 2017 by Simon Winchester

Visit our website at www.skyhorsepublishing.com.

10 9 8 7 6 5 4 3 2

Library of Congress Cataloging-in-Publication Data is available on file.

The author will donate all proceeds from the book's royalties to nonprofit organizations serving military veterans, their families, and other victims of war and violence.

For an updated list of U.S. military bases abroad, see: http://dx.doi.org/10.17606/M6H599

Maps by Kelly Martin Design
Designed by Kelly S. Too

Cover design by Rain Saukas
Cover photo credit: AP Images

Print ISBN: 978-1-5107-2881-3

Printed in the United States of America

This book is dedicated
to the memory of my grandparents,
Tea Eichengruen Stiefel and Master Sergeant Erwin Stiefel and
Gloria Simon Vine and Lieutenant Colonel Theodore Roosevelt Vine,
and to the memory of
U.S. Army Specialist Russell E. Madden,
who died of combat injuries in Afghanistan, June 23, 2010

A residential neighborhood for U.S. military personnel and their families at U.S. Naval Station Guantánamo Bay, Cuba.

CONTENTS

PART V: CHOICES

Foreword

The true nature of the hundreds of American overseas bases can present a troubling enigma. Do they constitute 1) an overwhelmingly comforting presence, all bubble gum and apple pie, 2) an American-taxpayer-funded guarantee of peace, security, and freedom for which all so protected should be grateful, or 3) are they an existential threat, an affront to local sovereignty and an unseemly reminder of postwar American corporate imperialism?

The readiest answer from the policymakers in Washington is that offered up to anyone who manages to win access to the Operations Room of U.S. Pacific Command, deep in the heart of Camp H. M. Smith outside Honolulu. There, young naval officers, all white clad and ocean-tanned and armed with impeccable manners, will dim the lights, switch on the projector, and present with practiced ease a slideshow that will convince even the most skeptical that theirs is a mission devoted to creating and maintaining all for the best in the best of all possible worlds.

The show usually begins with a monochrome picture of Seoul in the winter of 1953—ruined buildings, scarecrow-like figures pushing handcarts through a blasted Arctic landscape, a wailing and ill-nourished child clinging to its mother's arms. You consider the image for five seconds—and then up comes the next, in color: Seoul today, gleaming ziggurats of neon and prosperity, crowded freeways, contented crowds in fashionable beachwear lazing on the grassy banks of the Han River,

the nearby coffee shops doing a bustling trade, the internet lights wink-
ing in broadband heaven.

Much the same is then shown for Tokyo, Manila, and Shanghai, then
and now, hardscrabble poverty on the one hand, happy thousands on
the other, purses, stomachs, and minds all amply filled. It continues for
cities farther afield: Bombay and Jaipur, Bangkok and Jakarta, Auck-
land, Port Moresby and Melbourne. All places now fully recovered from
the scourges of conflict or history or occupation or just a pathological
lack, a want of some ineffable something.

After which comes the drumroll, and the images suddenly switch
their tone and pace: now the young sailors are showing pictures of sleek
American warships gliding through Hockney-blue lagoon waters, of
U.S. marines helicoptering aid to the survivors of a tropical cyclone, of
soldiers from Texas or Montana or New York downing K-rations in
some lonely jungle outpost and keeping an insurrection at bay, the local
people safe and sound in their longhouses or their newly made suburban condominiums.

Then the lights go up and the script begins. Without our presence,
secured by treaties here since the end of the last war, the cities you have
seen—Tokyo to Bombay to Nanjing and Perth—would never have come
to enjoy the prosperity and liberty they now take for granted. Our mission here is clear: our presence is demanded; our effect unquestioned,
profound, and beneficial.

And yet. And yet. Time and again, in my own long wanderings
around the Pacific and Indian and Atlantic Oceans, from my own mem-
ories of years spent in Europe and on the Indian subcontinent and in
China and her neighbors, I have to wonder if such assurances, so confi-
dently expressed and so arrogantly assumed, have quite as much basis in
fact as their slick presentations suggest.

I remember quite vividly, for example, standing open-mouthed in
astonishment in the middle of Oxford, buying coffee in the central market. It was soon after dawn on April 14, 1986—and two enormous
American fighter-bombers were suddenly roaring overhead, afterburn-
ers shooting gouts of fire behind them as they sped into the sky—and
off, we learned later, to bomb Libya. They had taken off moments before
from U.S.A.F. Upper Heyford, a base a few miles away in the rural peace

of Oxfordshire—and suddenly all the shoppers around me were saying the same thing: *Bloody Americans, why are they here? If you're going to bomb Libya, do it from your own country, not ours.*

I remember being on Kwajalein in the Marshall Islands, where the U.S. Army runs a base—the Ronald Reagan Missile Test Center—to help develop interceptor rockets. There had long been Marshall Islanders living on the atoll, peaceably fishing, growing crops, harming no one. These days, ten thousand of them are compelled to crowd onto just one of the atoll's islands, Ebeye, now the fifth most densely populated place on earth—filthy, sewer-less, crime-ridden. The base, all mown grass and tennis courts and air-conditioned barrack-blocks is forbidden to them, even though they are the islands' original inhabitants. *Bloody Americans,* the islanders say, with an impotent rage, *why are they here? If they want to test their missiles, why not do it on their own soil?*

Such a refrain seems to me to be endlessly repeated, with local objections voiced for reasons peculiar to each set of bases, to each country. To the Koreans, it is the massage parlors and seedy bars and diseases that cluster outside the great bases at Itaewon and Osan. To the Okinawans, it is the violence they all too often experience, much of it directed against these gentlest of people, and so often perpetrated by drunken U.S. marines who insist they have more right to be on the island than do the originals. Small wonder that the Filipinos now fret about the Americans returning to newly leased bases to deal with the new supposed threats in the South China Sea. All too many in the Philippines recall the cesspit that was Olongapo, outside the Subic Bay Naval Station, and the degradation of the citizenry in the hamlets beyond the wire at Clark Air Base. Ash from a volcano—and local politics—closed both bases in the early 1990s. But times have changed, and America is now clamoring to return, and Filipinos worry.

Most brutal of all, most poignant, is the situation at the mother of all bases, the vast mid-ocean staging center of Diego Garcia, a British mid-Indian Ocean possession that London, perfidious in the extreme, leased to the Pentagon in the 1960s under the pretense that no one lived there. London lied. Washington lied. Two thousand peaceable and contented people had lived and worked in coconut mills on the islands for decades, and on the agreement's signing they were unceremoniously bundled up and herded off, made stateless and impoverished, just to accommodate an armada of American bombers and submarines and pre-positioned supply ships, which have littered the lagoon to this day. The islanders have been fighting a lonely battle ever since, and they have generally been losing—much as have people in the Philippines and Korea and Micronesia and the English countryside and scores of places besides. Losing for the simple reasons that, so far as politicians and statesman of the day are concerned, American power and American money seems to trump all too many things—the rights of the locals most prominent among them.

We may rail against the bases; I fear, however, they are, by and large, here to stay. At least until there is a major seismic shift in global power— and that is not going to happen for a long while to come. And still the question of their true nature—a comfort, a guarantee, a threat?—is to many who live in their shadows, a question neither fully answered nor even properly understood. A troubling enigma, indeed.

Simon Winchester

Introduction

From a hilltop at the Guantánamo Bay naval station, you can look down on a secluded part of the base bordered by the Caribbean Sea. There you'll see thick coils of razor wire, guard towers, search lights, and concrete barriers. This is the U.S. prison that has garnered so much international attention and controversy, with so many prisoners held for years without trial. But the prison facilities take up only a few acres of the forty-five-square-mile naval station. Most of the base looks nothing like the detention center. Instead, the landscape features suburban-style housing developments, a golf course, and recreational boating facilities. This part of the base has received much less attention than the prison. Yet in its own way, it is far more important for understanding who we are as a country and how we relate to the rest of the world.

What makes most of the naval station so remarkable is just how unremarkable it is. Looking out on Guantánamo Bay, a U.S. flag flies outside base headquarters. Nearby, an outdoor movie theater has a regular schedule of Hollywood blockbusters. Next door, there are bright-green artificial turf fields for football and soccer, at a new sports facility that also features two baseball diamonds, volleyball and basketball courts, and an outdoor roller-skating rink. In the air-conditioned gym, ESPN's *Sportscenter* plays on TV. Across the main road there's a large chapel, a post office, and a sun-bleached set of McDonald's golden arches. Neighborhoods with names like Deer Point and Villamar have looping drives and spacious lawns with barbecue grills and children's toys. There's a high school, a middle and elementary school, and a childcare facility. There are pools and playgrounds, several public beaches, a bowling center, barber and beauty shops, a Pizza Hut, a Taco Bell, a KFC, and a Subway.

From the hilltop you can also faintly see two nearby Cuban towns, but most everywhere else on base it's easy to forget you're in Cuba. What base residents call "downtown," for example, could be almost anywhere in the United States—or at another of the hundreds of U.S. military bases spread around the globe, which often resemble self-contained American towns. The downtown is where you find the commissary and the Navy's version of the post exchange, or PX—the shopping facility present on U.S. military bases worldwide. Surrounded by plentiful parking, the commissary and exchange feel like a Walmart, full of clothing and consumer electronics, furniture, automotive products, and groceries. At Guantá- namo, the base souvenir shop is one of the few reminders of where you really are. There, along with U.S. Naval Station Guantánamo Bay post- cards and mugs, you can buy a T-shirt bearing the words Detainee Operations.

During years of debates over the closure of Guantánamo Bay's prison, few have asked why the United States has such a large base on Cuban ter- ritory in the first place, and whether we should have one there at all. This is unsurprising.

Most Americans rarely think about U.S. military bases overseas. Since the end of World War II and the early days of the Cold War, when the United States built or acquired most of its overseas bases, Americans have considered it normal to have U.S. military installations in other coun- tries, on other people's land. The presence of our bases overseas has long been accepted unquestioningly and treated as an obvious good, essen- tial to national security and global peace. Perhaps these bases register in our consciousness when there's an antibase protest in Okinawa or an acci- dent in Germany. Quickly, however, they're forgotten.

Of course, people living near U.S. bases in countries worldwide pay them more attention. For many, U.S. bases are one of the most prominent symbols of the United States, along with Hollywood movies, pop music, and fast food. Indeed, the prevalence of Burger Kings and Taco Bells on many of our bases abroad is telling: ours is a supersized collection of bases with franchises the world over. While there are no freestanding foreign bases on U.S. soil, today there are around eight hundred U.S. bases in foreign countries, occupied by hundreds of thousands of U.S. troops.

Although the United States has long had some bases in foreign lands, this massive global deployment of military force was unknown in U.S. history before World War II. Now, seventy years after that war, there are still, according to the Pentagon, 174 U.S. bases in Germany, 113 in Japan, and 83 in South Korea. There are hundreds more dotting the planet in Aruba and Australia, Bahrain and Bulgaria, Colombia, Kenya, and Qatar, to name just a few. Worldwide, we have bases in more than seventy countries. Although few U.S. citizens realize it, we probably have more bases in other people's lands than any other people, nation, or empire in world history.

And yet the subject is barely discussed in the media. Rarely does anyone ask whether we need hundreds of bases overseas, or whether we can afford them. Rarely does anyone consider how we would feel with a foreign base on U.S. soil, or how we would react if China, Russia, or Iran built even a single base somewhere near our borders today. For most in the United States, the idea of even the nicest, most benign foreign troops arriving with their tanks, planes, and high-powered weaponry and making themselves at home in our country—occupying and fencing off hundreds or thousands of acres of our land—is unthinkable.

Rafael Correa, the president of Ecuador, highlighted this rarely considered truth in 2009 when he refused to renew the lease for a U.S. base in his country. Correa told reporters that he would approve the lease renewal on one condition: "They let us put a base in Miami—an Ecuadorian base."

"If there's no problem having foreign soldiers on a country's soil," Correa quipped, "surely they'll let us have an Ecuadorian base in the United States."[1]

THE SCALE

At the height of the U.S. occupations of Afghanistan and Iraq, the total number of bases, combat outposts, and checkpoints in those two countries alone topped one thousand.[2] With American troops largely withdrawn, almost all of those have been shut down. Yet officially, according to the most recent publicized count, the U.S. military currently still occupies 686 "base sites" outside the fifty states and Washington, D.C.[3]

While 686 is quite a figure, that tally strangely excludes many well-known U.S. bases, such as those in Kosovo, Kuwait, and Qatar. Less surprisingly, the Pentagon's count also excludes secret (or secretive) American bases, such as those reported in Israel and Saudi Arabia. There are so many bases, the Pentagon itself doesn't even know the true total.[4] By my count, eight hundred is a good estimate.

But what exactly is a "base"? Definitions and terminology vary widely, and each of the military's services has its own preferred vocabulary, including "post," "station," "camp," and "fort." The Pentagon defines its generic term *base site* as a "physical (geographic) location"—meaning land, a facility or facilities, or land and facilities—"owned by, leased to, or otherwise possessed" by an armed service or another component of the Department of Defense.[5] To avoid linguistic debates and because it's the simplest and most widely recognized term, I generally use "base" to mean any place, facility, or installation used regularly for military purposes of any kind.[6]

Understood this way, bases come in all sizes and shapes, from massive sites in Germany and Japan to small radar facilities in Peru and Puerto Rico. Other bases include ports and airfields of all sizes, repair facilities, training areas, nuclear weapons installations, missile testing facilities, arsenals, warehouses, barracks, military schools, listening and communications posts, and drone bases. While I exclude checkpoints from my definition, military hospitals and prisons, rehab facilities, paramilitary bases, and intelligence facilities must also be considered part of the base world because of their military functions. Even military resorts and recreation areas in places such as Tuscany and Seoul are bases of a kind; worldwide, the military runs more than 170 golf courses.[7]

The Pentagon says that it has just sixty-four "active major installations" overseas and that most of its base sites are "small installations or locations." But it defines "small" as having a reported value of up to $915 million.[8] In other words, small can be not so small.

The United States is not the only country to control military bases outside its own territory. Britain and France have about thirteen between them, mostly in their former colonies. Russia has around nine in former

Soviet republics and at least two in Syria. For the first time since World War II, Japan's so-called Self-Defense Forces have a foreign base, located in Djibouti alongside American and French bases. South Korea, the Netherlands, India, Australia, Chile, Turkey, and Israel reportedly have at least one foreign base apiece. In total, all the non-U.S. countries in the world combined have about thirty foreign bases among them— as compared to the United States and its eight hundred or so. If we add up all the troops and the family members living with them, plus the civilian base employees and their family members, the bases are responsible for over half a million Americans abroad.[9]

THE FORWARD STRATEGY

Since the end of World War II, the idea that our country should have a large collection of bases and hundreds of thousands of troops permanently stationed overseas has been a quasireligious dictum of U.S. foreign and national security policy. The opening words of a U.S. Army War College study bluntly declare: "U.S. national security strategy requires access to overseas military bases."[10]

The policy underlying this deeply held belief is known as the "forward strategy." These two words, this wonky term of art, have had profound implications. Cold War policy held that the United States should maintain large concentrations of military forces and bases as close as possible to the Soviet Union, in order to hem in and "contain" supposed Soviet expansionism. Suddenly, as the historian George Stambuk explains, "the security of the United States, in the minds of policy-makers, lost much of its former inseparability from the concept of the territory of the United States."[11]

Two decades after the Soviet Union's collapse, in a world without another superpower rival, people across the political spectrum still believe as a matter of faith that overseas bases and troops are essential to protecting the country. At a time when bipartisanship has hit all-time lows, there are few issues more widely agreed upon by both Republicans and Democrats alike. The George W. Bush administration, for example, proclaimed that bases abroad have "maintained the peace" and provided "symbols of . . . U.S. commitments to allies and friends."[12] The Obama

U.S. MILITARY BASES ABROAD, 2015

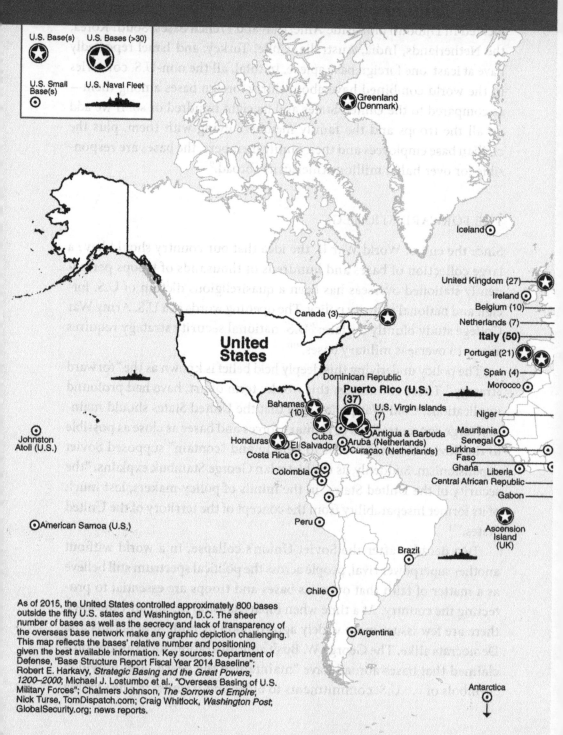

U.S. Base(s)

U.S. Bases (>30)

U.S. Small Base(s)

U.S. Naval Fleet

Greenland (Denmark)

Iceland

United Kingdom (27)

Ireland

Belgium (10)

Netherlands (7)

Italy (50)

Portugal (21)

Spain (4)

Morocco

Niger

Canada (3)

United States

Dominican Republic

Puerto Rico (U.S.) (37)

U.S. Virgin Islands (7)

Bahamas (10)

Cuba

Antigua & Barbuda

Mauritania

Senegal

Johnston Atoll (U.S.)

Honduras

El Salvador

Aruba (Netherlands)

Curaçao (Netherlands)

Burkina Faso

Costa Rica

Ghana

Liberia

Colombia

Central African Republic

Gabon

American Samoa (U.S.)

Peru

Ascension Island (UK)

Brazil

Chile

Argentina

Antarctica

As of 2015, the United States controlled approximately 800 bases outside the fifty U.S. states and Washington, D.C. The sheer number of bases as well as the secrecy and lack of transparency of the overseas base network make any graphic depiction challenging. This map reflects the bases' relative number and positioning given the best available information. Key sources: Department of Defense, "Base Structure Report Fiscal Year 2014 Baseline"; Robert E. Harkavy, *Strategic Basing and the Great Powers, 1200–2000*; Michael J. Lostumbo et al., "Overseas Basing of U.S. Military Forces"; Chalmers Johnson, *The Sorrows of Empire*; Nick Turse, TomDispatch.com; Craig Whitlock, *Washington Post*; GlobalSecurity.org; news reports.

administration, for its part, declared that "forward-stationed and rotationally deployed U.S. forces continue to be relevant and required" as they "provide a stabilizing influence abroad."[13]

And these are just two prominent examples. The forward strategy has been the overwhelming consensus among politicians, national security experts, military officials, journalists, and many others. It's hard to overestimate how unquestioned this policy has been and remains. Any opposition to maintaining large numbers of overseas bases and troops is generally pilloried as peacenik idealism, or isolationism of the sort that allowed Hitler to conquer Europe.

Superficially, it seems hard to argue against maintaining U.S. bases overseas. It seems logical enough that more bases mean more security. Since the bases have been there for decades, it's easy to assume that there must be good military reasons for them. U.S. leaders often portray our bases as a double gift to host countries, offering both security and economic benefits; thanks to the jobs and business contracts that bases provide and the money that U.S. military personnel and their families spend off base, many locals covet their presence. Why would anyone not want U.S. bases and troops in their countries? Many Americans assume that any "Yankee go home" sentiment must reflect a seething anti-Americanism. With bases in Europe and Asia, some might go so far as to invoke the old joke that if it weren't for us, the locals would probably be speaking German or Japanese right now.

Nevertheless, for the first time in decades, an unusually bipartisan group has slowly begun to question the conventional wisdom. "In a sense it's unnatural that any country be the host to large numbers of foreign forces," former Pentagon official and base expert Andy Hoehn told me. "It was a necessary condition for a long time. And it's a situation that we should be celebrating that we're able to make that change, not one that we should be bemoaning."

A TROUBLING RECORD

The most obvious reason to question the overseas base status quo is economic. Especially in an era of budget austerity, it makes sense to ask whether closing bases abroad can be an easy source of savings. Like many things far from home, overseas bases are very expensive. Even when host countries like Japan and Germany cover some of the costs, U.S. taxpayers still pay an average of $10,000 to $40,000 more per year to station a member of the military abroad compared to in the United States. The costs of transportation, the higher cost of living in some host countries, and the expense of providing schools, hospitals, housing, and other support to family members of military personnel abroad all contribute to the extra expense. With more than half a million troops, family members, and civilian employees on bases overseas, the expenses add up quickly.

By my very conservative calculations, the total cost of maintaining bases and military personnel overseas reaches at least $71.8 billion every year and could easily be in the range of $100–$120 billion. That's larger than the discretionary budget for every government agency except the Defense Department itself. And this number doesn't even include spending on bases in overseas war zones. If we include the cost of bases and troops in Afghanistan and Iraq, in 2012 the total easily topped $170 billion.

Other financial losses add up, too. When military personnel and family members spend their paychecks overseas rather than in communities at home, the U.S. economy is that much worse off. Allocating U.S. taxpayer dollars to build and run overseas bases means forgoing investments in areas like education, infrastructure, housing, and health care, which generally create more jobs and increase economic productivity far more than military spending does.

But beyond such financial costs, there are also human ones. The families of military personnel are among those who suffer from the spread of overseas bases, given the strain of distant deployments, family separations, and frequent moves. Overseas bases also contribute to the shocking rate of sexual assault in the military: an estimated one in three servicewomen is now assaulted, and a disproportionate number of these crimes happen at bases abroad. Outside the base gates, meanwhile, in places like South Korea, one often finds exploitative prostitution industries that frequently rely on human trafficking.

And once one begins to look closely at U.S. bases abroad, the list of problems only grows. Worldwide, bases have caused widespread environmental damage because of leaks, accidents, and, in some cases, the deliberate burial or discharge of toxic materials. In Okinawa, U.S. troops have repeatedly committed rapes and other crimes against the local population. In Italy, twenty died after a Marine jet severed a gondola cable. The military has also repeatedly built installations by displacing local peoples from their lands, in areas ranging from Greenland to the tropical island of Diego Garcia. Today, the disproportionate presence of bases in places that lack full democratic rights within the United States, such as Guam and Puerto Rico, helps perpetuate a twenty-first-century form of colonialism, tarnishing our country's ability to be a model for democracy.

Indeed, despite rhetoric about spreading democracy, the government's track record shows a clear preference for bases in undemocratic and often despotic states such as Qatar and Bahrain. The willingness to partner with unsavory characters for the sake of bases has also entangled the U.S. military with mafia organizations in Italy. Meanwhile, imprisonment, torture, and abuse at bases from Guantánamo Bay to Abu Ghraib have generated international anger and damaged the country's reputation. Similarly, drone bases enabled missile strikes that have killed hundreds of civilians, producing outrage, opposition, and new enemies. In Iraq, Afghanistan, and Saudi Arabia, foreign bases have created fertile breeding grounds for radicalism and anti-Americanism; the presence of our bases in the Muslim holy lands of Saudi Arabia was a major recruiting tool for al-Qaeda and part of Osama bin Laden's professed motivation for the September 11, 2001, attacks.

The hundreds of bases around the globe are a major (though largely unacknowledged) aspect of the "face" our country presents to the world, and bases often show us in an extremely unflattering light. Given the track record, it's little wonder that the base nation has frequently generated grievances, protest, and antagonistic relationships with others.

UNDERMINING SECURITY

Most crucially, it's not at all clear that U.S. bases overseas actually protect national security and global peace. During the Cold War, there was an argument to be made that to some extent U.S. bases in Europe and Asia played a legitimate defensive role. In the absence of a superpower enemy today, however, the argument that bases many thousands of miles from U.S. shores are necessary to defend the United States—or even its allies—is much harder to sustain. To the contrary, the global collection of bases has generally been offensive in nature, making it all too easy to launch interventionist wars of choice that have resulted in repeated disasters, costing millions of lives from Vietnam to Iraq and Afghanistan.

There are also questions about the degree to which bases actually increase host country safety. The presence of U.S. bases can turn a country into a target for foreign powers or militants. On Guam, a dark Cold War joke said that Soviet nuclear missile targeters were just about the only people who could locate the island on a map; with a China-focused U.S. military buildup under way, some are expressing similar concerns about Chinese missiles potentially targeting the island today.[14]

For those concerned that closing bases abroad might slow deployment times in case of a legitimate defensive war or peacekeeping operation, studies by the Pentagon and others have shown that in most cases, advances in transportation technology have largely erased the advantage of stationing troops overseas. Nowadays, the military can generally deploy troops just as quickly from bases in the continental United States and Hawaii as it can from many bases abroad.

Rather than stabilizing dangerous regions, foreign bases frequently heighten military tensions and discourage diplomatic solutions to conflicts. Placing U.S. bases near the borders of countries such as China, Russia, and Iran, for example, increases threats to their security and encourages them to respond by boosting their own military spending. Again, imagine how U.S. leaders would respond if Iran were to build even a single small base in Mexico, Canada, or the Caribbean.

Notably, the most dangerous moment during the Cold War—the Cuban missile crisis—revolved around the creation of Soviet nuclear missile facilities roughly ninety miles from the U.S. border. Similarly, one of the most dangerous episodes in the post–Cold War era—Russia's seizure of Crimea and its involvement in the war in Ukraine—has come after the United States encouraged the enlargement of NATO and built a growing number of bases closer and closer to Russian borders. Indeed, a major motivation behind Russia's actions has likely been its interest in maintaining perhaps the most important of its small collection of foreign bases, the naval base in the Crimean port Sevastopol. West-leaning Ukrainian leaders' desire to join NATO posed a direct threat to the base, and thus to the power of the Russian navy.

Perhaps most troubling of all, the creation of new U.S. bases to protect against an alleged future Chinese or Russian threat runs the risk of becoming a self-fulfilling prophecy. By provoking a Chinese and Russian military response, these bases may help create the very threat against which they are supposedly designed to protect. In other words, far from making the world a safer place, U.S. bases overseas can actually make war more likely and America less secure.

BEHIND THE FENCES

To cast light on this long-overlooked world of bases, I traveled around the world, conducting research over the course of six years at more than sixty current and former bases in twelve countries and territories, including Japan, South Korea, Italy, Germany, Britain, Honduras, El Salvador, Ecuador, Cuba, the United States, and the U.S. territories of Guam and the Northern Mariana Islands.

In many cases, U.S. officials were very helpful in accommodating my research, arranging base tours and interviews, and answering questions. At other times, bases denied my requests to visit, sent me from office to office in endless quests for visiting rights, or never responded to my inquiries. After exchanging more than fifty emails with military representatives over several months about visiting U.S. bases in Afghanistan, I am still waiting for an official response to my application.

At the naval station on Guam, I made it on base only by attending services for the Jewish holiday of Yom Kippur. On several occasions in Germany and Italy, I was stopped and questioned by police or private security guards while on public property outside a base. Outside the main *caserma* in Vicenza, Italy, I was taking photographs of a protest against the planned construction of a new base in the city when law enforcement seized my passport. After a few nervous moments and some brief questioning, the Italians and U.S. military personnel allowed me to enter the base—which was holding an open-to-the-public Fourth of July celebration. Within a few minutes I got another polite questioning from a civilian working on base, and I realized that I was going to be followed for the rest of the night by two friendly members of the Italian military police who asked me to call them "Starrrskeee and Huuutch."

Off base, I used a range of local contacts to meet as many people with as many perspectives as possible, including government officials, local residents, journalists, business leaders, academics, activists, military retirees, and many others both supportive of and opposed to bases in their communities. In Washington, D.C., and elsewhere in the United States, I interviewed Pentagon and State Department officials (one of whom, as you will see, I inadvertently helped get fired), military analysts, reporters, veterans, and many others with knowledge about overseas bases. In most cases, I recorded my interviews or took detailed notes. In the stories that follow, I have used quotation marks only when I know that I captured a speaker's exact words.

With the military having closed most of its bases and withdrawn most troops from Afghanistan after the longest war in U.S. history, we've reached a moment of transition in U.S. foreign and military policy. There's no better moment to ask whether the hundreds of overseas bases that keep on running whether the country is technically at war or at peace are a positive and necessary presence in the world, and whether they reflect how we should be engaging with the rest of the planet.

I say "we" because although I have written this book for readers worldwide, at times I address a U.S. audience directly. Ultimately, I believe all Americans bear responsibility for the base nation we've become and for the lives that our largely forgotten bases have shaped around the world. This book tells the stories of some of those lives—the U.S. troops and their families who live and work on foreign bases, the locals who live nearby, and others. And beyond the bases themselves, I examine the impact that the Pentagon's foreign-base strategy has on the lives of all of us in the United States and around the world, whether we know it or not.

In this respect, *Base Nation* is about more than bases alone. Overseas bases offer a lens through which we can look honestly and unflinchingly at our country, our place in the world, and how we interact with the rest of the planet. Examining America's sprawling collection of bases abroad can help us see how the United States has placed itself on a permanent war footing, with an economy and a government dominated by continuous preparations for battle.

Ultimately, the story of our bases abroad is a chronicle of the United States in the post–World War II era. In a certain sense, we've all come to live behind the fences—"behind the wire," as military folks say. We may think these bases have made us safer. Instead, they've helped lock us inside a permanently militarized society that in many ways has made all of us less safe and less secure, damaging lives at home and abroad.

PART I

· ·

FOUNDATIONS

View of Fort Keogh, Montana Territory, 1878, by U.S. Army soldier and painter
Hermann Stieffel.

1

The Birth of Base Nation

The base nation as we know it was born on September 2, 1940. It is a vastly underappreciated moment, generally treated as a small detail in World War II history books. But it was then, with the flash of a pen, that President Franklin Delano Roosevelt began the transformation of the United States from one of the world's major powers into a global superpower of unparalleled military might.

On that momentous day, more than a year before the United States entered the war, Roosevelt informed Congress that he was authorizing an agreement with Britain: the country would provide its nearly bankrupt ally with fifty World War I–era destroyers in exchange for U.S. control over a collection of air and naval bases in Britain's colonies.

Although such a pact should have required congressional approval, Roosevelt simply declared it done. Under what became known as the "destroyers-for-bases" agreement, the United States acquired ninety-nine-year leases and near-sovereign powers over bases in the Bahamas, Jamaica, St. Lucia, St. Thomas, Antigua, Aruba-Curaçao, Trinidad, and British Guiana, plus temporary access to bases in Bermuda and Newfoundland. Roosevelt called the agreement "the most important action in the reinforcement of our national security since the Louisiana Purchase."[1] Whether the deal was quite so important to national security is questionable. But in terms of its transformative effect, there was little exaggeration in comparing the acquisition of these bases to the 1803 treaty that nearly doubled the nation's size. The leases' ninety-nine-year length reflected similarly grand ambitions: President Roosevelt intended to cement the global power of the United States for at least a century to come.

The roots of Roosevelt's remarkable decision stretch back to the era surrounding the Louisiana Purchase. Beginning shortly after independence and continuing through the 1800s, the United States built up a small but significant collection of extraterritorial bases. This collection reflected the unabashedly imperial dreams of U.S. leaders and allowed the United States to join the ranks of the world's most powerful countries by the turn of the twentieth century.

The unprecedented profusion of U.S. bases that emerged from World War II, however, represented a quantitative and qualitative shift in the nature of American power, transforming the country's relationship with the rest of the world. By war's end, the size, geographic reach, and total number of U.S. bases had expanded dramatically. Never before had so many U.S. troops been permanently stationed overseas. Never before had U.S. leaders thought about national defense as requiring the permanent deployment of military force so far from U.S. borders. After World War II, the United States commanded an unparalleled global military presence, unmatched by any prior people, nation, or empire in history.

THE PRY BAR OF CONQUEST

Since the days of ancient Egypt, Rome, and China, military bases—especially bases abroad—have been a key foundation for imperial control over lands and people.[2] The Egyptian Middle Kingdom positioned military strongholds on the borders of its empire, while fortified cities were the norm across the fertile Middle East from Babylon to Jerusalem. The acropolis, which we now think of as the hilltop home of the Parthenon in Athens, originally referred to mountaintop citadels of the kind that appear from Israel's Masada to Machu Picchu in Peru.[3]

Rome, too, was an acropolis, and the Romans built temporary "Caesar's camps" and *castra stativa*—permanent bases—across the reaches of their empire. Some Roman fortresses later provided foundations for the castles built by England's Norman invaders. The Tower of London, one of Britain's iconic symbols, was originally a foreign base built by William the Conqueror shortly after 1066.[4] When Columbus first sailed to the

Americas, he ordered the construction of a fort on the island of Hispaniola, in today's Haiti, using the splintered timbers of the *Santa Maria*.[5] On the Genoese sailor's second voyage, in 1494, he anchored in the bay he called Puerto Grande and we now call Guantánamo.

Today, across the Americas, tourists still visit the remains of the Spanish, Portuguese, Dutch, French, and British bases that followed Columbus's first fort in Hispaniola. These tourist attractions are monuments to bygone empires and to the role that such fortifications played in the colonization of the Americas. France established its first bases near Parris Island, South Carolina, in 1562, and on the St. Johns River in Florida in 1564. The Spanish followed in Florida, San Juan, and Havana. Britain set up its own bases in North Carolina, Virginia, Massachusetts, and well beyond as its colonial power peaked in North America shortly before the American Revolution.[6]

While scholars generally identify Guantánamo Bay as the first U.S. military base abroad, they strangely overlook bases created shortly after independence. Hundreds of frontier forts helped enable the westward expansion of the United States, and they were built on land that was very much *abroad* at the time. Fort Harmar, built in 1785 in the Northwest Territory, was the first. Others appeared in today's Ohio and Indiana, including Forts Deposit, Defiance, Hamilton, Wayne, Washington, and Knox. Each of these bases helped waves of U.S. settlers move into the lands of Native American nations, pushing Indians progressively westward. By 1802, there was a chain of U.S. forts from the Great Lakes to New Orleans.[7] Native American groups' support for Britain in the War of 1812 brought only more displacement, expropriation, and base building.[8]

In 1830, President Andrew Jackson announced his "Indian removal policy," aimed at forcing all native groups to give up their lands east of the Mississippi River and relocate to the west. Fort Leavenworth, Kansas, was initially supposed to mark the "very western edge of civilization" and the "permanent Indian frontier." However, by protecting the start of the Santa Fe and Oregon trails, it only furthered the westward migration of Euro-American settlers, miners, traders, and farmers. The Army soon became what one historian has called the "advance agent" and "pry bar" of U.S. conquest.[9] A rapidly growing collection of western forts beyond

NATIVE LANDS AND EARLY U.S. MILITARY BASES ABROAD

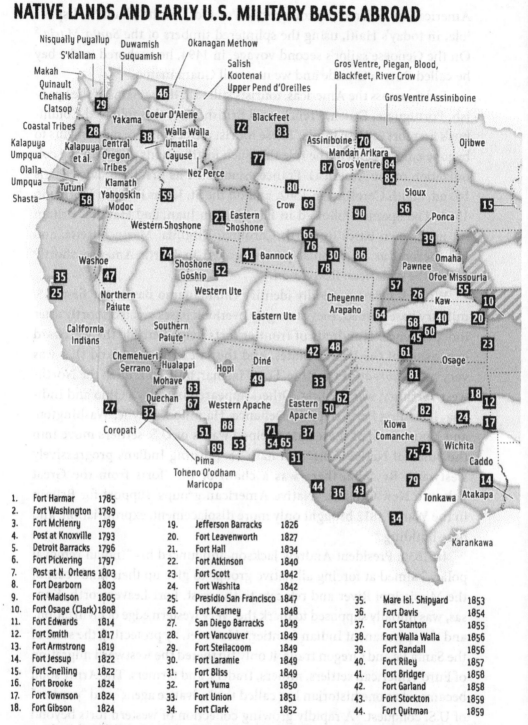

#			#			#		
1.	Fort Harmar	1785	19.	Jefferson Barracks	1826			
2.	Fort Washington	1789	20.	Fort Leavenworth	1827			
3.	Fort McHenry	1789	21.	Fort Hall	1834			
4.	Post at Knoxville	1793	22.	Fort Atkinson	1840			
5.	Detroit Barracks	1796	23.	Fort Scott	1842			
6.	Fort Pickering	1797	24.	Fort Washita	1842			
7.	Post at N. Orleans	1803	25.	Presidio San Francisco	1847	35.	Mare Isl. Shipyard	1853
8.	Fort Dearborn	1803	26.	Fort Kearney	1848	36.	Fort Davis	1854
9.	Fort Madison	1805	27.	San Diego Barracks	1849	37.	Fort Stanton	1855
10.	Fort Osage (Clark)	1808	28.	Fort Vancouver	1849	38.	Fort Walla Walla	1856
11.	Fort Edwards	1814	29.	Fort Steilacoom	1849	39.	Fort Randall	1856
12.	Fort Smith	1817	30.	Fort Laramie	1849	40.	Fort Riley	1857
13.	Fort Armstrong	1819	31.	Fort Bliss	1849	41.	Fort Bridger	1858
14.	Fort Jessup	1822	32.	Fort Yuma	1850	42.	Fort Garland	1858
15.	Fort Snelling	1822	33.	Fort Union	1851	43.	Fort Stockton	1859
16.	Fort Brooke	1824	34.	Fort Clark	1852	44.	Fort Quitman	1859
17.	Fort Townson	1824						
18.	Fort Gibson	1824						

Sources: Sam B. Hilliard / Dan Irwin / Southern Illinois University Cartographic Laboratory; University of Texas Libraries; United States Army Office

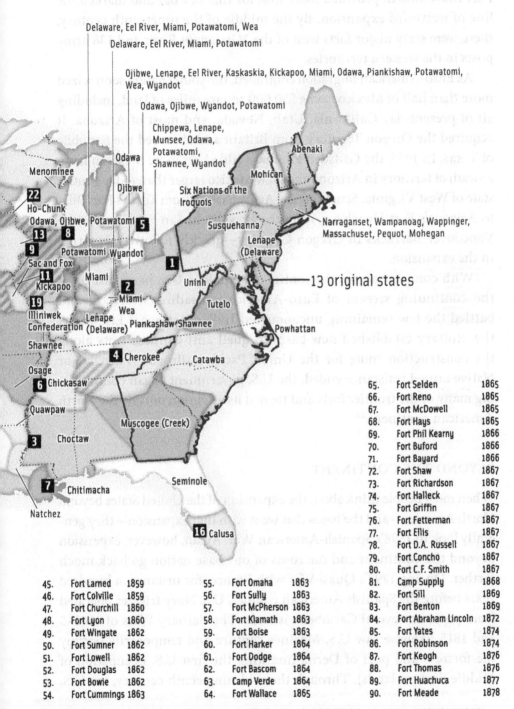

Delaware, Eel River, Miami, Potawatomi, Wea

Delaware, Eel River, Miami, Potawatomi

Ojibwe, Lenape, Eel River, Kaskaskia, Kickapoo, Miami, Odawa, Piankishaw, Potawatomi, Wea, Wyandot

Odawa, Ojibwe, Wyandot, Potawatomi

Chippewa, Lenape, Munsee, Odawa, Potawatomi, Shawnee, Wyandot

Abenaki

Odawa

Menominee

Ojibwe

Mohican

Six Nations of the Iroquois

22
Ho-Chunk

Odawa, Ojibwe, Potawatomi **5**

Susquehanna

Narraganset, Wampanoag, Wappinger, Massachuset, Pequot, Mohegan

13 **8**

9

Potawatomi Wyandot

Lenape (Delaware)

Sac and Fox

11

Miami

1

Kickapoo

2

Uninh

─13 original states

19

Miami

Tutelo

Illiniwek Confederation

Lenape (Delaware)

Wea

Piankashaw Shawnee

Powhattan

Shawnee

4 Cherokee

Catawba

Osage

6 Chickasaw

Quawpaw

Muscogee (Creek)

3 Choctaw

7

Chitimacha

Seminole

Natchez

16 Calusa

45.	Fort Larned	1859	55.	Fort Omaha	1863	81.	Camp Supply	1868
46.	Fort Colville	1859	56.	Fort Sully	1863	82.	Fort Sill	1869
47.	Fort Churchill	1860	57.	Fort McPherson	1863	83.	Fort Benton	1869
48.	Fort Lyon	1860	58.	Fort Klamath	1863	84.	Fort Abraham Lincoln	1872
49.	Fort Wingate	1862	59.	Fort Boise	1863	85.	Fort Yates	1874
50.	Fort Sumner	1862	60.	Fort Harker	1864	86.	Fort Robinson	1874
51.	Fort Lowell	1862	61.	Fort Dodge	1864	87.	Fort Keogh	1876
52.	Fort Douglas	1862	62.	Fort Bascom	1864	88.	Fort Thomas	1876
53.	Fort Bowie	1862	63.	Camp Verde	1864	89.	Fort Huachuca	1877
54.	Fort Cummings	1863	64.	Fort Wallace	1865	90.	Fort Meade	1878

65.	Fort Selden	1865
66.	Fort Reno	1865
67.	Fort McDowell	1865
68.	Fort Hays	1865
69.	Fort Phil Kearny	1866
70.	Fort Buford	1866
71.	Fort Bayard	1866
72.	Fort Shaw	1867
73.	Fort Richardson	1867
74.	Fort Halleck	1867
75.	Fort Griffin	1867
76.	Fort Fetterman	1867
77.	Fort Ellis	1867
78.	Fort D.A. Russell	1867
79.	Fort Concho	1867
80.	Fort C.F. Smith	1867

of the Chief of Military History, *Winning the West: The Army in the Indian Wars, 1865–1890*. Map by John Emerson and Siobhan McGuirk.

Fort Leavenworth provided more iron for that pry bar and marked the line of westward expansion. By the middle of the nineteenth century, there were sixty major forts west of the Mississippi River and 138 army posts in the western territories.

As Euro-American migration continued, the young nation soon seized more than half of Mexico: some 550,000 square miles of land, including all of present-day California, Utah, Nevada, and most of Arizona. It acquired the Oregon Territory from Britain and absorbed the Republic of Texas. In 1853, the Gadsden Purchase added yet more Mexican land, a swath of territory in Arizona and New Mexico larger than today's entire state of West Virginia. Scores of new Army bases—from Texas's Fort Bliss to Arizona's Fort Huachuca, from the Presidio in San Francisco to the Vancouver Barracks in Oregon Country—quickly followed, assisting in the expansion.

With conquest across the continent complete, U.S. bases protected the continuing stream of Euro-Americans heading westward and battled the few remaining unconquered Indian nations.[10] Elsewhere, the military established new bases to quell anti-Chinese riots along the construction route for the Union Pacific railroad. When major Native armed resistance ended, the U.S. government began consolidating many of the frontier forts and turned its attention outside the North American continent.[11]

BEYOND THE CONTINENT

When most people think about the expansion of the United States beyond North America—and the bases that went with that expansion—they generally look to 1898's Spanish-American War. Again, however, expansion beyond the continent and the roots of our base nation go back much farther. During 1798's Quasi-War with France, for instance, a hundred years before the Spanish-American conflict, U.S. Navy frigates operated from ports on several Caribbean islands. The Barbary Wars of 1801–5 and 1815 likewise saw U.S. Marines capture and temporarily occupy the fortress and port of Derna (marking the first U.S. occupation of Middle Eastern lands). Through the mid-nineteenth century, the U.S.

Navy used temporary bases to support military operations around the globe, in Taiwan, Uruguay, Japan, Holland, Mexico, Ecuador, China, Panama, and Korea.[12]

Even more significant than these temporary outposts were fleet stations that the Navy established in key strategic locations across five continents after the end of the War of 1812.[13] These patrol bases appeared at ports in Rio de Janeiro, Brazil; in Valparaiso, Chile, and Luanda, Angola; in Magdalena Bay, Mexico, and Panama City, Panama; on Portugal's Cape Verde and Spain's Balearic Islands; and in Hong Kong and Macau. The bases were positioned, as two prominent military analysts explain, "close to the 'nexus of US security and economic interests,' namely, important overseas markets."[14] While these modest "leasehold bases" generally supported relatively small fleets and used rented warehouse and repair facilities, they reflected and foreshadowed U.S. aspirations to global power.

These aspirations became clearer with the start of a "pivot" toward Asia: not the much-discussed recent effort by the Obama administration, but its original, pre–Civil War antecedent. In 1842, President John Tyler grew interested in establishing Pacific naval bases, and within two years, the country had opened up five Chinese ports to U.S. trade and military forces with the help of one of the many European and American "unequal treaties" imposed on China. Two base experts explain that although the treaties did not officially create bases, "they guaranteed forward access to US naval vessels, and enabled the Navy to purchase and establish warehouse facilities in any" of the ports. In total, the Tyler administration opened sixty-nine ports to U.S. military forces and trade.[15]

Commodore Matthew Perry accomplished much the same in Japan and Okinawa (which was then an independent kingdom) a century before their post–World War II occupation. In 1853, for fifty dollars, Perry purchased a plot of land on the island now known as Chi Chi Jima, near Iwo Jima in the western Pacific. He wanted the island to become a U.S. coaling station—necessary for new steam-powered military and commercial steamship travel operations. Perry also created the first U.S. military base in Okinawa. Although it lasted only a year, Perry used the base to help create additional U.S. enclaves and impose favorable treaties on

Okinawa and Japan.[16] After the Civil War, U.S. officials further increased the nation's Pacific presence and power by claiming and annexing Jarvis, Baker, Howland's, and Midway Islands to mine guano deposits and serve as coaling stations.[17]

The purchase of Alaska from Russia in 1867 led to the occupation of a former indigenous Tlingit and Russian fort in Sitka and the establishment of four more bases in the new territory along the northern edge of Asia.[18] By 1888, the United States had signed agreements to lease naval stations in the Kingdom of Samoa and in the Hawaiian Kingdom's Pearl Harbor. After the overthrow of the Hawaiian monarchy in 1893, the United States annexed the islands of Hawaii in 1898 and the newly renamed American Samoa in 1899. Naval bases appeared almost immediately.[19]

Meanwhile, in 1898 the United States declared war on Spain after the mysterious sinking of the USS *Maine* provided a pretext for intervening in Cuban efforts to win independence from the Spanish empire. The Navy decided that Cuba's Guantánamo Bay would make a good naval coaling station. Occupation of the bay helped U.S. forces seize control of the island and install a government to American liking. Others also saw the long-term advantages of Guantánamo: the *New York Times* declared, "the fine harbor there will make a good American base."[20] From Guantánamo Bay, the military launched its invasion of Puerto Rico, soon annexing that island and the Philippines, Guam, and Wake Island thousands of miles off in the Pacific.[21]

In 1903, U.S. officials pressured Cuban leaders into accepting thinly disguised U.S. rule in exchange for Cuba's official independence and the withdrawal of most (though not all) U.S. troops. The U.S.-penned Platt Amendment allowed the United States to invade Cuba at will to ensure stability and so-called independence, prevented Cuba from making treaties with other governments, and permitted the construction of U.S. "coaling or naval stations."[22] The two governments also signed a lease giving the U.S. military "complete jurisdiction and control" over forty-five square miles of Guantánamo Bay—an area bigger than Washington, D.C. Tellingly, the "lease" had no termination date, which effectively meant that Cuba had ceded the territory to its northern neighbor. In exchange, the United States agreed to build a fence, prevent commercial or industrial activities within the base, and pay a meager yearly fee of $2,000.*[23]

Cuban leaders would eventually annul the Platt Amendment, but U.S. officials insisted on a new treaty to hold on to Guantánamo Bay. The treaty continued the terms of the original lease and stipulated that Cuba could never force the United States to leave. Renters everywhere only wish they had such eviction-proof leases.[24]

By the end of the nineteenth century, the United States thus had a collection of overseas bases matched in size and global scope by only a few European colonial powers. This base network pales in comparison to what would emerge from World War II. But in displaying American leaders' ambitions for further economic, political, and military power, it presaged the base nation to come.[25]

FROM PANAMA TO SHANGHAI

One of the leaders responsible for the expansion of nineteenth-century bases outside North America was the man who came to be known as the "prophet" of the U.S. Navy, Admiral Alfred Thayer Mahan. A historian of eighteenth- and nineteenth-century Anglo-French competition for global preeminence, Mahan argued that great powers require strong navies capable of protecting a country's commercial shipping and opening foreign markets to trade. And to have a strong navy, he held, a country needed a far-flung network of support bases. Under his influence, Navy officials pushed for the creation of ever more coaling and repair stations.[26] In 1900, Navy warships steamed westward to crush the Boxer Rebellion and further open Chinese markets to U.S. businesses. Soon the U.S. Navy, which had become the world's second largest, established regular patrols from bases in Hong Kong, Hankow, and Shanghai.[27]

In 1903, the same year U.S. officials secured access to Guantánamo Bay, they did much the same in Panama. A treaty imposed on the newly independent country gave the United States what amounted to sovereign rights in perpetuity across 553 square miles that became the Panama

---

*The yearly checks now total around $4,000, though under Fidel Castro the Cuban government stopped cashing them. For years they apparently went directly into Castro's desk.

Canal Zone. The treaty also authorized other extensive powers, including land expropriation outside the Canal Zone and the authority to build bases. Panama would eventually host fourteen. As in Cuba, Panama's constitution allowed the United States to intervene militarily, and between 1856 and 1989, the U.S. military invaded twenty-four times.[28] With prominent U.S. bases occupying their land and enabling easy intervention, Panama and Cuba were effectively colonies.[29]

Elsewhere in Latin America, the military continued its pattern of intervention. In Nicaragua, Haiti, Honduras, Mexico, Guatemala, Costa Rica, El Salvador, and the Dominican Republic, U.S. troops were active on an almost yearly basis.[30] Each of these interventions and the often years-long occupations that followed involved the creation of bases for occupying American troops. Nicaragua alone, for instance, had at least eight U.S. garrisons stationed on its land between 1930 and 1932.[31]

Still, at the end of these Latin American occupations, the U.S. military packed up and went home. The same was true at the end of World War I, when the military closed its bases at war's end and brought hundreds of thousands of U.S. troops home (only in the U.S. Virgin Islands, bought from Denmark in 1917, did the military leave a small submarine base and communication outpost).

When the next world war came along, however, there would be no going home after the war. This time, the bases would stay.

A NATION TRANSFORMED

Even before World War II started, Roosevelt wanted to use far-flung bases to harness the newfound power of long-distance aircraft as an implicit threat to other powers and protection for the country. As early as 1939—before the destroyers-for-bases deal with Britain—Roosevelt expressed interest in obtaining new island bases in the Caribbean. After the war started, he pushed his military leaders to develop plans for a postwar network of military bases around the globe that could ensure U.S. dominance.[32] At Roosevelt's direction, military officials began preparing for the postwar period in November 1941, before the attack on Pearl Harbor and the U.S. entry into the war. By 1943, a Joint Chiefs of Staff paper declared that "adequate bases, owned or controlled by the United States, are essential and their acquisition and development must be considered as amongst our primary war aims."[33]

Once the United States entered World War II, the military worked to expand its base collection as quickly as possible. The government signed new deals to station U.S. forces in location after location: new bases were built or occupied in Mexico, Brazil, Panama, Northern Ireland, Iceland, Danish Greenland, Australia, Haiti, Cuba, Kenya, Senegal, Dutch Suriname, British and French Guiana, the Portuguese Azores, the Galápagos Islands, Britain's Ascension Island in the South Atlantic, and Palmyra Island near Hawaii.[34] By war's end, the military was building base facilities at an average rate of 112 a month. In five years, it built the largest collection of bases in world history.[35]

Importantly, achieving military dominance was not the only motivation for the growing number of bases. American leaders were also guided by political and economic considerations. Looking forward to what many assumed would be massive postwar growth in international air travel, Roosevelt and other officials were intent on supporting U.S. commercial airlines. They saw this as critical to ensuring U.S. economic dominance not just in the airline industry but also in accessing worldwide natural resources, international markets, and investment opportunities.[36] In 1943, for instance, the president sent a survey team to French-controlled islands in Polynesia to make plans for postwar bases and commercial airports connecting North America and Australia. Roosevelt wanted to determine what islands "promise to be of value as commercial airports in the future."[37]

Commercial and military planning often went hand in hand. Before the war, for example, Pan American Airways secretly acquired basing rights for the military throughout Latin America. It eventually built and improved forty-eight land and seaplane bases ranging from the Dominican Republic to Paraguay and Bolivia.[38] Pan Am thus provided the military with the foundation for rapidly expandable bases to use in the event of war. At the same time, Pan Am also provided itself and other U.S. airlines with the foundation for a significant competitive advantage after the war. The Joint Chiefs likewise saw that investments in overseas bases would provide powerful bargaining chips to obtain postwar commercial air rights. In this way, military and civilian planners pursued the development of bases and air routes that could serve both goals simultaneously.[39]

"Both for international military purposes and for commercial purposes the Northern, Central, and Southern trans-Atlantic routes should be completed and maintained," stated a Joint Chiefs of Staff study. "Present air routes to the South-West Pacific should be maintained and developed for military and commercial purposes."[40] As the base expert and retired Air Force colonel Elliott V. Converse explains, "From the beginning of the postwar planning process, [officials] hoped to integrate military and civil airfields into a vast network, assuring both physical and economic security for the United States."[41]

At the war's end, a partially completed base in Dharan, Saudi Arabia, illustrated the link between bases and economic interests, foreshadowing decades of Middle Eastern intervention to come. By June 1945, Germany had surrendered, and the military had determined that there was no need to use Dharan for the war against Japan. Still, the secretaries of war, state, and the navy pushed to continue construction at the site, arguing that "immediate construction of this field used initially for military purposes and ultimately for civil aviation would be a strong showing of American interest in Saudi Arabia and thus tend to strengthen the political integrity of that country where vast oil reserves now are in American hands."[42]

Shortly before the war's conclusion, President Harry Truman addressed the issue of postwar bases during the "Big Three" meeting in Potsdam, Germany. "Though the United States wants no profit or selfish advantage out of this war," Truman declared, "we are going to maintain the military bases necessary for the complete protection of our interests and of world peace."

And, he added pointedly, "Bases which our military experts deem to be essential for our protection we will acquire."[43]

"A PERMANENTLY MOBILIZED FORCE"

As World War II ended, the United States, like other world powers throughout history, was reluctant to give up what many considered the "spoils of war." Even if the military had little interest in using a base or a territory, many military leaders felt the United States should not cede its acquisitions. As justification, they generally invoked two military principles. The first, "redundancy," says it's always good to have backups. The second, "strategic denial," says it's smart to hold on to bases and territories simply to prevent enemies from using them.

The military felt especially justified in retaining captured Pacific islands because of the high human and financial costs of their acquisition. "Having defeated or subordinated its former imperial rivals in the Pacific," a group of base experts explains, "the United States military was in no mood to hand back occupied real estate."[44] Many in Congress agreed. No one, they felt, "had the right to give away land which had been bought and paid for with American lives." Louisiana representative F. Edward Hébert explained the logic prevalent after the war: "We fought for them, we've got them, we should keep them. They are necessary to our safety. I see no other course."[45]

The maintenance of such an extensive collection of military bases was also rooted in a widely held strategic belief that the security of the nation and the prevention of future wars depended on dominating the Pacific through a Mahanian combination of naval forces and island strongholds. "This imperial solution to American anxieties about strategic security in the postwar Pacific exhibited itself," writes the base expert Hal Friedman, "in a bureaucratic consensus about turning the Pacific Basin into an 'American lake.'"[46]

For General Douglas MacArthur, the Supreme Commander of Allied Forces in Japan, and other military leaders, securing the Pacific meant creating an "offshore island perimeter." The perimeter was to be a line of island bases stretching from north to south across the western Pacific. It would be like a giant wall protecting the United States, with thousands of miles of moat before reaching U.S. shores. "Our line of defense," MacArthur explained, "runs through the chain of islands fringing the coast of Asia. It starts from the Philippines and continues through the Ryukyu Archipelago, which includes its main bastion, Okinawa. Then it bends back through Japan and the Aleutian Island chain, to Alaska."[47] This plan found support from the architect of early Cold War strategy, the diplomat George Kennan. Kennan saw the island perimeter as equally beneficial for hosting airpower, which would, he thought, allow the control of East Asia without large ground forces.

Eventually, the grandest plans for postwar bases were trumped by concerns about costs and postwar demands for demilitarization. In the Pacific, the military abandoned the offshore island perimeter. Instead, to keep the Pacific an "American lake," the military would rely on key bases in Okinawa and in mainland Japan, Guam, Hawaii, and Micronesia. To the disappointment of military leaders, after the war, the nation ultimately returned about half its foreign bases.[48]

Still, the United States maintained what became a "permanent institution" of bases in peacetime.[49] In Germany, Italy, Japan, and France, U.S. forces retained occupation rights as a victor nation. After 1947, the military built 241 new bases in Germany, while Japan came to host as many as 3,800 installations.[50] The United States signed deals to maintain three of its most important bases, in Greenland, Iceland, and the Portuguese Azores; kept facilities in most of the British territories occupied under the destroyers-for-bases agreement; continued occupying French bases in Morocco; and gained further access to British facilities in Ascension, Bahrain, Guadalcanal, and Tarawa. When Britain wanted to grant complete independence to India and Burma, the U.S. State Department asked its ally to maintain control of three airfields in the former and one in the latter. U.S. bases turned the British Isles into one of several places around the world frequently referred to as an "unsinkable aircraft carrier."[51] Plus, the military enjoyed access to an even wider array of British and French bases still held in their colonies.

Among its own colonial possessions, the United States retained bases on Guam, the Northern Marianas, Samoa, Wake Island, Puerto Rico, and the Virgin Islands, as well as in Guantánamo Bay. When the Philippines gained its independence in 1946, the United States pressured its former colony into granting a ninety-nine-year rent-free lease on twenty-three bases and military installations.

A WORLD OF PERMANENT DANGER

The buildup of U.S. troops around the world was the result of a profound change in how U.S. leaders thought about the very idea of "defense," as well as a newly expansive concept of "national security." Even before the United States entered World War II, Roosevelt and other leaders had started developing a vision of the world as intrinsically threatening, in which any instability and danger, no matter how small or how far removed from the United States, was seen as a vital threat. "No attack is so unlikely or impossible that it may be ignored," argued Roosevelt in 1939. In a world of "permanent danger," the military thus needed to be a "permanently mobilized force" ready to confront threats wherever they might appear.[52] "If the United States is to have any defense," Roosevelt and others believed, "it must have total defense."[53]

In this way, the mentality of the Cold War started to take hold long before the Cold War had even begun.[54] After World War II, the result was a machinery of war centered on an expanding national security bureaucracy and a perpetually mobilized military patrolling the globe.[55] That the country needed a large collection of bases and hundreds of thousands of troops constantly stationed overseas, as close as possible to any potential enemies, was central to this "forward posture." A Navy strategic guide explained the first "Requirement of a Forward Strategy":

> U.S. forces are deployed overseas to be in position to engage promptly a hostile threat to the security of U.S. interests or allies. These forward deployed forces are a commitment which reassures our allies and deters the potential aggressor. Additionally, these forces provide a capability for flexible and timely response to other crises and contingencies [i.e., wars].[56]

While the motivations behind this strategy were diverse, the result was that U.S. bases overseas became a major mechanism of U.S. global power. While the total acreage of territory acquired may have been relatively slight, in the ability to rapidly deploy the U.S. military nearly anywhere on the globe, the basing system represented a dramatic expansion of American might.[57]

U.S. MILITARY BASES ABROAD, 1776–1903

U.S. Base
U.S. Naval Fleet or Squadron

U.S. Patrol Base or Other Small Installation

Fort Gibbon
Fort St. Michael   Fort Yukon
Fort Davis
Fort Egbert
Kenai Peninsula
Fort Seward
Fort Wrangell
Kodiak Island
Castle Hill
Alaska (U.S.)
Fort Liscum

United States

France
Villefranche-sur-Mer
Spain
Port Mahon
Portugal
Lisbon
Gibraltar (UK)

Midway Island (U.S.)
Hawaii (U.S.)
Pearl Harbor
Mexico
Magdalena Bay

Cuba
Guantánamo Bay
Haiti
Cap-Haïtien
Puerto Rico (U.S.)
Fort Buchanan
Danish West Indies
St. Thomas

Canary Islands
Tenerife

Cape Verde
Porto Praya

Panama
Panama City
Panama
Fort DeLesseps

American Samoa (U.S.)
Pago Pago

Peru
Callao

Chile
Valparaíso

Argentina
Buenos Aires

Brazil
Rio de Janeiro

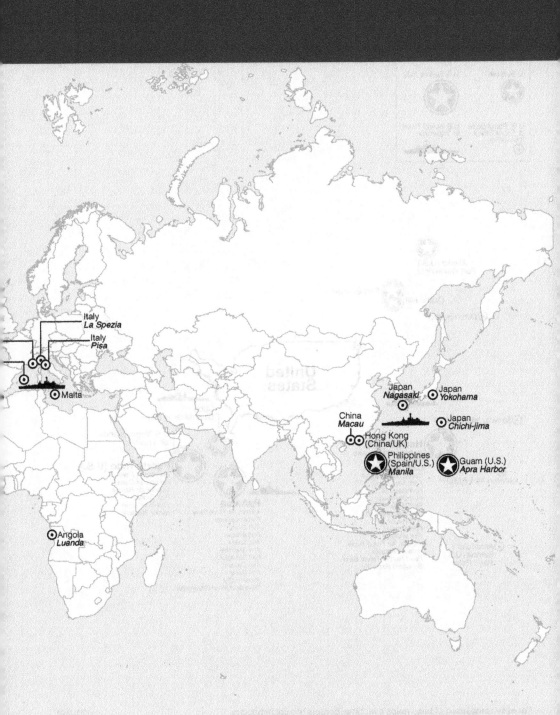

Italy
La Spezia

Italy
Pisa

Malta

Japan
Nagasaki

Japan
Yokohama

China
Macau

Japan
Chichi-jima

Hong Kong
(China/UK)

Philippines
(Spain/U.S.)
Manila

Guam (U.S.)
Apra Harbor

Angola
Luanda

For easy comparison of base maps over time, borders are contemporary.
Key sources: Stacie L. Pettyjohn, "U.S. Global Defense Posture"; U.S. Army Alaska;
Joint Base Elmendorf-Richardson; www.northamericanforts.com.

U.S. MILITARY BASES ABROAD, 1939

Key

U.S. Base

U.S. Bases (>3)

U.S. Patrol Base or Other Small Installation

U.S. Naval Fleet or Squadron

Alaska (U.S.)
Fort Wainwright

Fort Seward

Castle Hill

Dutch Harbor

United States

Midway Island (U.S.)

Johnston Atoll (U.S.)

American Samoa (U.S.)
Pago Pago

Hawaii (U.S.)
Bellows Army Airfield
Camp Kilauea
Camp Malakole
Camp Sand Island
Fort Armstrong
Fort Barrette
Fort DeRussy
Fort Hase
Fort Kamehameha
Fort Ruger
Fort Shafter
Fort Weaver
Hickam Air Force Base
'Iolani Barracks
Pearl Harbor Naval Base
Schofield Barracks

Cuba
Guantánamo Bay

Panama
Albrook Air Force Base
Fort DeLesseps
Fort Grant
Fort Amador
Fort Kobbe
Fort Sherman
Fort Randolph
Fort Clayton
Fort Davis
Panama City
Coco Solo Naval Reservation

U.S. Virgin Islands
St. Thomas

Puerto Rico (U.S.)
Borinquen Field
Camp Las Casas
Cuartel de Ballajá
Fort Brooke
Fort Buchanan
Henry Barracks

Antarctica
Ross Ice Shelf

For easy comparison of base maps over time, borders are contemporary.
Key sources: Robert E. Harkavy, *Strategic Basing and the Great Powers, 1200–2000*;
Stacie L. Pettyjohn, "U.S. Global Defense Posture";
U.S. Army Center of Military History, *The Panama Canal*; U.S. Army Alaska;
Joint Base Elmendorf-Richardson; www.northamericanforts.com.

China
Hankou

China
Shanghai

Hong Kong
(UK)

Guam (U.S.)
Guam Naval Base
Piti Navy Yard
Plaza de España
Sumay Barracks

Wake Island
(U.S.)

Philippines (U.S.)
Fort Drum
Fort Frank
Fort Hughes
Fort Mills
Fort Santiago, Manila
Fort Wint
Subic Bay Naval Reservation

U.S. MILITARY BASES ABROAD, 1945

Legend:
- U.S. Base(s)
- U.S. Bases (>30)
- U.S. Patrol Base(s) or Other Small Installation(s)
- U.S. Naval Fleet

ALASKA (U.S.) (68)

Canada (13)

Iceland (8)

Greenland (6)

Netherlands (15)

UNITED KINGDOM (58)

Newfoundland (7)

Belgium (20)

France (17)

ITALY (32)

Portugal (3)

Tunisia

Midway Island

French Frigate Shoals

Bermuda (3)

French Morocco (6)

French Algeria (2)

Bahamas (3)

Cuba (4)

Dominican Republic

Mexico

British Honduras

Haiti

Puerto Rico (U.S.)

HAWAII (U.S.) (32)

Guatemala (3)

Honduras (2)

Nicaragua (2)

Antigua & Barbuda (7)

U.S. Virgin Islands (2)

St. Lucia

Johnston Atoll (U.S.)

Palmyra Atoll (U.S.)

Costa Rica

Jamaica (2)

Aruba

Trinidad & Tobago (2)

French West Africa

Kiribati (2)

Line Islands

Clipperton Island

Panama (20)

Colombia

French Guiana

Dutch Guiana

Guyana

Liberia

Ecuador (3)

Venezuela

American Samoa (U.S.)

Society Islands

Peru

Brazil

Ascension Island

Cook Islands

Bolivia

Paraguay

Western Samoa

Wallis & Futuna

Tuvalu (3)

Uruguay

At the height of World War II, the United States controlled more than 2,000 bases and 30,000 installations overseas. This was the largest collection of bases possessed by one power in world history. This map reflects the relative number and positioning of these bases around 1945. For easy comparison of base maps over time, borders are contemporary.
Key sources: Robert E. Harkavy, *Strategic Basing and the Great Powers, 1200–2000*; Stacie L. Pettyjohn, "U.S. Global Defense Posture"; James Blaker, *United States Overseas Basing*; Department of the Navy Bureau of Yards and Docks, *Building the Navy's Bases in World War II*; John W. McDonald Jr. and Diane B. Bendahmane, *U.S. Bases Overseas*; news reports.

Norway

Denmark (6)

Luxembourg

GERMANY (148)

Austria (4)

Yugoslavia

Greece (10)

Malta

Libya

Cyprus

Iraq (2)

Iran (4)

Egypt

Palestine

Saudi Arabia

Bahrain (2)

Ethiopia

Kenya

South Rhodesia

INDIA (36)

Burma (8)

Thailand

French Indochina

Singapore

Ceylon

Christmas Island

China (30)

Republic of Korea (2)

Taiwan

Hong Kong

Philippines (U.S.) (11)

Indonesia

Australia (5)

JAPAN (53)

Marcus Island

Wake Island (U.S.)

Northern Mariana Islands (U.S.) (15)

Marshall Islands (3)

Palau

Guam (U.S.) (8)

Gilbert Islands (3)

Caroline Islands

Papua New Guinea (6)

Admiralty Islands

New Britain

Trobriand Islands

Fiji (3)

Tonga

New Zealand (3)

Woodlark Islands

Solomon Islands

New Hebrides

Vanuatu

New Caledonia (3)

U.S. MILITARY BASES ABROAD, 1989

Legend:
- U.S. Base(s)
- U.S. Bases (>30)
- U.S. Small Base(s)
- U.S. Naval Fleet

Greenland (Denmark) (2)

Iceland (8)

Canada (6)

United Kingdom (63)

Belgium (20)

Netherlands (8)

Luxembourg (3)

Italy (90)

Portugal (20)

Spain (9)

Morocco

Midway Island (U.S.)

Bermuda (4)

Puerto Rico (U.S.) (40)

Bahamas (12)

Cuba

U.S. Virgin Islands (6)

Antigua & Barbuda

Honduras (9)

Johnston Atoll (U.S.)

Panama (15)

Liberia

American Samoa (U.S.)

Ascension Island (UK)

United States

Argentina

Antarctica

At the end of the Cold War, the United States controlled around 1,600 bases overseas. This map reflects their relative number and positioning. For easy comparison of base maps over time, borders are contemporary. Key sources: Robert E. Harkavy, *Strategic Basing and the Great Powers, 1200–2000*; Department of Defense, "Base Structure Report 1989"; Stacie L. Pettyjohn, "U.S. Global Defense Posture"; James Blaker, *United States Overseas Basing*; John W. McDonald Jr. and Diane B. Bendahmane, *U.S. Bases Overseas*; news reports.

Norway
(2)

Denmark (5)

Germany (775)

Greece
(12)

Turkey
(24)

Cyprus (2)
Israel   Bahrain (2)
Kuwait
Egypt (2)

Oman (5)

Qatar
Saudi Arabia
Djibouti

Somalia
Kenya

Seychelles

Reunion
(France)

Diego
Garcia
(UK)

China

S. Korea
(125)

Japan
(150)

Guam
(U.S.)
(50)

Hong Kong (UK)

Federated
States of
Micronesia

Philippines (12)

Singapore

Northern
Mariana
Islands (U.S.)
(4)

Wake Island
(U.S.)

Marshall Islands
(11)

Australia (2)

New Zealand

Britain and other European empires had tied their expansionist success to the direct control of foreign lands. For Roosevelt and other leaders,
however, wide-scale colonial control was clearly no longer an option. The
European powers had already divided most of the world among themselves, and the ideological mood of the time was clearly against colonialism and territorial expansion.[58] The allied powers had made World
War II a war against the expansionist desires of Germany, Japan, and
Italy, and the United States had framed the conflict as an anticolonial
struggle, pledging to assist with the decolonization of colonial territories
upon war's end. The subsequent creation of the United Nations enshrined
the decolonization process and the right of nations and peoples to self-
determination and self-government.

Roosevelt and others saw that the United States would have to exert
its power through increasingly subtle and discreet means: the installation of bases as well as periodic displays of military might to keep as much
of the world as possible within the rules of an economic and political
system favorable to the United States.[59] In 1970, a Senate committee
found that "by the mid-1960s, the United States was firmly committed
to more than forty-three nations by treaty and agreement and had some
375 major foreign military bases and 3,000 minor military facilities
spread all over the world, virtually surrounding the Soviet Union and
communist China."[60] As the late geographer Neil Smith explains, "global
economic access without colonies" was the postwar grand strategy, with
"necessary bases around the globe both to protect global economic
interests and to restrain any future military belligerence."[61] Alongside U.S.
economic and political might, the base network became a major and
lasting mechanism of U.S. power, allowing control and influence over
swaths of the earth vastly disproportionate to the land actually occupied.

THE CARTER DOCTRINE

During the Korean War, the U.S. military built yet more overseas bases,
increasing their number by 40 percent. By 1960, the United States had
signed eight mutual defense pacts with forty-two nations, and executive
security agreements with more than thirty others, helping it secure base
access around the globe. Following some reductions after the Korean War,

there was a further 20 percent increase in base sites during the war in Vietnam.[62] By the mid-1960s, the United States had some 375 major foreign military bases and 3,000 minor military facilities spread worldwide. The bulk effectively surrounded the Soviet Union and China.[63]

Through the 1970s, the Middle East remained one of the few regions on Earth to see relatively little Cold War competition and a small U.S. base presence. For the most part, U.S. officials sought to increase American influence in the area by backing and arming the regional powers Israel, Saudi Arabia, and Iran under the shah. But after the Iranian revolution overthrew the shah in early 1979, and the Soviet Union invaded Afghanistan in December of that year, the approach changed dramatically. In his January 1980 State of the Union address, President Jimmy Carter announced a policy change that rivaled Roosevelt's destroyers-for-bases deal in its significance for the nation and the world. Enunciating what became known as the Carter Doctrine, President Carter spoke about the importance of the region "now threatened by Soviet troops." He warned the Soviet Union and other countries that "an attempt by any outside force to gain control of the Persian Gulf region will be regarded as an assault on the vital interests of the United States of America." He added pointedly, "Such an assault will be repelled by any means necessary, including military force."[64]

Carter soon launched what became one of the greatest base construction efforts in history. The Middle East buildup soon approached the size and scope of the Cold War garrisoning of Western Europe and the profusion of bases built to wage wars in Korea and Vietnam. U.S. bases sprang up in Egypt, Oman, Saudi Arabia, and elsewhere in the region to host a "Rapid Deployment Force," which was to stand permanent guard over Middle Eastern petroleum supplies.[65] Eventually, the Rapid Deployment Force grew into the U.S. Central Command, a geographic command like those overseeing Europe and the Pacific. The Central Command would soon lead three wars in Iraq and the war in Afghanistan, plus dozens of other military operations.

In the aftermath of the 1991 Gulf War in Iraq, thousands of troops and a significantly expanded base infrastructure remained in Saudi Arabia, Kuwait, Bahrain, Qatar, the United Arab Emirates, and Oman. The 2001 and 2003 invasions of Afghanistan and Iraq have led to yet another dramatic expansion of U.S. bases in the region. In the Persian Gulf alone, the U.S. military has built major bases in every country save Iran. Qatar's al Udeid Air Base has become home to the Central Command's air operations center for the entire Middle East; Bahrain is now the headquarters for the Navy's Fifth Fleet and its Middle Eastern operations; and Kuwait has become a particularly important staging area and logistical center for U.S. ground troops. The military has also maintained bases in Jordan and as many as six secret U.S. bases in Israel.[66] On a near-permanent basis, the Navy now maintains at least one aircraft carrier strike group—in effect, a huge floating base—in the Persian Gulf itself.

Elsewhere in the greater Middle East, the military has established a collection of at least five drone bases in Pakistan; expanded a critical base in Djibouti, at the strategic chokepoint between the Suez Canal and the Indian Ocean; and created or gained access to bases in Ethiopia, Kenya, and the Seychelles. Even in Saudi Arabia, where widespread anger at the U.S. military presence led to a public withdrawal in 2003, a small U.S. military contingent has remained to train Saudi personnel and keep bases "warm" as potential backups for future conflicts. In recent years, the U.S. military also established a secret drone base in the country.

In Afghanistan, meanwhile, the military will retain at least nine large bases after the official withdrawal of U.S. troops. Although the Pentagon failed in its effort to maintain as many as fifty-eight "enduring" bases in Iraq after the 2011 withdrawal from the country, the fortress-like embassy in Baghdad—the world's largest—is effectively a base. Base-like State Department installations and a large contingent of U.S. private military contractors have also remained.[67] And following the 2014 start of the new war in Iraq and Syria against the Islamic State, thousands of U.S. troops have returned to at least five military bases in Iraq.[68]

Stepping back, it's telling that the Carter Doctrine and the bases it spawned persisted despite the disappearance of the Soviet Union and any threat it may arguably have posed to Middle East oil. The U.S. military presence in a region that sits atop the world's largest concentration of petroleum and natural gas reserves is not a matter of Cold War exigency.[69] Rather, as the late base expert Chalmers Johnson explained, since World War II, "the United States has been inexorably acquiring permanent military enclaves whose sole purpose appears to be the domination of one of the most strategically important areas of the world."[70]

More broadly still, the Middle East base buildup reflects the continuation of a millennia-old strategy for pursuing power around the world. Like empires from ancient Egypt to imperial Britain, the United States has come to use its foreign bases to assert influence and dominate far-off lands, resources, and markets. But even more than its predecessors, including the empire upon which the sun never set, the United States since World War II has become defined by its unprecedented collection of bases encircling the planet.

Technical Sergeant Kenneth Bellard, U.S. Air Force

Entrance to the world's largest base exchange ("PX"), at Ramstein Air Base, Germany.

2

From Little Americas to Lily Pads

On the autobahn just outside Ramstein-Miesenbach, a small town in southwestern Germany, the exit sign simply says: air base. Once off the exit ramp, you find yourself on an isolated, arrow-straight stretch of "private state road" surrounded by the thick woods of the local Palatinate forest. The road widens, expanding until one can easily imagine airplanes landing on it in an emergency. The huge breadth of the secluded highway makes it feel surreal. A steady stream of cars moves in both directions; about a mile down the road lies the busy western entrance to the Air Force's "super base" in Europe, Ramstein Air Base.[1] It is the largest base in the middle of the largest concentration of U.S. citizens living overseas—some fifty thousand Americans spread over an area the size of Rhode Island.

The hundreds of U.S. bases spread around Germany and the rest of the world can be broadly divided into three groups. Most troops and family members overseas are stationed at giant city-sized garrisons often referred to as "Little Americas"—places like Ramstein, Kadena Air Base in Okinawa, and Camp Humphreys in South Korea. Smaller than those are medium-sized bases like the Soto Cano Air Base in Honduras, which retain amenities such as fitness facilities but rarely host family members, eliminating the need for schools and child care. And the smallest of all are the bases officially known as "cooperative security locations," more commonly referred to as "lily pads," after the flora that enable a frog to jump across a pond. Often secretive in nature, lily pads tend to have few if any U.S. troops, sometimes relying instead on private contractors. They frequently house drones, surveillance aircraft, or pre-positioned weaponry for the use of troops deploying from elsewhere. Generally, they are located in parts of the world that have previously seen relatively little U.S. military presence, giving U.S. forces access to new parts of the globe.

The battle zones in Iraq, Afghanistan, Syria, and elsewhere make the headlines. But behind the scenes, it is this far-flung base nation that has enabled the United States to wage war year after year in distant lands.

BURGER KINGS AND LEDERHOSEN

The Kaiserslautern Military Community, which includes Ramstein Air Base as well as Landstuhl Regional Medical Center, Rhine Ordnance Barracks, and numerous other bases, hosts roughly 45,000 U.S. troops, civilian employees, and family members, plus 5,000 retirees and their families and some 6,700 German civilians working for the U.S. military.[2] The city of Kaiserslautern itself, which military folks call K-Town, has a population of about a hundred thousand—only around twice the size of the U.S. presence.

Just steps from Ramstein's airfield are the shiny new passenger and cargo terminals of the Air Force's largest overseas cargo port. These terminals have been major logistical hubs for the wars in Afghanistan and Iraq: around 80 percent of the troops, weaponry, and supplies used in those wars have gone through Germany, the bulk of them through Ramstein.[3] Standing directly across from the passenger terminal that has ferried troops to and from the war zones is what some call the "Mall of America of the East." When it opened in 2009, the 844,000-square-foot Kaiserslautern Military Community Center was the largest single facility built by the military overseas, at a cost of more than $200 million.[4] The mall's "anchor tenant" is the world's largest base exchange (the combined Air Force / Army shopping facility formerly called the Post Exchange or "PX"). The 165,000-square-foot store is so large it's hard to see from end to end.[5]

A public affairs officer who gave me a tour of the Community Center explained that it is designed to add to the "quality of life" of military personnel and their families. This is particularly important, he said, when spouses and parents are deployed. It's a "retainment benefit" to keep people happy and in the military. And all of it, he said, is "on, quote-unquote, foreign soil."

Foreign soil or not, places like Ramstein tend to resemble insulated, self-contained small American towns that allow their inhabitants to hardly ever leave the base. These Little Americas have become both a symbol of American life and an exaggerated version of it. In many ways they resemble gated communities, with sprawling grounds, shopping malls, fast food, golf, and a car-based lifestyle. (Service members get their cars shipped overseas free of charge, and gasoline is heavily subsidized.) These "simulacrums of suburbia," as the architecture professor and former Air Force officer Mark Gillem calls them, subtly and not so subtly shape life around them, presenting the host nation with their particular vision of American culture and transforming local economies to reflect the consumption habits of U.S. troops.

Even in Afghanistan and, previously, in Iraq, the biggest bases have been Little Americas, absent family members but complete with tens of thousands of troops, fast-food outlets, sports facilities, swimming pools, and shopping.

"It's a little bit of Americana," an officer at Ramstein told me about the giant mall. It lets you buy things you just can't get off base. And while you're there, it also offers other things you might want—all for less than on the German market. There's even a vendor selling lederhosen in the middle of the mall and a "Ramsteiner" souvenir shop. "People go in there to buy German souvenirs," the officer said. "It's almost comical to me."

Understanding how the Little Americas became so complete that one can shop for German souvenirs on base requires going back to the arrival of U.S. troops in Germany at the end of World War II. At the time, Germany was in chaos. Most of the country's cities and towns had been battered by the war. Some were in near total ruin. "Much of Germany was just a mass of broken stones, and people found shelter among this rubble as best they could," a classic history of the war explains. "Millions upon millions of people were faced with the basic necessity of finding food, shelter, and work."[6]

Amid such destitution and destruction, tensions grew between occupiers and occupied. After years of bloody fighting, the first year of postwar occupation in particular was characterized by an aggressive Allied campaign to seize homes, automobiles, bicycles, wine, and other property from the locals. GIs called this "liberating" and spoke euphemistically of rape as "liberating a blonde."[7] Even when outright force was not involved, the nature of sexual relationships between GIs and German women—romance, prostitution, or assault—was often hazy at best.[8] Survival prostitution was widespread, with impoverished women sometimes congregating outside PXs and soldiers' camps. Venereal disease rates reflected as much. In April 1945, less than 6 percent of GIs had VD. Fifteen months later, the rate was over 30 percent.[9]

Rampant prostitution and venereal disease, GI theft and violence, a thriving black market, and racial hostility among Germans who objected to relationships between black GIs and German women became an increasing concern for the military. News of the Army's "disarray" in Germany began filtering back to the United States. *Life*, *Collier's Weekly*, and other popular news outlets published articles with titles like "Failure in Germany" and "Heels Among the Heroes." John Dos Passos wrote in *Life*, "Never has American prestige in Europe been lower. People never tire of telling you the ignorance and rowdyism of American troops."[10]

American officials decided that something had to be done. To reassert control and ease the tensions of the occupation, the Army employed a combination of harsh discipline and "wholesome" educational and recreational activities. As the economist John Willoughby writes in a book about the U.S. presence in Germany, the lifestyle that emerged was something "between boot camp and summer camp." Its norms have continued to this day.[11]

FAMILIES TO THE RESCUE

At the heart of the new lifestyle was the Army's decision in 1945 to allow families to join soldiers in Germany. Today it seems natural for spouses and children to join members of the military at bases worldwide. At the time, this was a radical decision. Traditionally, men in the U.S. military—as in most other militaries—deployed overseas alone. The idea that families might live with them somewhere abroad, let alone on the front lines of the Cold War amid the growing nuclear standoff between East and West, represented a profound change.

Until the end of the nineteenth century, after all, the U.S. military had made no formal provisions whatsoever for the lives or well-being of soldiers' partners and children. Military leaders generally referred to them as "camp followers." The only women allowed to live on post were a few officers' wives; the wives of ordinary soldiers had to live outside the walls. Only in the 1890s did the Army begin to create basic schools on posts for children and to provide food rations and other benefits to the families of enlisted men—benefits that barely foreshadowed the amenities to come. Indeed, until 1913 the Army actively discouraged its soldiers from marrying. A popular line has long said if the Army had wanted you to have a wife, it would have issued you one.[12]

Beyond improving relations with the occupied Germans, the 1945 decision to allow families to rejoin soldiers overseas was a response to growing demands in the United States to reunite families by bringing troops home. It was also a way to deal with the multiple problems associated with "fraternization." GIs' sexual relationships with locals not only created tension with German men, who were intent on maintaining patriarchal control over "their" women, but also left many women in the United States angry about continued deployments. "Thank you for telling us what fun it is to 'fraternize,'" one woman wrote to Life magazine in August 1945. "Too bad there aren't enough Nazi prisoners of war here in America for all of us wives with husbands in Germany to try it."[13]

U.S. leaders hoped that allowing family members to live with the GIs overseas would help address these problems, improve morale during continuing deployments abroad, and keep skilled soldiers from requesting redeployment to the United States. By October 1946, there were around four thousand wives and children in Germany. By the end of 1950, there were nearly thirty thousand.[14]

In the following decade, the numbers grew further. Beginning in 1951, following the outbreak of the Korean War, President Truman sent massive army reinforcements to Asia and Western Europe to contain "communist aggression." It was an early manifestation of the newly enshrined forward strategy. By the end of 1951, there were 176,000 U.S. troops in Germany, and there was almost no decline with the end of the Korean War. By

1955, Germany hosted more than 260,000 U.S. troops. Hundreds of thousands of wives and children followed. They would remain stationed for almost four decades across West Germany's south, where military planners thought a Soviet invasion was most likely.[15]

At first, the arrival of soldiers' family members in Germany actually inflamed tensions with locals because the presence of the newcomers meant the requisitioning of more German land. Attempts to ease the effects of the occupation on Germans—and to exert more control over soldiers—led the military to segregate GIs and their families on bases further removed from German society. As the military realized that the bases badly lacked medical facilities, schools, shopping, and other facilities for families, a massive building campaign followed in Germany and, soon, around the world. The aim was to create replicas of American towns so GIs and their families would feel at home overseas. Housing, shopping centers, recreational services, and hospitals sprang up on bases worldwide. The military established a Family Services Program and created an entire overseas school system.

"Commanders realized they needed to pay attention to quality of life issues in order to retain expensively trained personnel," explains Anni Baker, a historian who has lived on bases abroad as a family member and civilian employee. Otherwise, troops "would desert the military for better opportunities in the civilian world."[16] Because of the changes initiated in the early 1950s in Germany and elsewhere, family members once dismissed as "camp followers" are now described by the military as "force multipliers" who contribute to "overall readiness."[17]

The millions of dollars in base construction and spending that accompanied the buildup of Little Americas also helped improve relations with locals. Before the arrival of U.S. troops in Rheinland-Pfalz, for example, the rural state was Germany's "traditional poorhouse." After more than a hundred thousand GIs and family members arrived between 1950 and 1951, rapid construction created thousands of new jobs. Unemployment, which had been over 10 percent in the region and over 22 percent in the town of Baumholder, vanished amid a gold rush atmosphere. With a strong U.S. dollar, Americans splashed money around the local economy. By 1955, they were spending almost $5 million a year (the equivalent of $44 million today) in Baumholder alone, a town of around twenty-five hundred that came to host an average of thirty thousand U.S. troops and family members. People in Rheinland-Pfalz now remember the decade as the "Fabulous Fifties" and the "Golden Years."[18]

To many, the presence of wives and children living on the front lines of the Cold War in Germany, Japan, South Korea, and elsewhere was also a powerful sign of the U.S. commitment to defending its allies.*[19] Generally, people overlooked any problems such as airplane noise and damage caused by frequent exercises traversing city streets and farmers' fields. (In Baumholder, a permanent office in the city center paid compensation for training-related damage.)[20] Five years into the Korea buildup, a government survey indicated that a majority of Germans felt troop conduct and German-American rapport had improved.[21]

The family decision and the housing, schools, bowling alleys, and Burger Kings that followed it can seem superficial. They are anything but that, however, and their implications for the military and for the country as a whole have been profound. The Little Americas helped enable the permanent peacetime deployment of troops overseas, appeasing GIs, their families, and other Americans upset about the long-term presence of U.S. troops abroad. The city-sized bases that began growing in Germany, Italy, Japan, Britain, and beyond in the late 1940s and early 1950s also helped improve relations, legitimizing and normalizing what might have otherwise been seen as permanent occupation. They helped ensure a relatively friendly and stable local environment, thus allowing for the smooth operation of a military unencumbered by major protest or conflict with locals.[22]

"The success of the domesticating reforms," says the economist John Willoughby, "permitted President Truman to double the troop presence during the Korean War crisis with few complaints from the German state" or from U.S. citizens back home.[23] In short, the construction of Little Americas in Western Europe and Japan, the Philippines and South Korea, was critical to making the base nation a permanent feature of Cold

---

*Although officials did not publicize the fact, bases had detailed evacuation plans for families. They were never used in Europe but were employed in South Korea, South Vietnam, and Guantánamo Bay.

War life. When the Cold War ended, however, the Little Americas, and the permanent war footing they represent, would not disappear.

GLOBAL REALIGNMENT

With the dissolution of the Soviet Union, the U.S. presence overseas endured despite significant reductions. In the first half of the 1990s, the U.S. government gave up around 60 percent of its foreign bases and brought almost three hundred thousand troops back to the United States. The largest number of returnees came from the Army in Germany.[24] Between 1991 and 1995 the U.S. military returned around a hundred thousand acres of land to the German government—about twice the size of Washington, D.C.[25] Still, despite the disappearance of the Eastern Bloc, hundreds of U.S. bases and sixty thousand U.S. troops remained in Germany alone. Globally, in 2001—more than a decade after the end of the Cold War—around one thousand bases and hundreds of thousands of troops remained overseas.

As former deputy assistant secretary of defense for strategy Andrew Hoehn told me, with the end of the Cold War, the military reduced its overseas presence but failed to make any significant change in the nature of its forces abroad. There was "a lot of hedging at that moment," he said. "We shrank in place. But we really didn't reposition."

This did not please George W. Bush administration secretary of defense Donald Rumsfeld. The day after Bush's first presidential inauguration, Rumsfeld convened a small staff meeting. One of the staffers, Raymond DuBois, recounted how Rumsfeld told his staff, "We can no longer afford a post–Cold War [basing] apparatus."

Out of the meeting emerged a plan to transform "a global system of overseas military bases [developed] primarily to contain aggression by the Soviet Union." In late 2003, amid an intensifying insurgency in Iraq and warfare in Afghanistan, President Bush surprised many by declaring plans to "realign the global posture" of the U.S. military. The goal, Bush said, was to "ensure that we place the right capabilities in the most appropriate locations to best address" the world's security threats.[26]

The administration said it would eliminate more than a third of the nation's Cold War–era bases in Europe, South Korea, and Japan. In

Europe alone, the Pentagon identified around three hundred base sites for closure, most of them in Germany. The Pentagon would shift troops to be closer to current and predicted conflict zones, moving them from Europe and the Middle East to Asia, Africa, and South America. The administration planned to return as many as seventy thousand more troops stationed abroad—about 20 percent of the overseas total—as well as a hundred thousand family members to the United States. The remaining U.S. forces overseas, who would still number in the hundreds of thousands, were to be concentrated in a smaller collection of sprawling (and often enlarged) main bases like Ramstein, Osan Air Base in South Korea, and Marine Corps Air Station Iwakuni in Japan.

A move to consolidate troops at a smaller collection of very large bases had actually been under way for several years, thanks in part to a string of attacks beginning in 1996 that hit the Khobar Towers complex in Saudi Arabia, embassies in East Africa, and the USS *Cole*. In response, the military began closing small bases, bases in congested urban areas vulnerable to truck bombs, and other hard-to-protect facilities. The remaining Little Americas began growing larger, with taller walls, broader boundaries, and tighter security. Inside the gates, the military expanded shopping, food, and recreational offerings to provide troops and family members with most everything they might require.

"They are making these bases even more self-contained in an attempt to minimize the need for soldiers to go off-base" where security risks might arise, explains Mark Gillem in his book *America Town*. More than just idealized suburbia, these bases are now "necessarily like gated communities, with guards and walls designed to keep out the trouble-makers."[27]

"TEMPORARY BUT INDEFINITE"

Under the Bush administration's plan, rather than building new Little Americas in former Cold War zones, the military would instead generally focus on developing smaller and more flexible bases elsewhere. Mid-size "forward operating sites"—scattered from Singapore and Australia to Bulgaria and Djibouti—became increasingly important. These bases generally have been relatively compact, often rotating deployments of U.S.

troops, fewer amenities, and usually no family members. Crucially, the "operating site" nomenclature and the smaller size of the bases often let U.S. officials insist that there is "no U.S. base" in the area. Instead, officials refer to the base as just a "site," or, alternatively, as a "forward operating location" that's a guest of the host country.

The Soto Cano Air Base in Honduras, which predates the global posture realignment, exemplifies the small-to-midsize base the Pentagon increasingly favors. Ever since construction at Soto Cano began in 1982, U.S. officials have maintained that there is "no U.S. base in Honduras." They have said and still maintain that the more-than-three-decades-old base is "temporary," or, as some say, "temporary but indefinite."[28] Officials insist that U.S. forces there are "guests" on the site of the Honduran Air Force Academy, even though there are now more than thirteen hundred U.S. troops and civilians in Soto Cano, dwarfing the three-hundred-person academy. As numerous analysts have pointed out, calling the base "temporary" provides a rhetorical mechanism to circumvent the Honduras constitution's prohibition against the permanent stationing of foreign troops on Honduran soil.[29]

If there was any doubt about who really controls the base, a 2008 incident was revealing. At the time, Honduran president Manuel Zelaya proposed using Soto Cano's runway as part of a new international airport for joint civilian and military use. An embassy staffer in the Honduran capital told me that the U.S. response was, *No problem.* But U.S. officials added, "Oh, by the way, all the power, all the water, all the sewage, all the lighting, all the air traffic control stuff, the radar, is all controlled by the U.S., and our laws prohibit U.S. military funds supporting private enterprises. So, if you want to open up an international airport"—by building replacement facilities from scratch, that is—"by all means, go for it." The Honduran project went nowhere.

When I walked through the gate at Soto Cano in the summer of 2011, a handful of Puerto Rican National Guard soldiers rested at ease inside the guardhouse. A public affairs officer put a one-page letter (in English) approving my visit in front of the single Honduran guard. The slightest glance later, I was in.

Sgt. Timothy Edwards first showed me what he called, using air quotes, "the Honduran side." The Honduran Air Force Academy probably makes up less than one fifth of the base. It consists of a small array of aging class-room buildings and two-story concrete dorms. Grass and weeds sprout wildly along the road.

On the other side of the base, the grass is carefully manicured, as on U.S. bases worldwide. The "U.S. side" is not, however, a Little America kind of base. There are no suburban-style housing developments. There are a few fast-food vendors, but no shopping malls. Most signs on base were made in the 1980s with hand-painted stencils, and wood cabins are the base's dominant architectural feature, making it somewhat reminiscent of a large summer camp attached to an eight-thousand-foot runway. What troops call "hooches" (military slang dating back to the wars in Korea and Vietnam), with rusting corrugated iron roofs and shutters, are situated around communal toilets and bathrooms. Enlisted personnel sleep in the cabins; officers get more comfortable housing with indoor plumbing. More hooches are used as offices for the various tenant units on base. Still others house small restaurants and a few souvenir shops that may make Soto Cano the only U.S. military base in the world to sell Cuban cigars.

A military official who was in Honduras in the early 1980s told me that when he first came to the area, the Honduran Air Force was landing a few planes on dirt or on a little pavement. So, he said, "We came in and built it up." U.S. troops constructed a proper runway and assembled some tents and other basic living facilities. Soon there was an airplane ramp as well as hangars and the hooches. Over time they built a large runway capable of accommodating F-16 fighter jets and C-5 cargo planes, a pool, a gym, sports fields and other recreational facilities, twenty-two miles of roads, and extensive water, sewer, and electrical systems.[30]

If anything, the hooches and the "summer camp" feel of the base have helped maintain the pretense that U.S. troops might pack up and leave at short notice. But by 1989, operations at Soto Cano were so significant that some Pentagon officials referred to Joint Task Force Bravo, which commands the base, as having responsibilities and power almost matching an entire regional command, like the Southern or European Commands.[31] Two decades later, when I visited, millions of dollars in expansion and new construction was well under way; to some extent, officials have now dispensed with the charade of calling the base temporary.[32] Since

2003, Congress has appropriated at least $45 million to build "permanent facilities" in Soto Cano for almost seven hundred troops.[33] Between 2009 and 2011 alone, the base population has grown by almost 20 percent.[34] Construction workers were replacing the hooches with yellow aluminum-sided buildings, where enlisted soldiers would get single rooms with central air, furniture, a refrigerator, and a microwave. Elsewhere, they were building the foundation for new officers' housing.

Military planners generally design medium-sized bases like Soto Cano and others like it in Singapore, Djibouti, and Romania to be readily expandable. This allows short-term deployments of U.S. forces to visit for training purposes and operations of various kinds and also permits for more permanent construction of the kind that Soto Cano saw during the 1980s and is seeing today. All the while, officials at "forward operating sites" often repeat the mantra that their U.S.-funded, U.S.-operated facilities are not U.S. military bases at all. "This is *their* base," Sergeant Edwards emphasized to me before the end of my visit to Soto Cano. "Sometimes we forget that. But we're here to help them."

As Sergeant Edwards's admission suggests, the sincerity of such claims depends greatly on the power of a host country relative to the United States, with wealthy nations like Singapore toward one end of a spectrum and Honduras very much at the other. In many of the countries where one finds the smallest category of bases—the lily pads—the hosts often have similarly little power relative to their ostensible guests.

"NO FLAG, NO FORWARD PRESENCE, NO FAMILIES"

As with medium-sized forward operating sites (FOSs), U.S. officials strenuously avoid calling the third smaller group of installations "bases." They instead call them cooperative security locations, or lily pads. Like "forward operating site," the terms "cooperative security location" and "lily pad" seek to minimize perceptions about the size and significance of a base.

Beyond the terminology, lily pads generally occupy remote locations and are either secret or only tacitly acknowledged to avoid protests that might lead to restrictions on their use. They usually have limited numbers of troops, no families, and few amenities. Sometimes they rely mostly or entirely on private military contractors, whose actions the U.S.

government can more easily disown if necessary. To further maintain a low profile and preempt accusations about building "new U.S. bases," the Pentagon has often hidden its lily pads within existing host nation bases or on the margins of civilian airports.

With lily pads found in places as diverse as Colombia, Kenya, and Thailand, a principal aim of the new strategy is avoiding local populations, publicity, and potential opposition. "To project its power," former Air Force officer Mark Gillem says, the United States wants "secluded and self-contained outposts strategically located" around the world.[35] According to some of the strategy's strongest proponents at the conservative American Enterprise Institute, the goal should be "to create a worldwide network of frontier forts," with the U.S. military "the 'global cavalry' of the twenty-first century."[36]

Unbeknownst to most, the Pentagon has been trying to acquire as many lily pads as it can, in as many countries as it can, as fast as it can. Although statistics are hard to assemble, given the often secretive nature of such bases, the Pentagon has probably built upwards of fifty lily pads and other small bases in the past fifteen years, while exploring the construction of dozens more. While the collection of giant Cold War–era bases has shrunk, the proliferation of new lily pads (and FOSs) in recent years has meant that our base nation has actually grown in geographic scope.

In early 2001, the Pentagon official Ray DuBois traveled to the Philippines to negotiate new access to the country for the U.S. military. Some wondered whether this would mark a return to the days of giant American bases in the Philippines: Clark Air Base and Subic Bay Naval Base used to be the largest overseas U.S. military bases in the world. DuBois responded with an emphatic *no*. There would be "no flag, no forward presence, no families," he said. The phrase became his motto. It meant that host countries would maintain sovereignty over the lily pads; that there would be no large, permanent contingent of U.S. troops; and that there would be no family members or the extensive amenities that go with them.

Clark and Subic Bay closed in 1992 after the Filipino government refused to renew a lease on the bases and adopted a new constitution banning foreign bases. A few years later, after the 1999 reversion of the

Panama Canal Zone, the U.S. military lost its Panamanian bases as well. Responding to these losses, Bill Clinton's Pentagon started developing lily pads and other small and medium-sized bases in places such as Ecuador, Aruba, Curaçao, and El Salvador. As a Pentagon official explained in a 2009 presentation, the aim is to "lighten U.S. foreign footprints to reduce friction with host nations" and avoid offending "host nation and regional sensitivities."[37]

The Pentagon has various techniques for disguising its presence at cooperative security locations. In Pakistan, for instance, the military leased a base technically owned by the United Arab Emirates so the Pakistani government could deny the presence of a "U.S. base" on its territory.[38] In Thailand, a private contractor rents space on Utapao Naval Air Base, a facility of the Royal Thai Navy, and leases the space to U.S. forces. "Because of Delta Golf Global," writes the journalist Robert D. Kaplan, "the U.S. military was here, but it was not here. After all, the Thais did no business with the U.S. Air Force. They dealt only with a private contractor."[39] Thanks to this arrangement, the Thai lily pad has become a major logistical hub for aircraft and naval vessels heading to the wars in Iraq and Afghanistan. By 2008, almost nine hundred flights were passing through Utapao annually.[40] The military misleadingly calls Utapao a "disaster relief hub," which describes only a small portion of its activities.[41]

In even more countries, "access agreements" have given U.S. forces regular use rights at airfields, ports, and bases. As part of the global realignment, the Air Force signed more than twenty "gas-and-go" agreements with countries in Africa alone during Donald Rumsfeld's time as secretary of defense. These agreements allow planes to refuel and repair at locations across the continent. Between the end of the Cold War and the end of Rumsfeld's tenure in 2007, the number of agreements permitting the presence of U.S. troops on foreign soil more than doubled, from forty-five to more than ninety.[42]

"Access, not bases" has become a mantra for some—although sometimes, as in the Philippines since 2001, "access" can become just another euphemism for a base. Through the work of DuBois and other U.S. negotiators in the Philippines, as many as six hundred American special forces troops began operating in the country's south in early 2002, using perhaps as many as seven lily pads. Kaplan, one of the few journalists to visit the bases, noted that despite the Philippines' constitutional ban on foreign bases, the new deployment "had succeeded as a political mechanism for getting an American base-of-sorts up and running."[43]

The developments in the Philippines have been widely replicated with American lily pads flowering around the globe. The result appears to be a case of "back to the future," with the creation of what military analyst Robert Work likens to a "global coaling-station network" last seen in the nineteenth century.[44]

This new generation of smaller bases is appealing to many who hope that lily pads and other relatively small bases can avoid the controversies and protests that have often accompanied the large bases worldwide. But this has often not been the case. As we will see, military facilities small and large alike all too often harm local communities in ways that locals do not easily forget.

British agents announce the deportation of all Chagossians from Diego Garcia, January 1971.

3

The Displaced

While the U.S. military was welcoming the families of American soldiers to overseas bases in the decades after World War II, it had very different plans for another group of families living on a small atoll in the middle of the Indian Ocean. In the late 1950s, Navy officials began developing a plan to build a new U.S. base on the British-controlled island of Diego Garcia, in the Chagos Archipelago. During talks with their British counterparts, Pentagon and State Department negotiators insisted that the Chagos islands come under their "exclusive control (without local inhabitants)."[1]

This tiny parenthetical phrase amounted to an expulsion order. Between 1968 and 1973, the two governments forcibly removed Diego Garcia's entire indigenous population, deporting them to the western Indian Ocean islands of Mauritius and the Seychelles, twelve hundred miles from their homeland.

The exiled Chagossians received no resettlement assistance. Decades after their expulsion, they generally remain the poorest of the poor in Mauritius and the Seychelles, struggling to survive in places that outsiders know as exotic tourist and honeymoon destinations. The U.S. military, having claimed the Chagossians' former home, has nicknamed Diego Garcia "the Footprint of Freedom."

And Diego Garcia is not the only U.S. base with a sordid history of displacing indigenous populations. Military bases need land to exist, and throughout history, militaries have acquired such land through a variety of means. Sometimes, as in Germany and Japan, it comes with the aftermath of victory in war. Sometimes the land is bought or leased from locals or from a national government. But often, land has simply been taken.

STRATEGIC ISLAND CONCEPT

In a way, the idea for acquiring Diego Garcia dates to the winter of 1922, when eight-year-old Stuart Barber found himself sick and confined to bed at his family's home in New Haven, Connecticut. Stu, as he was known, was always a solitary boy, and he sought solace in a cherished geography book. He was particularly fascinated by the world's remote islands, and he developed a passion for collecting the stamps of far-flung island colonies. While the British-controlled Falkland Islands off the coast of Argentina was his favorite, Barber noticed that the Indian Ocean off the east coast of Africa was also dotted with islands claimed by Britain.

Thirty-six years later, Barber would once again be consulting lists of small, isolated colonial islands from every map, atlas, and nautical chart he could find. The year was 1958. Thin and spectacled, Barber was a civilian working in the Navy's long-range planning office.

At this time of decolonization and Cold War confrontation between East and West, Barber and other officials in the growing national security bureaucracy were concerned about what would happen as colonized nations gained their independence. Postwar independence movements were vocally opposed to foreign military facilities, and U.S., British, and French bases were also increasingly criticized by the Soviet Union and the United Nations. U.S. officials were particularly worried that losing overseas bases would diminish American influence in the so-called Third World, where they predicted future military conflicts would likely take place.

"Within the next 5 to 10 years," Barber wrote to the Navy brass, "virtually all of Africa, and certain Middle Eastern and Far Eastern territories presently under Western control will gain either complete independence or a high degree of autonomy," making them likely to "drift from Western influence."[2] The inevitable result, Barber predicted, would be the withdrawal of U.S. and allied European military forces and "the denial or restriction" of Western bases in these areas.[3] The Cold War's "forward strategy" was premised on maintaining large numbers of bases and troops as close as possible to the Soviet Union, but Barber and others feared that the United States would soon face eviction orders across much of the globe.

Barber's solution to this perceived threat was what he called the "Strategic Island Concept." Barber had served as an intelligence officer in Hawaii during World War II and had seen the importance of having scores of Pacific island bases in defeating Japan. Island bases near hot spots in the "Third World," he said, would increase the nation's ability to rapidly deploy military force wherever and whenever officials desired. His plan was to avoid traditional base sites located in populous mainland areas, where bases were vulnerable to local opposition. Instead, he wrote, "only relatively small, lightly populated islands, separated from major population masses, could be safely held under full control of the West."[4]

With the decolonization process unfolding rapidly, Barber argued that if the United States wanted to protect its "future freedom of military action," government officials would have to act fast to "stockpile" basing rights, grabbing as many islands as possible as quickly as possible to retain territorial sovereignty in perpetuity. Just as a sensible investor would "stockpile any material commodity which foreseeably will become unavailable in the future," Barber said, the United States had to find small, little-noticed colonial islands around the world and either buy them outright or ensure that Western allies maintained sovereignty over them. Otherwise the islands could be lost to decolonization forever.[5] Once officials secured the islands, the military could then prepare them for base construction whenever future needs required.[6]

Barber told his superiors that the Navy should specifically look for small islands with good anchorages where the Navy could build airstrips, fuel storage tanks, and other logistical facilities capable of supporting minor peacetime deployments and major wartime operations. Island bases insulated from local "population problems" and "decolonization pressures" were the key to maintaining U.S. global dominance for decades to come.

Barber first thought of the Seychelles and its more than one hundred islands before exploring other possibilities in the Atlantic, Pacific, and

Indian Oceans. In and around the Indian Ocean alone, there were Phuket, Cocos, Masirah, Farquhar, Aldabra, Desroches, Salomon, and Peros Banhos. After finding all of them to be "inferior sites," Barber settled on "that beautiful atoll of Diego Garcia, right in the middle of the ocean." Its isolation made it safe from attack, yet it was still within striking distance of a wide area of the globe, from southern Africa and the Middle East to South and Southeast Asia.

Others in the national security bureaucracy quickly embraced Barber's idea. In 1960, the Navy settled on Diego Garcia as its most important acquisition target. As Barber had recognized, the V-shaped island was blessed with a central location, a protected lagoon that offered one of the world's great natural harbors, and enough land for a large airstrip.

Since it was first settled in the late eighteenth century, Diego Garcia and the rest of the Chagos Archipelago had been a dependency of initially French and then British colonial Mauritius. The U.S. Navy's highest-ranking officer, Chief of Naval Operations Admiral Arleigh Burke, initiated secret conversations about the islands with his British counterparts, who were quickly receptive to the idea. By 1963, the proposal to create a base on Diego Garcia had gained support among powerful officials in the Kennedy administration, including the Joint Chiefs of Staff, the Pentagon of Robert McNamara and Paul Nitze, Dean Rusk's State Department, and the National Security Council (NSC) of McGeorge Bundy.

Prodded in particular by the NSC's Robert Komer, the Kennedy administration persuaded the British—in contravention of international agreements forbidding the division of colonies during decolonization—to create a new colony by detaching the Chagos Archipelago from colonial Mauritius and additional islands from colonial Seychelles. They called it the British Indian Ocean Territory, and it was to be devoted solely to military use. In exchange for the detached islands, the British government agreed to build an international airport for the Seychelles, and in 1965 it paid £3 million to Mauritius. A British official described the compensation as "bribes" to ensure that both colonies would quietly acquiesce to the plan.[7]

A year later, the U.S. and British governments confirmed the arrangements with a little-noticed "Exchange of Notes." This effectively constituted a treaty, but unlike a treaty, it required no congressional or parliamentary approval—allowing both governments to keep the plans hidden. Representatives of the two governments signed the agreement, as one of the State Department negotiators told me, "under the cover of darkness," the day before New Year's Eve 1966.

According to the Notes, the United States would gain use of the new colony "without charge."[8] In confidential agreements accompanying the Notes, however, the United States agreed to secretly transfer $14 million to Britain. Secretary of Defense Robert McNamara had approved the transfer of funds a year earlier, circumventing the congressional appropriations process.[9]

"A NEGLIGIBLE NATIVE POPULATION"

A fundamental part of Stuart Barber's Strategic Island Concept was the idea of avoiding antibase protests. The Navy, Barber thought, needed to ensure it would have bases without "political complications" like those increasingly arising in the decolonizing world. Any targeted island would have to be "free of impingement on any significant indigenous population or economic interest," Barber wrote. He was pleased to note that Diego Garcia's population was "measured only in the hundreds."[10] The CIA's assessment of the population size was even more telling: a report described it as "NEGL"—negligible.[11] A Navy memo later concurred: "The selection of these islands was based on unquestioned UK sovereignty and a negligible native population."[12]

Barber's numbers were not entirely correct. There were around one thousand people in Diego Garcia alone in the 1960s. With the other Chagos islands, the population of the archipelago actually numbered between fifteen hundred and two thousand. The Chagossians had been living there since the time of the American Revolution, when they were brought to the previously uninhabited islands as enslaved Africans and indentured Indians to work on French coconut plantations. After slavery was abolished in the territory in 1835, this diverse group had developed into its own society, with a distinct culture and a language known as Chagos Kreol. They called themselves the Ilois—the Islanders.

But none of that mattered to U.S. officials. Navy Admiral Horacio Rivero approved the Diego Garcia acquisition plan and helped champion

Barber's idea to the Navy and the national security bureaucracy. According to Barber, Rivero insisted "emphatically" that the new base have "no dependents."[13] Other officials agreed. They wanted the Chagossians gone. Or as one document said, they wanted the islands "swept" and "sanitized."[14]

Once British officials had agreed and base construction appeared imminent, any Chagossians who left Chagos after 1967 for medical treatment or a routine vacation in Mauritius were barred from returning home. Agents for the steamship company that connected the islands told the travelers that their islands had been sold and that they could never return. The Chagossians were marooned in Mauritius, separated from many of their family members and almost all their possessions.

British officials soon began restricting the flow of food and medical supplies to Chagos. As conditions deteriorated, more Chagossians began leaving the islands, hoping to return when the situation improved. Meanwhile, British and U.S. officials designed a public relations plan aimed, as a British bureaucrat wrote, at "maintaining the fiction" that Chagossians were migrant laborers rather than a people whose roots on Chagos stretched back across many generations. One British official called them "Tarzans" and, in a similarly racist reference, "Man Fridays."[15]

By 1970, the U.S. Navy secured funding for what officials told Congress would be an "austere communications station."[16] Internally, though, Navy officials were already planning to ask Congress for additional funds to expand the facility into a much larger base. Construction on Diego Garcia began in 1971. In a memo of exactly three words, the Navy's highest-ranking admiral, Elmo Zumwalt, confirmed the Chagossians' fate: "Absolutely must go."[17]

With the help of U.S. Navy Seabees, British agents began the deportation process by rounding up the islanders' pet dogs. They gassed and burned them in sealed cargo sheds as Chagossians watched in horror. Then the authorities ordered the remaining Chagossians onto overcrowded cargo ships. During the deportations, which took place in stages until May 1973, most of the Chagossians slept in the ship's hold atop guano—bird shit. Horses stayed on deck. By the end of the five-day journey, vomit, urine, and excrement were everywhere. At least one woman miscarried. Some compare conditions to those on slave ships.[18]

Upon arrival in Mauritius and the Seychelles, most Chagossians were literally left on the docks. They were homeless, jobless, and had little money. Most were able to bring only a single box of belongings and a sleeping mat. In 1975, two years after the last removals, the *Washington Post* exposed the story for the first time in the Western press. A reporter found the people living in "abject poverty," victims of what the paper called an "act of mass kidnapping."[19]

Aurélie Lisette Talate was one of the last to go. "I came to Mauritius with six children and my mother," Aurélie told me. The family arrived in Mauritius in late 1972. "We got our house near the Bois Marchand cemetery, but the house didn't have a door, didn't have running water, didn't have electricity," she said. "The way we were treated wasn't the kind of treatment that people need to be able to live. And then my children and I began to suffer. All my children started getting sick."

Within two months of arriving in Mauritius, two of Aurélie's children were dead. The second was buried in an unmarked grave because she lacked money for a burial. "We didn't have any more money. The government buried him, and to this day, I don't know where he's buried."

Aurélie herself experienced fainting spells and couldn't eat. She had been "fat" in her homeland, she recounted, but in Mauritius she soon became alarmingly skinny. "We were living like animals," Aurélie said. "Land? We had none. . . . Work? We had none. Our children weren't going to school." The Chagossians had lost almost everything, for no reason other than the happenstance of living on an island desired by the U.S. Navy.

THE BIKINI TESTS

The Navy's expulsion of the Chagossians was not its first experience taking over tropical islands. After World War II, it had been given the responsibility of searching the planet for places to host the country's first postwar nuclear weapons tests. "We just took out dozens of maps and started looking for remote sites," explained Horacio Rivero, one of two officers charged with examining locations—the same Rivero who would later insist "no dependents" remain on Diego Garcia. "After checking the Atlantic, we moved to the West Coast and just kept looking."[20]

Rivero knew something about islands. He was born in 1910 in Ponce, Puerto Rico, and during World War II he had served on the USS *San Juan* as it battled for islands across the Pacific, including Kwajalein, Iwo Jima, and Okinawa. After the war, Commander Rivero moved to the Los Alamos nuclear weapons laboratory. There he worked for William "Deak" Parsons, who had helped drop the atomic bomb on Hiroshima as a crew member on the *Enola Gay*.

In Rivero's search for nuclear test sites, he considered more than a dozen potential locations around the world's oceans. Officials ruled out most of them because the waters surrounding the islands were too shallow, the populations too large, or the weather undependable. Rivero even considered the Galápagos, but the Interior Department struck Darwin's famed islands from the list. Eventually he settled on the Bikini Atoll in the Marshall Islands, then under U.S. control as a UN "trust territory." The Navy was particularly pleased that Bikini had an indigenous population of only about 170 people.[21]

The Navy sent Commodore Ben H. Wyatt, known as "Battling Ben," to "ask" the Bikinians for use of their islands. The answer was a foregone conclusion: President Harry Truman had already approved the removal, and preparations for a nuclear test on the islands had already begun. For their part, the Bikinians had been awed by the U.S. defeat of Japan and were grateful for the help the United States had provided since the war. They "believe[d] that they were powerless to resist the wishes of the United States," according to Jonathan Weisgall, an attorney who has represented the group for decades.[22]

On March 7, 1946, less than one month after posing its question, the Navy completed the removal of the Bikinians to the Rongerik Atoll, elsewhere in the Marshall Islands. Within months it became clear that the move to Rongerik had been a disastrously planned mistake, leaving the Bikinians in dire conditions. The *New York Times* wrote in classically ethnocentric language that the Bikinians "will probably be repatriated if they insist on it, though the United States military authorities say they can't see why they should want to: Bikini and Rongerik look as alike as two Idaho potatoes."[23]

By 1948, the Bikinians on Rongerik were running out of food and suffering from malnutrition. After planning to move them to Ujelang Atoll, the Navy sent them to a temporary camp on Kwajalein Island, near a major U.S. base. Later that year, the Navy moved the islanders to a new permanent home on Kili Island. By 1952, as conditions again deteriorated, the government was forced to make an emergency food drop on Kili. Four years later, the United States paid the Bikinians $25,000—in one-dollar bills—and created a $3 million trust fund making annual payments. These totaled about $15 per person. "The Bikinians were completely self-sufficient before 1946," explains Weisgall, "but after years of exile they virtually lost the will to provide for themselves."[24]

Meanwhile, back on Bikini, the Navy conducted sixty-eight atomic and hydrogen bomb tests between 1946 and 1958. On March 1, 1954, the first U.S. hydrogen bomb test spread a cloud of radiation over 7,500 square miles of ocean, leaving Bikini Island "hopelessly contaminated" and covering the inhabitants of the Rongelap and Utirik Atolls. The Navy ultimately displaced people from six island groups in the Marshalls in addition to Bikini, including Ailinginae, Enewetak, Lib, Rongelap, and Wotho. In addition to deaths and disease directly linked to radiation exposure, the Navy's evictions led to a veritable catalog of societal ills for the displaced, including declining social, cultural, physical, and economic conditions, high rates of suicide, poor infant health, and the proliferation of slum housing, among other debilitating effects.[25]

For his work in selecting Bikini for the nuclear tests, the Navy rewarded Horacio Rivero by making him an admiral—the first Latino admiral in Navy history. His next promotion made him the director of the Navy's long-range planning office, where he would discover Stuart Barber's "brilliant idea" for Diego Garcia.[26]

A CENTURY OF DISPLACEMENT

That the Navy would expel indigenous peoples from both Diego Garcia and Bikini is no coincidence. Around the world, often on islands and in other isolated locations, the U.S. military long displaced indigenous groups to create bases. In most cases the displaced populations have ended up deeply impoverished, like the Chagossians and Bikinians.

After a century of displacement in North America, there have been at least eighteen documented cases of base displacement outside the

THE DISPLACED, 1898–2015

U.S. Base(s)

U.S. Nuclear Testing Facilities

Greenland
Thule
(1953, with Denmark)

United States

Alaska
Aleutian and Attu Islands
(1942)

Hawaii
Pearl Harbor
(1898)

Hawaii
Kahoolawe
(1941–1942)

Panama
Canal Zone
(1908–1931)

Puerto Rico
Vieques
(1941–1961)

Puerto Rico
Culebra
(1941–1970)

Bases and other military facilities whose establishment or expansion has displaced local peoples. During the eighteenth and nineteenth centuries, bases in North America assisted in the displacement of millions of Native American peoples. See David Vine, *Island of Shame*.

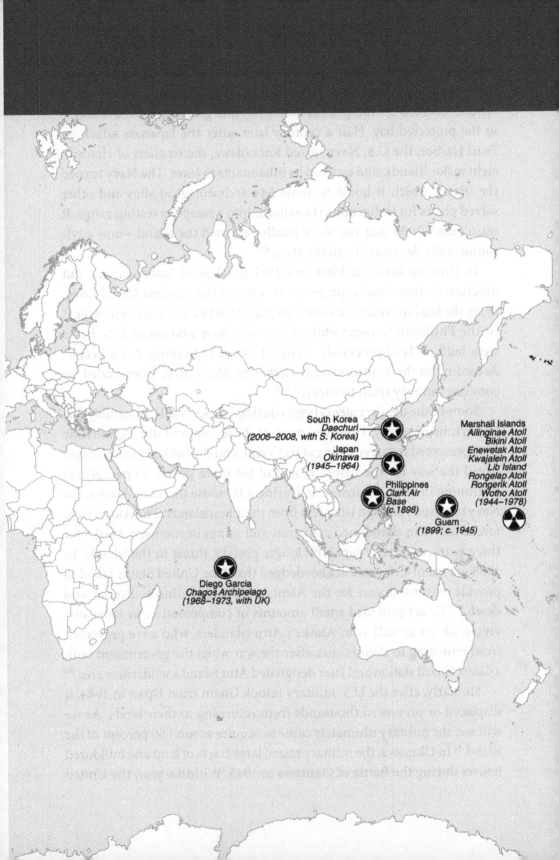

South Korea
Daechuri
(2006–2008, with S. Korea)

Japan
Okinawa
(1945–1964)

Philippines
*Clark Air
Base
(c. 1898)*

Diego Garcia
Chagos Archipelago
(1968–1973, with UK)

Guam
(1899; c. 1945)

Marshall Islands
Ailinginae Atoll
Bikini Atoll
Enewetak Atoll
Kwajalein Atoll
Lib Island
Rongelap Atoll
Rongerik Atoll
Wotho Atoll
(1944–1978)

continental United States since the late 1800s. In Hawaii, for instance, the United States first took possession of Pearl Harbor in 1887, when officials coerced the indigenous monarchy into granting exclusive access to the protected bay. Half a century later, after the Japanese attack on Pearl Harbor, the U.S. Navy seized Kahoolawe, the smallest of Hawaii's eight major islands, and ordered its inhabitants to leave. The Navy turned the island, which is home to some 544 archaeological sites and other sacred places for indigenous Hawaiians, into a weapons testing range. It wasn't until 2003 that the Navy finally returned the island—now environmentally devastated—to the state.[27]

In Panama between 1908 and 1931 the United States carried out nineteen distinct land expropriations around the Panama Canal Zone, using the land to create not only the canal itself but also fourteen bases.[28] In the Philippines, meanwhile, Clark Air Base and other U.S. bases were built on land previously occupied by the indigenous Aetas people. According to the anthropologist Katherine McCaffrey, "they ended up combing military trash to survive."[29]

Some of the displacements began during World War II, ostensibly due to wartime necessity. However, most of those removed during wartime were prevented from returning at war's end, and the initial evictions often paved the way for the displacement of yet more people in peacetime. Beginning in 1942, for instance, fearing a Japanese threat to Alaska, the Navy removed Aleutian islanders from their homelands. The Aleuts were forced to live in abandoned canneries and mines in southern Alaska for three years, even after Japan no longer posed a threat to the islands. In 1988, an act of Congress acknowledged that "the United States failed to provide reasonable care for the Aleuts, resulting in illness, disease, and death." The act provided small amounts of compensation to some surviving Aleuts as well as to Alaska's Attu islanders, who were prevented from returning to their homes after the war when the government built a Coast Guard station and later designated Attu Island a wilderness area.[30]

Similarly, after the U.S. military retook Guam from Japan in 1944, it displaced or prevented thousands from returning to their lands. As we will see, the military ultimately came to acquire around 60 percent of the island.[31] In Okinawa, the military seized large tracts of land and bulldozed houses during the Battle of Okinawa in 1945. Within a year, the United

States had taken 40,000 acres and 20 percent of the island's arable land. By the 1950s, the military had seized more than 40 percent of Okinawa's farmland, ultimately displacing around 250,000 people, or nearly half the island's population. A common refrain among Okinawans is that they lost their land by "bulldozer and bayonet."[32] A Navy officer would later say to the high-ranking Pentagon official Morton Halperin, "The military doesn't have bases in Okinawa. The island itself is the base."[33]

With the part of Okinawa left for civilians growing increasingly overcrowded, between 1954 and 1964 the United States induced at least 3,218 Okinawans to resettle 11,000 miles away, in landlocked Bolivia. (This was not entirely unheard of at a time when Japan arranged with several Latin American countries to accept its migrants.)[34] The government promised them farmland and financial assistance. Instead, most found disease, jungle-covered lands, incomplete housing and roads, and none of the promised aid. By the late 1960s, the displaced Okinawans began heading to Brazil and Argentina and back to Okinawa and Japan.[35]

Closer to home, in Admiral Rivero's homeland of Puerto Rico, the Navy carried out repeated removals on the small island of Vieques. Between 1941 and 1943, and again in 1947, the U.S. Navy displaced thousands from their lands, seizing three quarters of Vieques for military use, and squeezing the Viequeños into a small portion of the middle of the island. Military occupation brought few benefits. As productive local economies were disrupted, stagnation, poverty, unemployment, prostitution, and violence became the rule. In 1961, the Navy announced plans to seize the rest of Vieques and evict its remaining eight thousand inhabitants. Officials canceled the expulsion plans only when Governor Luis Muñoz Marin convinced President Kennedy that the expulsion would fuel UN and Soviet criticisms of the colonial relationship between the United States and Puerto Rico.

On Puerto Rico's neighboring island Culebra, the Navy seized 1,700 acres in 1948 for a bombing range. By 1950, the island's population, which had numbered four thousand at the turn of the century, had shrunk to just 580. The Navy controlled one third of the island and its entire coastline, encircling civilians with the bombing range and a mined harbor. In the 1950s, the Navy drafted plans to remove the rest of Culebra's inhabitants. Although those plans were never executed, in 1970 it tried to remove the islanders again. When the issue became a cause célèbre for the Puerto Rican independence movement, the Navy stopped using the range. Bombing increased in Vieques as a result, until a campaign of civil disobedience stretching from Puerto Rico to New York City finally forced the Navy to leave Vieques in 2003.

In 1953, in a case echoing the Anglo-American expulsion of the Chagossians, U.S. officials signed a secret agreement with the Danish government to remove 150 indigenous Inughuit (Inuit) people standing in the way of expanding an American air base in Thule, Greenland. Inughuit families were reportedly given four days to move or face U.S. bulldozers. The Danes gave the Inughuit some blankets and tents and left them in exile in Qaanaaq, a bleak village 125 miles away.[36] The expulsion severed the people's connection to a homeland to which they, like the Chagossians, were intimately linked. The relocation led to the loss of ancient hunting, fishing, and gathering skills and caused significant physical and psychological harm. In recent years, Danish courts have ruled the Danish government's actions illegal and a violation of the Inughuits' human rights. Still, the Danish Supreme Court said they have no right to return.[37]

The displacement of indigenous groups for nuclear testing at Bikini also has its echoes elsewhere. Between the end of World War II and the 1960s, the U.S. military displaced hundreds of people to create a missile testing base in the Marshall Islands' Kwajalein Atoll. Most were deported to the small island of Ebeye, where the population increased from twenty people before 1944 to several thousand by the 1960s living on 0.12 square miles of land. In 1967, with overcrowding a major problem, governing U.S. authorities removed fifteen hundred people from Ebeye.[38] Following protests from the Marshallese government, they were later allowed to return. By 1969, *Newsday* called Ebeye "the most congested, unhealthful, and socially demoralized community in Micronesia." A population of more than forty-five hundred lived in what has widely been called the "ghetto of the Pacific."[39] Today, there are around ten thousand people living on the island, making its population density greater than that of the world's densest city, Mumbai.[40]

John Seiberling, a U.S. Congress member from Ohio, compared the conditions on Ebeye and military-occupied Kwajalein when he visited the islands in 1984:

The contrast couldn't be greater or more dramatic. Kwajalein is like Fort Lauderdale or one of our Miami resort areas, with palm-lined beaches, swimming pools, a golf course, people bicycling everywhere, a first-class hospital and a good school; and Ebeye, on the other hand, is an island slum, over-populated, treeless filthy lagoon, littered beaches, a dilapidated hospital, and contaminated water supply.[41]

Seiberling's description aptly captures not only the situation in the Marshall Islands, but the distance between the lives of troops at bases like Diego Garcia and the lives of Chagossians and other victims of displacement whose former lands the bases now occupy.

"NOBODY CARED VERY MUCH"

Former Pentagon official Gary Sick testified to Congress about the Chagossians' expulsion in 1975, on the one day Congress has ever examined the issue. "The fact is," Sick told me years later, "nobody cared very much about these populations."

"It was more of a nineteenth-century decision—thought process—than a twentieth- or twenty-first-century thought process," Sick said. "I think that was the bind they got caught in. That this was sort of colonial thinking after the fact, about what you could do." And U.S. officials, Sick added, "were pleased to let the British do their dirty work for them."

A former State Department official, James Noyes, who was involved in the creation of the base, told me that he and others considered the Chagossians a small "nitty gritty" detail that they thought the British were handling. "The ethical question of the workers and so on," Noyes told me, "simply wasn't in the spectrum. It wasn't discussed. No one realized, I don't think . . . the human aspects of it. Nobody was there or had been there, or was close enough to it, so. It was like questioning apple pie or something."

In the minds of many U.S. officials, the supposed gains to be realized from a base justified what they saw as the limited impact of removing a small number of people. Henry Kissinger is widely reported as having said of the inhabitants of the Marshall Islands, "There are only ninety thousand people out there. Who gives a damn?"[42] Stu Barber's Strategic

Island Concept was largely predicated on the same assumption: Who gives a damn? But from the perspective of the Chagossians and a long list of other peoples, there was of course nothing limited about the impact of their expulsion.

In her study of Vieques, Katherine McCaffrey notes that "bases are frequently established on the political margins of national territory, on lands occupied by ethnic or cultural minorities or otherwise disadvantaged populations."[43] While the military is generally driven by strategic considerations when deciding what regions should have bases, within a given region the selection of specific base locations is heavily influenced by the ease of land acquisition. The ease with which the military can acquire land tends to be strongly linked to the relative powerlessness of that land's inhabitants, which in turn is usually linked to factors such as their nationality, skin color, and population size.

"Across history," writes the former Air Force officer Mark Gillem, "displacements and demolitions are the norm."[44] Removing locals promises the ultimate in stability and freedom from what government officials generally consider "local problems." U.S. officials displaced the Chagossians, the Bikinians, and others because the military prefers not to be bothered by local populations, and because it has the power to enforce its preference.

The displacement has not stopped. In 2006, in South Korea, the U.S. military wanted to expand Camp Humphreys, which already occupied two square miles, as part of the consolidation of U.S forces south of Seoul. At the behest of the military, the South Korean government used eminent domain to seize 2,851 acres of farmers' land from Daechuri village and other areas near the city of Pyongtaek. When the farmers resisted, the government sent police and soldiers to enforce the evictions. Riot police went into Daechuri with bulldozers and backhoes, beating protesters, destroying a local school, and tearing up farmers' rice fields and irrigation systems. When many still refused to leave, the government surrounded the village with police, soldiers, and barbed wire. In April 2007, the last villagers finally were forced to go. "I can't stop shedding tears," one older resident said. "My heart is totally broken."[45]

The South Korean government has also seized a delicate and rare volcanic beachfront in the heart of a beautiful seaside village on its "Island of Peace," Jeju. Despite years of passionate struggle by Gangjeong villagers and supporters, the government has dynamited much of the beach to build a Korean naval base. Given that the U.S. military has access to all South Korean bases and operational control over South Korean forces, many suspect that the new base is intended for U.S. forces.[46]

The displacement of Chagossians, Marshallese islanders, and other groups demonstrates the vulnerability of small, isolated populations whose forcible relocation U.S. officials have so often treated as a matter of negligible concern. The story of another group of islands underscores the decisive role that ideas about race have played in such decisions.[47] Before World War II, Japan's Bonin-Volcano (also known as Ogasawara) islands, which include Iwo Jima, had a population of roughly seven thousand. The islanders were the descendants of nineteenth-century settlers, most of whom had come from Japan but also from the United States and Europe. In 1944, Japanese officials evacuated all the Bonin-Volcano islanders to Japan's main islands to protect them from impending U.S. attack. After the U.S. capture of the Bonin-Volcanos, American officials prohibited the locals from returning in order to give the military unhindered use of the islands. In 1946, however, officials modified the decision: they would "permit the return of those residents of Caucasian extraction who had been forcibly removed to Japan during the war and who had petitioned the United States to return."[48]

U.S. authorities subsequently assisted with the repatriation of approximately 130 Euro-American men and their families to the Bonin-Volcano islands. The Navy helped them establish self-government, allowed children to attend a Navy school, and created a cooperative trading company to market agricultural products on Guam and a Bonin-Volcano Trust Fund to provide financial support.[49] The only differences between this community and the Chagossians were the color of their skin and their ties to the United States.

STRUGGLE AND *SAGREN*

After years of protest, including a series of five hunger strikes led by women like Aurélie Talate, Chagossians finally received small amounts of compensation from the British government, ten and fifteen years after the last expulsions. The compensation consisted of small concrete block houses and small plots of land for some of the Chagossians, and money totaling less than $6,000 per adult. Others, including all those living in the Seychelles, received nothing.[50] Many of those who did receive compensation used the money to pay off large debts accrued since the expulsion. For most, conditions improved only marginally.

Numbering more than five thousand today, most Chagossians remain impoverished. They are still struggling to win proper compensation and the right of return. In 2002 they secured the right to full UK citizenship, and since that time well over one thousand Chagossians have moved to Britain in search of better lives. Even the ones who have found housing and employment there, though, are often stuck working long hours in low-wage service sector jobs.[51]

Aurélie Talate had no interest in moving anywhere except back to her home on Diego Garcia. Unfortunately, she will not see the day when Chagossians return to their homeland. She died in 2012 at the age of seventy, succumbing to what Chagossians call *sagren*—profound sorrow.

"I had something that had been affecting me for a long time, since we were uprooted," Aurélie told me a few years before her death. "This *sagren*, this shock. It was this same problem that killed my child," she said. "We weren't living free like we did in our natal land. We had *sagren* when we couldn't return."

Stu Barber also will not see the Chagossians return. Before his death, however, Barber discussed the prospects of a return in a 1991 letter to the *Washington Post*. "It seems to me to be a good time to review whether we should now take steps to redress the inexcusably inhuman wrongs inflicted by the British at our insistence on the former inhabitants of Diego Garcia and other Chagos group islands," Barber wrote.

> There was never any good reason for evicting residents from the Northern Chagos, 100 miles or more from Diego Garcia. Probably the natives could even have been safely allowed to remain on the east side of Diego Garcia atoll . . . Such permission, for those who still want to return, together with resettlement assistance, would go a long way to reduce our deserved opprobrium. Substantial additional compensation for 18–25

past years of misery for all evictees is certainly in order. Even if that were to cost $100,000 per family, we would be talking of a maximum of $40–50 million, modest compared with our base investment there.[52]

Barber's letter went unpublished and he received no reply from the *Post*. Similar letters imploring a former Navy supervisor and the British embassy in Washington to help return the Chagossians to Chagos also received no answer.

In yet another letter, to former Alaska senator Ted Stevens, Barber confessed, the expulsion of the Chagossians "wasn't necessary militarily."[53]

David Vine

A *lusong* (mortar) among the archaeological remains at Pågat, the ancient indigenous village and sacred burial ground on Guam where the U.S. Marine Corps proposed building a shooting range.

4

The Colonial Present

Outright expulsion such as that faced by the Chagossians and other indigenous peoples has been far from the only method used by military leaders wanting to maintain control over "their" island bases after World War II. When the United States granted the Philippines independence in 1946, for instance, it did so on the condition of maintaining a ninety-nine-year rent-free lease on sixteen bases and military installations, including Subic Bay and Clark Air Base and even more bases in cases of "military necessity." (Nationalist protest later forced revision of the agreement; in 1966, the base leases were changed to expire in 1991.) The agreement effectively continued colonial rule over the bases themselves, where the United States retained sovereignty and control over Filipino workers, criminal prosecutions, taxation, and the entire city of Olongapo, adjacent to the Subic Bay Naval Base.[1] In Japan, the United States occupied and ruled Okinawa until 1972, when it allowed Japan to regain formal sovereignty but likewise ensured the long-term tenancy of U.S. bases there.

Elsewhere in the Pacific, the United States made sure it retained basing rights when the UN granted it "trusteeship" over the Trust Territory of the Pacific Islands, which had been "mandated" to Japan after World War I. This territory included the Marshall Islands, Palau, and islands that decades later became the Federated States of Micronesia. The trusteeship gave the United States the right to establish military facilities in the islands, and until 1951, the Navy governed the territory.[2] Even after the Department of the Interior became the governing authority, the arrangement still amounted to what British constitutional law expert Stanley de Smith called "de facto annexation."[3]

Eventually the Trust Territory islands gained their formal independence by signing "compacts of free association" with the United States. These compacts gave responsibilities for defense to the United States, which allowed the U.S. government to retain military control over the islands.[4] In addition to the nuclear testing that was carried out in the Marshall Islands over the decades, the military still uses the islands for the Ronald Reagan Ballistic Missile Defense Test Site—a facility that provides a target for missiles launched from California, thousands of miles away. In Palau and the Federated States of Micronesia, the military uses islands for training and has broad base construction rights during wartime.[5]

At the urging of the military after the war, the government maintained its control over possessions once called colonies, including Guam, American Samoa, the Northern Mariana Islands, Puerto Rico, and the U.S. Virgin Islands, as "territories" of the United States. These islands have neither full independence nor the full democratic rights that would come with incorporation into the United States. They highlight how, even in the twenty-first century, our base nation still relies on the perpetuation of colonial relationships, albeit under new guises and with new vocabulary. From the military's perspective, Guam and the other territories offer unmatched autonomy. "This is not Okinawa," Major General Dennis Larsen told a reporter at Guam's Andersen Air Force Base. "This is American soil in the midst of the Pacific. Guam is a U.S. territory. We can do what we want here, and make huge investments without fear of being thrown out."[6]

A TINY FOOTNOTE . . . AT THE CENTER OF POWER

The ability to do whatever it wants without fear of eviction—and with greater ease than in the fifty states—is a major part of why the military likes Guam so much. Located some eight thousand miles from Washington, D.C., Guam is about one fifth the size of Rhode Island, the smallest of the fifty states. At one point, military facilities took up nearly 60 percent of the island; today, they still account for almost 30 percent.

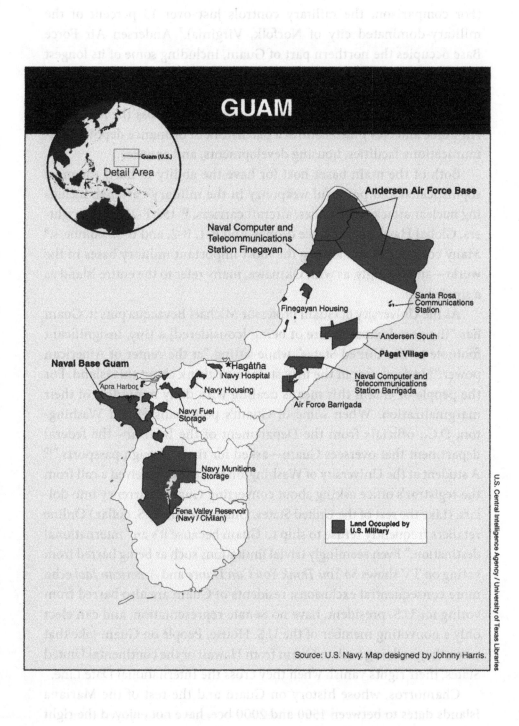

Source: U.S. Navy. Map designed by Johnny Harris.

(For comparison, the military controls just over 15 percent of the military-dominated city of Norfolk, Virginia).[7] Andersen Air Force Base occupies the northern part of Guam, including some of its longest and most beautiful beaches. Naval Base Guam occupies Apra Harbor, one of the largest in the western Pacific, along the southwest coast, where Guam's second-largest village once stood. Across the island, the Air Force and Navy also control a patchwork of ordnance depots, communications facilities, housing developments, and annexes.

Both of the main bases host (or have the ability to host) the most sophisticated and powerful weaponry in the military's arsenal, including nuclear attack submarines, aircraft carriers, F-15s, F-22 stealth fighters, Global Hawk surveillance drones, and B-1, B-2, and B-52 bombers.[8] Many consider Guam among the most important military bases in the world—and tellingly, as with Okinawa, many refer to the entire island as a single base.

As the University of Guam professor Michael Bevacqua puts it, Guam has "the paradoxical nature of being [considered] a tiny, insignificant footnote to the United States" while sitting "at the center of American power."[9] Indeed, few in the fifty states ever think about this island. For the people of Guam this means dealing with daily reminders of their marginalization. When some of Guam's politicians visited Washington, D.C., officials from the Department of the Interior—the federal department that oversees Guam—asked for their "foreign passports."[10] A student at the University of Washington told me he received a call from the registrar's office asking about converting Guam's currency into dollars. (Like the rest of the United States, Guam uses the U.S. dollar.) Online retailers frequently refuse to ship to Guam because it's an "international destination." Even seemingly trivial limitations such as being barred from voting on TV shows *So You Think You Can Dance* and *American Idol* echo more consequential exclusions: residents of Guam are also barred from voting for U.S. president, have no Senate representation, and can elect only a nonvoting member of the U.S. House. People on Guam joke that when they're flying back to Guam from Hawaii or the continental United States, their rights vanish when they cross the International Date Line.

Chamorros, whose history on Guam and the rest of the Mariana Islands dates to between 1500 and 2000 bce, have not enjoyed the right to self-determination in nearly five hundred years. The Spanish arrived in 1521, claiming Guam and the Marianas as a Spanish possession four decades later. Like the indigenous peoples of the Americas, Chamorros were decimated by disease and violence.[11] Spain ruled Guam as a colony for more than two hundred years until the U.S. Navy seized the island and its small military garrison as a prize of the 1898 war. The United States did not, however, occupy the other Spanish-controlled islands in Guam's Mariana Islands chain. Instead, Spain sold them to Germany, dividing the Chamorros between two occupying powers.

Guam was now a U.S. colony, and the Navy designated the entire island a U.S. naval station. Technically, at that point, the whole island really was one large military base. Naval officers served as governors and generally ran Guam like a ship. Signs appeared saying english only will be spoken here. In a series of cases, the Supreme Court ruled that Guam's people (as well as Puerto Ricans and Filipinos) were entitled to neither U.S. citizenship nor the full protection of the Constitution.[12]

Before its inhabitants finally became citizens, Guam became one of the only pieces of U.S. territory occupied during World War II. Two days after the Japanese attacked Pearl Harbor on December 7, 1941, thousands of Japan's troops overwhelmed about four hundred defenders on Guam. Chamorros would have to endure not just one day but thirty-two months "which will live in infamy" during the Japanese occupation. The Japanese government changed the island's name to Omiya Jima, introduced the yen, and forced Chamorros to learn Japanese. "You must bow to us" became the law; violence became the means of enforcement. The Japanese military put as many as twenty thousand Chamorros into concentration camps. There was rape, sexual slavery, and other forced labor. Hundreds were killed by machine gun, grenade, and sword.[13]

President Roosevelt's government celebrated the Chamorros for their exceptional heroism under occupation. For two and a half years, locals hid and kept alive a member of the U.S. defense force who refused to surrender after the Japanese invasion. When the Japanese learned there was an American in hiding, Chamorros suffered torture and execution to keep his secret.[14]

The battle to retake Guam began in July 1944 with one of the war's longest and largest naval bombardments.[15] The bombardment, which planners designed to weaken Japanese defenses before an amphibious assault, showed little concern for the local population. Ironically, many Chamorros survived the bombing only because they were in concentration camps and not in their villages. By the time the U.S. military had regained control of Guam, some 1,170 Chamorros were dead.[16]

After the battle, the military seized Chamorro land to build bases that would help launch attacks on more Japanese-controlled islands as the military moved across the Pacific toward Japan. When the war ended, the land was not returned. Rather, the military seized more Chamorro land after the war, including 2,850 acres of the best land in one swoop. Guam's agricultural economy never recovered from the fighting and the land seizures. Whereas Guam had been self-sufficient before the war, after the war it imported 90 percent of its food; Spam became a culinary staple. Some Chamorros received small amounts of compensation for their land, but money was not guaranteed.[17] To this day, many feel cheated. In 1986, the federal government paid $40 million in compensation to landowners but set the payments using land values from 1940, which represented only a fraction of the land's current value.[18] Some continue to press for war reparations from the U.S. and Japanese governments for their lost land and the suffering experienced under Japanese rule.

Chamorros on Guam expected their bravery and loyalty during the war at least to be rewarded with citizenship and self-rule. The Navy thought otherwise. Adding insult to an array of injuries, it reestablished military rule, and Chamorros had to struggle for years to win U.S. citizenship. Only when State Department officials grew concerned that the policy was creating "an island of anti-American radicals," and there were widespread acts of civil disobedience and threats of a general strike, did the Truman administration authorize the control over Guam to be transferred from the Navy to the Department of the Interior.[19] In 1950, Guam became an "unincorporated territory," giving the island limited rights to self-governance. The U.S. Congress maintained ultimate control. To this day, Guam remains one of just seventeen non-self-governing territories in the world, as tracked by the UN. (Others on the list include American Samoa and the U.S. Virgin Islands, along with territories like French Polynesia and Gibraltar.) In the words of the Department of the

Interior, Guam became an "area in which the United States Congress has determined that only selected parts of the United States Constitution apply."[20]

THE BUILDUP

Despite Guam's marginalization, the military enjoys almost unparalleled support on the island. Enlistment rates on Guam generally top those of nearly every U.S. state and territory. This is in no small part because Guam's unemployment and poverty rates tend to top the nation's as well. Currently, unemployment is around 13 percent, with the poverty rate around 20 percent. At $39,000 a year, median household income is less than three quarters of the U.S. average.[21] Nearly everyone on the island has a family member or close friend connected to the military in some way, whether as a member of the military, a veteran, or an employee on base or in a base-dependent industry.

In 2006, Pentagon officials announced a major multibillion-dollar buildup of new base infrastructure on Guam. The buildup would accommodate up to nine thousand marines and tens of thousands of family members and civilians moving from Okinawa in the face of continued protests against the U.S. base presence. Around the same time, the Air Force announced plans to increase its presence on the island by naming it one of four major global hubs for its strike forces, which it called "Guam Strike." Meanwhile, the Navy made plans to expand Apra Harbor's ability to host nuclear aircraft carriers and submarines; the Army National Guard planned new construction to accommodate its planned force expansion; and the Pentagon selected Guam as a key site for its ballistic missile defense system. The island thus became the centerpiece of the most significant transformation in the structure of U.S. forces in Asia since at least the departure from the Philippines and perhaps since the end of the war in Vietnam. Planners anticipated nearly eighty thousand people, including almost twenty thousand construction workers, moving to Guam in a four-year period.[22] Since Guam's entire population is only around 160,000, that would mean an almost 50 percent population increase.

Given the island's high poverty and unemployment rates, there is little surprise that many on Guam expressed enthusiasm about the economic benefits anticipated from the buildup. Military representatives promised tens of millions of dollars in additional tax revenues, government aid, and infrastructure investments.[23] For a time, at least, a gold rush atmosphere prevailed. Email solicitations with subject lines like "Opportunity of a Lifetime!" proclaimed, "The tiny little island of Guam is about to become a great big deal! . . . There's Work to be Done and Money to be Made!"[24]

The Guam Chamber of Commerce, among others, trumpeted both the economic benefits of the buildup and the security rationale for the move. To provide evidence of the need for the buildup, a 2011 Chamber report outlined a long list of threats ranging from North Korean missiles and China's cyberwar capabilities to violent extremism, transnational criminal organizations, pandemics, and natural disasters. In the face of these dangers, the business organization wrote, Guam offers "permanent sovereign facilities" to demonstrate U.S. "strength, presence, [and] engagement" in Asia, thus helping to "avoid confrontation and conflict" by deterring potential adversaries.[25]

Given such high levels of support for the military on Guam, many were surprised when growing numbers of people started expressing concerns about the buildup. Along with established activists, some of the most prominent voices of opposition came from young people, mostly in their twenties. They formed a group called We Are Guåhan, after the Chamorro name for the island, to monitor the buildup. As the group and others scrutinized the plan, their work seemed to reveal just how much the military takes for granted the kind of nearly unchecked power it has enjoyed on the island since Guam became a U.S. colony in 1898. We Are Guåhan and others pointed out the dangers of the planned population boom on an island with an already strained infrastructure. Guam's public school system was expected to have its student population grow by up to 26 percent. Demand for the island's sole public hospital was expected to increase by 20 percent.

The military's own assessment predicted that at its height the buildup would strain and exceed the island's wastewater treatment capacities. Given what the military called "the current poor state of the utilities infrastructure on Guam," civilians would also face a shortage of millions of gallons of drinking water per day, requiring the military to share some of its surplus. Opponents noted that while the military hadn't budgeted to expand Guam's civilian facilities, the buildup plan included money to build new military schools, a new military hospital, and other base infrastructure.[26] The military's offer to share water to meet civilian needs only underlined the island's inequalities and many locals' feelings of being second-class citizens.

When the Environmental Protection Agency (EPA) looked at the buildup plan, it had many of the same concerns. In a scathing report, the agency found the buildup would likely damage "Guam's existing substandard drinking water and wastewater infrastructure, which may result in significant adverse public health impacts." Dredging to expand Apra Harbor would cause "unacceptable impacts" to seventy-one acres of coral reef. The EPA deemed the buildup plan "environmentally unsatisfactory," saying it "should not proceed as proposed."[27]

Many Chamorro activists were particularly upset that the Marines wanted to acquire 1,800 additional acres of Guam's land to build a gun range on the remains of Pågat, a sacred indigenous village and burial ground dating to at least 900 ce. We Are Guåhan spokesperson Cara Flores-Mays compared the Marines' plan for Pågat to "putting a firing range on Arlington Cemetery. You would never think to do that," she said. "We have a lot of responsibility for our ancestors and those who came before us, and so you can understand why some people would get angry."[28]

Today, one can still find the remains of the village along a secluded jungle path on Guam's northeast coast. Beyond a trailhead nearly obscured by tall grasses, weeds, and branches, a trail lined with moss-covered rocks leads the way. The former village sits near a cliff topped by a naturally occurring stone arch overlooking a cove and the ocean beyond. Steps away there's an entrance to an underground cave containing a large, clear pool of water. On the ground in the jungle stand *lusongs*—heavy stone mortars for grinding herbs and food—and *latte* stones, pillars topped by stones shaped like a cup. The *lattes* once formed the foundation of Chamorro houses and today are a powerful cultural symbol across the Marianas.

"There's this portion of society that will make a lot of money on the buildup," Flores-Mays said. "But I think there's a growing number of people who are realizing that money is not everything and that there are parts of our island that we'll lose that will be irreplaceable and that are much more valuable than money."

Leevin Camacho, another We Are Guåhan spokesperson, noted that in addition to Pågat itself, the surrounding jungle is also important to Chamorros. "That's our culture, to believe we have a connection to the land and the people who lived there," Leevin told me. "Part of being Chamorro," he said, means that "you have to ask permission" of the ancestors if you're going to disturb anything in the jungle. "These spirits are everywhere," Leevin said. If you ask their permission, "that's supposed to protect you. Like a guardian angel." And now the Marines were planning to build a firing range by clearing the jungle atop Pågat, he said. "What could be more disrespectful than bulldozing and digging up remains?"

Opposition to the buildup "doesn't translate into hating the military," noted Leevin, whose father has been an enlisted soldier for more than twenty years. It just means you're "worried about your home."

Local opinion was also inflamed when several military officials were overheard during a lunch meeting strategizing about how best to market the buildup. The group, which had gathered at the popular Mermaid Tavern in Guam's capital, Hagåtña, included buildup spokesperson Marine Corps Major Aisha Bakkar. In an account that Bakkar later confirmed, Cara Flores-Mays heard the officials discuss plans "to 'use' the mayors to hold community pocket meetings where they can 'control' the [buildup's] messaging," and "to 'use' the stories of our man'amko"—revered elders—to attract local support. The officials laughed about an older man from the indigenous Chamorro community, mocking his accent and his degree from the University of Guam. "So, how many teeth does he have left? Three?" one official asked.[29]

Ultimately, We Are Guåhan, with the help of the National Trust for Historic Preservation and the Guam Preservation Trust, went to court to challenge the Marines' planned Pågat shooting range. In a closed-door meeting, Major General David Bice, who headed the office trying to build support for the buildup, was reported to have told members of the National

Trust and the Guam Preservation Trust that if the military didn't get its preferred site for the shooting range, "Your children will die."[30] Undeterred, the opposition groups showed the U.S. federal district court in California that despite already controlling nearly one third of Guam, the military hadn't considered any alternative range sites.[31] The court agreed and forced the Marines to conduct another environmental impact assessment to study other locations.

Amid recent national efforts to curtail Pentagon spending and government debt, others have grown critical of the buildup's costs and financial planning. Three influential members of the Senate Armed Services Committee called the plan "unrealistic, unworkable and unaffordable." The Government Accountability Office has repeatedly shown that the Pentagon's budgets for the move dramatically underestimate expenses and are simply "not reliable." The GAO's cost estimate of $23.8 billion is more than double the Pentagon's $10.3 billion figure. The GAO pointed out that although Congress asked for a master plan for the move, the Pentagon still did not have one almost a decade into one of the largest and costliest military transformations in history.[32]

"WE CAN DO WHAT WE WANT HERE"

In 2014, in the face of this growing opposition, the military finally backed down on its desire to build a shooting range at Pågat, recommending instead that it be located on Andersen Air Base. Revised buildup plans also suggested that it would no longer be necessary for the military to acquire additional land, that total population growth would be ten thousand rather than eighty thousand, and that the buildup could be slowed to spread its effects over thirteen years rather than seven. In the new plans, only five thousand marines from Okinawa would relocate to Guam, while roughly four thousand others would disperse to bases in Hawaii, Australia, and Southeast Asia.[33] And though the marines from Okinawa were originally scheduled to move to Guam in 2014, in the new scheme they likely won't arrive before 2021 (in part because of the longtime stalemate over the construction of a new base in Okinawa).

Were it not for the resistance of a small group of hardworking activists like We Are Guåhan, along with the Okinawa stalemate and Congress's fiscal concerns, the military might have gotten its way completely on Guam. While we will see that the military's brazenly poor planning of the buildup is far from unique to Guam, the carelessness also reflects something larger than decades of Pentagon profligacy. The major elements of the buildup that generated so much opposition—the idea of building a shooting range on sacred indigenous land without even considering an alternative; seizing 1,700 acres of additional private land; planning to increase Guam's population by 50 percent without the civilian infrastructure to handle the growth; embarking on a major buildup without a master plan—all come back to the same root cause: for more than a century, "we can do what we want here" has been the military's core attitude toward Guam.

As the cases of base displacement show and as other evidence will reveal, the military has frequently adopted a "we can do what we want here" attitude in Guam, Diego Garcia, Okinawa, Puerto Rico, the Philippines, Panama, Greenland, and well beyond. The attitude shows us how the base nation has relied on continuing colonial relationships in the twentieth and twenty-first centuries, albeit under new guises and with new terminology. After all, in the post–World War II age of decolonization, with rare exceptions, maintaining large colonies became impossible. But as the Strategic Island Concept shows, the government and a few of its European allies found ways to maintain a handful of small mostly island colonies, largely because of their strategic value as base sites. From the military's perspective, ongoing colonial relationships have allowed officials to "do what we want" without many of the restrictions faced in the fifty states or in fully independent nations. From the perspective of the Chamorros on Guam and others trapped in similar colonial relationships today, the military's attachment to overseas bases means that they still lack the basic democratic rights and freedoms taken for granted by most of their fellow citizens.

At a public meeting held by the military at a local public high school, We Are Guåhan's Cara Flores-Mays pointed out that the United States was founded by people seeking freedom. Standing up, her eyes welling with tears, she asked, Where do the people of Guam go to obtain that freedom that all other Americans enjoy? Where do we go? I'm an American citizen just like any other, she said. I want constitutional rights like everyone else. Do I have to move to be a real American?

What you're fighting for, she told the military officials, we don't have here.

A U.S. marine training Honduran troops, Puerto Castilla, Honduras, 2011.

5

Befriending Dictators

The lack of full democracy in Guam and other places where one finds U.S. bases overseas is only the beginning. In their quest to secure base access around the globe, government officials have repeatedly collaborated with murderous, antidemocratic regimes and ignored widespread evidence of human rights abuses. The history of U.S. involvement in Honduras—where the "temporary but indefinite" Soto Cano Air Base has been operating since the 1980s—dramatically demonstrates just how much the military's actions contradict the very ideals that it is supposedly dedicated to protecting.

The passions surrounding the U.S. presence in Honduras quickly became clear to me on a visit to Soto Cano a few years ago: within hours of stepping off the plane, I got tear-gassed. It was June 28, 2011, the second anniversary of the military coup that overthrew the government of President Manuel Zelaya. I was walking outside the base, in a broad valley about fifty miles from the Honduran capital, Tegucigalpa, alongside a group of around three hundred protesters.

The protest had been under way for about forty-five minutes, and the marchers were only about halfway from the base's southern boundary to its main entrance. Peeling off from the march, four young men walked toward the base's gray concrete wall with spray paint in hand. Several Honduran soldiers—mostly teenagers—and black-clad riot police rushed to block them. One raised his baton over his head, while a senior officer with an M-16 pushed the graffiti artists back against the wall. Protesters rushed toward the rapidly escalating confrontation.

Suddenly a cop swung his baton at one of the young men. A police commander grabbed the man in a chokehold and started dragging him away before tripping and falling, pulling the protester down with him. People started shouting. Another cop pulled a second protester down, smacking his legs with his baton.

And then the tear gas canister exploded, a plume of white smoke engulfing us. Protesters, soldiers, and cops alike started running (only a few of the riot force had gas masks). One cop pointed a tear gas launcher at the retreating protesters. Two others pulled out semiautomatic pistols, pointing them back and forth from protester to protester. Knowing protesters had been killed during demonstrations after the coup, I thought I was about to see someone shot. I, too, began to run.

Just when I thought I had escaped the gas, I felt the burning in my eyes and lungs. I began rubbing my face, and someone shouted, "Don't touch your eyes!" As people coughed and doused red, swollen faces with water, tensions somehow eased. Most of the protesters went back to marching, undeterred. To the tune of "Guantánamera," they loudly sang *"Los Yanquis van para fuera!"*—Yankees get out.

At the base's entrance, a line of police and soldiers was blocking the gate, some with equipment marked "U.S.A." and shields saying police in English. Inside the base's gates, English street signs read do not enter and yield. Two American soldiers looked briefly at the protest as they cruised by in a golf cart. The protesters had good reason to be at Soto Cano. During the 2009 coup against Zelaya, the Honduran military flew the president from Tegucigalpa to Soto Cano before sending him into exile in Costa Rica, fueling suspicion about a U.S. role in the overthrow. "The United States participated directly in the planning and management of the coup," a leading human rights advocate, Bertha Oliva, told me. After coup leaders seized Zelaya, she noted, the next stop that they made was at the base. "That says everything. You don't need documents to understand that there's participation on behalf of the United States." I would later meet a high-ranking Honduran Air Force officer who said he directed the pilot to stop at Soto Cano for fuel.

The U.S. government, for its part, has denied any involvement in the coup. Indeed, the U.S. military still persistently downplays its presence in Honduras, even though it has spent millions on barracks construction and "permanent facilities" at Soto Cano. In 2012 alone, the Pentagon would spend a record $67.4 million on military contracts in Honduras and authorize $1.3 billion in military electronics exports to the country, among other spending.[1] Officials say the increased activity is merely aimed at countering skyrocketing drug trafficking in Central America and providing disaster relief and humanitarian assistance.

As speeches started at the protest march, a small group of U.S. human rights observers asked the *comandante* of the small Honduran Air Force Academy—which sits adjacent to Soto Cano—whether they could enter the base and speak with the U.S. commander. No, he said. There is "no U.S. base" here. There is only a "task force inside Honduran territory."

"Where is the U.S. base?" a Honduran journalist asked incredulously, looking toward the expansive U.S. facilities.

The *comandante* closed his eyes momentarily and shook his head slightly. "Well," he said, clearly embarrassed, "I don't know."[2]

THE ORIGINAL "BANANA REPUBLIC"

Foreigners have long exercised enormous power in Honduras and the rest of Central America. U.S. domination in the region has been virtually unchallenged for almost two hundred years, ever since President James Monroe's 1823 doctrine proclaimed "the American continents . . . are henceforth not to be considered as subjects for future colonization by any European powers." At the beginning of the twentieth century, President William Taft was more direct about U.S. intentions when he said, "The day is not far distant when . . . the whole hemisphere will be ours in fact as, by virtue of our superiority as a race, it already is ours morally."[3]

Since the 1850s, U.S. military interventions, primarily to protect U.S. economic interests, have been a recurring fact across Latin America. In Honduras, U.S. forces have intervened or occupied the country eight times—in 1903, 1907, 1911, 1912, 1919, 1920, 1924, and 1925.[4] The U.S. military also intervened militarily in the nearby Dominican Republic, Cuba, Haiti, Mexico, Guatemala, El Salvador, Nicaragua, and Panama, in some cases occupying them for decades at a time. (There's a reason many of today's best baseball players come from Latin America.)[5]

One of the first invasions of the twentieth century was actually carried out not by the U.S. military but by a private one. The army's financial backing came from "Banana Man" Sam Zemurray. When Zemurray arrived in Honduras in 1905 from Mobile, Alabama,[6] the country was already weak and debt-ridden from a British railway construction fraud that had produced no railway.[7] Seizing the moment, the businessman launched a coup and replaced the Honduran government with one more "sensitive to Zemurray's every wish"—namely, land and tax concessions for his banana plantations.[8] Within five years of arriving in Honduras, he controlled more than five thousand acres of plantations. A few years later, it was fifteen thousand.[9] By 1913, Zemurray and his closest rivals, the Vacarro brothers from New Orleans (whose Standard Fruit Company later became Dole), accounted for two thirds of Honduran exports.

The banana companies "bought up lands, built railroads, established their own banking systems, and bribed government officials at a dizzying pace," writes the historian Walter LaFeber. "If Honduras was dependent on the fruit companies before 1912, it was virtually indistinguishable from them after 1912. In 1914 the leading banana firms held nearly a million acres of the most fertile land. Their holdings grew during the 1920s until the Honduran peasants had no hope of access to their nation's good soil."[10] The wealth of the country was hauled off to the United States. Honduras was left with low-wage jobs in the banana groves and with proceeds from export duties, which were often evaded and, when they did get paid, were in any case mostly pocketed by a small group of Honduran elites.[11]

Thus did Honduras become the prototypical "banana republic." In popular usage (clothing company aside), the term nowadays mostly calls to mind buffoonlike Third World despots in the mold of Woody Allen's comedy *Bananas*. We tend to forget its original meaning. After living in Honduras, the writer O. Henry coined the phrase to refer to weak, marginally independent countries facing overwhelming foreign economic and political domination. In other words, a banana republic is a colony in all but name.

The basic pattern established in Zemurray's time continued after World War II. U.S. aid largely succeeded in increasing the economy's reliance on a few export products, while Citibank, Chase Manhattan, and Bank of America took over the financial system.[12] Honduras became "the closest ally to the United States," writes LaFeber, "while remaining the poorest and most underdeveloped state in the hemisphere other than Haiti."[13]

In 1954, the CIA used a banana plantation on Honduras's particularly impoverished north coast to train a U.S.-backed rebel army that went on to overthrow the democratically elected government of Guatemala. The Guatemalan government had been guilty of threatening the near-monopoly powers of the United Fruit Company, which had bought out Sam Zemurray's firm and made him its top official.[14] The Honduran plantation where the rebels trained was also owned by United Fruit—known today to banana consumers as Chiquita.

THE "USS HONDURAS"

During Central America's bloody civil wars of the 1980s, the U.S. presence in Honduras was so great that the country was nicknamed the "USS Honduras": it was like a stationary, unsinkable aircraft carrier, strategically anchored at the center of the war-torn region. From the Soto Cano Air Base, the Pentagon and CIA orchestrated support for regimes in Guatemala and El Salvador, which were responsible for hundreds of thousands of deaths, and for the murderous Nicaraguan Contra insurgency, which became part of the biggest American political scandal since Watergate.

In Nicaragua, the Contras were the U.S. government's primary weapon against the Sandinistas, who had ousted the longtime U.S.-backed Nicaraguan dictator Anastasio Somoza Debayle. "I speak in the name of President Ronald Reagan," Duane Clarridge, the CIA chief for Latin America, told a group of Somoza loyalists in 1981. "We want to support this effort to change the government of Nicaragua."[15]

Others in the room with Clarridge that day included Colonel Mario Davico, the vice chief of Argentine military intelligence, and Colonel Gustavo Alvarez Martínez, one of the most powerful officers in the

Honduran military. The meeting produced a plan to support the Contras known as "La Tripartita." As a Contra commander explained: "The Hondurans will provide the territory, the United States will provide the money, and Argentina will provide the front" to hide U.S. involvement.[16]

Honduras provided sanctuary for the Contras, and in exchange U.S. military aid to the country more than tripled between 1981 and 1982, from $8.9 million to $31.3 million. By 1984, military aid had more than doubled again, rising to $77.4 million (the equivalent of $175.9 million in today's dollars).[17] As the Honduran military received new U.S. weaponry, it transferred its old weapons to the Contras.[18]

There was never any real hope the Contras would overthrow the Sandinistas. Instead, in a post-Vietnam environment where direct U.S. military intervention was nearly impossible, U.S. officials saw the Contras as a second-best option. They were, in the words of former foreign service officer Todd Greentree, "a classic guerrilla counterweight who could harass and bleed the Sandinistas and whom the Sandinistas could not defeat."[19] Their "real political boss" was the CIA. President Reagan infamously described the group as the "moral equivalent of the Founding Fathers." Greentree, like others, says that they had "the reputation of being brigands and brutes who raped women, executed prisoners, and enjoyed murdering civilians."[20]

Within a year of La Tripartita's creation, the CIA helped set up six Contra bases in Honduras and started landing cargo planes filled with weapons. CIA operatives, U.S. and Argentine military advisers, Israelis, and Chileans began training the rebels. (According to former Army Special Forces operative William Meara, he once heard a U.S. Special Forces team refer to their students as "LBGs"—little brown guys.)[21] The Argentines brought the "Argentine method" of "disappearing," torturing, and killing political opponents.[22] The Contra force was soon so large it virtually took over whole Honduran provinces near the Nicaraguan border.[23]

In 1982, an addendum to a 1954 U.S.-Honduras military agreement gave the United States authority to base troops in Honduras, to build up airfields in country, and to build *any* "new facilities and installation of equipment as may be necessary for their use"—pretty much carte blanche.[24] The military used the freedom to build bases for Contra, Honduran, and U.S. forces far beyond Soto Cano. These included, by my count, at least thirty-two Contra bases alone, in Honduras, Nicaragua, Costa Rica, and even Florida. There were also at least sixteen bases for Honduran forces and at least nine U.S. bases in addition to Soto Cano and several secret CIA installations.[25]

"When Congress refused to fund the construction of new military bases in Honduras, the Pentagon built them anyway," explains the historian William LeoGrande. Often they used military exercises as a cover.[26] "When the exercises were over, the improved facilities and leftover supplies could be given to the Hondurans and the Contras."[27] Elsewhere, the military and CIA used Honduran bases to provide the Contras with supplies Congress hadn't authorized and simply told Congress otherwise.[28] By decade's end, Honduras was "little more than a vast U.S. military base" and "a virtual U.S. protectorate."[29]

In the United States, the Contras eventually became part of the biggest presidential scandal since Nixon when reporters and Congress revealed that the Reagan administration had covertly sent money and weapons to the Contras by using proceeds from secret sales of weaponry to Iran. The revelations were triply shocking: the United States had officially condemned Iran as a sponsor of international terrorism; Congress had explicitly prohibited funding the Contras; and Congress's Iran-Contra hearings confirmed that the CIA had known since at least 1984 that the Contras were trafficking drugs into the United States.[30]

While the scandal eventually passed, the effects of the wars in Central America were horrific. Honduras itself, though less affected than its neighbors, suffered a decade of death squads, extrajudicial killings, and torture. Between 1980 and 1984 alone, there were 274 unsolved killings and disappearances of leftists and other dissidents.[31]

Most of the "disappeared" were never heard from again. Oscar and Gloria Reyes are among the few Honduran victims who lived to tell their story. As a U.S. court found in 2006, soldiers working under the Honduran director of national intelligence took the couple from their home and subjected them to beatings, mock execution, forced nudity, electric shocks on their genitals, and confinement in rooms covered in feces, blood, vomit, and urine. In court testimony, Gloria Reyes said, "I am unable to explain how I was able to withstand it."[32]

Elsewhere the toll was higher: 50,000 dead in Nicaragua, 75,000 dead in El Salvador, and 240,000 dead or disappeared in Guatemala in what is widely considered a genocide. The majority of the victims were poor civilians. They died, as foreign service officer Greentree writes, in "large and indiscriminate numbers, families, clans, entire villages, the victims of torture, of bombardment, of massacre, of crossfire."[33] Hundreds of thousands of refugees flooded to neighboring countries and to the United States, whose government had provided the bullets that forced many to flee in the first place. Entire nations were left traumatized in ways that reverberate to this day.

THE ATTRACTIVENESS OF DICTATORS

The end of the Cold War effectively ended the wars in Central America. With U.S. funding for the Contras withdrawn, a GAO report declared, "The original reasons for the establishment of U.S. presence at Soto Cano no longer exist."[34] Many U.S. military and diplomatic officials agreed that the contributions made to new U.S. policy goals in the region by this "expensive, semi-permanent logistics base" were "incidental and not reason enough to maintain the presence." Officials saw that any counternarcotics or disaster relief operations in the region could be conducted just as effectively from domestic bases.

In some ways, the GAO found, Soto Cano's continued existence was actually counterproductive to U.S. policy.[35] The GAO recommended closing the base.[36] A study supported by the military's own National Defense University agreed. It concluded that the base "does not have a significant impact on regional stability, is potentially a political problem between U.S. and Honduran governments, and unnecessarily costs the U.S. taxpayer millions of dollars."[37]

Still, Soto Cano didn't close. While overall U.S. military spending in Honduras declined significantly, "exercises were continuing through sheer bureaucratic inertia," one former Army and Foreign Service officer explains. "Even though the original rationale for the base was disappearing, no one seemed to be considering packing up and going home."[38]

In fact, the persistence of the base was due not just to bureaucratic inertia. There were also concerted efforts to create new missions and justifications for the supposedly temporary base and for the military's entire

Southern Command. After the Cold War, the combatant command responsible for Latin America found itself marginalized and with little to do. Southcom discovered its salvation in disaster and drugs.[39]

The first opportunity came with the damage caused in Nicaragua by 1998's Hurricane Mitch. The Command coordinated a $30 million relief effort for America's former enemy and used the opportunity to expand its operations in the region.[40] The following year, Southcom used the closing of bases in Panama as a pretext to set up four new U.S. air bases in Ecuador, Aruba, Curaçao, and El Salvador.[41] And with the "war on drugs" providing a public rationale for broadening U.S. military activities in Latin America, by the end of the 1990s Southcom saw its budget expand more than any of the other regional commands.[42]

After the 2009 military coup removed President Zelaya from power, the Obama administration declared an official policy of no contact with the Honduran military. Nevertheless, U.S. and Honduran military officials maintained close relations. As U.S. embassy personnel in Honduras told me, high-ranking U.S. and Honduran officers still had one another's cell phone numbers and crossed paths in malls and other public places in Honduras. Contact continued at Soto Cano—where the Honduran military technically hosts the U.S. presence—and in other places where the two militaries interacted regularly. There was a brief dip in aid after the coup, but soon U.S. assistance to Honduran security forces began to rise again. In 2012, for example, Congress appropriated $56 million in U.S. military and police aid for Honduras.

The rising aid has come despite strong evidence that the Honduran military and police forces are connected to the skyrocketing violence in the country.[43] (Honduras has the world's highest murder rate—higher than that in Afghanistan and Iraq, more than four times that of Mexico, roughly twenty times the U.S. rate, and ninety times greater than western Europe's.)[44] Allegations have included the revival of 1980s-style death squads, and suspicions that the government's tough-on-crime "iron fist" policing program has led to the murder of thousands of young people labeled "delinquents" or "gang members." In a country with a population of only 6.7 million, the nongovernmental organization Casa Alianza / Covenant House has documented 9,641 people under age twenty-three murdered between 1998 and January 2014.[45] The Associated

Press reported in 2013 at least two hundred "formal complaints about death squad–style killings" in Honduras's two largest cities over a three-year period, while the National Autonomous University counted 149 civilians killed by police in 2011–2013.[46]

Military violence, too, has escalated since the coup against President Zelaya. Human rights groups have identified more than four thousand human rights violations after Zelaya's ouster, including arbitrary detention, torture, and political assassinations, with the de facto government implicated in scores of abuses.[47] Opposition members, journalists, and activists have continued to be the victims of shootings, beatings, death threats, and political intimidation. In the lead-up to the 2013 national elections, eighteen candidates for the party led by Zelaya and his wife, Xiomara Castro, were murdered.[48] While many of the facts are still unclear, there's growing reason to fear that providing money and resources to the Honduran military and police forces contributes to rising levels of violence and insecurity throughout the country.

There should be little surprise about the U.S. military's close relationship with undemocratic Honduran governments responsible for murders, torture, and widespread human rights abuses, both in the 1980s and after the 2009 coup. Despite frequently invoking rhetoric about spreading democracy and maintaining peace and security, the U.S. government has often shown few qualms about collaborating with repressive regimes to maintain access to overseas bases.

"Gaining and maintaining access to U.S. bases," the base expert Catherine Lutz explains, "has often involved close collaboration" with corrupt, antidemocratic, and sometimes murderous governments. Since World War II, the United States has supported undemocratic and authoritarian base hosts in Afghanistan, Bahrain, Djibouti, Greece, Iraq, Kuwait, Kyrgyzstan, Morocco, Pakistan, Panama, the Philippines, Portugal, Qatar, Saudi Arabia, South Korea, Spain, Thailand, Turkey, and Uzbekistan, to name only a few. A large-scale study of U.S. bases created since 1898 confirms that autocratic states have been "consistently attractive" to U.S. officials as base hosts. "Due to the unpredictability of elections," on the other hand, democratic states prove "less attractive in terms [of] sustainability and duration."[49]

In some cases, U.S. officials have reacted to this unpredictability by intervening in ostensibly democratic processes to produce outcomes to their liking and ensure ongoing base access. In the lead-up to Italy's crucial 1948 national elections, for instance, the CIA, the State Department, and other agencies of the U.S. government used propaganda, smear campaigns, threats to withdraw aid, and the appearance of warships off Italy's coasts, among other tactics, to help the Christian Democracy party defeat Italy's favored communist and socialist parties. The Christian Democrats, who maintained a client relationship with the U.S. government and provided widespread base access, then dominated Italian politics for the next five decades. (Their rule ended only when a massive 1994 corruption scandal reshuffled all of Italian politics.)

The U.S. government also provided similar covert and overt support in the aftermath of World War II for the right-wing Liberal Democratic Party in Japan and for dictatorial governments in South Korea. This support ensured that of the four countries worldwide hosting the largest number of U.S. bases, three saw virtually unbroken one-party rule for half a century or more. The other, Germany, had twenty years of one-party rule after the war.[50]

More recently, the U.S. government offered only tepid criticism of the government of Bahrain during its violent crackdown on pro-democracy protesters. According to Human Rights Watch and others (including an independent commission of inquiry appointed by King Hamad bin Isa al-Khalifa), the government has been responsible for abuses including the arbitrary arrest of protesters, torture and ill treatment during detention, torture-related deaths, the prosecution of political opponents, and growing restrictions on freedoms of speech, association, and assembly.[51]

After the 2013 military coup in Egypt, which has a relatively small U.S. base presence plus broader military and political ties related to the Arab-Israeli conflict, U.S. officials took months to withhold some forms of military and economic aid despite more than 1,300 killings by security forces and the arrest of more than 3,500 members of the Muslim Brotherhood. Despite these steps, according to Human Rights Watch, "little was said about ongoing abuses."[52] Likewise in Thailand, the U.S. has retained deep connections with the Thai military, even though it has carried out twelve coups since 1932.[53]

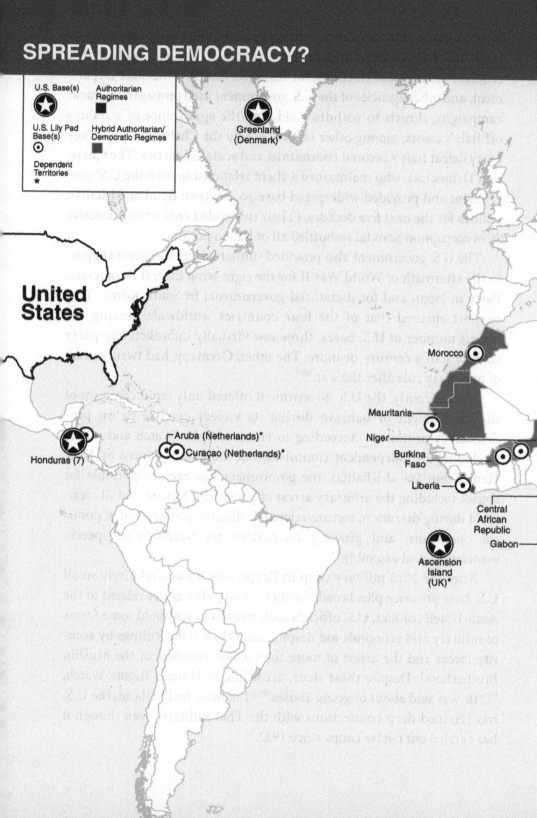

SPREADING DEMOCRACY?

U.S. Base(s) ✪

U.S. Lily Pad Base(s) ⊙

Dependent Territories ✱

Authoritarian Regimes ■

Hybrid Authoritarian/ Democratic Regimes ■

Greenland (Denmark)*

United States

Morocco

Mauritania

Niger

Burkina Faso

Liberia

Central African Republic

Gabon

Honduras (7)

Aruba (Netherlands)*

Curaçao (Netherlands)*

Ascension Island (UK)*

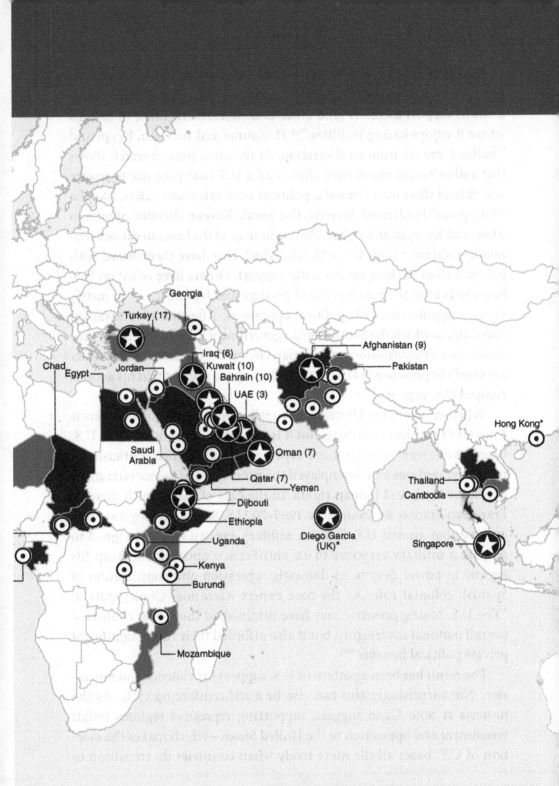

Turkey (17)

Georgia

Chad

Egypt

Jordan

Iraq (6)

Kuwait (10)

Bahrain (10)

UAE (3)

Afghanistan (9)

Pakistan

Saudi
Arabia

Oman (7)

Qatar (7)

Yemen

Dijbouti

Ethiopia

Uganda

Diego Garcia
(UK)*

Hong Kong*

Thailand

Cambodia

Singapore

Kenya

Burundi

Mozambique

Bases in countries and territories with limited or no democratic rule.
Key source: Economist Intelligence Unit, "Democracy Index 2013."

Research by the Johns Hopkins political scientist Kent Calder confirms the "dictatorship hypothesis": consistently, "the United States tends to support dictators [and other undemocratic regimes] in nations where it enjoys basing facilities."[54] Honduras and Bahrain, Egypt and Thailand, are far from an aberration. At the same time, research shows that authoritarian rulers have often used a U.S. base presence to ensure and extend their own domestic political survival. Some rulers, like the Philippines' Ferdinand Marcos, the South Korean dictator Syngman Rhee, and Kyrgyzstan's Askar Akayev, have used the bases to extract economic assistance from U.S. officials, which they have then shared with political allies to shore up domestic support. Others have relied on U.S. bases to bolster their international prestige and legitimacy or to justify violence against domestic political opponents. After the 1980 Kwangju massacre, in which the South Korean government killed around 240 prodemocracy demonstrators, strongman General Chun Doo-hwan explicitly cited the presence of U.S. bases and troops to suggest that his actions enjoyed U.S. support.[55]

Whether or not the United States really supported Chun's actions is a matter of continuing debate. But it is clear that in countries with U.S. bases, American officials have repeatedly muted their criticism of repressive regimes and downplayed the promotion of democratization, decolonization, and human rights. In the case of the Spanish dictator Francisco Franco, for example, a 1969–70 U.S. Senate investigation discovered that annual U.S.-Spanish military exercises were designed to prepare a military response to an anti-Franco uprising and keep his regime in power despite its domestic repression and continuation of Spanish colonial rule. As the base expert Alexander Cooley puts it, "The U.S. basing presence may have diminished these host countries' overall national sovereignty, but it also afforded their rulers significant private political benefits."[56]

The result has been a pattern of U.S. support for violence and repression. Not surprisingly, this can also be a self-reinforcing cycle. As the protests at Soto Cano suggest, supporting repressive regimes builds resentment and opposition to the United States—which makes the eviction of U.S. bases all the more likely when countries do transition to democratic rule.[57] Knowing this, the U.S. military has even more incentive to prevent that transition from taking place.

BLOWBACK

While some defend the presence of U.S. bases in repressive, undemocratic countries as necessary for supporting "U.S. interests" (that is, generally, corporate economic interests), backing dictators and autocrats frequently harms not only host nation citizens but also the United States and U.S. citizens as well. Honduras provides a telling example of what the CIA would call "blowback" from U.S. support for repressive regimes during Central America's civil wars.[58] Popularized by the onetime CIA analyst Chalmers Johnson, the term "blowback" refers to the unintended consequences of covert operations whose causes the public cannot understand precisely because the precipitating operations were covert. Put simply, the United States reaps what it secretly sows.[59]

In the 1980s, the U.S. government helped fuel Central America's dirty wars through its covert and overt support for brutal, drug-dealing Contras and repressive regimes in Honduras, Guatemala, and El Salvador. These wars killed and injured hundreds of thousands, frayed and destroyed social relations, and increased poverty, insecurity, and drug trafficking in the region. The wars also led to widespread forced migration, including widespread flight to the United States.

These refugees typically ended up in the poor neighborhoods of cities like Los Angeles. Once there, many impoverished boys and young men (and, to a lesser extent, girls and young women) found themselves joining U.S.-born-and-bred gangs. In addition to terrorizing U.S. neighborhoods, these refugee gang members were often arrested and deported back to their home countries, where they soon established new branches of their U.S.-based gangs.[60] In turn, these gangs became centrally involved in the growth in drug trafficking in Central America—which the Contras helped kick-start—as drug traffickers took advantage of the region's poverty and instability to create a new transshipment hub between South American producers and North American points of sale.[61] The main result of the U.S. drug war has been merely to shift transportation routes while increasing violence and doing little to affect consumption. Squeezing trafficking in one place has created a "balloon effect," pushing the trade from the Caribbean to Honduras and other parts of Central America. Today, an estimated 90 percent of the cocaine shipped from Colombia and Venezuela to the United States goes through Central America, with more than one third of that total going through Honduras.[62]

The drug trade's violence and the proliferation of gangs have been mutually reinforcing. Combined with the violence of living in the second-poorest country in the hemisphere, there should be little surprise that Honduras has the world's highest murder rate (followed by El Salvador, Belize, and Guatemala in the top five).[63] Amid such deteriorating and desperate conditions, there should be equally little surprise that the United States has seen so many Central American migrants arriving at our borders. Like the migrants who arrived at U.S. borders in the 1980s, these new refugees are in part a kind of second and third wave of blowback from decades of supporting repressive governments with bases and military aid.

The United States is not responsible for all the problems in Honduras and Central America. But the country's violence and insecurity today are directly linked to the violence and insecurity produced by almost two centuries of continuous U.S. domination, including the "USS *Honduras*" period of the 1980s.

There was a missed opportunity for the United States in Latin America at the end of the Cold War. After supporting a violent, repressive regime in Honduras and using the country to support even more murderous regimes in El Salvador and Guatemala, the United States should have completely withdrawn its bases and forces from Honduras and the rest of Latin America once peace came. There was no need for them in a region facing almost no external security threats or cross-national conflicts. Any humanitarian, training, and counternarcotics operations in Honduras could have been carried out from bases in the United States, just as the military does in many other countries.

The same remains true today. There is simply no reason for Soto Cano to exist. As long as it continues to exist and as U.S. forces become ever more entrenched at Soto Cano and elsewhere in Honduras, the United

States becomes increasingly complicit with the military that carried out the 2009 coup and with military and police forces implicated in murders and other serious human rights violations. The only question now is what bloodshed and blowback will occur in the future thanks to the U.S. military's growing involvement in Honduras today.

States becomes increasingly complicit with the military that carried out the 2009 coup and with military and police forces implicated in murders and other serious human rights violations. The only question now is what bloodshed and blowback will occur in the future thanks to the U.S. military's growing involvement in Honduras today."

New York City Police Department

Charles "Lucky" Luciano, notorious leader of New York and Naples mafias, in a 1931 mug shot.

6

In Bed with the Mob

"It looks like an outlet mall!" my friend Sonia blurted out in surprise as we crested a hill on a quiet rural road. We had gotten lost driving through the southern Italian countryside before finally sighting "Yankee City"—the sprawling U.S. military base north of Naples, on the outskirts of a small town called Gricignano di Aversa.[1]

The contrast between the base and its surrounding landscape was dramatic. Amid fields of peaches, apricots, and grapes, the base was ringed by a razor-wire-topped fence, security cameras, and motion detectors. Inside, there were perfectly ordered roads, large swaths of manicured and lavishly watered grass, shaded picnic areas and barbecue pits, children's playgrounds, skate parks, pools, neat apartment blocks, and row upon row of parking. The only signs of anything out of order at this gated community were trash bins overflowing with garbage spilling onto the ground.

The uncollected garbage reminded us that we were wending our way through Campania, the agriculturally rich and economically poor region controlled by the Neapolitan mafia, the Camorra. Less well known than Sicily's Cosa Nostra, the Camorra is Italy's oldest existing criminal organization, dating to at least the late eighteenth or early nineteenth century.* Out of the spotlight, the Camorra has thrived, inflicting devastating costs

---

*One origin story dates the Camorra to 1825 and men imprisoned, ironically enough, in a military base—Naples's Castel Nuovo.

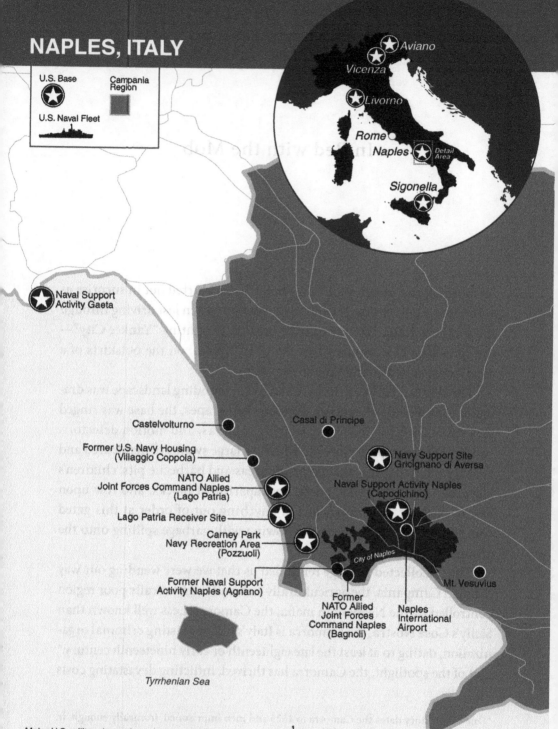

NAPLES, ITALY

U.S. Base

Campania Region

U.S. Naval Fleet

Aviano

Vicenza

Livorno

Rome

Naples — Detail Area

Sigonella

Naval Support Activity Gaeta

Castelvolturno

Casal di Principe

Former U.S. Navy Housing (Villaggio Coppola)

Navy Support Site Gricignano di Aversa

NATO Allied Joint Forces Command Naples (Lago Patria)

Naval Support Activity Naples (Capodichino)

Lago Patria Receiver Site

Carney Park Navy Recreation Area (Pozzuoli)

City of Naples

Mt. Vesuvius

Former Naval Support Activity Naples (Agnano)

Former NATO Allied Joint Forces Command Naples (Bagnoli)

Naples International Airport

Tyrrhenian Sea

Major U.S. military bases in and around Naples.
Inset shows major U.S. base locations in Italy.
Key source: U.S. Naval Support Activity Naples.

in blood and corruption. As Sonia and I drove toward the base, I recalled the words of Roberto Saviano, the Italian investigative journalist who has lived in hiding since publishing *Gomorrah*, his famed Camorra exposé. "Never in the economy of a region," Saviano writes, "has there been such a widespread, crushing criminal presence as in Campania in the last ten years."[2] The Camorra has been responsible for more than 3,600 deaths in the last four decades—far more deaths than Italy's other major criminal organizations (Sicily's Cosa Nostra, Calabria's 'Ndrangheta, and Puglia's Sacra Corona Unita).[3] And no other Italian region has as many cities under observation for mafia infiltration. Between 1991 and 2006, out of a total of 170 judicial decrees in Italy dissolving local governments that had been infiltrated by organized crime, 75 of them—nearly half the total—were from Campania alone.[4]

The Camorra system (mafia members typically call their organization *il sistema*) and its clans have integrated themselves into nearly every part of the social, political, and economic life of Campania. The U.S. military is no exception. A short drive down the potholed road from Gricignano's sibling base, the U.S. Navy facility at Naples International Airport, sits one of Europe's largest open-air drug markets, dominated by the clans.[5] To help describe Campania, Saviano turned to the words of a magazine for U.S. military personnel: "Imagine yourself in a Sergio Leone film. It's like the Wild West. Somebody gives orders, there are shoot-outs and unwritten, yet unassailable laws. Don't be alarmed . . . Nevertheless, leave the military compound only when necessary."[6]

I first started trying to make sense of the presence of major U.S. facilities and the roughly ten thousand troops, civilians, and family members in this mafia heartland after an otherwise uneventful interview with an American official in Naples. After I turned off my audio recorder, the official (who has asked not to be named, for obvious reasons) told me the Navy has had a problem of getting "into bed" with the wrong people. And they've been doing it, he said, ever since the Allies arrived in Naples during World War II. Rather than work with ex-Fascist officials, the Navy found people who could get things done—the Camorra.

A ROUGH-EDGED CITY

Naples's reputation is generally as bad as Saviano suggests. Before arriving there, I was warned to be careful. Friends living in Rome—one of whom grew up in Naples—cautioned me about walking the city's streets, known for their skilled thieves riding two to a motorbike to snatch bags and belongings. They even briefly considered recommending I avoid the city's most famous pizzeria, Da Michele, because of its rough neighborhood.

Aside from pizza, crime, and poverty, Naples has become synonymous with garbage. In 2007 and 2008, trash went uncollected for weeks at a time. It lined roadsides, clogged city streets, and piled into mountains surrounding communal collection areas. Six million metric tons of garbage remain scattered at dumpsites around Campania.[7]

While there's no confusing Naples with the tourist havens of Florence and Venice or the grandeur of Rome, the city is remarkable precisely because of its rough edges. Scooters, cars, and pedestrians duck and weave along the city's roads. Vespas and Asian-made motorbikes fly around the boulevards and the narrowest of stone-paved alleyways, sliding between cars, deftly adjusting their trajectories at the last possible second to avoid passersby, hitting their high-pitched horns in a nearly constant chorus of Road Runner beeps. Cars are parked and double-parked at every possible angle on the roads and sidewalks. Pedestrians make their way protected only by courage and faith that drivers will stop (which mostly they do).

Naples, which is Italy's third-largest city after Rome and Milan, was founded by Greeks around 600 bce as "Neapolis," or New City. During much of Europe's Renaissance and under Spanish rule, when southern Italy was far wealthier than the north, Naples was a center of art and culture, rivaled in size only by London and Paris. Today, its old city remains largely intact. It is full of arched passageways tagged with centuries of graffiti, apartments covered in chipped pink and peach hues, balconies overflowing with laundry lines and potted plants, tiny shops and crowded vendors' tables. Beneath lies an underground city of Greco-Roman catacombs, caves, waterways, and temples to worship the dead.

Aboveground, the aromas of dark Neapolitan espresso, sweet cream-filled *sfogliatelle*, and folded sidewalk pizza designed for eating while walking compete with the odors of heavy pollution and the port. Outside the old city and surrounding areas, much of Naples now consists of an unremarkable business core and brutalist public housing blocks on the city's periphery. The varied neighborhoods are united perhaps most of all by a passionate love for the local soccer team, SSC Napoli—and by the controlling power of the Camorra.

THE MILITARY AND THE MOB

Charles "Lucky" Luciano, one of the gangsters portrayed on the HBO television series *Boardwalk Empire*, is known for having transformed the mafia in the United States. What's less well known to Americans is the role Sicilian-born Luciano played in the history of Naples and the U.S. military's presence in the city.

One of the most notorious gangsters in the New York City mafia, Luciano—along with close associates Meyer Lansky and Benjamin "Bugsy" Siegel—organized the American mob into a powerful and wealthy national crime syndicate boasting a corporate structure and command over drugs, prostitution, and a range of other rackets.[8] Eventually Luciano ended up in prison, but he managed to gain an early release by helping Navy officers who were concerned about protecting New York harbor from Axis spies and saboteurs during World War II.[9] Luciano had close ties to the unions that controlled the docks. From his cell, he recommended that fellow mafiosi aid in the wartime campaign, and he had Lansky introduce them to Naval Intelligence officials.*[10]

Although the Navy long tried to cover up the story, Luciano also aided preparations for the Allied invasion of Sicily. There's debate about exactly how much help the mafia provided, but at the very least, Luciano and others supplied information about the island and local contacts to help with the landing and to ensure social order would be maintained after the Allies took control.[11] It was an early example of the links between the

---

*Later, Luciano claimed he was responsible for the arson that triggered the military's concern about sabotage in New York Harbor in the first place. If true, it would be "classic Mafia style," as historian Salvatore Lupo says: "Threat and protection from the same source!"

military and the mob. Luciano's reward for all this wartime usefulness was a 1946 letter of clemency from New York governor Thomas Dewey, and immediate deportation from New York to Italy.

After the Allies landed in Sicily, the mob connections deepened. Allied leaders drew on the assistance of local mafia bosses, who had been the targets of a brutal crackdown by Mussolini. In some cases, the Allies appointed the mafiosi as mayors. One, Calogero Vizzini, had been accused of (though not tried for) thirty-nine murders, six attempted murders, seventy-three robberies and thefts, and sixty-three cases of extortion.[12] Soon, according to one mafia expert, the Allied administration was "riddled with Mafiosi."[13] Bosses were serving as brokers between the Allies and locals, providing interpretation, and fulfilling other important roles. Once the mafiosi declared themselves anti-Fascist, the historian Tom Behan notes, the Allies had "trusted partners who were able to police society very effectively."[14]

After the Allies occupied Naples, connections with organized crime expanded. When Colonel Charles Poletti, head of the Allied Military Government and former lieutenant governor of New York, arrived in Naples, he selected Vito Genovese as his interpreter and counselor.[15] Poletti was undoubtedly familiar with the mafia boss who had managed Lucky Luciano's New York drug and gambling operations before fleeing to Italy to escape a murder charge.[16] Soon, Genovese was at the center of the expanding underground.

Through Genovese's influence, Poletti's military government appointed Camorra mayors in Campania towns, which remain Camorra-dominated to this day. Within fifty miles of Naples, Genovese reigned.[17] He and Vizzini used Genovese's relationship with Colonel Poletti to smuggle oil, sugar, and other goods from the Naples docks in Allied military trucks. In Sicily and Naples, the looting and skimming of Allied food and supplies became endemic.[18] In a devastated Naples where hundreds of thousands were homeless and hungry, up to 60 percent of unloaded goods may have disappeared. Up to 65 percent of locals' income derived from underground sales.[19]

An entire contraband system for food, clothing, cigarettes, appliances, and other goods took root in Naples, despite largely disappearing elsewhere in Italy after the war. It became so efficient that penicillin and other medical supplies were readily available there even when there were short-ages in military hospitals.[20] GIs even joined the ranks of customers frequenting brothels and buying contraband in the famed and feared Quartieri Spagnoli neighborhood (originally built in the sixteenth century to house Spanish troops).[21] By April 1944, the British writer Norman Lewis, then an intelligence officer, wrote of the underground market, "It is becoming generally known that it operates under the protection of certain high-placed Allied Military Government officials."[22]

In August 1944, the U.S. Army was sufficiently embarrassed to arrest Genovese and return him to New York. After the prosecution's prime witness was poisoned to death, though, Genovese went free. He eventually became the leader of Lucky Luciano's New York crime family—which soon bore the Genovese name.[23] In Naples, meanwhile, Genovese's arrest left an opening. It was filled by Luciano himself, newly returned to Italy after Governor Dewey's clemency.[24] The bosses simply switched places.

Following a temporary reduction in U.S. and Allied forces after the war, the American presence in Italy was soon on the rise. The right-wing Christian Democracy party, which had overcome Italy's favored communist and socialist parties in 1948 elections thanks to massive U.S. support, repaid the favor by actively advocating for U.S. and NATO bases in Italy and Italian participation in NATO. In 1954, the Christian Democrats established the foundation for the growing U.S. presence by signing the Italian-American "Bilateral Infrastructure Agreement." (The terms of the agreement are classified to this day; a former Italian Ministry of Defense official has suggested that the secrecy is a function of some of the agreement's violating the Italian constitution.)[25] Around the same time, the CIA appears to have also supported the Sicilian Mafia as fears grew about the power of the communist and socialist parties. "Because of its anti-communist nature," writes Victor Marchetti, a former high-ranking CIA official turned critic, the Mafia was "one of the elements which the CIA use[d] to control Italy."[26]

In and around Naples, U.S. forces built bases in Gaeta, Ischia, Lago Patria, Varcaturo, Marinaro, Grazzanise, Mondragone, Montevergine,

Nisida, and Carney Park[27]—a slightly surreal amusement-park-cum-sports-center secluded in the forested crater of an extinct volcano near Lake Averno, once believed to be the entrance to the underworld.[28] The Navy concentrated many of its facilities in a part of Naples called Agnano. Elsewhere in Italy, the military built or occupied bases from Aviano to Sicily, plus a large base and recreation facility on the Tuscan coast not far from Pisa. Today, the Pentagon counts fifty bases, more than twelve thousand U.S. troops, and thousands more civilians and family members stationed with them across Italy. After Germany, Japan, and South Korea, there are now more U.S. bases in Italy than anywhere else outside the United States.

Boosted by its relationships with U.S. forces and the mafias in Sicily and America, the Camorra eventually surpassed the economic power and influence of the Sicilian Cosa Nostra. Growing beyond underground markets, small-scale extortion, and racketeering, the Camorra became an international business syndicate.[29] The biggest expansion in scale and scope came in the 1970s, when the Camorra clans found lucrative opportunities in construction, concrete, public contracts, waste disposal, and especially international drug trafficking. This turned the Camorra into a global economic powerhouse, grossing an estimated $16 billion per year and employing twenty thousand people, with affiliates across Europe, South America, and the United States.[30]

Lucky Luciano, the gangster who helped the Allies connect with the Camorra in the first place, didn't live to see it reach these heights. He passed away in 1962, officially of a heart attack. Some say it was really poison. When he died, he was sitting in the Naples International Airport, a few hundred yards from the Navy's eventual home.[31]

RUBBLE IN THE PINE GROVES

After seeing the Gricignano base with Sonia, I went to visit a place where thousands of Navy sailors and their families had once lived. I found the remains of Villaggio Coppola—Coppola Village—standing along the Mediterranean coast north of Naples, secluded between a verdant pine forest and the bright blue sea.

When I arrived, I suddenly felt as if I had entered a scene out of Mel

Gibson's postapocalyptic classic *Mad Max*. Shabby high-rises were interspersed with abandoned, decaying four-story apartment blocks. The Villaggio's road to the water ended in a rutted mess of broken pavement, gravel, and a pile of dumped trash. I parked near the trash heap and walked onto a beach dotted with tall patchy grass, garbage, and a rusted car wreck.

Some of the Villaggio Coppola had been torn down years ago, and several of the remaining apartments lacked walls and rooftops. Windows and shutters on many of them were gone, too. In places, twisted rebar jutted out through eroding concrete. I was surprised to see clothes flapping in the wind on a few surviving balconies. Although the apartments are officially unoccupied, I was told that if you know a Camorrista, you can find somewhere to stay.

The Villaggio, which has been called "the City of Abuse,"[32] was built by the Coppola family in the 1960s, largely to house U.S. military personnel. The family, whose most prominent members are the brothers Cristoforo and Vincenzo, hails from the Camorra stronghold of Casal di Principe. "Compared to Casal di Principe," Saviano notes, the town of Corleone—the Sicilian community made famous by the *Godfather* movies—"is Disneyland."[33]

Of the Coppolas' Villaggio, Saviano says it is like nothing else in Italy. "They did not ask for authorization. They didn't need to. Around here construction bids and permits make production costs skyrocket because there are so many bureaucratic palms to grease. So the Coppolas went straight to the cement plants. One of the most beautiful maritime pine groves in the Mediterranean was replaced by tons of reinforced concrete."[34] The Camorra provided the building materials. The project helped the Coppolas become the "richest and most powerful" construction group in Campania.[35]

With the help of cooperative politicians, the family built more than half of the Villaggio illegally on public land. The rest was built on private land acquired by one illegal means or another. Litigation followed, but the Coppolas got away with a nominal fine—assessed by a judge with an apartment in one of the Villaggio high-rises.[36] The development was a perfect illustration of the Camorra's deepening relationships with local politicians and businesses like the Coppolas' firm, all united by a shared goal of making huge profits from public contracts and illegal construction.[37]

And this is where thousands of U.S. military personnel and their families lived for decades. It was only in the 1990s that the commanding officer in Naples, Admiral Michael Boorda, finally ordered them to leave "because of the poor condition of the buildings and high crime."[38] Unfazed, Cristoforo Coppola and a member of the particularly murderous Casalesi clan cofounded a business that would bid on contracts to revitalize the environmental and economic life of the coast, which the Villaggio itself had helped destroy. When some of the Villaggio's towers were torn down after barely four decades of occupancy, Vincenzo Coppola did the demolition work.[39] For the Coppolas, it was profit upon profit upon profit—thanks in no small part to Camorra connections.

YANKEE CITY

To replace the Villaggio Coppola and other housing, the Navy convinced Congress to build a new housing development and naval station around Naples. To whom did the military turn when it was looking for a developer? To the Coppolas. Or at least to Cristoforo and four of his children, who control the Mirabella construction company following a contentious split between Cristoforo and Vincenzo.

The Navy had been working on plans for a new base ever since a series of earthquakes hit Agnano in 1982. The Navy's initial plan, "Project Pronto"—Project Quick—moved slowly. In 1988, the U.S. Congress finally rejected it because of its high costs. Two years later, Congress approved a two-pronged plan to build an operations base at the Naples airport and the support site in Gricignano di Aversa that Sonia and I later visited, with its housing, school, shopping, and other amenities.

For the Gricignano site, Congress and the Navy decided to use a procedure called "lease-construction." Rather than buying land and paying for construction through congressional appropriations, the Navy invited developers to build the support site to its specifications. In exchange, the Navy promised to lease the site from the developer for thirty years. After that, the developer would get the buildings back, with the right to rent them to the Navy or anyone else. The initial costs to the U.S. government would be nearly zero—the developer would pay all the construction and land acquisition costs while getting the security of guaranteed future rent. Congress, on the other hand, would be on the hook for thirty or more years of lease payments.

In 1993, the Navy awarded the first of four contracts for the support site to Cristoforo Coppola's Mirabella. Why it did so is the subject of some dispute. A letter from a Pentagon official to the chairman of Mirabella, Cristoforo's son Francesco, suggests that Mirabella's "friends," the powerful congressmembers Ron Dellums and Tom Foglietta, may have helped win the contract.[40] Others say Coppola paid a politically connected Italian restaurateur in Washington with good ties to the military to secure the deal. (The restaurateur was charged but acquitted of wrongdoing.)[41]

After construction at Gricignano began, the discovery of Bronze Age archaeological remains described as "priceless" and potentially a "new Pompeii" slowed the building process only briefly.[42] "The Americans . . . were in a hurry," one Italian journalist explained. "Cristoforo proceeded with construction like a tank to spend as little as possible and avoid paying millions in fines."[43] The Navy official overseeing construction admitted that "Mirabella developed a strategy it wouldn't have if not for the Navy's timetable" to begin construction as quickly as possible.[44]

While archaeological discoveries couldn't stop Coppola, Naples prosecutors did. In 1999, prosecutors investigated multiple allegations of crime and corruption at Gricignano. Some of the allegations came from Vincenzo Coppola, whose own company had lost the construction contract to his brother. Vincenzo claimed Cristoforo had won the contract illegally and that the Navy had changed its rules during the bidding. The Navy denied the charge. However, prosecutors also discovered that Gricignano's municipal government helped Mirabella get two hundred acres of farmland by changing local zoning laws. Prosecutors said the changes could only have happened through criminal dealings. According to the *Stars and Stripes* newspaper, which covers the U.S. military worldwide, a former Camorra boss "hinted that organized crime did, in fact, influence Gricignano town policy."[45] A former town councillor said that the land was expropriated from farmers at a cut-rate price.[46]

Meanwhile, six known Camorristi—including two confessed murderers—said that when they failed to win the base construction contract, they began extorting money from Mirabella's subcontractors. (None directly implicated Mirabella or Cristoforo, who at the time was finishing three months of house arrest for an unrelated tax fraud conviction.)[47] According to another witness, the Camorra demanded 3 percent payoffs from subcontractors, or about $10,000 per month. *Stars and Stripes* reported that the witness "confessed to murders and implied some were related to the construction." Another Camorra witness testified he killed someone who collected the payoffs.[48]

The Navy said it would not vouch for the legality of the parties involved in the construction, and added that Mirabella had cleared the Italian government's mafia check. "We're not here on behalf of the Italian government to make sure none of these parties are shady," insisted the Navy officer overseeing construction.[49] Eventually a Naples appeals court allowed construction to continue. The prosecutors appealed to the Italian Supreme Court but soon found themselves replaced on the case. The new prosecutors dropped the charges, saying they lacked evidence.

The allegations didn't end there. In 1996, Admiral Boorda, the former Naples commander who got the Navy out of the Villaggio Coppola and later became the Navy's highest-ranking officer, died at the Washington Navy Yard. According to the Navy and news reports, Boorda committed suicide by shooting himself in the chest with his son-in-law's .38-caliber revolver.[50] Navy and other government officials officially attributed Boorda's suicide to a *Newsweek* investigation into his improperly wearing two Vietnam-era decorations for serving in combat (he had stopped wearing the medals a year before his death). Some reports say he died, unusually, of two shots to the chest, but the Navy never released an autopsy.[51] Citing Boorda's wife's privacy, officials also never released what they said were two typed suicide notes. In the days before his death, Boorda had learned that Navy investigators were ready to arrest twenty-one sailors in Naples on heroin and cocaine smuggling charges.[52] The Italian journalist Riccardo Scarpa reported that some U.S. officials told him the suicide might have been related to Boorda's discovery of corruption at Gricignano.[53] Unanswered questions and JFK-style assassination theories circulate to this day about Boorda's death (including unsubstantiated speculation about Camorra involvement).[54]

CAMORRA LANDLORDS

Gabriella, a stylish Italian woman in her twenties with two degrees and remarkable English skills, suggested we meet at an outdoor café in the fashionable Piazza Vanvitelli to talk about the Navy presence in Naples. She said she had dated two "Navy guys," and described herself as a little "obsessed" with dating Americans. On several occasions, she said, she had spent time with her boyfriends at the Gricignano base.

"The Gricignano base is in an area that is very, very Camorra controlled," Gabriella told me. Interestingly, she found that some Navy guys living off base actually seem to feel safer renting homes from the clans. When they look for housing off base, she explained, the Navy's Housing Office tries to show them nice apartments and houses. And members of the Camorra own some of the nicer ones.

Once she asked some sailors if they felt safe living off base. "No," one told her, "but our landlords are mafia, or Camorra, so we feel safe because they wouldn't let anybody do any damage to us . . . Nobody would ever dare enter into my house to steal something or scratch my cars because they know that my landlord is mafia."

"Ohh-kaay," Gabriella said sarcastically, "if *you* feel safe . . . I try not to go there at all . . . because *I* don't feel safe."

Gabriella's experience is not unusual. In October 2008, the major Italian daily *Corriere della Sera* published the results of an investigation by Naples antimafia officials showing that the Navy has been renting multiple properties owned by Camorra money laundering fronts. For many years, for example, Navy officers had been renting a house at number 10 Via Toti in San Cipriano d'Aversa, about seven miles from the Gricignano base. The building, a two-story villa surrounded by fortresslike walls and security cameras, had been purchased in 1986 in the name of the mother of Camorra boss Antonio Iovine with what investigators believe were his criminal earnings. Iovine is listed as one of the thirty most dangerous criminals in Italy and was one of five Camorra leaders the U.S. Treasury put on a sanctions list to combat transnational criminal organizations.[55] In other words, it was as if the Navy were renting from the mother of Al Capone.

Beyond Iovine, investigators discovered that of some fifty villas seized from another Camorra clan, U.S. personnel were renting at least forty. Police suspected there were probably "hundreds more."[56] The Navy— and U.S. taxpayers—were paying the Camorristi from $2,000 to as much as $8,000 per month for the homes. (They were paying these rents to other landlords, too, at two to three times local averages.) "We know full well that many of the large villas in the Caserta area and those near military bases have dubious owners, and have often been built illegally with money originating from criminal activities," said Sergio de Gregorio, the Italian senator responsible for relations with NATO forces. "These are princely villas with swimming pools and huge gardens surrounded by high walls."[57]

"Absurd, isn't it?" said Franco Roberti, the head of the Naples antimafia squad. "Italy contributes to NATO, and [U.S. forces belonging to NATO] are helping fill the coffers of the Camorra."[58]

In November 2008, Italian authorities surprised Navy officials when they appeared at the Navy's Housing Office. The Italian agents produced a court order for records regarding six homes leased by U.S. personnel and discovered to be owned by Camorra families. The agents also asked for access to the Navy's entire housing database. The Navy refused, seemingly to avoid further embarrassment.[59] The head of the antimafia squad faulted the Navy for knowingly renting from suspected mob bosses.[60] Italian media reports in recent years suggest that the Navy and other NATO forces have continued renting from people with Camorra connections.[61]

"PHILOSOPHICAL ABOUT THE SITUATION"

The relationship between the U.S. military and the Camorra is neither a coincidence nor an aberration. Indeed, the construction project at Gricignano probably couldn't have been better designed to ensure Camorra involvement.

To begin with, any construction in the Campania region was likely to attract the Camorra given its infiltration of the industry. Beyond that, the Navy's "lease-construction" contract meant there was even more pressure than usual on the developer to keep construction costs as low as possible. The contract's structure meant the developer wouldn't be paid until construction was complete and the lease payments started. This meant taking on considerable debt in the meantime, as opposed to a standard contract that would have paid the developer at intervals during construction. Keeping costs—and thus debt—to a manageable amount, especially around Naples, meant acquiring land as cheaply as possible (by means legal or otherwise) and reducing construction and labor costs as much as possible (by means legal or otherwise).

In other words, in a place well known for the Camorra's presence in the construction business, the Navy's contract plainly encouraged cutting corners at best and illegalities at worst. A "cost reimbursement" contract, clearly specifying estimated labor and materials reimbursement rates and providing greater contracting oversight, would almost surely have been preferable.

Something similar had happened at the Navy's former home in the Villaggio Coppola. There, the Coppolas acquired much of their land illegally (it's cheaper that way) and without permits, which would have cost money in fees, bribes, and construction delays. Then they built such poorly constructed buildings that the Navy was moving out after just three decades. A similar story unfolded at the Agnano base, where the Navy employed much the same lease-construction technique and got poorly constructed facilities with "serious maintenance problems," like a hospital with a leaky roof, sporadically operating air-conditioning, and an X-ray machine with a protective shield that fell from the ceiling.[62] The Camorra's Zagaria family, another target of U.S. anti–organized crime sanctions, even built NATO's radar base in Lago Patria, outside Naples.[63]

U.S. bases in Sicily have also remained closely linked to the Mafia since World War II. In the 1980s, at the now closed Comiso base, firms controlled by the Cosa Nostra won most of the base construction contracts; many of the subcontracts went to Sicilian companies with Mafia ties; and many of the temporary construction workers came from Mafia-controlled firms in western Sicily. Locals quickly understood, as the anthropologist Laura Simich explains, "that base construction was not effectively under the jurisdiction of Italian law."[64]

In the 1990s, three major janitorial, grounds keeping, and maintenance contractors at Sicily's Sigonella naval base were revealed to have Mafia ties. According to court rulings, the controlling partner in the three companies, Carmelo La Mastra, was part of attempts to intimidate a competitor into withdrawing a contract bid. A U.S. court found that it was "probably in connection with that bid" that another firm's owner was killed. La Mastra's companies were placed under legal receivership, and he was indicted for his role in a "Mafia-type association" and bid rigging. Yet in 1999, the Navy awarded La Mastra's three companies a major base maintenance contract, stating they had they had "a satisfactory record of performance, integrity, and business ethics."[65]

Ties between the military and the Mafia may not have been simply the result of questionable oversight, but a deliberate decision. "It has even been suggested that the decision to install nuclear cruise missiles at Comiso was because the Mafia could be relied on to protect the site in return for the inevitable rake off it could extract on the hundreds of millions of dollars in construction contracts for roads, housing and so on," the New York Times's Flora Lewis wrote at the time. "Max Raab, the U.S. ambassador in 1983 when the site was being built, was said by aides to be philosophical about the situation, holding that the corruption was a problem for the Italian, not the U.S., government and that in any case the dollars would help stimulate the bedraggled Sicilian economy."[66]

In Sicily and Naples alike, the repeated connections between the Navy and organized crime should be an expected, not a surprising, part of the U.S. military's presence in the country. As we have seen around the world, the military has long sought base locations with a friendly and stable political and economic environment. Military officials have employed various means to achieve such stability. In places like Honduras and Bahrain, collaborating with repressive regimes has ensured long-term tenancy. In places like Germany, bringing over families and building segregated Little Americas has helped smooth and stabilize relations. In Diego Garcia and elsewhere, the military has simply gotten rid of locals.

Locating bases in poor and marginalized areas like Naples, ridden with organized crime, is part of the same pattern. U.S. officials have assumed that the promise of jobs and money will help secure a long-term presence free of protest or dissent. This has indeed largely been the case in Naples, as the Navy, over the course of more than sixty years, has embedded itself in the regional political economy. The Camorra, of course, is even more deeply embedded in the local political economy, leading the two organizations to become increasingly entwined over the years. As the Italian military analyst Antonio Mazzeo explains, the "proliferation of U.S. and NATO bases" has helped "strengthen the political and economic power of criminal organizations."[67]

In the Italian government, U.S. officials have also had a partner agreeable to most military requests. What's more, the Italian government has usually been available to take the blame for anything that might go wrong, such as uncomfortable revelations of ties with organized crime. And plenty of American officials, like Ambassador Raab, seem to have been "philosophical" about working with the Camorra, the Cosa Nostra, and other mafias. Given the crime families' success in cutting costs, providing stability and protection, avoiding bureaucratic, legal, and political hurdles, and quickly getting concrete on the ground, many U.S. officials have been happy to ignore evidence of mafia involvement.

THE TRIANGLE OF DEATH

Before Sonia and I returned to Naples from the Gricignano support site, we stopped to buy and quickly devour something unavailable at the Gricignano base itself: freshly made buffalo mozzarella. This Campania specialty is known worldwide in its own right and is an essential component of true Neapolitan pizza. The lusciously smooth, soft cheese is strikingly different from the shredded or rubbery plastic-wrapped versions sold in American grocery stores, and even from tasty well-made cow's milk mozzarella.

Slightly high on the rich, sweet cheese, Sonia and I drove back to Naples, passing more peach orchards, apricot trees, and some of those transcendent water buffalo grazing near the highways. We also passed heaps of trash lining the roadways and strewn around bridge overpasses. We saw trash fires in the fields clouding the air, and huge bales of compacted plastic-wrapped trash waiting for incineration in Campania's planned but nonexistent incinerators. It was impossible not to think about what was buried and hidden just below the surface of the Campania plains. It was impossible not to wonder just what the buffalo were grazing on.

Gricignano and surrounding areas where Navy personnel live are at the center of an area where the Camorra has engaged in the illegal dumping of garbage and toxic waste since the 1980s. Garbage has become gold for the Camorristi, in what is now a $20-billion-a-year illicit industry.[68] The Camorra has solved many of the waste disposal problems for businesses in northern Italy and beyond, cheaply ridding companies of manufacturing and other hazardous waste by burying the refuse in illegal dumps, pumping dangerous chemicals into hidden underground ditches, and burning trash on a nightly basis in secluded areas around Naples. A Camorra boss's recently declassified 1997 testimony said his clan alone had buried "millions of tons" of toxic waste from the north and truckloads of nuclear waste from Germany in areas around Gricignano.[69]

Since the 1980s, studies have consistently shown elevated cancer rates in Campania compared to Italian national averages. Researchers publishing in the major scientific journal Lancet Oncology named an area near Gricignano the "triangle of death."[70] Elevated levels of radiation, nitrates, fecal coliform bacteria, arsenic, and chemicals used in cleaning solvents have been found in well water, air, and soil. The highly toxic industrial chemical dioxin has been found in sheep, which stagger and hobble through trash-littered fields until they expire, mangy and skeletal.[71] After my visit, I learned that dangerous levels of carcinogens have been found in Campania's water buffalo.

The Navy has become so concerned about local conditions that it has spent millions of dollars on studies investigating asthma, birth defects, cancer rates, and water, air, and soil quality. The Gricignano base now prohibits sailors from using tap water, and the base commissary carefully labels the origin of Italian produce.[72] The only buffalo mozzarella for sale is from northern Italy.

The way that Camorristi solve waste disposal problems for northern Italian businesses is rather like the way the Camorra and Camorra-linked companies have cheaply and efficiently solved base construction problems for the U.S. military, building and maintaining Navy facilities with minimal hassle and expense. The moral implications of the U.S. military and U.S. taxpayer dollars supporting such a murderous criminal organization are troubling, to say the least. That U.S. troops are now facing the same garbage-related health risks that Campania locals face around the "triangle of death" is just one more reminder of the shortsightedness of the U.S. military's relationship with the Camorra. In some cases, almost literally, you reap what you sow.

Munitions debris from some of the decades of weapons testing on Vieques, Puerto Rico.

Currents magazine, U.S. Navy

7

Toxic Environments

You know nothing good is coming when a Navy lawyer responds to a question about the destructive impacts of bombing practice with "It depends what you mean by 'destroy'. . ."

It was 2011, and the Navy was holding a public meeting on Saipan, the largest of the Northern Mariana Islands, some 130 miles north of Guam. The meeting was part of an environmental impact statement process for proposed military training and testing around Guam and the Northern Marianas. Many locals were especially concerned about the bombing of Farallon de Medinilla, known as FDM, a two-hundred-acre uninhabited island in the Northern Marianas that is home to numerous species of migratory birds. When the Northern Marianas negotiated with the U.S. government in the 1970s to end its UN trust territory status and become a U.S. commonwealth (like Puerto Rico), part of the deal involved giving the military full use of FDM and two thirds of the island of Tinian. Much like at Puerto Rico's Vieques, the military then used FDM for years as a live-fire range to test two-thousand-pound bombs, precision-guided munitions, and various other large guns, cannons, mines, and missiles. In 2002, several environmental groups successfully sued to stop the bombing, but the Pentagon found exemptions to environmental regulations and was allowed to resume testing.[1]

At the meeting on Saipan, a Navy video was playing in a loop behind the environmental lawyer for the Navy's Pacific Fleet. "For decades the Mariana Islands have provided a safe training and testing environment for the military," a woman's voice intoned, as images of exotic birds, whales, coral reefs, and the Marianas' beaches alternated with photos of ships, submarines, fighter jets, troops, and weapons. A sailor in uniform told the camera, "If we can't train, then we would not be prepared for the real scenario." The narrator continued, "The military is committed to protecting the islands' natural and cultural resources and heritage and strives to minimize the effects of its training and testing activities on the environment."

People inside and outside the military often laud the environmental record of the Pentagon and the armed services. Many point to the protection some large military bases and training ranges provide for wilderness areas and wildlife. With control over tens of millions of acres of land, bases indeed do in some cases (primarily in the contiguous United States) shield the nonhuman environment from the expansion of cities, suburbs, highways, and parking lots.[2]

Since the George H. W. Bush administration, the Pentagon has also made progress in "greening" itself at home and abroad to lessen the military's environmental footprint. In 1989, secretary of defense and future vice president Dick Cheney noted the poor environmental conditions on bases and initiated a "Defense and the Environment" initiative to make the Pentagon "the federal leader in agency environmental compliance and protection."[3] By 1995, the Pentagon reported reducing energy usage on bases by an average of 14 percent and fuel usage by 20 percent over levels a decade earlier. In 1998, the Environmental Protection Agency gave the Pentagon an award for reducing its pesticide use by 50 percent; two years later, it credited the military with "significant decreases" in greenhouse gas emissions. In 1999, the military reported reducing toxic chemical disposal by 77 percent in five years. During the George W. Bush administration, the Pentagon reported reducing hazardous waste disposal by 68 percent since 1992 and diverting 41 percent of its solid waste to recycling.[4]

While the downsizing of the military by almost one third during the 1990s contributed to these reductions,[5] the Pentagon has shown an unusually high level of environmental awareness compared to most of the U.S. government. Years ago, for example, long before many in the civilian world, the Pentagon identified global warming and climate change as

serious threats to national security. The military has made investments in solar power and other alternative energy sources for everything
from its bases to the Pentagon itself. According to the Army, the new U.S.
base in Vicenza, Italy, was the first base in the world to receive LEED
Green Building certification.[6] The armed services hold Earth Day events,
the Pentagon mentors other federal agencies in environmental management, and even Guantánamo Bay has three wind turbines to produce
clean energy.

Regardless of the progress the U.S. military has made in improving
its practices, there is no underestimating the profound environmental
damage caused by most military bases and the significant risks they pose
to humans and the rest of the natural environment. By definition, most
bases store large quantities of weapons, explosives, and other inherently
dangerous tools of war; nearly all of them contain toxic chemicals and
other hazardous waste. Pollution, contamination, and other forms of
environmental harm are found at nearly every base.[7] Any town, city, or
other large concentration of people causes some degree of environmental
harm, but bases magnify those effects, both inadvertently—through toxic
leaks, accidental ordnance detonation, and other dangerous accidents—
and through the intentional discharge of weapons and other environment damage caused during training. Bases storing nuclear weapons are
especially dangerous.

Even the greenest military installation has a carbon footprint vastly
disproportionate to the number of people living and working on base.
Bases are, after all, usually home to large concentrations of extraordinarily fuel-inefficient trucks, tanks, aircraft, and naval vessels. All of these
require massive supplies of fuel, oil, lubricants, and other petroleum products for frequent training and exercises, not to mention wartime activities. The military also uses huge amounts of energy to air-condition, heat,
and power its bases' tens of thousands of buildings and structures. The
military's thirst for petroleum is so great that on a worldwide basis,
the U.S. armed services consume more oil every day than the entire
country of Sweden.[8] This means that with the exception of a handful of
countries, the U.S. military probably produces more greenhouse gas
emissions and other forms of pollution than almost any other organization, corporation, or entity on earth.

WIDESPREAD DAMAGE

Before the introduction of national environmental legislation, the environmental damage caused by military bases was even worse than it is today. At home and abroad, bases regularly dumped toxic substances into rivers and streams, including asbestos, leaded paint, and other hazardous materials. Bases habitually oiled down dirt roads to contain dust.[9] Some dumped hazardous waste at sea, including materials associated with nuclear, biological, and chemical weapons. An Army spokesperson admitted that in waters off eleven states around the country, the Army "secretly dumped 64 million pounds of nerve and mustard gas agent in the sea, along with 400,000 chemical-filled bombs, landmines, and rockets, and more than 500 tons of radioactive waste either tossed overboard or packed into the holds of scuttled vessels."[10] By 2000, the military estimated that its bases in the United States alone contained 28,538 toxic waste sites, with nearly twenty-seven million acres of contaminated property. The estimated cleanup costs are nearly $50 billion.[11]

The military offered no count of toxic sites abroad, but there is little reason to believe its record there is any better. In fact, it's likely that the situation overseas is considerably worse. After all, as we have seen, in the minds of many military leaders, one of the advantages to having bases abroad is the freedom they offer—and part of that freedom is in not being constrained by environmental regulations. Some countries, such as Germany, have strict environmental protection laws and "status of forces" agreements requiring high levels of environmental compliance for U.S. bases. But in most other host nations, environmental protection in local laws and status of forces agreements is often weak or nonexistent. In many cases, the military does not have to meet standards that would be required under U.S. law.[12] (This is also sometimes true at domestic bases, as when courts have granted the Pentagon waivers from U.S. environmental laws.)

When environmental regulations do exist abroad, a host nation often has no mechanism for ensuring a base's compliance. Frequently, the military can return property to a host nation without cleaning up its environmental damage. For example, in Japan, which otherwise has strict environmental laws, the U.S. military has no obligation to remediate environmental damage on its bases, and some of the bases returned to Japan in recent years have featured widespread contamination.[13] Globally, the military has generally refused to clean up any environmental damage unless required to do so by a bilateral agreement.[14]

In Afghanistan and Iraq, bases have regularly used open-air burn pits despite the military's prohibiting their use outside emergencies. At Camp Leatherneck, one of the largest U.S. bases in Afghanistan, investigators found that solid waste was being burned in open-air pits despite the construction of four incinerators costing $11.5 million.[15] For years, military leaders denied any significant risk from the practice of burning waste in outdoor settings. A leaked 2011 Army memo, however, shows the Army warning that breathing air affected by the burning of waste could cause "long-term adverse health conditions" including "reduced lung function or exacerbated chronic bronchitis, chronic obstructive pulmonary disease (COPD), asthma, atherosclerosis, or other cardiopulmonary diseases." At Bagram Air Base in Afghanistan, a base hosting up to forty thousand troops and contractors, hundreds of thousands on and off the base may have been affected by open-air burn pits during the U.S.-led occupation.[16]

At training ranges, unexploded conventional bombs and shells can be a major problem. In places like Afghanistan, children living near ranges have been maimed and killed by unexploded munitions. If munitions cases crack open or degrade, they can also leak toxins into the soil and groundwater. One study suggests that there may be sixteen thousand U.S. military sites worldwide containing unexploded ordnance. The Pentagon has challenged this precise figure but acknowledged that it could cost $14 billion or even "several times that much" to deal with the problem.[17]

Leaks in storage tanks and pipelines are also a regular danger. At Diego Garcia, to mention just one example, four separate incidents between 1984 and 1998 spilled more than 1.3 million gallons of jet fuel, polluting soil and groundwater.[18] For perspective on just how bad such leaks can get, a jet fuel leak at Kirkland Air Force Base in Albuquerque, New Mexico, started around 1953 and was only discovered by the Air Force in 1999. The spill grew to an estimated twenty-four million gallons—more than twice the size of the eleven-million-gallon Exxon Valdez oil spill—and is currently threatening Albuquerque's water supply.[19]

Bases can also be dangerously loud. Air bases hosting jets and helicopters, and bases where training involves tanks and large artillery, are particularly prone to causing harmful noise pollution. From Ansbach, Germany, to Okinawa and other parts of Japan, noise has been the source of considerable friction with local communities. More than twenty-two thousand residents living around Okinawa's Kadena Air Force Base are now suing the Japanese government in the third citizens' suit seeking the reduction of aircraft noise.[20] Although some dismiss the effect of persistent exposure to helicopter or jet engine operations as "just noise," research shows that noise pollution can be a serious public health hazard, damaging both physical and psychological well-being. In Japan, for example, jet noise from U.S. bases has been linked to stress, low educational performance, and poor health outcomes for infants.

In many cases, bases have made efforts to limit noise and its impact on locals. At Ramstein Air Base, there is a permanent "Aircraft Noise Complaint Hot Line." A Noise Abatement Committee meets twice a year with base commanders. The German government has funded window replacements to better soundproof local homes, and the base generally limits its nighttime flying hours and low-altitude flights and avoids flying over villages. Still, complaints persist. As one local told me, "It goes without saying that an airport in operation per se emits a high noise level."

Even seemingly quotidian issues like ordinary trash disposal illustrate the damaging environmental effects of overseas military bases. The problem is simple: U.S. bases abroad produce lots and lots of garbage. Local civilians also produce garbage, of course. But whereas the average Okinawan, for instance, produces 590 pounds of trash per year, the average GI in Okinawa produces some 1,500 pounds annually—almost three times as much. At Camp Leatherneck in Afghanistan, the average marine produces eight pounds of trash a day, adding up to 2,290 pounds a year.[21] And this is actually a low number for troops at war. Across war zones, U.S. troops average nine to twelve pounds of waste per day.[22]

DUMPING GROUNDS

Unless you personally live near a base that poses a health risk or is known to have caused serious environmental damage, understanding the experience of others in this position can sometimes be challenging. In my case, though, I can simply walk out the door of my office at American University, in Washington, D.C. That's because my university and the surrounding Spring Valley neighborhood (where I happened to spend part of my childhood) are built atop the remnants of a World War I base that tested and produced chemical weapons.

In its heyday, the American University Experiment Station was the world's second-largest chemical weapons production facility. Some call it World War I's Manhattan Project. Almost two thousand chemists, engineers, and technicians tested hundreds of chemical substances there, including arsenic trichloride, ricin, and 498 variations of mustard gas.[23] The station created the war's deadliest chemical weapon—seven times deadlier than mustard gas. Its name was Lewisite, the "dew of death." A single drop could kill.[24] After the war's end, the then tiny American University gave the Army permission to bury large quantities of munitions, weapons material, and chemicals on its grounds in exchange for leaving some of the base infrastructure for university use.

Decades later, among the children growing up in tree-filled Spring Valley were siblings Nancy and Robert Dudley Jr. Nancy and Robert loved playing in their yard and the nearby woods. They ate almost year-round from their mother's garden, which was fed by a small creek running through their property.[25] But in 1993, local construction workers began stumbling upon buried munitions, some of which were armed and filled with chemicals. Six years later, after the Army Corps of Engineers declared a cleanup complete—and after Nancy and Robert had moved away from Spring Valley—the Army found a 75-millimeter bomb six inches beneath the surface of Nancy and Robert's former yard. The bomb contained mustard gas. Over time, the Army uncovered 680 more remains linked to chemical weapons where Nancy and Robert once lived, including live explosives and shells that had leaked mustard gas and arsenic. Some of the soil at their former home was literally smoking. The Army made similar discoveries at neighboring homes.[26]

Nancy and Robert remembered how, as children, they and their four siblings had serious skin problems. Robert's were so bad at times that he would lie awake scratching all night. "Sometimes I had to sleep with restraints on my arms," Robert recalled, "to keep me from tearing up my skin." They started to wonder if there might be a connection between the chemical munitions and the deaths of their parents. Their mother had died in 1984 of colon cancer. Two years later, their father, Robert, died of prostate cancer. Several of their neighbors had contracted cancer as well. Their uncle and aunt, who'd lived just a few houses away, also both died of cancer.[27]

"That's the earth where I grew up," said Nancy, "and I am wondering what may have been in the soil."

About one hundred yards from my office, the Army Corps has erected a containment tent where it is completely demolishing the house next to the Dudleys' and removing all the soil down to bedrock.[28] The Army hopes to find a major burial pit, a hole dubbed "Hades" in an old photograph of the base. Christine Dieterich lives across the street from the excavation. Like the Dudleys, she's worried. "How can they expect me to have peace of mind and have my children play in the front yard while they are digging for chemical-warfare agents 20 feet away?"

"I wake up at 3 a.m. in a cold sweat," Dieterich said. "It frightens the hell out of me. Nobody knows what's under the ground."[29]

Until the Army finds the hole called Hades, the most toxic burial pits found to date remain those at the Dudleys' old home. Today, it's the residence of the South Korean ambassador.

There's an irony to the fact that the remains of a U.S. Army base have contaminated the Korean ambassador's home. In South Korea itself, American bases have caused widespread harm because of chemical, fuel, and other toxic waste leaks, spills, and, in some cases, deliberate burial. At fourteen of the thirty-four bases the U.S. military recently agreed to return to South Korea, the levels of chemicals linked to cancer in humans exceeded South Korean standards.[30] According to the military's own reports, one base in South Korea has contaminated surrounding soil and groundwater as a result of the haphazard storage and disposal of pesticides, herbicides, solvents, battery acid, and petroleum products.[31]

In 2011, underground water at Camp Kim in Seoul had almost a thousand times the allowable level of petroleum hydrocarbon, which includes gasoline and other oil by-products.[32] What's more, three veterans say they followed orders in the late 1970s to bury hundreds of leaky barrels of

Agent Orange at the base.[33] Agent Orange is now known to contain a dioxin that is carcinogenic in humans. Scientists have linked the compound to diseases in troops and locals alike, including chronic lymphocytic leukemia, Hodgkin's and non-Hodgkin's lymphoma, multiple myeloma, prostate cancer, several respiratory cancers, and some soft tissue sarcomas. "It haunts me," one of the veterans, Steve House, says. "We basically buried our garbage in their back yard."[34]

The South Korean environmentalist Chung In-cheol commented, "If Agent Orange was dumped in 1978, the toxic substance could have contaminated the soil and underground water," as well as a water source for two major cities in the area. Cancer rates near the base have exceeded the national average by as much as 18.3 percent.[35]

In another case (dramatized in the 2006 film *The Host*), a soldier at an Army base in the middle of Seoul dumped twenty gallons of formaldehyde—a chemical that causes cancer in some animals and may cause cancer in humans—into the capital's Han River. After the incident sparked national outrage, the U.S. ambassador in Seoul took five months to express personal regret about the contamination. The Army announced it would spend $100 million to replace fuel tanks at bases throughout South Korea to avoid leaks and improve its environmental reputation.[36]

The trail of environmental damage is hardly confined to South Korea. When construction of the base on Diego Garcia started in 1971, Navy Seabees used bulldozers and chains to rip coconut trees from the ground. They blasted the island's reef with explosives to excavate thousands of tons of coral for building a runway. Diesel fuel sludge began fouling the water.[37] Billions of dollars in construction has followed, resulting in considerable environmental damage: additional large-scale blasting and deep dredging of eleven square miles of coral reef; clear-cutting of thousands of trees and other vegetation, including the habitat for threatened wildlife species; radioactive contamination due to leaks from nuclear-propelled ships and submarines; and the likely contamination of soil and groundwater following the widely reported use of Agent Orange to clear jungle foliage.[38]

Recently, British media revealed that U.S. naval vessels dumped waste and treated human sewage into Diego Garcia's protected coral lagoon for three decades. Nitrogen and phosphate levels are up to four times normal and may be damaging some of the world's most pristine coral.[39] Meanwhile, during the bombing of the Tora Bora cave complex in Afghanistan in late 2001, a B-1 bomber loaded with ordnance crashed after takeoff from Diego Garcia. The crew ejected, and the pilotless plane ended up at the bottom of the Indian Ocean along with its payload of bombs, which could total more than 85 hundred-pound munitions.[40]

In Okinawa, on land that was once part of Kadena Air Base, investigations in 2013 and 2014 uncovered more than eighty barrels containing dioxin and other contaminants. The barrels were buried under a soccer field adjacent to two schools. And just as in South Korea, over the decades Okinawa has apparently been polluted by Agent Orange: although the military denies the defoliant was ever present on the island, more than 250 veterans have testified since 2001 to having seen it sprayed, stored, and buried on Okinawa during the Vietnam War.[41]

When the Navy and Air Force left the Philippines in 1992, they left behind asbestos, unexploded ordnance, heavy metals, leaking fuel tanks, dangerous pesticides, and other hazardous materials.[42] The military has admitted to dumping untreated water and sewage at Subic Bay.[43] Similarly, when the military left Panama, it left an estimated hundred thousand pieces of unexploded ordnance in the Canal Zone despite being required to remove such ordnance under the Canal Treaty. On San José Island, Panamanians found mustard gas bombs.[44]

The Navy's use of Puerto Rico's islands of Vieques and Culebra as bombing and training ranges has also been an environmental disaster. On Vieques, the Navy dumped almost two million pounds of military waste in mangrove swamps and other sensitive wetland areas. Research has shown elevated levels of cadmium, lead and other heavy metals, mercury, nitrates, uranium, and other toxic chemicals in the food chain and locals' bodies as well as in the water and soil.[45] In 2005, the EPA included Vieques on its National Priorities List of the most hazardous contaminated sites requiring cleanup. The Navy's estimated total cleanup costs were just $30 million in 2004 but have climbed to around $350 million.[46]

COLONIAL CONTAMINATION

It is no coincidence that places under colonial or semicolonial rule, such as the Philippines, Panama, Okinawa, and Puerto Rico, have experienced some of the worst environmental damage from U.S. bases. The same disregard for the environment that the military has shown at bases abroad has also been the case on bases in U.S. territories lacking the full protections of the Constitution.

Many in the Northern Marianas and Guam view the environmental damage caused by military bases in recent decades as part of a long history of often unremediated damage dating to World War II. As with Guam, the battle to take Saipan from the Japanese military devastated the island.[47] In many cases, munitions, debris, and military equipment remained for years where they lay at the battle's end. Across Saipan, Tinian, and Guam, unexploded ordnance still lies buried under the soil or exposed to the elements. On the grounds of a recently proposed housing development on Saipan, for example, residents uncovered more than one thousand World War II–era bombs.[48] In other cases, the military disposed of hundreds of thousands of pounds of ordnance locally through detonation, burning, or dumping at sea.[49]

Since the war, the long-term presence of bases and troops has inflicted even broader damage. When the military began testing nuclear weapons in the Marshall Islands in 1946, it used Guam to clean naval vessels and other remnants of the tests. (Investigators have also discovered nuclear waste from similar post-test cleaning at the Hunters Point Naval Shipyard in San Francisco.) There's evidence that radioactive materials carried from the Marshalls in the air and rain after nuclear testing there may have directly affected people on Guam.[50]

On Saipan in the 1960s, U.S. troops dumped used radar equipment containing PCBs in the village of Tanapag. Never informed about the danger, local residents transformed radar parts into boundary markers, windbreaks, rooftop decorations, and even cemetery headstones. After finally telling the government of Saipan about the materials in 1988, the Pentagon had to ship away more than a million tons of contaminated soil for treatment on the mainland. Others have identified at least four dumping sites that still likely contain tons of military debris. Some believe the military stores Agent Orange on Saipan as well.[51]

On Guam, the military has long stored toxic materials including Agent Orange, mustard gas and other chemical weapons, cleaning fluids, insecticides, and pesticides found to be carcinogenic or otherwise harmful to humans. In 1988, a nuclear submarine discharged radioactive reactor water in the harbor at Naval Base Guam. Navy officials never informed locals, who learned of the accident only after it was reported in a San Diego newspaper.[52]

A dumpsite near Guam's Andersen Air Force Base has leached dangerous compounds including antimony, arsenic, barium, cadmium, lead, manganese, dioxin, and PCBs. Like Vieques, Andersen is on the EPA's National Priorities List identifying the worst cases of environmental contamination nationwide.[53] During my visit in 2012, workers clearing foliage from around the runway were surprised to stumble upon the buried wreckage of a B-52 bomber; the plane was likely pushed off the runway, hazardous materials and all, with other military debris during the war in Vietnam.

An environmental problem of a different kind is presented by brown tree snakes on Guam, which were accidentally introduced by military cargo flights in the 1950s. The snakes have no natural predators on the island, and they have devastated other animals, driving eight species of birds into extinction. They also cause electrical outages when they slither into power substations. The snakes grow to between three and six feet in length, and today there are an estimated two million of them on Guam. The military is now spending millions of dollars a year on eradication efforts; recently, it has been trying to kill them by airdropping thousands of dead neonatal mice implanted with acetaminophen tablets that are deadly to the snakes.[54]

In the Northern Marianas, meanwhile, the military recently announced new plans to create additional live-fire military ranges and training areas on the islands of Pagan and Tinian. Unlike Tinian, much of which was paved during World War II, Pagan is a gorgeous and pristine volcanic island with archaeological remains dating back two thousand years. It is home to numerous rare and endangered birds, snails, bats, lizards, crabs, and other species. Michael Hadfield, a biologist who headed a 2010 U.S. Fish and Wildlife Service survey of Pagan, has urged the military not to use the island for target practice as it has done on Farallon de Medinilla and other islands. "There is ample evidence," Hadfield says, "that when Marines take an island for live-fire training, they ultimately destroy it."[55]

As at so many base locations around the world, many on Guam and the Marianas fear that the military's pollution has affected human health. Research shows that as a group, Chamorros have "significantly higher" cancer rates than other ethnic groups. The incidence of mouth and pharynx, lung and bronchus, cervix, uterus, and liver cancers among Chamorros all exceed U.S. averages.[56] And while there has been no comprehensive study definitively establishing a link between illness and base pollution, there are some clear correlations. At Camp Lejeune in North Carolina, for instance, where leaks and chemical dumping left toxic materials in the ground and the local water system, a federal study of people who worked and lived on the base has revealed unusually high rates of cancer and birth defects.

Such statistics can only be considered suggestive; even under the most clear-cut and infamous circumstances, such as Love Canal or veterans' exposure to Agent Orange, it is extraordinarily difficult to conclusively connect the disease of any one individual to a specific chemical or contaminant.[57] Still, given how many Chamorros can reel off long lists of relatives afflicted by cancer, it is easy to understand why so many are concerned about environmental damage on tropical islands—especially since, with the exception of the military's presence, these islands have largely remained untouched by industrial pollution.

TIED TO THE LAND

The overrepresentation of U.S. bases in current and former colonies means that the environmental damage caused by bases tends not to be shared equally. Consistently, those most often harmed—such as the Chamorros in the Northern Marianas and Guam—are economically and politically disadvantaged or marginalized groups, indigenous peoples, the poor, and non-Western people of color.[58] Bases in Italy, Germany, Britain, and elsewhere in Europe have also caused environmental damage, of course, but the military is increasingly interested in moving some of its bases from western Europe to poorer countries in eastern Europe, Africa, and elsewhere. And part of that interest stems from those countries' limited environmental regulations.

At the Saipan public meeting I attended, a Chamorro couple, Miguel and Janice Mueller, told a military representative, the Air Force's Mark Petersen, that they were worried about the bombing of Farallon de Medinilla and the military's other impacts on the land, air, and water of the Marianas. Petersen tried to assure Miguel that the military would be looking at all the impacts of the training "in detail." But the answer didn't satisfy. "We're tied to the ocean and the land," Miguel told him. But you are connected "only by your job."

There will be "ample monitoring of water quality," Petersen said, cutting Miguel off and ending the conversation.

Later, I asked Miguel and Janice if they felt their concerns were heard at the meeting. "No," Janice replied. To her, it seemed the military was just trying to persuade people to go along with their plans. "I feel like they have an agenda. I honestly feel like they were trying to sell a product," she said. "It's a product I don't want to buy."

Offering a comparison to a different island in the United States, Janice asked how Manhattanites might feel about having live explosives tested so close to their home. "Maybe they can come back after twenty-five years, and how do they feel when there's some unexploded ordnance there?" she said. "Tell me. Tell me after twenty-five years and maybe we can sit down and maybe we can share the same lens.

"But at this point, they can't see what I'm seeing or even have an inch, an inkling of how it feels to live in this remote area, being a United States citizen and part of the American family, and you don't really matter," Janice said.

"I think that's wrong."

PART III

LABOR

A U.S. Army National Guard soldier says goodbye to his wife and child before deploying to Iraq, January 2008.

8

Everyone Serves

At many bases I visited, people often invoked Mayberry, the mythical small town in the *Andy Griffith Show*, to describe base life. Beyond the comfortable living arrangements and the numerous amenities, they meant the comparison to capture feelings of security, community, and connection on base. George Reeves, a civilian working at Naval Station Guantánamo Bay told me that living on base was like being in "any small town in America." "You know everyone or you know of those you don't know," he said.

George and his wife, Mary Reeves, who also worked on base, were living with their three teenaged children in a three-bedroom house with a large backyard in one of Gitmo's suburban-style housing developments. "It's like America. An American city," George explained. But it's "a city without crime. You don't worry about your kids," he said. "They can jump on the shuttle [which provides a free way to get around base], and you don't worry about them."

The schools on base are good, George told me, with small class sizes and teachers who really care about their students. For single parents, there's pretty cheap child care, with reduced rates for people at lower ranks. "You have a lot of support," George said, adding that people are always looking out for you. "It's like you have a family." As a blogger at MilitaryBases.com, one of many websites dedicated to base life, puts it, "There is a thread of oneness and camaraderie that connects everyone."[1]

People on base also tend to be extraordinarily polite: one quickly learns to always say "Thank you, sir" and "Thank you, ma'am." Income inequality is shockingly low for the United States: the highest-ranking general makes only around ten times the pay of the lowest-ranking private. (The average S&P 500 CEO, on the other hand, makes 354 times the average worker's salary.)[2] And unlike lily-white Mayberry and most of the United States, the bases are unusually diverse and ethnically integrated, in keeping with the overall diversity of the military.

On the other hand, some ethnic segregation endures: Euro-Americans are overrepresented among military officers, and a form of class segregation is strictly enforced in on-base housing. Rank and pay grade determine the size and quality of one's quarters, and officers are usually housed in different neighborhoods or residential complexes from the enlisted troops. Officers also often have their own clubs, dining halls, and even gym changing rooms.[3]

On many bases, an even lower class of segregated housing exists for people termed "third country nationals." These are the citizens of countries other than United States and the host nation of the base, who frequently cook, clean, and keep the physical infrastructure of bases running every day. Most often, they are Filipinos. At Gitmo, the Filipinos live in dormitories that usually have four bunk beds to a room; Jamaicans have slightly better housing, formerly occupied by U.S. troops. At bases in Afghanistan and Iraq, many of the contractors have been from Nepal, Bangladesh, and as far away as Fiji. The journalist Sarah Stillman described them as "the Pentagon's invisible army: more than seventy thousand cooks, cleaners, construction workers, fast-food clerks, electricians, and beauticians from the world's poorest countries who service U.S. military logistics . . . Filipinos launder soldiers' uniforms, Kenyans truck frozen steaks and inflatable tents, Bosnians repair electrical grids, and Indians provide iced mocha lattes."[4]

While the nationalities of the people who make up this invisible army tend to change from country to country (aside from the widespread presence of Filipinos), the amenities and services they provide and the facilities they maintain are remarkably similar at most bases. The comforts provided for the benefit of families help ensure that bases look and function like small American towns, making the adjustment to life overseas and from base to base as easy as possible.

Despite the benefits, however, family members make significant sacrifices to their lives when a spouse or parent is posted abroad. Even in an era when women join the military in large numbers—they account for about 15 percent of the force—most of these sacrifices are borne by women: around 95 percent of military spouses are female.[5] Even though war can feel surprisingly distant on U.S. bases, amid the yoga classes and intramural basketball games, these women can usually attest more than anyone else how the proximity of death hangs over base life.

"A REALLY FAIR SYSTEM"

Today there are around 233,000 spouses, children, and adult family members of military personnel living on and around bases and other facilities outside the United States. Family members, in fact, outnumber the total number of troops overseas by more than 55,000.[6] When the first wives arrived on bases abroad in the late 1940s, their living conditions were nothing like today's. Women had to make do with surplus food and makeshift commissaries. Many military men were hardly enthusiastic about their presence. An Army report from 1946 sarcastically contrasted the days of wartime combat with the postwar period: "Then the emphasis was placed on ammunition, clothing and food for fighting men, while today such interesting items as cleaning materials for household use, clothing and feeding of our civilian employees who are natives of the occupied countries and the problem of fresh milk for dependents' children occupy our attention."[7]

Soon, many of those same military men began realizing the importance of caring for the growing population of family members as part of building Little Americas around the globe. Thus began the construction of family housing, schools, hospitals, commissaries and shopping centers, recreational facilities, and much more support infrastructure. After the Vietnam War, during which conditions and morale deteriorated across the military, leaders placed renewed emphasis on improving the lives of families. In an era without conscription, troops were, on average, older and more likely to have a wife and children. The Pentagon realized that a major reason personnel were leaving the military before retirement was the poor quality of life for families. Unhappy families mean unhappy troops, and unhappy troops mean not enough troops to fight.[8] Family support thus became a significant labor issue for the military.

Life overseas had, for example, long been boring for women. One medical officer in the 1950s reported getting a large number of "neurotic complaints from women who had nothing to do all day but visit the clubs." Women in Okinawa often spent much of their days drinking and losing money in the slot machines that were ubiquitous in clubs on overseas bases.[9] Reacting to the rise of the feminist movement of the 1970s, the Pentagon created programs to address domestic violence, to allow women to collect child support and alimony, and to provide on-base child care. A 1985 hiring preference law giving spouses preferential access to on-base jobs helped address the problem of wives having to give up jobs and careers to follow their husbands overseas. (Many women married to military personnel teach in the Pentagon's overseas school system, and since there are schools at most large bases worldwide, this makes following a partner's military transfers somewhat easier.) By 1988, the military was investing $8 billion a year in family programs around the globe.[10]

As a result, base life is now generally very good for families, particularly on bases abroad. Most domestic bases tend to be comfortable, too, but because of the challenges that overseas postings create for families, bases abroad usually offer even greater comforts and family supports. Children usually have an extensive array of extracurricular opportunities, including competitive sports, music and dance, clubs, and spelling bees that often offer opportunities for additional travel. Football teams in Okinawa, for example, fly to play against teams at bases in South Korea, Guam, and on Japan's other islands. Tennis and soccer teams in Italy cross the Alps to play teams at bases in Germany. Research shows that on the whole, children appear to benefit, rather than suffer, from their nomadic lifestyle and separations from one or more of their parents.[11]

For families as a whole, living overseas is also financially advantageous. In addition to the regular salary earned by a member of the military, personnel generally receive an overseas cost-of-living adjustment. (The adjustment is also given in Hawaii and Alaska.) The average adjustment is about $300 per month; worldwide, the adjustments total around $2 billion annually.[12] The military also pays for troops' housing. Some live on base, but in most countries, the majority of troops and their families live off base. Overseas housing allowances are usually generous, so families often live in homes far larger than they could afford in the United States. Because military personnel lose any money from their housing allowances that they don't use, most rent the largest and most expensive home their allowance will buy. (The generosity of the Pentagon's rental payments tends to drive up area rents, to the frustration of many local renters, if not the owners. In places like Guam, nineteen- and twenty-year-olds will sometimes pool their money to live in luxurious beachside homes that are out of reach for most locals.)

On top of it all, there's the military's single-payer health care system, providing universal coverage to families. There are extensive education opportunities, both online and off. There's the adventure of living overseas, complete with opportunities for tourism, cross-cultural interaction, language learning, and vacations at military resorts. For "military children," as the Pentagon calls them, there are generally high-quality, well-funded Pentagon-run public schools. Depending on how one calculates expenses, annual per-pupil spending is almost twice the national public school average of $12,608 and may be more than $20,000 higher.[13] And that's just the start of the inventory of amenities and benefits.

"It's the purest application of socialism there is," Wesley Clark, the retired four-star general, has said with a sense of irony. "It's a really fair system, and a lot of thought has been put into it, and people respond to it really well."[14]

SACRIFICE

During my first visit to Gitmo, there was a telling moment during the playing of morning reveille. As the tinny recording sounded over loudspeakers around the base, the wife of a sailor wondered aloud if she had to stop and salute the flag like her husband.

Technically, the answer to her question is no. But the fact that the question occurred to her at all highlights the ambiguous role that spouses and other family members have on base. Although they are not formally part of the military, living on base still shapes their time, their behavior, even their thoughts and feelings. And the unacknowledged costs can be remarkably high.

In one of my classes, a self-identified "Army brat" (a term most embrace) described how, despite the advantages of the globe-trotting lifestyle, the life can be a "very insular" one. Until recently, for instance, she didn't know what a grocery store was, having always gone to the commissary. "Military children are impacted by the constant change of schools," she wrote. "It is hard to constantly be the new kid, to constantly be catching up, to constantly just be different." During a class presentation, she admitted that the feeling of being different, of being a constant outsider had persisted into her college years. "Sometimes, I have days when I go into my dorm room and cry."

For spouses, too, frequent moves from base to base tend to interrupt their lives. Living in foreign countries where spouses typically can't work in the local economy, many struggle to maintain careers outside the home despite spousal hiring preferences that help some. In 2012, the unemployment rate for spouses of active duty troops was 25 percent. When they do find work, military spouses tend to earn around 60 percent less than peers married to civilians.[15]

As for childrearing and housekeeping, the twenty-four-hour-a-day nature of military life likewise places heavy burdens on spouses—who are, again, 95 percent women. While military spouses usually have excellent access to around-the-clock child care compared to most parents in the United States, they also must be ready to assume 100 percent of the parenting and other household duties with next to no notice if their partner is deployed.

During deployments to war zones, and temporary or long-term postings to locations where families can't join military personnel (such as Honduras, Qatar, and Thailand), spouses become single parents in most ways. Like civilian families facing separation, these periods can harm spouses, children, and service members alike, as well as entire family dynamics. That military personnel have demanding jobs typically involving a greater chance of death than most careers only adds to the impact of separations.

Dr. Suzanne Rogers, an Army child psychologist (who asked me to use a pseudonym), has witnessed the problems that children of soldiers face during deployments and other separations. Being aware of these challenges, she was surprised when her children had many of the same problems during their father's deployment to Iraq. "They were still more stressed out than I'd imagined and about as much as what I was seeing in my office," she told me during a posting in Ansbach, Germany. "I train people to help their kids through this! But still, using all the tools, you can't make it not impact them."

Even technologies like Skype and email that ease some of the challenges of separation can also backfire, Rogers found. "If you have an awful lot of Skyping, seeing Daddy over the television screen—and yet [a child says], 'I can't have him.' 'He's not tucking me in.' 'I can't put my arms around him.' 'You're not watching my baseball game.' That can really piss a kid off."

"You take the father away," Rogers said, "it's gonna have an impact."

Whether or not a service member is deployed, spouses bear much of the psychological and social burden of having a partner in an unusually stressful and all-consuming career. As the base expert Catherine Lutz explains, spouses, like the troops themselves, "are effectively on call to the military."[16]

Military spouses are also on call to perform significant work outside the home. Mayberry-like feelings of community on bases don't magically appear from nowhere. They develop in no small part because of the work spouses do to build community, especially at overseas locations. While there are no formal requirements for spouses to participate in base activities or directly support a service member's job, subtle pressures suggest that not participating might affect their partner's performance reviews.

In years past, the wives of high-ranking officers created "wives' clubs" with a hierarchy paralleling their husbands' ranks. The woman married to the highest-ranking officer was considered the "mother" to the women "under her," just as her husband exercised patriarchal authority over his uniformed subordinates. The other officers' wives, in turn, were unofficially expected to mentor the wives of lower-ranked personnel, creating an entire support network for families.[17] Today, each of the armed services maintains official support organizations for units and connected family members. In the Army, family members are automatically enrolled in Family Readiness Groups that rely heavily on the volunteer labor of spouses to organize support activities and communication networks for families. Like wives' clubs of old, each group's leader is often the spouse of a unit's highest ranking officer.

Other family support roles are now filled by paid "Morale, Welfare, and Readiness" staff, as well as psychologists and other civilian employees dedicated to supporting troops and families. But the wives of officers still face expectations to lead and mentor the families of lower-ranking officers and enlisted personnel. "To decline these responsibilities, many wives worry, might harm a husband's career," writes the historian and former military family member Anni Baker.[18] Retired Army colonel Douglas Macgregor explains, "There's the expectation that the commanding officer—whether he's a captain, colonel or general—that his wife will set an example by doing things consistent with her husband's responsibilities . . . Wives are under enormous pressure."[19] The wives of enlistees frequently face similar pressures to participate in base life and support other families in ways ranging from emergency child care to offering comfort and help during deployments and in the wake of a service member's death.

TOTAL INSTITUTIONS

In part, the pressures spouses face stem from the fact that the military is what sociologists refer to as a "total institution." Total institutions—like the military, boarding schools, prisons, and asylums—have power over virtually every part of a person's life. They usually have the power to keep an individual under nearly constant surveillance. They have control over an individual's body. They have the ability to compel a person to follow orders (and in the military, these orders could result in death).[20] The U.S. military's power as a total institution has been so far-reaching that soldiers once had to ask permission to marry. Even recently, some have felt compelled to ask permission to get pregnant.[21]

Until 2011, the military also exercised broad control over its members' sex lives and sexuality, by prohibiting same-sex intercourse and identification as anything other than heterosexual. At some bases, MPs would cruise by the parking lots of gay bars to record the license plates of service members.[22] Of course, plenty of service members did maintain surreptitious same-sex relationships, and sometimes they weren't even all that surreptitious. The power of any total institution is not limitless. Still, the psychological, social, and other effects of forcing people to stay in the closet should not be underestimated.

Bases are the physical manifestation of the military as a total institution (as are naval vessels). After all, while bases are designed to keep enemies out, like prisons and asylums they can also control their inhabitants by keeping them in. Commanders always have the power to make a base literally like a prison by ordering subordinates to stay inside or by simply locking the gates.

What this means for spouses and other family members is that they, too, are subject to much of the military's power as a total institution. Though they are not in the military themselves, the military has the power to shape significant parts of their lives, especially if they live on base. The military shapes the food family members eat, the clothes they wear, the purchases they make, the education they receive, the ideas they're exposed to, and the media they consume (from Fox News often playing on TVs around base to everyone from Rush Limbaugh to National Public Radio on the American Forces Network Radio). And on bases overseas, where family members are separated from their homes, communities, and larger social networks and living in societies where they often don't speak the local language, the military's power over them is particularly pronounced.

Just as troops are under near constant surveillance, so, too, spouses and other family members are subject to high levels of daily observation. Little on base is private, and not everything off base is, either. "On or off base, there is great pressure to conform to common standards of behavior, from home decorating styles to dress to recreational activities," says Baker, who experienced these pressures as a family member overseas. "When a family problem arises, it is more than likely that those in the chain of command will get to know" about it.[23] Commanding officers have long called "unruly spouses" into their offices[24] or told GIs to "control" their wives. In recent years the orders have become subtler and less explicit, but they have not gone away.[25]

A KNOCK AT THE DOOR

During Dr. Matt Rogers's fifteen-month deployment to Iraq, one of his duties was to identify troops in body bags and officially declare them deceased. Back at his base in Ansbach, Germany, he has been part of several death notification teams responsible for informing spouses of the death of a deployed service member. He and others describe it as one of the most difficult things they have to do. Usually, Rogers (also a pseudonym) told me, the spouse breaks down completely, and the highest-ranking officer can't make it through the prescribed lines: "The Secretary of the Army has asked me to express his deep regret that . . ."

Throughout my visits to various bases, I repeatedly had to remind myself about the role they play in waging war—such is the distance one can feel from conflict in these manicured Little Americas, with all their comforts and conveniences. And while military personnel and their families surely have a harder time forgetting the connection between bases and bloodshed, many of them mention a similar distance. At Gitmo, people describe forgetting about the prison on the other side of the base, let alone the wars raging thousands of miles away. Even within war zones, military personnel testify that Internet access, Skype, and other amenities make it possible to forget you're in the middle of a war. They make it possible to regard the "bloody snarl of combat," as the former Army public affairs officer and novelist David Abrams put it, as if "through a telescope . . . at a safe, sanitized distance."[26]

But the truth is inescapable. Usually, Rogers told me, the notification team pulls up to a family's home in a dark SUV. They try to be inconspicuous, but the sight of a notification team turns heads in every direction on base. There are pretty much just two occasions when a soldier wears a "Class A" dress uniform: having official photographs taken and participating in a death notification team. So when a spouse or another family member sees a group of soldiers in Class A's approaching, on base or off, it can mean only one thing.

Generally, wives already know that someone is going to get a visit. After a death, there's a three-day blackout on Internet and phone contact with the unit that has lost a member. When that happens, everyone knows someone has died. The only question left is, "Which family is going to get the knock on the door?"[27] Which leaves the wives at the windows of their homes, waiting. Until they know *who*, it's as if time stops on base.

In the Army, Rogers explained, there are usually at least three people on a death notification team. Each must be an officer or a high-ranking enlisted soldier. A casualty notification officer delivers the news to a spouse, a parent, or other next of kin. A military chaplain is there to offer spiritual support. A casualty assistance officer will inform kin about Army benefits, assist with paperwork, and offer a phone with unlimited calling to the United States to help make necessary arrangements.

Rogers said the team usually also alerts a close friend, to have someone on hand immediately to provide support for the spouse. So far, he told me, he's only had to notify women, and he's glad. People say that after getting the news, widows will hurt themselves, while widowers will hurt others.

Rogers told me that he and other doctors are included in notification teams both because of their stature as officers and because they can prescribe medications. Sleep aids and antidepressants can be helpful if a woman can't sleep or can't function, especially when children are involved, he said. There's been some talk on post about the doctors over-medicating wives, he added, but it's no good having a mother unable to care for her kids.

After the notification team has visited the family, the affected unit will send out a "red line message" to families on base and off. The brief official script, listing the name of the deceased and the date of death, will make its way around the unit with the help of a phone tree that's usually run by soldiers' wives.

When they get the red line message, spouses likely feel a brief sensation of relief, because they know the officers in the Class A's didn't knock at their door. And then they feel the pain of knowing that another family has had that dark SUV pull up in front of their home. Putting aside their feelings as best they can, spouses usually spring into action, organizing memorial services on base, offering support for the families, bringing them food, sitting with them, listening to their grief. Some units have freezers prestocked with food, ready for the next family.

But until they get that message, until they know it's someone else, spouses wait, looking out their windows, wondering if it's their door the team in the Class A's will be knocking on this time.

Soldiers walk past Filipina women known as "juicy girls" outside Camp Casey, South Korea.

9

Sex for Sale

Women's labor, though often unacknowledged and overlooked, has long been essential to the workings of the U.S. military, as with most militaries across time and place. This has been true with women who wash the laundry, cook the food, and nurse injured soldiers back to health. This has been true with soldiers' wives, who are expected to perform an outsized share of the childrearing and to create feelings of community on military bases.[1] And it has also been true with sex. Throughout history, women's sex work has been used to help make male troops happy—or at least happy enough to keep working for the military.

Commercial sex zones have developed around U.S. bases worldwide. Many look much the same, filled with liquor stores, fast-food outlets, tattoo parlors, bars and clubs, and prostitution in one form or another. The evidence is just outside the gates in places such as Baumholder and Kaiserslautern in Germany, and Kadena and Kin Town on Okinawa. Even during the U.S. wars in Afghanistan and Iraq, there have been multiple reports of brothels and sex trafficking involving U.S. troops and contractors.[2]

Domestic bases like Fort Bragg, North Carolina, have also given rise to red-light districts nearby. But the problems associated with the sex trade are particularly pronounced overseas—especially in South Korea, where "camptowns" that surround U.S. bases have become deeply entrenched in the country's economy, politics, and culture. Dating to the 1945 U.S. occupation of Korea, when GIs casually bought sex with as little as a cigarette, they are at the center of an exploitative and profoundly disturbing sex industry.

"STIGMATIZED TWILIGHT ZONES"

As World War II came to a close, U.S. military leaders in Korea, just like their counterparts in Germany, worried about the interactions between American troops and local women. "Americans act as though Koreans were a conquered nation rather than a liberated people," wrote the office of the commanding general. The policy became "hands off Korean women"—but this did not include women in brothels, dance halls, and working the streets.[3] Instead, with venereal disease and other communicable infections widespread, the U.S. military government created a VD Control Section that instituted regular inspections and treatment for "entertaining girls." This category included licensed prostitutes, dancers, "bar girls," and waitresses. Between May 1947 and July 1948, medical personnel examined almost fifteen thousand women.[4]

Most troublingly, U.S. military authorities occupying Korea after the war took over some of the "comfort stations" that had been central to the Japanese war machine since the nineteenth century. During its conquest of territory across East Asia, the Japanese military forced hundreds of thousands of women from Korea, China, Okinawa and rural Japan, and other parts of Asia into sexual slavery, providing soldiers with "royal gifts" from the emperor. With the assistance of Korean officials, U.S. authorities continued the system absent formal slavery, but under conditions of exceedingly limited choice for the women involved.[5]

The arrangements were further formalized after the 1950 outbreak of the Korean War. "The municipal authorities have already issued the approval for establishing UN comfort stations in return for the Allied Forces' toil," wrote the *Pusan Daily*. "In a few days, five stations will be set up in the downtown areas of new and old Masan. The authorities are asking citizens to give much cooperation in coming days."[6]

After the signing of the 1953 Korea-U.S. Mutual Defense Treaty (still the legal foundation for U.S. troops' access to U.S. and Korean bases), camptowns boomed. In the 1950s alone, eighteen new camptowns were created. As the political scientist and camptown expert Katherine Moon explains, they were "virtually colonized space where Korean sovereignty was suspended and replaced by the U.S. military authorities." The livelihoods of Koreans in the camptowns were almost completely dependent on GIs' buying power, and sex work was a core part of the camptown economy. The camptowns became "deeply stigmatized twilight zones" known for sex, crime, and violence. By 1958, there were an estimated three hundred thousand sex workers in a country whose entire population was just 22 million. More than half worked in camptowns.[7] In the middle of downtown Seoul, where the Army occupied the 640-acre Yongsan Garrison originally built by Japanese colonizers, the Itaewon neighborhood filled with bars and brothels. GIs named it "Hooker Hill."[8]

"Cohabitating marriage," resembling European-style colonial concubinage, also became popular. "Many men have their steadies," commented one military chaplain. "Some of them *own* their girls, complete with hooch [small house] and furniture. Before leaving Korea, they sell the package to a man who is just coming in."[9]

After a military junta seized power in South Korea in a 1961 coup, Korean officials created legally recognized "special districts" for businesses catering to U.S. troops and off-limits to Koreans. American military police could arrest sex workers without health inspection cards, and U.S. doctors treated women with sexually transmitted diseases at detention centers given names such as "the monkey house." In 1965, 85 percent of GIs surveyed reported having "been with" or "been out with" a prostitute.[10]

Camptowns and prostitution thus became critical parts of a South Korean economy struggling to emerge from the devastation of war. Government documents show male officials strategizing to encourage GIs to spend their money on women in Korea rather than Japan during leave time. Officials offered classes in basic English and etiquette to encourage women to sell themselves more effectively and earn more money. "They urged us to sell as much as possible to the G.I.'s, praising us as 'dollar-earning patriots,'" recounts former sex worker Ae-ran Kim. "Our government was one big pimp for the U.S. military."[11]

There was indeed considerable competition for GI dollars in Okinawa, South Vietnam, Thailand, and the Philippines. In Okinawa, prostitution was legal through the end of the U.S. occupation in 1972. Within three months of the start of the Korean War, Okinawan authorities created the Yaejima Approved Prostitution Zone, and by 1969, 7,400 women—about 2 percent of all Okinawan females between ten and sixty years old—were involved in prostitution around the bases.[12] Meanwhile, the U.S. war in Vietnam helped transform Thailand's Pattaya Beach into one of the world's largest red-light districts. It was a favored spot for R&R, or, as some called it, I&I—intoxication and intercourse. When the military withdrew from South Vietnam, it left behind an estimated seven hundred thousand sex workers.[13]

"Prostitution was obviously a racket," a U.S. official at the embassy in Seoul told me, describing the time when he'd been stationed in Korea in the early 1980s. "It kind of had a dirty feel to it." And "even the married guys" were taking part. (Unlike in Japan, Germany, Italy, and many other base locations, 90 percent of troops on tours of duty in Korea have, until recently, been unaccompanied by families because the Korean War has technically never ended.)[14] "It was kind of a bonding thing to go out and bar hop. You'd go from bar to bar to bar."

"The women were readily available," the official told me. And they wouldn't ask you to buy them a drink—they asked you to take them home. "There was kind of a joke" where guys "would take out a $20 bill and lick it and stick it to their forehead." They said that's all it took to get a girl.

Today, many of the women who once worked in the system still live in the camptowns, so strong is the stigma attached to them. One of the sex workers, who would identify herself to a reporter only as "Jeon," moved to a camptown in 1956 as an eighteen-year-old war orphan. Within a few years she became pregnant, but she gave up her son for adoption in the United States, where she hoped he would have a better life. In 2008, now a U.S. soldier, he returned to find her. Jeon was surviving on public assistance and selling things from the trash. She refused his help and said he should forget about her. "I failed as a mother," Jeon says. "I have no right to depend on him now."[15]

"Women like me were the biggest sacrifice for my country's alliance with the Americans," she says. "Looking back, I think my body was not mine, but the government's and the U.S. military's."[16]

"JUICY GIRLS"

Since the mid-1990s, the dramatic growth in the South Korean economy has largely allowed Korean women to escape the exploitative conditions of the camptown bars and clubs. In their place, Filipinas and, to a lesser extent, women from Russia and former Soviet republics have generally replaced Korean women as the primary camptown sex workers. The South Korean government's creation of the E-6 "entertainer" visa has allowed Korean "promoters" to import Filipinas and other women on a legal basis. The E-6 visa is the only Korean visa for which an HIV test is mandatory; venereal disease tests are required every three months.[17] Over 90 percent of women with the visas are estimated to work in the sex industry.[18]

The promoters who recruit women often promise to find them work as singers or dancers—applicants must submit videos demonstrating singing ability. The agents then bring the women into South Korea, charging them a fee that the women must pay off by working in camptowns and other bars and clubs.[19]

The women sign a contract in their home country specifying an employer and a salary, but they often end up in different clubs and working for a lower salary than promised. The promoters and owners often charge hidden fees or deduct money from the women's salaries, keeping them in perpetual debt. Often the housing and food promised in contracts is little more than a decrepit shared room above the bar and ramen noodles. In some clubs, owners force women to perform sex work in "VIP rooms" or other locations. In other clubs, indebtedness and psychological coercion force the women into sex. Speaking little Korean, the women have little recourse. Promoters and bar owners often hold the women's passports. Leaving their place of employment would subject them to immediate arrest, fines, imprisonment, or deportation by the South Korean state and potentially violent retribution from those to whom they are indebted.[20]

In 2002, a Cleveland television station exposed how military police officers were protecting the bars and the GIs in them, and interacting with women they knew had been trafficked and sold at auction.[21] "You know something is wrong when the girls are asking you to buy them bread,"

one soldier said. "They can't leave the clubs. They barely feed them."
Another commented, "There are only Americans in these clubs. If they're
bringing these women over here to work for us, they should get paid a
fair wage. They should have the right to a day off."[22] (Most of the women
get one day off a month.) In a 2002 report, the State Department confirmed that South Korea was a destination for trafficked women.[23] And
in 2007, three researchers concluded that U.S. bases in South Korea have
become "a hub for the transnational trafficking of women from the Asia
Pacific and Eurasia to South Korea and the United States."[24]

In the wake of these revelations, there has been growing public
criticism of prostitution around U.S. bases in South Korea. Feminists,
religious groups, and congressmembers demanded change. The South
Korean government began a crackdown, and the Pentagon quickly
announced a "zero tolerance" policy for trafficking.[25] In 2004, the South
Korean government outlawed prostitution, and the following year President George W. Bush signed an executive order making prostitution illegal under the Uniform Code of Military Justice. The military began
more strictly monitoring bars and clubs in the camptowns and placing
those believed to be involved in trafficking on "off-limits" lists for military personnel.

At least one vet told me, though, that lists like these give troops at bases
ideas about where *to* go rather than where *not* to go. And instead of shutting down prostitution, bars and clubs have simply responded with new
tactics to vaguely disguise the nature of their business. At so-called juicy
bars, for instance, men buy small glasses of supposedly alcoholic juice
for scantily clad "juicy girls," most of whom have been trafficked from the
Philippines or the former Soviet Union. The rules differ slightly from bar
to bar, but basically, if a man buys enough juice, he can arrange to take a
woman out. There's no explicit exchange of money for sex at the bar, but
once the two are off the premises, a deal is done.

The subterfuge is fairly superficial. After the military's *Stars and Stripes*
newspaper published another exposé, a soldier who blogs about the
military in Korea wrote, "Here is some shocking news for everyone, the
Stars & Stripes has investigated and confirmed that (gasp!) juicy bars
are fronts for prostitution!"[26]

Just outside Camp Stanley and the Uijeongbu camptown, a former *mamasan*, Mrs. Kim, told me how the new system works. If you're a man, "you've got to buy her a drinky," she said. They cost $20 to $40 each, or even $100 at some clubs. "One drinky, twenty minutes," she continued. The *mamasan* will tell you to buy more when your time's up.

If the man buys enough, Kim said—usually at least $150 in juicys— he can ask, "Tomorrow can I take you lunchy?" He also pays the *mamasan* a "bar fine" to let the woman miss the next day of work, offsetting what she would make selling juicys. Sometimes, a man will pay a bar fine to leave immediately—often for a hotel. In either case, the man and the woman usually negotiate a separate price for sex.

"Officially they do not say 'prostitution'" when they go to lunch, Kim said. "Where they go, no one knows. It's her choice." Maybe the next day they go to buy clothes or shoes. "Later what they do, nobody knows."

"She has a choice if she goes to lunch?" I asked.

"It's her choice," replied Mrs. Kim. But if she says no, the man "is crying," and "he doesn't come to [the] club . . . They don't come no more." "*Shit!*" exclaimed Mrs. Kim, imitating the men.

I imagined how an owner might say "Shit!" too, after losing a customer—and the pressure that that might place on a woman's choice, on top of the financial pressure to pay off debts.

Youngnim Yu, the director of Durebang, or "My Sister's Place," a South Korean organization that has assisted women in the sex industry since 1986, joined our conversation. While the rules differ at every bar, she explained, a woman usually has to bring in a minimum of around $200 a night. If she doesn't make the minimum, the owner charges her a "bar fine" as well. She has to go with a man to make up the difference.

Once a month, the promoter who imported the women comes for their salaries. The bar owner pays him a percentage of drink sales, and the promoter usually takes at least half. He tells the government that he pays the women South Korea's minimum monthly wage, about $900. Typically, the women actually make around $300 to $500 a month.

"THEY ARE SCARED"

Around noon on a scorching hot day in July, I was on the streets of the camptown in Songtan, outside the gates of Osan Air Base. Songtan is one of as many as 180 camptowns in South Korea today. Within four hundred yards of Osan's main gate, there are some ninety-two bars—about one every twenty-six feet. In a 2007 count, there were twenty-one hotels in the area with rooms by the hour.[27]

I was in Songtan to accompany two women from Youngnim Yu's organization Durebang, whom I will call Valeria and So-hee. They were there to reach out to sex workers in this "special tourist district" and offer the organization's support.

Special tourist districts are technically off-limits to Koreans not working in them, so most of the people on the streets were from Osan. With the bars and clubs still quiet at midday, we saw airmen and -women out walking in their uniforms and a few casually dressed families with strollers. Some men in civilian clothes walked alongside young Filipinas toward fast-food outlets and other restaurants. A few men walked hand in hand with Korean women.

Every few minutes, we came across a Filipina woman. Some were with children. When we did, Valeria and So-hee offered them a Durebang business card written in Tagalog, some toiletries, and a "korea" shirt donated by supporters. On Songtan's main pedestrian walkway, we stopped to talk with other outreach workers near Club Join Us, advertising "Filipino Food / Filipina Women." A couple of young Filipinas walked by, saying they were in a rush. Two more walked hurriedly from a Western Union bearing a sign proclaiming cheaper to send to the philippines! in Tagalog.

I asked Valeria what the women discuss with her. They complain of not receiving salaries, she said. Some talk about being hurt by owners or customers. Some want to get out but don't know how. Most have gone deep into debt to get a visa to go to Korea, and most are supporting children and other family members back home. "They cling to the clubs," she said. The clubs provide apartments, usually on the premises of the bar. Most owners allow the women to leave for just two hours a day. Otherwise, she said, "someone is always watching."

Most of the women don't know Korean, and they're illegal if they leave the bar, Valeria said. Durebang can provide some legal assistance and, in some cases, financial help. "We cannot do anything" about their visa status, said Youngnim, who had joined our group. So if they leave a club, she said, they're likely to be deported or put in an immigration jail.

"There are some nasty clubs where women are locked in, but mostly women don't leave because they are scared," Veronica, a twenty-four-year-old Russian, told one reporter. A club owner in Songtan agreed, saying, "Some of the women are locked up. If a fire breaks out, they can't escape. But the main method of coercing them is psychological. They know no one. They have no money. The only way they can get money is by prostituting themselves."[28] Reydelus Conferido, the labor attaché at the Philippine embassy, says he tries to explain to people, "If you take somebody far from home, under certain conditions, you can get them to do whatever you want . . . . It could happen to anybody."[29]

Youngnim explained that the women often "try to get out of the clubs" by finding a GI. It's a hard life with a different client every day. So they go and live with GI boyfriends. But "practically 90 percent of the women are abandoned," she said. Many get pregnant and have babies. Some get married, and then the soldier disappears without a word when his tour is done in South Korea, leaving the woman in financial and legal trouble. Having left their clubs, many women are suddenly without a sponsor required to live in Korea. Sometimes they are stuck in legal limbo without an official divorce, and some can't claim child support.[30] In other cases, Youngnim said, the men get the women to sign documents they don't understand, and these turn out to be divorce papers that leave them with nothing.

Since the 1970s, GIs have also been involved in sham marriages used to bring Korean women to the United States to perform sex work in Korean massage parlors. Korean divorcées from legitimate marriages have also been vulnerable to recruitment into massage parlors. In fact, researchers and law enforcement officers suggest that most Korean women working in U.S. massage parlors were once married to GIs.[31]

Later in the evening, after I left the Durebang outreach workers, I met a woman who said she was from Okinawa. With her flowing all-white clothes, very pale skin, and long black hair, she looked like a ghost. She said she was "a bum," pointing to a large duffel bag and several stuffed plastic bags laid out on the sidewalk. She said she needed help. She had been married to a sailor, but now she couldn't get her money out of the Navy's bank. They wouldn't let her on base anymore. They wouldn't let her onto Osan either. She had "bad karma," she said. "Bad karma."

There have been more than half a million marriages between Asian women and male GIs since World War II, but language barriers, stereotypes and prejudice, familial disapproval, cultural differences, and other challenges combine to make them particularly fragile. Military personnel tend to be very young when they marry: almost 20 percent of enlisted Army soldiers are married, compared to just 5 percent of civilians their age. In some ways, it should be no surprise that an estimated 80 percent of GIs' Asian-American marriages end in divorce.[32]

One hears similar stories about American soldiers, like men in other militaries, abandoning women and children throughout the world: Japan, Honduras, Germany, and just about everywhere else one finds a base. Between failed marriages and GIs simply leaving mothers and children overseas, U.S. bases abroad have produced generations of abandoned offspring. In Okinawa, GIs have abandoned an estimated four thousand children; many have ended up in orphanages and foster homes.[33] Approximately ninety thousand "illegitimate" children were born during the occupation of West Germany alone, in part because German-American marriages were banned until December 1946.[34] And U.S. bases in Germany continue to produce abandoned offspring. Indeed, a number of soccer players who have played on the U.S. men's national team grew up never knowing their American servicemen fathers, who left their mothers in Germany.[35]

GLOBAL INEQUITIES

That night in the Songtan camptown outside Osan Air Base, I wandered through streets that were getting louder and more crowded now that the sun had set. There were still a fair number of couples and children on the streets, passing the juicy bars on their way to shop or eat. As the night progressed, hip-hop boomed out of bars along the main pedestrian mall and from second-floor clubs with neon-lit names like Club Woody's, Pleasure World, Whisky a-Go-Go, and the Hook Up Club. Many of the bars have stages with stripper poles for women to gyrate (clothed) to the flash

of stage lights and blasting music. In other bars, groups of mostly Filipina women in tight skirts and dresses talked to one another, leaning
over the table as they shot pool. Some were chatting with a handful of
GIs, young and old. Groups of younger GIs walked together through the
red-light-district-meets-pedestrian-mall scene, peering into bars and
considering their options. Bright signs for cheap hotels beckoned. Near
a small food cart, a sign read man only massage prince hotel.

I thought about going into one of the bars, but enough journalists have
done it already. I can let them testify to what happens when a man goes
to a juicy bar.

> It took less than an hour and $40 in glasses of juice for the pretty young
> woman working at the noisy bar to offer up her cell phone number and
> a promise that "the pleasures of a Filipina" could be had for the right
> price . . . The woman repeatedly touched a patron suggestively and offered
> a proposition as thinly veiled as she was scantily clad.[36]

On another occasion, a *Stars and Stripes* reporter quickly collected the
telephone numbers of five Filipinas.

> Three of the women said they were open to "having a boyfriend" and
> another said she wanted to "talk personally" over lunch about what it
> would take to accompany him back to his hotel room . . . In one bar, a
> young woman introduced herself by grinding her buttocks against a
> customer.[37]

Until recently, the camptown sex trade wasn't hidden. Few thought
there was anything to hide. Tom Merriman, the journalist whose 2002
exposé helped start calls for reform, explained it was "no super secret
hidden camera operation. We walked in as tourists." Everything was
"wide open."[38]

It sadly makes perfect sense that Filipina women fill most of the bars
and clubs in South Korea. The sex industry boomed in the Philippines
after U.S. troops colonized the country in 1898. By the time the Filipino government evicted the U.S. military, in 1992, the country's sex
industry had become one of the world's largest, with as many as twenty

thousand sex workers around Subic Bay Naval Base alone.[39] Given how impoverished the Philippines was under U.S. colonial rule, and the persistence of poverty after the country declared independence in 1946 and the U.S. shifted to less overt forms of control, it's easy to understand why prostitution remains a huge industry for many Filipina migrant laborers.

Earlier in the day, toward the end of my walk around Songtan with the Durebang outreach workers, I asked Valeria whether some of the women know what they're getting into before they arrive.

"Nowadays, they know about the system," Valeria said. "Most . . . they know what they're doing."

As Valeria, who has lived in the Philippines, explained, "They come here because of the promise of big money. Dollars." Many come from the poorest southern regions of the Philippines, and they have to support their families. "They have to endure it," she said. "They could never earn this kind of money in the Philippines."

At the root of the camptown sex industry, then, are gender inequalities and global economic inequalities that shape who has money and who does not. As South Korea's economy has grown, Korean women have largely left the relatively low-paying world of camptown sex to be replaced by women further down the global economic ladder, such as those from the Philippines.

The experiences of these women upon arrival in South Korea appear to fall along a spectrum. While many women now seem to know the general nature of the work that usually comes with an entertainer visa, deceptive recruiting strategies, outright misrepresentation, and employers violating contracts with impunity are the norm. As poor migrants who don't speak Korean and need to pay off debts and support families at home, the women find themselves in a position of extreme vulnerability. This leaves them open to a range of exploitation including wage theft, the withholding of passports, abusive working and living conditions, violence, and rape. In some instances, conditions appear to constitute sexual slavery; in almost all cases, the women are living under conditions of extremely limited power and agency.

A woman named Lori, who got an entertainer visa in the Philippines to go to South Korea in 2005, says that she was among those who did not know the true nature of "the system" before arriving. She "thought that we really have to sing because we sign a contract as a singer," she says. Now, she feels stuck at the club, hating the sex work but unable to leave for financial reasons. "I talked with some girls and said, 'I really can't take it anymore. I don't want to go, I don't want to go with any guy,'" Lori recounts. "A girl told me, 'As long as you think about your family, your child, or other people you love, you will take all the men, and you won't think about yourself.' I was thinking if I don't have a debt to pay in the Philippines, I would go back in the Philippines and not stay here even for a second."[40]

"SOLD HOURLY, NIGHTLY, OR PERMANENTLY"

A case from the U.S. Army's operations in Bosnia illustrates the extreme end of the spectrum. After six years in the Army, Ben Johnston got an aircraft maintenance job with major military contractor Dyn-Corp at Camp Comanche in Bosnia in late 1998. Soon he began hearing some of his co-workers bragging about buying women as sex slaves. "You could get basically any girl you wanted," Ben Johnston later told a Texas court. "A lot of people said you can buy a woman and how good it is to have a sex slave at home." One man bragged, "My girl's not a day over twelve." Another forty-five-year-old man "owned a girl," Johnston said, "who couldn't have been more than fourteen."[41]

After trying unsuccessfully to get DynCorp officials to do something, Johnston reported to the Army's Criminal Investigation Command, known as CID, that eight DynCorp employees talked openly of buying women. Johnston explained how DynCorp employees and Serbian mafiosi brought women and girls into Bosnia from other countries, mostly in eastern Europe. "DynCorp leadership was 100 percent in bed with the mafia over there," Johnston said. His boss, John Hirtz, "would take new employees to the brothels and set them up," and then "the Serbian mafia would give Hirtz the women free."[42]

Another employee, Kevin Werner, admitted to investigators that he bought a woman. "Harley's is a nightclub that offers prostitution," Werner told CID. (In Bosnia, prostitution is illegal.) "Women are sold hourly, nightly, or permanently." Werner said he bought the woman and an Uzi machine gun for the equivalent of $740. "Ever since then [she] has lived with me as a housemate. She does not speak much English but knows that she could leave any time she wanted," he claimed.[43]

This was not the first time DynCorp had been confronted with such behavior by its employees. In 1999, months before Johnston spoke to CID, another group of five DynCorp employees was identified by Bosnian media as having bought women and their passports from the Serbian mafia. And around the same time, Kathryn Bolkovac, a DynCorp employee working as part of a UN police force, was airing similar accusations about the involvement of DynCorp employees and members of the international community in sex trafficking. After interviewing some of the victims during her UN posting, Bolkovac revealed stories of women trafficked from the east and forced to work off debts to pimps, as well as examples of what appeared to be rape, beatings, and torture. At one club, she and a local police officer discovered "seven young women there who were huddled together on bare mattresses on the floor. Condoms strung over the garbage can, plastic bags of their street clothes and working clothes, just terrified. Beaten and terrified."[44]

Following instructions from the Army, DynCorp officials removed at least eighteen of its employees from Bosnia, firing at least twelve. Emails show that DynCorp officials knew the problem was even more widespread than these individual cases but that they took little other action. Instead, one official commented that the swift firings had allowed DynCorp "to turn this into a marketing success." And along with firing people like John Hirtz, the boss who got women from the Serbian mafia, DynCorp also fired Johnston and Bolkovac, the two whistleblowers. According to Johnston's letter of discharge, he was fired for bringing "discredit to the company and the U.S. Army."[45]

Bolkovac and Johnston both sued DynCorp for wrongful termination. (Their stories form the basis for the 2011 film *The Whistleblower*.) Bolkovac eventually won a judgment in a British court, while Johnston settled with DynCorp for an undisclosed sum. In Bosnia, the Army CID referred the case to local police and closed its investigation without examining the trafficking allegations or speaking to any of the women involved. None of the accused were prosecuted, and no DynCorp official faced prosecution.[46]

It was not for lack of evidence. During the investigation, the Army CID uncovered a video of John Hirtz having sex with two women. In one case, a woman could be heard repeatedly saying "no" to him.[47]

"Did you have sexual intercourse with the second woman on the tape?" a CID investigator asked Hirtz.

"Yes," he replied.

"Did you have intercourse with the second woman after she said 'no' to you?"

"I don't recall her saying that. I don't think it was her saying 'no.'"

"According to what you witnessed on the videotape played for you," the investigator continued, "did you have sexual intercourse with the second woman after she said 'no' to you?"

"Yes," said Hirtz.

"Did you know it is wrong to force yourself upon someone without their consent?"

"Yes."

The videotaped rape was never investigated further. A CID report concluded that "the offense was committed by a civilian who is no longer subject to the [Uniform Code of Military Justice], there are no violations of federal criminal statutes with which the person can be charged, and no other Army interest exists."

WHAT GOES ON IN THE CAMPTOWNS . . .

Over the centuries, militaries have attempted to solve their constant labor needs in a variety of ways. After providing troops with cash, food, and housing, plying them with easy access to commercial sex has been one of the most popular strategies. That troops generally have had to pay for this readily available sex has only benefited militaries further: as working-class men burn through their pay (and, not infrequently, go into debt), their dependence on a military salary helps keep them enlisted.

Unlike cash, food, and housing, however, sex brings risks for military leaders. Sexually transmitted diseases are one obvious concern. Another is the conflict over women that can arise between male soldiers, or between the soldiers and local men. Less obviously, sex brings with it the possibility that a partner and children could challenge the military's monopoly on troops' time, loyalty, and emotional attachments.

Hence, military leaders across the centuries have endeavored not just to provide troops with sex but also to control their access to it. Controlling access to sex has meant controlling women and their sexual labor: restricting them to particular areas, mandating health inspection cards, and so forth. In colonial India, Britain's 1864 Cantonment Acts gave British commanders the power to bring Indian sex workers into military camps, license them as prostitutes, subject the women to medical exams, and house them in brothels called *chaklas* within view of soldiers' barracks. The former Air Force officer and base expert Mark Gillem observes how this kept the women "conspicuously close" to the soldiers but "conveniently out of the barracks." Just as in the camptowns of the twentieth and twenty-first centuries, the aim has ultimately been the control of men and men's labor, which allows a military to function. To paraphrase the political scientist Cynthia Enloe, military leaders have made brothels as important to bases as their dry docks.[48]

No matter one's opinions about the legality and morality of sex work, patronizing the sex industry means violating both military law and the laws of most countries in which U.S. bases and troops are located (with the exception of Germany, the Netherlands, and a few other countries). Given the prevalence of sex trafficking in the industry,[49] troops also violate national and international prohibitions on supporting human trafficking.

The dangers of patronizing the sex industry can be broader still, as was made clear to me when I visited a bar just outside the gates of Kadena Air Base on Okinawa. There I met a fairly tipsy woman who, within seconds of meeting, told me she had two kids and a pilot husband recently back from Guam and Thailand. He thought he could go on temporary duty, she exclaimed, and no one would know what he was doing—"until I got gonorrhea!"

Now, she said, she doesn't know what to do. Although she wants to leave her husband, she's staying home with her kids, living in a foreign country, and dependent on her husband financially. She also doesn't want to separate the kids from the father they love.

Ultimately, the effects of military prostitution are felt not just by women abroad whose bodies are used and too often abused, trafficked, and exploited. They're also felt by the family members, co-workers, and others who share the troops' lives. Unlike the Las Vegas fantasy, what goes on in the camptowns doesn't stay in the camptowns. And as we will see, the attitudes fostered by commercial sex zones and by the military more broadly about men and women, dominance and power carry over dangerously into GIs' lives—both on base and at home.

Dallas Cowboys cheerleader Megan Willsey performs at a United Service Organization (USO) show for troops deployed during the second U.S. war in Iraq, 2003.

10

Militarized Masculinity

It's easy to condemn GIs for taking advantage of an often exploitative sex industry in places like South Korea. But as a soldier who runs ROK Drop, a popular blog about the military in South Korea, points out, it's wrong to blame the soldiers alone. "Despite all the rhetoric by [United States Forces Korea] about fighting human trafficking, prostitution, and alcohol abuse," he writes, "USFK's own policies continue to ensure this type of activity will continue around the US camps."[1] It's hypocritical, he says: training programs are "telling soldiers to drink responsibly and stay away from juicy girls, but what environment do we create for the soldiers to spend most of their free time in? A ville [camptown] filled with cheap booze and prostitutes."[2]

The dearth of other recreational opportunities on Korean bases may be a factor. But at issue is also the broader American military culture, and the sexism and patriarchy found society-wide in the United States, Korea, and much of the world. The behavior of men who take advantage of exploitative sex industries is often excused as a matter of "boys will be boys"—as merely natural behavior for male soldiers. In fact there's little that's natural about the behavior. Men on military bases and women in camptowns find themselves in what is a highly *unnatural* situation, one that's been created by a series of human decisions made over time (mostly by male military and government officials). Those decisions have created a predominantly male military environment, in which women's visible presence is overwhelmingly reduced to one role: sex. When researchers studied GIs in South Korea in the 1960s, they found that "one of the forces exerting pressure on them to 'try a prostitute'" was peer pressure from other Americans. Consider the powerful message communicated, for example, when a medical officer gathers a ship's men before docking in the Philippines or Korea and throws condoms "as if they were Hallmark cards," as one sailor recounted.[3]

Cynthia Enloe has helped show how this world of institutionalized camptown sex helps shape the identities and behavior of male soldiers *as men* and in the process helps the military to function. Institutionalized military prostitution draws on existing gender norms—cultural ideas about what it means to be a man and a woman—but it also intensifies these norms. It trains men to believe that using the sexual services of women is part of what it means to be a soldier and part of what it means to be a man. It helps shape what Enloe and others have called a "militarized masculinity," involving feelings of power and superiority over women and a willingness to inflict violence on anyone deemed inferior.[4]

The ROK Drop blogger describes how these kinds of feelings and ways of seeing the world can develop. "You got 18–20 year old soldiers in a club with [a mamasan] pushing alcohol," he writes, "and half naked Russian & Phillipino [*sic*] drinky girls on them making the soldiers feel like a king. A lot of them cannot resist the temptation at their age. So the soldiers drink, get involved with these drinky girls, and take this I'm king of the ville attitude with them everywhere else they go in Korea."[5]

This "I'm king" attitude implies a hierarchy, of the kind that is fundamental to military training. Researchers have shown that one of the most difficult challenges militaries face is that of teaching human beings to kill other human beings, and that doing so requires dehumanizing others by promoting the belief that another human is somehow a "lesser" creature. As we will see, one of the central forms of dehumanization promoted by military training and the culture of daily life in the military has been the supposed inferiority of women—that women are less than men. Institutionalized military prostitution provides one important source for this dehumanization of women and the militarized masculinity that helps perpetuate it. In places where there is an ethnic difference between GIs and sex workers, military prostitution can also reinforce societal beliefs about supposed racial and ethnic superiority, and the naturalness of some people serving and others being served.[6]

Given the ubiquitous nature of camptown prostitution in South Korea in particular, men deployed to the country frequently have their ideas about what it means to be a man transformed—just as boys do in all-male boarding schools, summer camps, sports teams, and fraternities. Thus, when we try to understand recurring incidents of rape and sexual assault perpetrated by troops in places such as Okinawa, or the high rates of sexual assault and violence against women in the military, we cannot overlook men's experiences in the camptowns. As one advocate for the victims of military sexual violence explains, "You can't expect to treat women as one of your own when, in the same breath, you as a young soldier are being encouraged to exploit women on the outside of that base."[7]

"I COULDN'T RAISE MY VOICE"

Yumi Tomita grew up near Kadena Air Base in Okinawa.[8] One day, she was walking by herself home from high school. Along a sidewalk on a narrow side street near a red dirt ball field, she saw a car parked nearby. "The soldier in the car asked me for directions to his friend's house," she recounts. "I tried to give directions in my broken English, but he didn't seem to understand what I said."

"So I got closer to the window and tried to give directions again. Another soldier, who was hiding, came behind me, pointed a knife at my back, and said, 'I can kill you.'" Being interviewed for a documentary some two decades years later, Yumi wears large black sunglasses to disguise her identity. During the Korean War, she says, the Kadena area had been turned into a bar district "to 'protect' Okinawan women because so many were being raped. Before that, armed U.S. soldiers often barged into people's homes looking for women. Locals used to ring a warning bell whenever a soldier was nearby. People protected women by hiding them in closets whenever they heard the bell."

The dangers didn't go away after the war. When she was a schoolchild, Yumi said, "Sometimes I'd be walking down the street, and I'd be chased by a U.S. soldier. I had heard of women being raped in our area, but those incidents were not reported [to the police]."

On the sidewalk that day, the soldiers forced her into their car, took her to a nearby park, and raped her. "I heard people's voices in the playground just beyond the trees," Yumi said. "But I couldn't raise my voice for the whole time. Later I managed to get up and go home." She felt she couldn't ask her parents for help. Eventually she talked to her brother's friend, who was studying law. He told Yumi the police would take her back to the crime scene and would make her reenact what happened in front of male police officers. If the case went to court, she would have to repeat it again. "He asked me if I could do that. And I thought I couldn't. So I didn't report it to the police.

"When I heard that a sixth-grade Okinawan girl was raped by three U.S. soldiers near a U.S. base," Yumi said, "I thought I was partly responsible because I didn't tell anyone what had happened to me."

Yumi Tomita's case was one of around three hundred and fifty rapes, sexual assaults, and other crimes that GIs have committed against Okinawan women between 1945 and 2011, according to documentation compiled by the group Okinawa Women Act Against Military Violence. (Since sexual assaults are especially prone to underreporting, this is likely an undercount of the true number of incidents.)[9] The rape of the sixth grader that Yumi mentioned was the most notorious among these. On September 4, 1995, marines Rodrico Harp and Kendric Ledet and Navy seaman Marcus Gill grabbed the twelve-year-old girl at knifepoint off the streets of Kin Town, near the Marine Corps' Camp Hansen. They threw her in a rental car, taped her eyes and mouth shut, bound her arms and legs, and then repeatedly raped her, discarding her bloodied body when they were finished.[10]

After the twelve-year-old dragged herself to safety, she gave a detailed description of the men and the car. Within hours, the three were taken into U.S. military custody. News coverage emerged slowly, but once it did, outrage grew. The commander of U.S. forces in the Pacific, Admiral Richard C. Macke, further inflamed the situation when he said of the rape, "I think that it was absolutely stupid. I have said several times: For the price they paid to rent the car they could have had a girl."[11]

Two of the perpetrators, Gill and Harp, received seven-year prison sentences. The third, Ledet (who claimed he faked raping the girl because he feared Gill), received a six-and-a-half-year sentence. Three years after the men were released from Japanese prison, Ledet committed suicide. Police in Kennesaw, Georgia, found him next to a former co-worker whom he had sexually assaulted, bludgeoned, and strangled to death.[12]

MILITARY SEXUAL ASSAULT

In addition to camptown-style prostitution, pervasive sexually objectifying entertainment in the military plays a role in the victimization of locals who have suffered rapes and assaults committed by the very people whose presence in their countries is supposed to provide security. Like the camptowns that grew around bases in South Korea and elsewhere, the "camp show" tradition dates to World War II. Under the auspices of the United Service Organizations, hundreds of musicians, actors, and comedians began going on tours designed to boost troop morale overseas. USO shows have since become an iconic staple at bases abroad, featuring the likes of Bob Hope, John Wayne, and Stephen Colbert, as well as "pinup girls" such as Marilyn Monroe, Rita Hayworth, and Betty Grable. In a 2005 USO show at Camp Victory in Iraq, Al Franken did a comedy routine about Army chow; then, two scantily clad Dallas Cowboys cheerleaders in their trademark short-shorts, halter tops, and cowboy boots took the stage to dance before throngs of troops.[13]

Along with Playboy Bunnies, the Dallas Cowboys cheerleaders rank among the most famous of USO performers. Francis Ford Coppola's *Apocalypse Now* immortalized the tradition, showing a scene in which three bikini-clad Playmates perform for hundreds of cheering male GIs in Vietnam. Not long after the show gets started, to shouts of "Take it off!" and "You fucking bitch!" GIs storm the stage, forcing the women to retreat into a helicopter to escape the chaos.

Few have questioned the effects of these government-funded shows. But in a series of articles on "Women in the Battlefield and the Barracks," the environmental health expert H. Patricia Hynes notes that these forms of sexually objectifying entertainment have helped shape the epidemic of sexual assault and harassment now roiling the military. The pervasive pornography found in the armed services—a soldier told me that pornography was so valued by troops in Iraq, it was like currency—has had a similar effect.[14]

The problem officially known as "military sexual trauma," or MST, has been particularly acute during the recent wars in Afghanistan and Iraq. During these wars, despite their unprecedented role in direct combat situations, American women have been more likely to be raped at the hands of a fellow member of the military than killed by enemy fighters. Estimates suggest that as of 2012, seventy thousand women had been victimized, almost all of them on bases in and around the two countries.[15] As one woman said, "The mortar rounds that came in daily did less damage to me than the men with whom I shared my food."[16] Another female soldier said, "They basically assume that because you are a girl in the Army, you're obligated to have sex with them."[17]

At Camp Victory—the base where the two Dallas Cowboys cheerleaders performed with Al Franken—several women died of dehydration in their barracks during the first years of the occupation of Iraq. They died because, despite 120-degree heat, they stopped drinking water every afternoon. They stopped drinking water because they feared being raped by other GIs while using the unlit latrines at night.[18] Hynes and others call it a "war on two fronts," in which women in Afghanistan and Iraq have had to fight "a second, more damaging war—a private, preemptive one in the barracks."[19]

Around two thirds of incidents of unwanted sexual contact take place on military installations, and the problem has become a veritable pandemic.[20] According to a 2003 Army-funded study of female veterans who were in the military between the Vietnam War and the 1991 Gulf War, almost one in three was raped during her time in the military. That's almost twice the rate found across the United States over women's *entire lifetimes*, even though the women veterans were in the military for, on average, just two to six years. Of those reporting an experience of rape in the military, 37 percent reported having been raped two or more times; 14 percent reported having been gang-raped. And 80 percent of female vets across the military have reported being the victim of sexual harassment.[21] The most recent Pentagon data show that in the 2014 fiscal year alone, an estimated nineteen thousand service members experienced a sexual assault. That figure represents 4.3 percent of female and 0.9 percent of male service members (although these statistics include neither sexual assaults committed by intimate partners nor assaults committed against children).[22]

Overseas bases seem to be particularly dangerous for women. Although only about 17 percent of U.S. military personnel were posted overseas (including those in war zones) in 2013, approximately one quarter to one third of all sexual assaults in the armed forces reported that year took place abroad.[23] Sexual assaults on bases in and around Afghanistan and Iraq were particularly prevalent, but even outside war zones, bases overseas appear to present a greater risk of sexual assault than bases in the United States. Some in the military suggested to me that unaccompanied postings like those in South Korea, where troops are far from family members and home communities, make crimes of all kinds more likely.[24]

In 2011, the Service Women's Action Network held a conference to address the problem of military sexual trauma. One of the speakers was retired brigadier general Thomas Cuthbert, who has advised the military services on the issue. During his presentation to an audience of survivors of military sexual trauma, other veterans, and members of the media, Cuthbert said military law "works pretty well." Audible laughs and hisses erupted from the crowd.

A few minutes later, the general mentioned two decades of Navy and Army sexual assault scandals. He said of the women involved, "Nobody had taught them properly how to say no." This elicited more groans and widespread head shaking. When Cuthbert added that people need to report sex crimes to their supervisors, a chorus of loud objecting coughs went around the room. An audience member asked angrily what someone should do when a supervisor says, "When you get raped, don't report it."

"The other thing you do is go to the CID," Cuthbert responded. The reference to the widely criticized Criminal Investigation Command spawned a burst of laughter and sarcastic clapping. In 2011, less than half of assaults reported to the CID were considered suitable for disciplinary proceedings. Less than 8 percent went to trial. An estimated 10 percent of the accused were able to escape prosecution entirely by resigning from the military.[25] And along with these low rates of prosecution and conviction, there is widespread evidence of retaliation against women reporting assaults or harassment.[26]

Much of the military's male leadership appears to have been unable to grasp the nature of the sexual assault problem, to take steps to protect female troops, and to enforce its own laws. In 2012, after numerous female Air Force cadets were sexually assaulted by their instructors, the Air Force considered allowing only women to train women—instead of making male trainers comply with rules, regulations, and laws on sex.[27] In a similarly revealing moment, the Wisconsin Army National Guard introduced an "Ask her when she's sober" campaign; a spokesperson said that this approach will "avoid legal trouble (for the initiator)." As Patricia Hynes points out, the implicit message is that the men don't have to be sober to discuss sex, and that "the military's top concern is how to prepare a male soldier to defend himself in a rape charge, not how to prevent rape and protect women soldiers."[28]

At the conference, a man in the audience received loud applause when he asked why the military isn't locking up perpetrators and putting them on sexual offender lists. Why, he said, doesn't the military have an ad on TV saying that rape is not acceptable? "How are we going to police the world," he asked, "if we can't police our own people?"

PENETRATION AND DOMINANCE

Military sexual trauma does not affect women alone. Although the odds of any particular man being sexually assaulted in the military are much lower than for a woman, in absolute terms, more men than women are victimized.[29]

Aaron Belkin, an expert on sexuality in the armed forces, was once told by a U.S. Naval Academy professor that male students at the academy rape each other "all of the time."[30] Belkin initially assumed she was speaking metaphorically, but the professor insisted, "I meant what I said." Years of subsequent research by Belkin, at the Naval Academy and elsewhere in the armed forces, graphically confirmed the truth of that assertion. "Male American service members," he writes, indeed "penetrated each other's bodies 'all of the time.'"

They forced broom handles, fingers and penises into each other's anuses. They stuck pins into flesh and bones. They vomited into one another's mouths and forced rotten food down each other's throats. They inserted tubes into each other's anal cavities and then pumped grease through the tubes.[31]

The prevalence of these various forms of abuse suggests how central penetration—with all its complex connotations of dominance—is to the military, and thus part of the unseen world of life on base. On bases throughout the world, penetration and dominance are central to an ideal form of military masculinity, one that's prized and actively groomed among troops.

In the context of military training, where troops are drilled to overcome societal prohibitions on killing, leaders generally equate penetration and dominance with men and masculinity while they equate penetrability and subordination with women and femininity.[32] A soldier who shared his diary from boot camp with me recorded a telling incident.

We got a semi time-killing/inspirational speech by a drill sergeant today. He had some hilarious jokes. He said that all men had a clit until graduation and as graduation got close our clit moved faster and faster as we got more excited and finally at graduation our clits turned into penises and we became Men. What an eloquent analogy.

The speech demonstrates the close relationship in the military between ideas about being a warrior and ideas about gender, sex, and sexuality. To become a soldier, according to the drill sergeant, is to shed all that is feminine, making a grunt into a man in one orgasmic process of transformation.

Men are not naturally rapists, and the majority of men in the military—whatever their degree of obedience—do not commit sexual assault. But across human societies, certain conditions enable rape and make sexual assault more likely. These are the conditions generally found in the U.S. military and on bases worldwide. This is an environment where females are considered inferior; where women are frequently reduced to sex objects in camptowns, in pornography, and in USO shows; and where men are trained and encouraged to enact a masculinity centered on demonstrating one's strength and dominance over others who are considered weaker, inferior, and deserving of being dominated.

There's no ambiguity about the general disdain for all that's female in a military where words like "pussy," "bitch," "dyke," and "girl" are common insults.[33] During the war in Vietnam, Hynes notes, the military appears to have "deliberately infused" training with "misogynist language and imagery and phallic allusions to weapons . . . to build battlefield aggression and improve the rate of weapon use." In many ways, little has changed. As Hynes points out, "when sexist epithets and misogynist chants are used in drill exercises, and when women are singled out and harassed by drill sergeants, it gives license to male recruits to do likewise, and it seasons the recruits and sets the culture for future military sexual harassment and assault."[34]

This conditioning, this kind of unofficial training that men experience in the military, is reflected in statistics showing that men who have spent time in the U.S. military are much more likely than their civilian counterparts to be imprisoned for sexual offenses. This is particularly striking because, compared to adult males without military experience, male veterans are much *less* likely to be imprisoned for other violent crimes, theft, robbery, and drug offenses. Sex crimes are the one exception.[35] There appears to be something about what happens on base and in the barracks that makes it significantly more likely that a man will sexually victimize another person.

The risk of rape in such a culture of misogyny is only compounded by the fact that a disproportionate number of men in the military have themselves been the victims of violence. In two studies, half the men enlisting reported having suffered physical abuse, and one in six reported sexual abuse. Eleven percent reported both. Assorted research shows that victims of abuse are more likely to become abusers in turn.[36] This makes it unsurprising that, beyond sexual assault, domestic violence rates in the military may be five times civilian rates, according to one study. One in three Army families may be affected.[37]

The problem of sexual assault appears to have been exacerbated by the wars in Afghanistan and Iraq. There were simply too few troops to fight two wars, so the armed forces relaxed many of their standards to draw in more recruits. By 2006, the military had issued "moral waivers" to one in five enlisted troops, including those convicted of sexual assault and domestic violence.[38] A growing epidemic of substance abuse in what is a stressful work/life environment has also contributed to the problem of physical and sexual violence.[39]

While the amenities and rituals of life on base make many of them look and feel like idyllic 1950s-era Mayberry, closer examination reveals a reality more akin to the dark suburban underbelly seen in David Lynch's *Blue Velvet* and *Twin Peaks*. Simply put, bases are dangerous, unhealthy places to be.

• •

PART IV

MONEY

Mine-Resistant Ambush Protected (MRAP) vehicles and Humvees at Camp Arifjan, Kuwait, a major deployment base during the second war in Iraq.

11

The Bill

It's impossible to quantify the human costs that our overseas bases have inflicted on locals, military personnel, and their family members alike. However, we can try to add up the financial costs, though even this simple-seeming task quickly proves to be anything but.

One of the first people I went to talk to in my quest to tally the base nation's bill was Andy Hoehn, a former deputy assistant secretary of defense in the George W. Bush administration. In his office at the government-funded RAND Corporation, Hoehn told me that many people who "advocate a forward presence" assume that the host countries are paying most of the costs.

But, Hoehn said, they're not accounting for a lot. There's the cost of buying airplane tickets for family members and shipping over all their belongings, for example. Plus you've got overseas housing and cost-of-living allowances, hotel rooms while waiting for permanent billeting, meals, per diems, and so on. When you have families, Hoehn added, the base also needs to build a school, a clinic, a church, and much more.

"It adds up," I said.

"It adds up. And it's routine," Hoehn said. "And often these tours [abroad] are fairly brief. Three years and sometimes shorter."

The problem is, Hoehn said, no one has really bothered to calculate the costs. Ultimately, he added, even "the services don't know."

In 2013, Hoehn's RAND Corporation finally did a calculation. A nearly five-hundred-page study of overseas bases showed that "despite substantial host-nation financial and in-kind support, stationing forces and maintaining bases overseas produces higher direct financial costs than basing forces in the United States."[1] In Europe, for example, the Air Force's estimated average annual cost just for running a base (before adding the costs of having any personnel there) is more than $200 million. That's more than double the costs of an Air Force base in the United States.[2]

When it comes to personnel, the Air Force's cost *per person* on an overseas base is almost $40,000 per year more, on average, than on a domestic base. The Navy's annual cost per person in Europe is almost $30,000 more than domestically, while in Japan, the Army pays on average nearly $25,000 more per person every year than at home.[3] Even in the least expensive case, that of the Marines in Japan, it costs $10,000 to $15,000 more per year for every marine stationed there compared to locations in the continental United States. For eleven thousand marines, that adds up to an extra $110 million to $165 million that taxpayers are spending every year to keep marine forces in Japan rather than in America.[4] When one considers all the deployments globally, the numbers are staggering.

Another way to get a sense for the magnitude of the costs is this: because of the hundreds of bases overseas, the U.S. military is probably the world's largest international moving company. Why? Because when stationed abroad for any period other than a temporary assignment, every member of the military generally has the right to ship his or her entire household and a personal vehicle to and from an overseas station.[5] With tours generally lasting between one and three years, about one third of the military moves in any given year.

Among other things, this means the military is shipping tens of thousands of privately owned vehicles to and from bases overseas every year.[6] Based on recent contracts, this is costing the government, and taxpayers, around $200 million every year.[7]

And that's in addition to shipping every last piece of furniture, every book, every television, every kitchen pot and pan, every fork and spoon, every bicycle and children's toy, and every other item in a uniformed service member's household, up to a weight limit of 5,000 to 18,000 pounds (depending on rank and on whether one has family members).[8] Which is in addition to the long-term storage of household goods for troops overseas, for which the military also pays. Which is in addition to miscellaneous expenses such as pet quarantine fees— which the military will also cover, up to $550 per move.[9] Overall, the total annual moving costs alone easily stretch into the hundreds of millions of dollars.

THE OFFICIAL BILL

While overseas bases are clearly more expensive than domestic bases, the total bill for maintaining hundreds of bases and hundreds of thousands of troops abroad remains a mystery.[10] In theory, we should know the total: by law, the Pentagon must tell Congress what it spends on all the military's activities at bases, embassies, and other facilities abroad in an annual report called the "Overseas Cost Summary" (OCS).[11] This means calculating all the costs of building, running, and maintaining every last base site, garrison, airfield, port, warehouse, ammunition dump, radar station, and drone base, plus the costs of paying for and maintaining every U.S. service member and family member abroad, including all their salaries, housing, schools, teachers, hospitals, moving costs, lawn mowing, utilities, and much, much more.

For the 2012 fiscal year, the Overseas Cost Summary put the total at $22.7 billion.[12] That's a considerable sum, roughly equal to the entire budget of the Department of Justice or the Department of Agriculture. It's also about half the entire 2012 budget of the Department of State— significant portions of which actually go to arms sales, foreign military training, and other military (rather than diplomatic) purposes overseas.[13]

At the same time, however, the Pentagon's official figure contrasts sharply with the only other recent estimate available. In 2009, the economist Anita Dancs estimated total spending on bases and troops abroad at $250 billion—a more than tenfold difference.[14] Part of the discrepancy stems from Dancs's including war spending in her total, whereas at Congress's direction, the OCS doesn't include the billions spent on the wars in Iraq, Afghanistan, and elsewhere around the globe. But even without war spending, her figure comes to around $140 billion—still almost $120 billion more than the Pentagon suggests.

Faced with such a significant disagreement, I wanted to figure out the real costs of keeping so many bases and troops overseas. Trying to get a handle on the numbers, I talked to budget experts and current and former Pentagon officials, as well as budget officers at bases abroad. Many of the people I spoke to politely suggested this was a fool's errand, given the number of bases involved, the complexity of distinguishing overseas from domestic spending, and the secrecy of Pentagon budgets. The "frequently fictional" nature of Pentagon accounting also poses a problem: the Department of Defense remains the only federal agency unable to pass a financial audit.[15] Congress first ordered the Pentagon to make itself auditable in 1997; it has since missed numerous deadlines, and the goal is now 2017.[16]

Ever the fool, I plunged into the world of Pentagon budgets, where ledgers sometimes remain handwritten and $1 billion can be a rounding error.[17] I reviewed thousands of pages of budget documents, government and independent reports, and hundreds of line items for everything from shopping malls to military intelligence to mail subsidies. Wanting to err on the conservative side, I decided to follow the basic methodology Congress mandated for the OCS[18] while also including overseas expenses the Pentagon or Congress might have forgotten or ignored. It hardly seemed to make sense to exclude, for example, spending for troops in Kosovo, the price tag of bases in Afghanistan, or the costs of bases in overseas U.S. territories.[19] Here's an abbreviated version of my quest to establish the real costs.

MISSING COUNTRIES AND CONSTRUCTION

Although the Overseas Cost Summary initially seemed quite thorough, I quickly realized that countries widely known to host U.S. bases go completely unnamed in the report. In fact, around a dozen countries and foreign territories from the Pentagon's own list of overseas bases appear to be missing from the summary. While they may be lumped into the "Other" category, for "countries with costs less than $5 million or unspecified overseas locations," the absence of places such as Kosovo, Bosnia, and Colombia is surprising. The military has had large bases and hundreds of troops in the Balkans since the late 1990s; in a different Pentagon report, 2012 costs in Kosovo and Bosnia were listed as $313.8

million.[20] According to the same report, I discovered that the OCS understates costs for bases in Honduras and Guantánamo Bay by about a third, or $86 million.

The OCS also reports costs of less than $5 million apiece for Colombia, Yemen, Thailand, and Uganda. Given current levels of military activity in each country, this seems highly unlikely. The costs of the military presence in Colombia alone could easily reach into the tens of millions a year, in the context of more than $9 billion in Plan Colombia funding since 2000. Unsure of the true spending in these countries, however, I decided to be conservative and not to replace the OCS figures with what would have been, at best, educated guesses. However, the real totals in those countries could add many tens of millions more.

Primed to look more carefully at the OCS, I found other oddities. In places like Australia and Qatar, the Pentagon reported having funds to pay troops' salaries but no money for "operations and maintenance." This would mean not having funds to turn the lights on, feed people, or do regular repairs. In other places, like Diego Garcia, there were no funds reported to pay personnel. Clearly, the report had either omitted the relevant figures or hadn't gathered the data to include them. Using costs reported in other countries as a guide, I estimated another $35 million in spending for such locations. As a start, I found *$435 million[21] for missing countries and costs.*

This is a relatively insignificant sum in the context of the Pentagon's $22 billion estimate and certainly not much in the context of the entire Pentagon budget, but this was just the beginning.

TERRITORIES, POSSESSIONS, AND PACIFIC ISLAND NATIONS

At Congress's direction, the Overseas Cost Summary omits the costs of bases in the oft-forgotten parts of the United States lacking full democratic representation—places such as Puerto Rico, Guam, American Samoa, the Northern Mariana Islands, and the U.S. Virgin Islands. This is strange because these areas are, of course, literally overseas, and because the Pentagon considers them "overseas" for accounting and other purposes.

Even more relevant for the purposes of calculating the base nation's

bill, as Dancs points out, is the fact that "the United States retains territories ... primarily for the purposes of the military and projecting military power." As we have seen, since World War II the government has
largely hung on to this collection of islands because they're home to critical bases like Andersen Air Force Base on Guam and the Saipan and Tinian bases in the Northern Marianas. Given this fact, one could reasonably
regard all the federal spending in each territory as the cost of maintaining bases and troops there. Federal transfer payments to Puerto Rico
alone were more than $17 billion in 2010, with the total for all the terri-
tories probably nearing $20 billion.[22] To be conservative, however, I deci-
ded to focus strictly on explicit military spending. Spending on Guam is
particularly high at a conservatively estimated $1.4 billion, including
monies appropriated to the Pentagon and other agencies for the planned
transfer of U.S. forces from Okinawa.[23] I estimate that total spending
for the remaining islands lacking full democratic representation reaches
$1.2 billion.[24] This brings us to around $2.6 billion more that's not
included in the OCS.

And beyond current U.S. territories such as Guam and Puerto Rico,
one also needs to account for the Pacific Ocean island nations that were
once U.S. "strategic trust territories": the Marshall Islands, the Federated
States of Micronesia, and Palau. Eventually those areas gained their
formal independence by signing compacts of free association with the
United States. These compacts gave responsibilities for defense to
the United States and allowed the U.S. government to retain military
control over the islands; in exchange, the island nations get yearly aid
packages, and their residents have greater rights to live in the United
States than citizens of other countries. (They also have the right to join
the U.S. military; per capita, the Federated States of Micronesia has a
higher rate of enlistment and of death at war than any U.S. state.)[25] Aside
from the Ronald Reagan Ballistic Missile Defense Test Site in the Marshall Islands' Kwajalein Atoll, there is currently little military activity in
the islands; the U.S. government is basically paying for the site and for
base construction rights during wartime.

So what does that cost? Every year, the Department of the Interior's
Office of Insular Affairs makes payments as part of the compact of free
association agreements. The transfers include rent to landowners in the

Kwajalein Atoll and funds to provide health care and ongoing cleanup assistance to Bikinians and other Marshallese affected by nuclear testing. The Insular Affairs office is also responsible for such expenditures as the ongoing effort to control the invasive brown tree snakes that military cargo flights accidentally introduced to Guam. For 2012, such payments totaled $570.6 million, bringing the total cost here to *$3.2 billion for territories and Pacific island nations.*

SHIPS AND PERSONNEL OUTSIDE U.S. WATERS; PRE-POSITIONED SHIPS AND STOCKS

In a way, it's strange, given the name of the Overseas Cost Summary, that it excludes (at Congress's instruction) the costs of maintaining naval vessels overseas. After all, Navy and Marine Corps vessels are essentially floating and submersible bases used to maintain a powerful military presence across the planet's waters. About 3.5 percent of Navy and Marine Corps personnel are afloat outside U.S. waters at a given time, so given total Navy and Marine Corps personnel and operations and maintenance costs of $108 billion, an estimate based just on that personnel percentage adds another $3.8 billion to the overseas budget. Of course, given the costs of far-flung operations and a total Navy and Marine Corps budget of $181 billion, this is an extremely conservative number; spending on fuel and other necessities away from home is likely to be considerably higher outside U.S. waters than domestically.[26]

Then there are the costs of Navy ships pre-positioned at anchor around the world in places like Diego Garcia and Saipan. These are like warehouse bases at sea, stocked with weaponry, war matériel, and other supplies. The Army also has pre-positioned stocks, in locations including Kuwait and Italy, that likewise aren't included in the OCS. Together, these come to an estimated $600 million a year. The Pentagon also appears to omit some additional $860 million for overseas "sealift" and "airlift" and "other mobilization" expenses.[27]

Some might argue that the costs of maintaining a global navy, pre-positioned equipment, and sealift and airlift capacity shouldn't be included in the cost of bases abroad, because those resources are what the military would "fall back to" if it closed all the overseas bases. This argument, of course, assumes that the United States *must* maintain military power around the globe, which is by no means self-evident. And whether or not one agrees with this proposition, the costs of pre-positioned equipment and vessels outside U.S. waters are clearly incurred overseas, rather than domestically, and should be counted here. All told, the bill grows by *$5.3 billion for Navy vessels and personnel plus seaborne and airborne assets.*

HEALTH CARE; MILITARY AND FAMILY HOUSING CONSTRUCTION; PX AND POSTAL SUBSIDIES

The Overseas Cost Summary includes the pay and extra allowances for military personnel abroad, but I confirmed with the Pentagon that, strangely, it doesn't include health care and other benefits paid to troops.[28] The Defense Health Program and other military personnel benefits, excluding those that are war-related, cost $31.2 billion and $51.8 billion, respectively, in 2012 worldwide.[29] With 14 percent of all U.S. military personnel overseas, not counting troops directly involved in U.S. wars, I conservatively estimate that the same percentage of costs occurs overseas. This adds up to a little over $11.6 billion. Meanwhile, the Navy's Expeditionary Health Services System costs some $66.2 million per year; since some of that spending is domestic, I add only half that amount to the overseas budget. This yields $11.7 billion for health care and benefits overseas.

While the OCS includes military and family housing construction costs submitted by each branch of the armed forces, it appears not to include military and family housing construction spending from Department of Defense–wide budgets. Such spending totals $3.6 billion, and since 15 percent of base sites are overseas, one can expect a roughly similar percentage of construction to take place there.[30] This gives us an estimated $537.6 million in additional construction costs. There is also a much larger $4.6 billion in military construction spending at "unspecified locations" worldwide found in the Pentagon budget but missing from the OCS.[31] Without knowing what proportion of this spending occurred at locations overseas, I again conservatively assume 15 percent (in fact, most of the spending may be abroad). This adds another $690 million in costs.

A much smaller, but significant, omission appears in the form of quality-of-life subsidies paid by the U.S. taxpayer. Take, for instance, the Post Exchange, or PX, which has long been an iconic feature of Army life on military bases at home and abroad. (Similar exchanges are called BXs by the Air Force, NEXs by the Navy, and MCXs by the Marine Corps.) These Walmart-like shopping malls are run by congressionally mandated government resale entities that enjoy retail rights on bases worldwide. In exchange for agreeing to return a portion of "reasonable earnings" to fund sports, libraries, and other recreational facilities and programs on bases, the Army and Air Force Exchange Service (AAFES) and its Navy and Marine counterparts enjoy buildings and land free of charge, free utilities, and free transportation of goods to overseas locations. They also operate tax free, which partly explains why they have generated thriving black markets and "PX economies" for decades.[32]

While no one appears to have estimated the value of buildings, land, and utilities that taxpayers provide, AAFES and its counterparts do report some information about the subsidies they enjoy. In fiscal year 2012, the three Exchange companies received approximately $258 million in transportation subsidies, "contributed services," and taxpayer reimbursements.[33] Forgone federal, state, and local taxes would add tens of millions more to that figure. Meanwhile, postal subsidies to transport mail to and from overseas bases add up to at least $130.7 million.[34] In total, you have *$13.3 billion for health care, military and family housing construction, and shopping and postal subsidies.*

"RENT" PAYMENTS AND NATO CONTRIBUTIONS

Another exclusion from the OCS is money paid to other countries whose land the Pentagon occupies. Although a few countries pay the United States to subsidize our bases, far more common, according to the base expert Kent Calder, "are the cases where the United States *pays* nations to host bases."[35] Though it is not officially framed as such, we can think of this effectively as a form of rent.

Given the secretive nature of basing agreements and the complex economic and political trade-offs involved in base negotiations, precise figures for these quasirental payments are impossible to find. However, it's safe to conclude, as Calder says, that "the United States generally pays a lot of money for its foreign bases."[36] Using a representative sample, Calder calculates that when a country allows the United States to create a new base on its territory, military and economic aid to that country increase by an average of 218 percent and 164 percent, respectively, over the first two years of the base's existence. After the creation of a base in Uzbekistan in 2001, U.S. military aid jumped from $2.9 million to $37.1 million the following year; economic aid leaped from $62.3 million to $167.3 million. (By contrast, when a country forces a U.S. base to close, military and economic aid decline during the first two years after closure by an average of 41 and 30 percent.)[37]

Calder's research illustrates just how expensive gaining access to bases can be. Because his calculations are based on a small sample and because I prefer to err on the conservative side, I instead use an estimate from James Blaker, a former deputy assistant secretary of defense. Using Pentagon and other government data, Blaker calculates that around 18 percent of total foreign military and economic aid—subtracting Agency for International Development (USAID) funding—goes to buying base access.[38] Given $31.5 billion in aid in 2012,[39] this adds around $5.7 billion to total overseas costs.

On the other side of the accounting ledger, the OCS also omits cash payments the United States receives from countries such as Japan, Kuwait, and South Korea that help sustain U.S. bases on their territory. Budget documents from 2012 indicate the U.S. government received $889 million in "burden-sharing" payments and $225 million in "host nation support" for the relocation of bases—totaling approximately $1.1 billion paid for the U.S. overseas presence that year.[40] Some countries also provide in-kind contributions of utilities and services rather than cash payments, but such contributions are not income received by the United States, so I have excluded them from these calculations.[41]

Aside from U.S. "rent" expenditures and "burden-sharing" receipts, the OCS also omits U.S. spending on the North Atlantic Treaty Organization (NATO). During fiscal year 2012, the Pentagon budget included $247.6 million for U.S. contributions to the NATO Security Investment Program, which went toward "the acquisition and construction of military facilities and installations (including international military head-quarters) and for related expenses for the collective defense of the North Atlantic Treaty Area."[42] The Pentagon also paid $3 million for the U.S. military mission to NATO in Belgium,[43] while the Army, Navy, and Air Force spent a combined $533.7 million to support NATO and to provide "miscellaneous support to other nations."[44] And the United States contributed $889 million of its own burden-sharing payments to support NATO member countries and other allies.[45]

In sum, $5.7 billion in estimated quasirental payments and $1.7 billion in NATO contributions, weighed against $1.1 billion in receipts from other countries, yields *$6.3 billion in NATO expenditures and net "rent."*

COMBATANT COMMANDS

The OCS also appears to overlook operations and maintenance funds and other spending that go directly to the Pentagon's cross-service Unified Combatant Commands.[46] Six of those commands—Africa, Central, European, Northern, Pacific, and Southern—divide the globe among them, and all of them operate in whole or in part overseas. So do the Special Operations and Transportation Commands.

The Northern Command mainly focuses on the continental United States, but it also patrols parts of Mexico, the Gulf of Mexico, the Caribbean, Canada, and the Arctic. Conservatively estimating that 5 percent of the Northern Command's budget[47] and half of funding for the other seven commands go to operations abroad adds an estimated *$2.8 billion in funding for the combatant commands overseas operations.*[48]

COUNTERNARCOTICS, HUMANITARIAN, AND ENVIRONMENTAL PROGRAMS; OVERSEAS RESEARCH

Although the OCS must report the costs of *all* military operations overseas, I confirmed with the Pentagon that it omits around $550 million for counternarcotics operations.[49] It also excludes the money spent on humanitarian and civic aid. Some of the humanitarian aid can be considered truly nonmilitary, but as a budget document explains, humanitarian operations crucially help "maintain a robust overseas presence" and obtain "access to regions important to U.S. interests."[50] Again erring on the conservative side, I include only half of the humanitarian spending in my calculations, which adds $54 million. The Pentagon also spent $24 million on environmental projects abroad to monitor and reduce its on-base pollution, to dispose of hazardous and other waste, and for "initiatives . . . in support of global basing/operations."[51]

The military also maintains a large collection of research laboratories overseas. Given the CIA's use of a fake childhood vaccination campaign to help locate and kill Osama bin Laden, it is doubtful that all these research activities are purely scientific. At the very least, they constitute another way the Pentagon builds military-to-military ties, gains influence, and broadens the U.S. military presence abroad.

Funding for these labs is hard to find within the overall Pentagon budget, but the Cooperative Biological Engagement program offers one visible example. This $259 million program builds and operates labs and other activities to counter the threat of biological weapons in countries such as Afghanistan, Azerbaijan, and Burundi.[52] While some of this program's funding seems to be spent domestically, any overestimate here is likely offset by harder-to-locate funding for other overseas labs. The bill now grows by *$887 million for counternarcotics, humanitarian, and environmental programs, and overseas research.*

CLASSIFIED PROGRAMS, MILITARY INTELLIGENCE, AND CIA PARAMILITARY ACTIVITIES

Not surprisingly, the Pentagon tally omits the cost of secret bases and classified programs overseas. In 2012, the Pentagon's classified budget was estimated at $51 billion.[53] Applying the OCS methodology, I focused on the operations and maintenance spending portion of that total, which was estimated at $15.8 billion.[54] As elsewhere, I conservatively estimate the overseas portion of that spending at 15 percent (the percentage of base sites overseas), adding $2.4 billion to the cost of bases abroad. Since classified spending is more likely to take place overseas than domestically, this is almost surely an underestimate.

Then there's the $21.5 billion Military Intelligence Program.[55] Given that U.S. law generally bars the military from engaging in domestic spying (NSA revelations notwithstanding), I estimate that half this spending—$10.8 billion—took place overseas.

Since the onset of the war on terror, CIA paramilitary activities have grown dramatically.[56] These activities have included the creation of secret bases in places such as Pakistan, Somalia, Libya, and elsewhere in the Middle East, as well as the CIA's drone assassination program.[57] In short, the intelligence agency has become a major war fighting force. With thousands killed by CIA operations, it only makes sense to consider its expenditures as military costs. In the fiscal year 2013 black budget, released by the *Washington Post*, the CIA received $2.6 billion for "covert action," which would include the drone program and other paramilitary operations abroad, and about $2.5 billion for its war operations.[58] Because adding these two figures may double-count some spending, I use only half of the "covert action" costs. In total, this yields *$17 billion for classified programs, military intelligence, and CIA paramilitary activities.*

THE TOTAL BILL

Having started with the OCS figure of $22.6 billion, my total now reaches $71.8 billion, which is more than three times the Pentagon's calculation. Given my very conservative estimates, the true total could easily be much higher. For example, the Pentagon never replied to my inquiries asking whether all the costs of Department of Defense schools overseas are included in the OCS. If they are not, school costs could add more than $1.3 billion more to my total.[59]

Far more significantly, my $71.8 billion calculation does not include the costs of maintaining bases and troops in war zones such as Afghanistan and Iraq. Congress instructs the OCS to exclude all of the costs of maintaining bases and personnel overseas if those costs are funded by war appropriations, which appear in a separate annual Overseas Contingency Operations budget. On the other hand, one could argue that the *entire* war budget should be counted: after all, war spending crucially helps maintain the physical security and political legitimacy of U.S. bases in Afghanistan, Iraq, and beyond. Calculating the overseas base expenses without including the immense costs of the "contingency operations" revolving around those bases is a bit like setting up a family budget without accounting for the cost of a luxury vacation beachfront rental, or discussing the finances of the New York Yankees while excluding the cost of the team's big free-agent signings.

Still, in determining how much war spending has supported bases and military personnel overseas, I stuck with the OCS methodology. I excluded funding for procurement, research, and similar activities, and focused on the costs of military personnel, operations and maintenance, military construction, and health care. Those costs represent approximately 75 percent of the total war budget.[60] Using data for fiscal year 2012 to match the other calculations in this chapter, I applied that percentage to Congress's $107.5 billion in war appropriations for Afghanistan and the final months of the U.S. occupation of Iraq. This yields an estimated $80.6 billion in additional war spending.[61]

The official $107.5 billion war appropriations figure for fiscal year 2012 is itself arguably a significant underestimate. There are many other costs of war that Congress does not include in the Overseas Contingency Operations budget, including medical and disability care for veterans, interest payments on past appropriations, and perhaps even additions to the Department of Homeland Security budget necessitated by the increased threat of terrorist attacks launched in response to U.S. military actions. Using numbers provided by Brown University's Costs of War project, such considerations might have brought the actual war spending total to almost $130 billion in 2012 alone.[62] Future costs for veterans' medical and disability care would bring the total even higher.

To err again on the conservative side, I have not included these unacknowledged expenses in my calculation. However, my $80.6 billion figure is also incomplete in another way: war funding only pays for "incremental" costs, above those found in the normal Pentagon budget. So I also had to account for war zone troops' basic salaries and other personnel costs, which I calculated at around $14.3 billion (employing a widely used $125,000 per troop per year cost estimate). I also found another $74.9 million in "Wounded Warrior Care" health costs tucked away in the Pentagon budget.[63] Finally, I calculated almost $2 billion in "rental" costs—in the form of military and economic aid—for bases in Afghanistan and Iraq, using the previously detailed methodology from James Blaker.[64]

With those additions, my estimate of war zone costs for 2012—including appropriations for military construction and maintenance, troop salaries, and so on—was $97 billion. My estimate for the total costs to maintain U.S. bases and troops around the globe—both within war zones and outside them—thus reached some $170 billion for fiscal year 2012.

CALCULATING THE COSTS OF U.S. MILITARY BASES AND U.S. MILITARY PRESENCE ABROAD

PENTAGON TOTAL AND OMITTED SPENDING	TOTAL
Pentagon "Overseas Cost Summary" Total	$22,670,400,000
Missing Countries	435,404,000
Territories, Possessions, and Pacific Island Nations*	3,181,672,562
Navy Outside U.S. Waters; Pre-positioning; Sealift, Airlift, and Mobilization	5,244,562,000
Health Care, Military/Family Housing Construction, PX, Postal Subsidies	13,403,114,900
"Rent" Payments and NATO Contributions (Less Funds from Other Nations*)	6,230,063,000
Combatant Commands Funding	2,844,743,150
Counternarcotics, Humanitarian, Environmental, and Research Programs	887,628,000
Classified Programs, Military Intelligence, and CIA Paramilitary Activities	16,875,558,250
TOTAL	$71,773,145,862
Additional Costs in War Budget (Operations and Maintenance, Military Construction, Personnel)	$96,996,568,660
TOTAL (Including War Budget Costs)	$168,769,714,522

All data FY2012 unless indicated by * when the most recent data are from 2004, 2008, or 2011.

Since 2012, Pentagon spending has fallen somewhat, due to the end of U.S. operations in Iraq, the gradual withdrawal of troops from Afghanistan, and Congress's sequestration process. Accounting for those declines and adjusting my estimate for the latest complete fiscal year, 2014, yields an estimate of $64.4 billion for the costs of bases and troops abroad outside war zones. Adding the costs of bases and troops in Afghanistan and other war zones would bring the total to around $136 billion for 2014.

Even if one excludes spending on the war in Afghanistan from the final bill for the base nation, there seems little reason to ignore billions of dollars in war funding that has actually gone to funding bases, troops, and regular operations in countries other than Afghanistan, including places in the Persian Gulf, Central Asia, Africa, Europe, and elsewhere. In recent years, the Pentagon has increasingly used war budgets to evade spending caps on its regular "base" budget imposed by sequestration's Budget Control Act. In fiscal year 2014, for example, at least $19.9 billion funded "in-theater support" *outside* Afghanistan.[65] Adding that figure to my $64.4 billion estimate for 2014 shows that, at a minimum, the full cost of maintaining bases and troops overseas that year was some $85 billion.

Plus, there's more spending for which I couldn't account. In addition to money surely hidden in the nooks and crannies of the budget, there are Pentagon expenses that clearly support overseas bases but are too difficult to estimate reliably. Examples include the cost of offices and personnel who are supporting bases and troops overseas but who are located at the Pentagon itself, in embassies, and in other government agencies. Overseas bases also make use of (and thus incur expenses for) training facilities, depots, hospitals, and even cemeteries in the United States. Other costs could include the costs of Coast Guard operations overseas; foreign currency exchange fees; attorneys' fees and damages won in lawsuits against military personnel abroad; short-term "temporary duty assignments" overseas; U.S.-based troops participating in overseas exercises; some of NASA's military functions; the Pentagon's space-based weapons; a percentage of recruiting costs required to staff bases abroad; interest paid on the debt attributable to the past costs of overseas bases; and Veterans Administration costs and other retirement spending for military personnel who worked abroad.

Even with recent reductions in military spending, the annual cost to taxpayers to maintain bases and troops overseas in coming years could easily reach $100 billion or more given the conservative nature of my calculations and the Pentagon's use of war budgets to fund nonwar activities. At these levels, if Pentagon spending abroad were its own government agency, it would have a larger discretionary budget than every other federal agency except the Department of Defense itself. Including the costs of maintaining bases and troops in war zones of Afghanistan and Iraq could bring the base nation's total bill to $160–$200 billion—which is two to three times the size of the discretionary budget of the Department of Education, for example.[66]

SPILLOVER COSTS

We also have to remember that these estimates represent just direct costs to the U.S. government's budget. The total costs to the U.S. economy of keeping bases and military forces abroad are even higher. Consider where the (taxpayer-funded) salaries of troops go when they eat or drink at a local restaurant or bar, buy clothing, or rent a home in Germany, Italy, or Japan. These are what economists call "spillover" or "multiplier effects." When I visited Okinawa in 2010, Marine Corps representatives bragged how their presence contributes $1.9 billion to the local economy through base contracts, jobs, local purchases, and other spending. While there are reasons to be skeptical about the accuracy of this particular figure (for example, a considerable portion of marines' economic impact comes from Japanese government rental payments and subsidies), the scale of the impact makes it easy to understand why some members of Congress want to bring overseas bases home, where more of that spending would go into the economies of their districts and states instead.[67]

The true costs of the base world are even higher when one considers the trade-offs, or opportunity costs, involved. Military spending creates fewer jobs per billion dollars expended than the same billion dollars invested in education, health care, or energy efficiency—less than half as many jobs as investing in schools, for example.[68] Even worse, while military spending provides direct benefits to military contractors such as Lockheed Martin and KBR, these investments don't boost long-run economic productivity the way infrastructure investments do.[69]

In 1953, President Dwight Eisenhower famously said,

> Every gun that is made, every warship launched, every rocket fired signifies, in the final sense, a theft from those who hunger and are not fed, those who are cold and are not clothed. This world in arms is not spending money alone. It is spending the sweat of its laborers, the genius of its scientists, the hopes of its children. The cost of one modern heavy bomber is this:
>
> A modern brick school in more than 30 cities.
> It is two electric power plants, each serving a town of 60,000 population.
> It is two fine, fully equipped hospitals.
> It is some 50 miles of concrete highway.
> We pay for a single fighter with a half million bushels of wheat.
> We pay for a single destroyer with new homes that could have housed more than 8,000 people.[70]

So, too, every base that is built overseas signifies a theft from American society. Reallocating the $75 billion to $100 billion in total annual expenditures on overseas bases would allow the country to roughly double federal education spending, for example. Today, Eisenhower might say the cost of one modern base is this:

> A college scholarship for a year for 63,000 students.
> It is 295,000 households with renewable solar energy for one year.
> It is 260,000 low-income children getting health care for one year.
> It is 63,000 children getting a year of Head Start.
> It is 64,000 veterans receiving health care for a year.
> It is 7,200 police officers for one year.[71]

Meanwhile, the costs to host countries are also steep. They include financial expenses, like the money spent cleaning environmental damage, soundproofing homes, and paying damages for crimes committed by U.S. troops.[72] They also include, as we have seen, nonfinancial forms of spillover, ranging from environmental damage to the support offered for repressive governments to sexual assault and rape. These, in turn, impose on the United States and its citizens what the economist Dancs calls the "costs of rising hostility," reckoned in the damage done to the country's international reputation and its standing in the world.

From the billions of dollars wasted to the human costs that can't be quantified, we all pay. The question that remains, then, is who's benefiting from all this spending?

KBR employees preparing food for troops, Camp Fallujah, Iraq, November 2008.

Lance Corporal Grant Walker, U.S. Marine Corps

12

"We're Profiteers"

"You whore it out to a contractor," Major Tim Elliott said bluntly. It was April 2012, and I was at a swank hotel in downtown London attending "Forward Operating Bases 2012," a conference for contractors building, supplying, and maintaining military bases around the world. IPQC, the private company running the conference, had promised that the conference would be "attended by senior officials and decision-makers from industry worldwide" and "bring together buyers and suppliers in one location." It was pitched as "an excellent platform to initiate new business relationships" through "face-to-face contact that overcrowded trade shows cannot deliver."[1] Companies sending representatives included major contractors such as General Dynamics and the food services company Supreme Group, which has won billions in Afghan war contracts, as well as smaller companies such as QinetiQ, which produces acoustic sensors and other monitoring devices used on bases. "We're profiteers," one contractor representative said to the audience in passing, with only a touch of irony.

Aside from the corporate representatives, a few officers from NATO member militaries were on hand to speak. Major Elliott, of the Royal Scots Brigades, had offered his stark "whore it out" assessment while explaining how to build a military base that allows a base commander to "forget the base itself"—that is, the work of running the place—and instead maximize his effectiveness outside the base walls.[2]

Of course, Elliott said, in wartime you won't get contractors to run a base without "a shitload of money." And at times, he said, vast amounts of "time, effort, and resources" are expended "just to keep a base running." In Afghanistan, Elliott said, he saw situations so bad that on one base there were private security guards protecting privately contracted cooks, who were cooking for the same private security guards ... who were protecting the privately contracted cooks ... who were cooking for the private security guards ... and so on it went.

After an extensive examination of government spending data and contracts, my calculations show that just from late 2001 (when the war in Afghanistan began) to 2013, the Pentagon has disbursed around $385 billion in taxpayer-funded contracts to private companies for work outside the United States. Most of this money has gone to overseas bases. And while some of the contracts are for nonbase items such as weapons procurement, the thousands of contracts believed to be omitted from these tallies thanks to accounting errors make the entire $385 billion figure a reasonable reflection of the funds flowing to private contractors to support the country's global base collection. Indeed, because of the Pentagon's poor accounting practices and the secrecy surrounding military budgets, the true total may be significantly higher.

Almost a third of the total—more than $115 billion—was concentrated among the top ten corporate recipients alone. Many of the names scoring the biggest profits are familiar: the former Halliburton subsidiary Kellogg Brown & Root, the private security company DynCorp, and BP. Others are less well known: Agility, Fluor, Bahrain Petroleum Company. The complete list includes major transnational construction firms, large food service providers, the world's biggest oil corporations, and thousands upon thousands of smaller companies receiving government contracts.

All this base spending has been marked by spiraling expenditures, the increased awarding of noncompetitive contracts (and contracts lacking incentives to control costs), and outright fraud. Even companies with well-established histories of fraud and abuse have repeatedly been awarded noncompetitive sweetheart contracts. Financial irregularities have been so common that any attempt to document the misappropriation of taxpayer funds at overseas bases would be a mammoth effort. The Commission on Wartime Contracting, which Congress established to investigate waste and abuse, has estimated that there has been $31 billion to $60 billion in contracting fraud in the Afghanistan and Iraq Wars alone, with most of it involving bases in and around the two countries.[3] In Singapore, at least four Navy officials have recently been charged with receiving bribes—in the form of cash, gifts, and sexual services—in exchange for providing a contractor with inside information and helping to inflate the company's billing. Globally, billions of dollars are likely wasted or misused every year.

Proponents of outsourcing the work of building, running, and supplying bases overseas argue that contractors save the government and taxpayers money, and that, as Major Elliott suggested, they allow the military to focus on its combat duties. But research suggests that this is often not the case. On base and off, contractors tend to provide services at higher costs than the military itself.[4] Around the globe, military bases have become an important source of corporate profit making, diverting hundreds of billions of taxpayer dollars from domestic needs.

PEELING POTATOES AND BRINGING HOME THE BACON

Once upon a time, the military, not contractors, built and ran U.S. bases. Soldiers, sailors, marines, airmen, and airwomen built the barracks, cleaned the clothes, and peeled the potatoes. But this started changing during the Vietnam War, when Brown & Root began building major military installations in South Vietnam as part of a contractor consortium. Brown & Root enjoyed deep ties with President Lyndon Johnson dating back to the 1930s, leading to well-founded suspicions that Johnson personally steered contracts to the company.[5]

The use of contractors grew as the war in Vietnam continued. Amid nationwide resistance to the draft, contractors were one way to solve the military's labor problem, which became permanent with the end of conscription in 1973. In the era of the all-volunteer force, hiring contractors reduced the need for the military to recruit new troops. Instead, it passed the labor problem to the contractors, who have frequently searched the globe for the cheapest possible workers. Often, these have been Filipinos and other non-U.S. citizens from formerly colonized parts of the world who are willing to work for much less than uniformed troops. By recruiting foreign workers, the government and contractors could also often avoid paying for the health care, retirement, and other benefits provided to U.S. troops. A general trend toward the privatization of government services only accelerated this trend in the military.

Without forced conscription, the military was also under pressure to retain recruits once they joined. Keeping troops and their families happy with a growing array of comforts played an important part in retaining the military's labor force. Especially at bases abroad, military leaders sought to mitigate the challenges of overseas tours with a generally cushier lifestyle than troops could afford at home. As time passed, troops, families, and, importantly, politicians came to expect elevated—and ever rising—living standards not just at peacetime bases, but also in war zones. To deliver this lifestyle, the military would pay contractors with increasing generosity.

During the first Gulf War in 1991, one out of every hundred deployed personnel was a contractor. Later in the 1990s, during military operations in Somalia, Rwanda, Haiti, Saudi Arabia, Kuwait, and especially the Balkans, Brown & Root received more than $2 billion in base support and logistics contracts, covering construction and maintenance, food services, waste removal, water production, transportation services, and much more.[6] In the Balkans alone, Brown & Root built thirty-four bases. The largest, Camp Bondsteel in Kosovo, covered 955 acres and included two gyms, two movie theaters, extensive dining and entertainment facilities, coffee bars, and a PX for shopping. Speaking of off-duty soldiers, a U.S. Army representative told USA Today, "We need to get these guys pumping iron and licking ice cream cones, whatever they want to do." By contrast, military personnel from other NATO countries lived in existing apartments and factories.[7]

By the second Gulf War, contractors represented roughly half of all deployed personnel in Iraq. Brown & Root, now known as KBR, employed more than fifty thousands people in the war zone—the equivalent of five divisions or one hundred army battalions.[8] For most in the military, the days of peeling potatoes are long gone.

CONTRACTS, CONTRACTS, CONTRACTS

Figuring out who has been profiting from this increasingly comfortable military lifestyle has not been easy. Because the government does not compile many aggregated lists of contract winners, I had to pick through hundreds of thousands of individual records from publicly available data and research scores of companies worldwide. With these lists in hand, I adopted the methodology for tracking funds used by the Commission on Wartime Contracting.[9] Ultimately, for the period between October 2001 and May 2013, I put together a list of every Pentagon contract with a "place of performance"—that is, the country where most of a contract's work is performed—outside the United States.

There were 1.7 million of them.

Generally, the companies winning the largest contracts were those providing one or more of five things: construction, operations and maintenance, food, fuel, and security. Scrolling through all 1.7 million rows (more than can be handled by a single Microsoft Excel spreadsheet) offered a dizzying feel for the immensity of the Pentagon's activities and the amount of money being spent worldwide. The breadth was remarkable. There was one contract for $43 for sand in South Korea, another for a $1.7 million fitness center in Honduras. There was $23,000 for sports drinks in Kuwait, $53 million in base support services in Afghanistan, and everything from $73 in pens to $301 million for army industrial supplies in Iraq.

Cheek by jowl I found the most basic services, the most banal purchases, and the most ominous acquisitions. The Pentagon paid contractors for concrete sidewalks, a traffic light system, diesel fuel, insect fogger, showerheads, black toner, a 59-inch desk, a 50-inch plasma screen, unskilled laborers, chaplain supplies, linen for "distinguished visitor" rooms, easy chairs, gym equipment, flamenco dancers, and the rental of six sedans. There were funds for phone cards, billiards cues, Xbox 360 games and accessories, Slushie machine parts, and a hot dog roller. There were payments for scallops, shrimp, strawberries, asparagus, and toaster pastries, as well as for hazardous waste services, a burn pit, ammo and clips, bomb disposal services, confinement buildings, and blackout goggles for detainees.

Not surprisingly, given the recent wars, contractors have won the most taxpayer dollars in Afghanistan and Iraq. With more than thirteen hundred installations between the two countries, corporations received around $160 billion in contracts there between 2001 and 2013. In Kuwait, which hosted hundreds of thousands of troops deploying to

Iraq, corporations enjoyed $37.2 billion in contracts. The next four countries where contractors have secured the most money are those that have generally been home to the largest numbers of bases and troops since World War II: Germany ($27.8 billion in contracts), South Korea ($18.2 billion), Japan ($15.2 billion), and the United Kingdom ($14.7 billion).[10]

Given a federal data system that has been called "dysfunctional," the real totals are almost surely higher.[11] Black budgets and CIA contracts for paramilitary activities could also add tens of billions of dollars in overseas base spending.[12]

Even the data that have been recorded and made available are unreliable and opaque. This is highlighted by the fact that the top recipient of Pentagon contracts abroad is not a company at all, but "miscellaneous foreign contractors."[13] In other words, almost a quarter of a million contracts, totaling $47.1 billion—some 12 percent of the total—have gone to recipients that the Pentagon has not identified publicly. As the Commission on Wartime Contracting explains, "miscellaneous foreign contractors" is a catchall "often used for the purpose of obscuring the identification of the actual contractor."[14]

Complicated subcontracting arrangements, the use of foreign subsidiaries, frequent corporate name changes, and the general lack of corporate transparency make identifying the value of contracts received by specific companies yet more difficult. But in general, a troubling pattern emerges: the majority of benefits have gone to a relatively small group of private contractors. Indeed, almost a third of the $385 billion spent around the world has gone to just ten contractors. Putting aside the "miscellaneous foreign contractors" topping the list, it's helpful to examine the top recipients in some detail.

KBR

Among the contracting companies bringing home billions, Kellogg, Brown & Root dominates. It has almost five times the contracts of the next company on the list, and it is emblematic of broader problems in the contracting system.

KBR is the latest incarnation of Brown & Root, the company that built U.S. military installations during the Vietnam War. From its

TOP 25 RECIPIENTS OF PENTAGON CONTRACTS ABROAD

CONTRACT AWARDEE	TOTAL IN BILLIONS
1. Miscellaneous Foreign Contractors	$47.1
2. KBR, Inc.	44.4
3. Supreme Group	9.3
4. Agility Logistics (PWC)	9.0
5. DynCorp International	8.6
6. Fluor Intercontinental	8.6
7. ITT/Exelis, Inc.	7.4
8. BP, PLC	5.6
9. Bahrain Petroleum Company	5.1
10. Abu Dhabi Petroleum Company	4.5
11. SK Corporation	3.8
12. Red Star Enterprises (Mina Corporation)	3.8
13. World Fuel Services Corporation	3.8
14. Motor Oil (Hellas), Corinth Refineries S.A.	3.7
15. Combat Support Associates Ltd.	3.6
16. Refinery Associates Texas, Inc.	3.3
17. Lockheed Martin Corporation	3.2
18. Raytheon Company	3.1
19. S-Oil Corporation (Ssangyong)	3.0
20. International Oil Trading Co./Trigeant Ltd.	2.7
21. FedEx Corporation	2.2
22. Contrack International, Inc.	2.0
23. GS/LG-Caltex (Chevron Corporation)	1.9
24. Washington Group/URS Corporation	1.6
25. Tutor Perini Corporation (Perini)	1.5
SUBTOTAL	$201.8
All Other Contractors:	$183.4
TOTAL	$385.2

Note: Numbers may not add up due to rounding.

beginnings in 1919, when it got its start paving roads in Texas, Brown & Root eventually grew into the largest engineering and construction firm in the United States. In 1962, it was bought by Halliburton, an international oil services company. Dick Cheney, who helped significantly increase the Pentagon's reliance on private contractors when he was President George H. W. Bush's secretary of defense, became Halliburton's president and CEO in 1995. During the five years when Cheney ran the company, KBR, as it was now known, won $2.3 billion in U.S. military contracts—compared to $1.2 billion in the previous five years.[15]

Later, when Cheney was vice president of the United States, Halliburton and its KBR subsidiary won by far the largest wartime contracts in Iraq and Afghanistan. It is difficult to overstate KBR's role in the two conflicts. Without its work, there might have been no wars. In 2005, Paul Cerjan, a former Halliburton vice president, explained that KBR was supporting more than two hundred thousand coalition forces in Iraq, providing "anything they need to conduct the war." That meant "base support services, which includes all the billeting, the feeding, water supplies, sewage—anything it would take to run a city." It also meant taking care of Army "logistics functions, which include transportation, movement of POL [petroleum, oil, and lubricants] supplies, gas supplies . . . spare parts, ammunition," and more.[16]

Most of KBR's contracts to support bases and troops overseas have come under the multibillion-dollar Logistics Civilian Augmentation Program, known as LOGCAP. In 2001, KBR won a one-year LOGCAP contract to provide an undefined quantity and an undefined value of "selected services in wartime." Thanks to a series of one-year contract extensions, the company then enjoyed nearly eight years of work without facing a competitor's bid. Overall, between 2001 and 2010, the number of Pentagon contracts issued without competitive bidding nearly tripled. "It's like a gigantic monopoly," a representative from Taxpayers for Common Sense said of LOGCAP.[17]

The work KBR performed under LOGCAP also reflected the Pentagon's frequent use of "cost-plus" contracts. These reimburse a company for its expenses and then add a percentage of the costs on top of that as the company's fee. In other words, as the Congressional Research Service explains, "increased costs mean increased fees to the contractor," and therefore there is "no incentive for the contractor to limit the government's costs."[18] As one Halliburton official bluntly told a congressional committee, the company's unofficial mantra in Iraq became, "Don't worry about price. It's 'cost-plus.'"[19]

In 2009, the Pentagon's top auditor testified that KBR accounted for "the vast majority" of wartime fraud.[20] The company has faced accusations of overcharging for everything from delivering food and fuel to providing housing for troops and base security services.[21] This shouldn't have been a surprise: back in 2006, Halliburton/KBR paid $8 million to the government to settle lawsuits charging double billing, inflating prices, and other fraud connected to its work at Camp Bondsteel in Kosovo.[22]

After years of bad publicity, in 2007, Halliburton spun KBR off as an independent company and moved its own headquarters from Houston to Dubai. But despite KBR's track record, which includes a 2009 guilty plea for bribing Nigerian government officials to win gas contracts, the company has continued to receive massive Pentagon money. Its latest LOGCAP contract could be worth up to $50 billion through 2018.[23]

In early 2014, the Justice Department sued KBR and two subcontractors for exchanging kickbacks and filing false reimbursement claims for costs "that allegedly were inflated, excessive or for goods and services that were grossly deficient or not provided." The suit also charged KBR with transporting ice for troops' consumption in unsanitized trailers previously used as temporary morgues.[24]

SUPREME GROUP

Next on the list of top Pentagon contractors is the company that has been described as the "KBR for the Afghan War." Supreme Group has won well over $9 billion in contracts for transporting and serving meals to troops and supplying fuel at bases in Afghanistan and other countries worldwide.[25] The company's growth perfectly symbolizes the soldiers-to-contractors shift in who peels the potatoes.

Supreme was founded in 1957 by an Army veteran, Alfred Ornstein, who saw an opportunity to provide food for the hundreds of growing U.S. bases in Germany. After expanding over several decades into the Middle

East, Africa, and the Balkans, the company won multibillion-dollar "sole source contracts" that gave it a virtual monopoly over wartime food services in Afghanistan. In the decade since the start of the war in 2001, the company's revenues grew more than fiftyfold to $5.5 billion. Its profit margins in 2008–2011 ranged between 18 and 23 percent. Wartime contracts account for 90 percent of revenues for the company, which, like KBR, is now based in Dubai. They have made its majority owner, the founder's son, Stephen Ornstein, a billionaire.

Supreme's chief commercial officer, the former Army lieutenant general Robert Dail, provides a prime example of the revolving door between the Pentagon and its contractors. From August 2006 to November 2008, Dail headed the Pentagon's Defense Logistics Agency, which awards the Pentagon's food contracts. In 2007, Dail presented Supreme with DLA's "New Contractor of the Year Award." Four months after leaving the Pentagon, he became the president of Supreme Group USA.

The Pentagon now says Supreme overbilled the military by $757 million. Others have started to scrutinize how the company won competition-free contracts and charged service fees as high as 75 percent of costs. Supreme, for its part, denies overcharging and instead claims the government owes it $1.8 billion. In 2013, Supreme sued the Pentagon for awarding a new $10 billion Afghanistan food contract to a competitor that underbid Supreme's offer by $1.4 billion. The lawsuit failed.[26]

AGILITY LOGISTICS

After Supreme comes Agility Logistics, a Kuwaiti company formerly known as Public Warehousing Company KSC and PWC Logistics. It won multibillion-dollar contracts to transport food to troops in Iraq. When the Pentagon decided against awarding similar contracts in Afghanistan to a single firm, Agility partnered with Supreme in exchange for a 3.5 percent fee on revenues. Like Supreme, Agility hired a former high-ranking Defense Logistics Agency official, Major General Dan Mongeon, who now serves as its U.S. president of defense and government services. He joined the company just months after it won its second multibillion-dollar contract from DLA, where Mongeon was director of operations.[27]

In 2009 and 2010, grand juries indicted Agility on criminal charges for $6 billion in false claims and price manipulation.[28] In 2011, a grand jury subpoenaed Mongeon as part of investigations into new charges against Agility.[29] With the litigation ongoing, the Pentagon suspended the company and 125 related companies from receiving new contracts. Agility, in turn, has filed a $225 million suit against the DLA for breach of contract. But strangely, the Army and the DLA have continued to do business with Agility, extending contracts on at least seven occasions via "compelling reason" determinations that override the company's suspension.[30]

THE REST OF THE TOP TEN: A PATTERN OF MISCONDUCT

Things do not get much better farther down the list. DynCorp International and Fluor Intercontinental, the next two companies in the top ten, won the latest LOGCAP contracts along with KBR. Awarding this work to three companies rather than one was intended to increase competition. In practice, according to the Commission on Wartime Contracting, each corporation has enjoyed a "mini-monopoly" over logistics services in Afghanistan and other locations. DynCorp, which has also won large wartime private security contracts, has a history littered with charges of overbilling, shoddy construction, smuggling laborers onto bases, sexual harassment, and sex trafficking. Meanwhile, a Fluor employee pleaded guilty in 2012 to conspiring to steal and sell military equipment in Iraq.

On the positive side, Fluor is the only defense firm in the world to receive an A on Transparency International's anticorruption index, which rates companies' efforts to fight corruption. On the other hand, ITT/Exelis, number seven on the list, received a C for its anticorruption efforts. So did KBR and DynCorp.[31]

Rounding out the Top Ten list are BP (which tops the Project on Government Oversight's federal contractor misconduct list)[32] and the petroleum companies of Bahrain and the United Arab Emirates. In total, ten of the top twenty-five firms are oil companies, with contracts for delivering oil overseas totaling more than $37 billion. The military consumed five billion gallons of oil in fiscal year 2011 alone.[33]

The Pentagon and the government generally justify the use of so many contractors based on their supposed efficiency, but reality appears to be the opposite. Research shows that contractors cost two to three times as much as Pentagon civilians doing the same work. More than half of Army contracts go to administrative overhead rather than contract services.[34] Military comptrollers acknowledge that when it comes to the use of contractors, "growth has been unchallenged."

"The savings are here," the comptrollers conclude.[35]

PERKS AS PATRIOTISM

Among the speakers at the Forward Operating Bases 2012 (FOB2012) conference in London was U.S. Marine Corps Major Patrick Reynolds. After talking about an energy-saving forward operating base that the Marines are experimenting with, Reynolds ended his presentation by alerting the contractors to a list of upcoming contract opportunities. "RFP to be posted on FEDBIZOPPS soon!" read one of his PowerPoint slides, referring to the website advertising government procurement opportunities.

"I know you guys from the industry pay a lot to be here," Reynolds said. So he thought it was right to offer some "food for thought [to] give you something to walk away with" from the conference. Suddenly there was a noticeable surge in energy in the room. People sat up in their chairs, and for the first time during his talk, many in the audience began taking notes on their mostly blank notepads.

Equally telling was Reynolds's explanation of how bases tend to expand dramatically over time. "You start out small" with an outpost, he said, "thinking you'll only be there for a week . . . And then it's two weeks. And then it's a month. And then it's two months." In the process, bases add facilities, fancier food, and recreational amenities: steak and lobster, flat screen TVs, and Internet connections. The major said he and others in the military refer to these comforts collectively as "ice cream."

Right now, he told the audience, "there's no 'ice cream'" at small outposts. It's just at headquarters and forward operating bases. "But eventually you'll get to the point where it's out" at the outposts, too, he said. "It's a building block process."

The process Major Reynolds described is precisely what happened on bases in and around Afghanistan and Iraq. According to a Congressional Research Service report, the Pentagon "built up a far more extensive infrastructure than anticipated to support troops and equipment." Funds for the operation and maintenance of bases, including food and amenities, grew three times as fast as the number of deployed troops would suggest.[36]

During a Q&A session, a Supreme Group representative asked Reynolds if the Marines were thinking about cutting back on the TVs and the other amenities.

I'd love to do that, the major replied. Is it going to happen? "Sort of, kind of, not really . . . Do we need ice cream? Do we need cable TVs? Do we need high-speed Internet and all the crap? No," he said. But there are senators and congressmen coming out and "visiting their constituents and they want to help." Reynolds paused. "That's probably all I'll say on that."

Reynolds's circumspect phrasing pointed to some of the political players shaping the base world. In Afghanistan and Iraq, congressmembers have used base amenities as a public way to demonstrate their patriotism and support for the troops. One former soldier told me his reaction to arriving at Iraq's Camp Liberty was, "This is awesome!" Like thousands of others, he found comfortable rooms, beds, and amenities that eventually included unrestricted Internet access, thanks to a favor from a KBR contractor. "It was really plush," he said. "It was dope." Later, he admitted, "I felt ashamed it wasn't harder."

The perks of the overseas base life are even greater for the generals and the admirals, who often enjoy personal assistants, chefs, vehicles, and private planes. And beyond such authorized perks, there are cases like that of the former Africa Command commander General William "Kip" Ward. Pentagon investigators found Ward "engaged in multiple forms of misconduct"—including billing the government for hundreds of thousands of dollars of personal travel and misusing government funds on luxury hotels, five-car motorcades, and spa and shopping trips for his wife. Ward also accepted free meals and tickets to a Broadway musical from an unnamed "construction management, engineering, technology and energy services company" with millions in Pentagon contracts.[37]

ELECTION DONATIONS

In addition to their illegal efforts to influence base contracting, contractors have also contributed millions of dollars to congressmembers' election campaigns. According to the Center for Responsive Politics, individuals and PACs linked to military contractors gave more than $27 million in election donations in 2012 alone and have donated almost $200 million since 1990.[38]

Most of these donations have gone to members of the committees on appropriations and armed services in the Senate and House of Representatives. These committees have most of the authority over awarding military dollars. For the 2012 elections, for example, Virginia-based DynCorp's political action committee donated the legal maximum of $10,000 to both the chair and ranking member of the House Armed Services Committee. It also made additional donations to thirty-three other members of the House and Senate Armed Services Committees and to sixteen members of the two appropriations committees.[39]

As they try to sway military budgeteers and policymakers, contractors also pay millions more to lobbyists. KBR and Halliburton spent nearly $5.5 million on lobbying between 2002 and 2012.[40] This included $420,000 in 2008, when KBR won the latest LOGCAP contract, and $620,000 the following year, when it protested being barred from bidding on contracts in Kuwait.[41] Supreme spent $660,000 on lobbying in 2012 alone.[42] Agility spent $200,000 in 2011, after its second indictment on fraud charges.[43] Fluor racked up nearly $9.5 million in lobbying fees from 2002 to 2012.[44] Overall, the ten leading military contractors spent more than $32 million on lobbying in 2001 alone.[45]

AVOIDING TAXES

While the contractors have enjoyed billions in taxpayer funds, many have sought to use both legal and illegal means to minimize U.S. taxes paid on their profits. Across the entire aerospace and military industry, the effective tax rate as of 2010 was just 10.6 percent, compared to the top federal statutory corporate tax rate of 35 percent and an average effective tax rate for large profitable U.S. companies of 12.6 percent.[46]

In 2004, the Government Accountability Office found that 27,100 Pentagon contractors—about one in nine—were illegally evading taxes while still receiving money from government contracts. Privacy rules prevented the government from naming names, but in one case a contractor providing base services owed almost $10 million in taxes while receiving $3.5 million from the Pentagon. The government estimated the total taxes owed by military contractors at $3 billion.[47]

In recent years, major military contractors have also increasingly created foreign-chartered subsidiaries to lower their taxes legally. At bases overseas, foreign companies frequently receive a significant proportion of base contracts, meaning these contractors legally pay little if any U.S. taxes at all. Some U.S. companies have taken advantage of this situation by creating foreign subsidiaries to do much of the work on base contracts abroad. KBR, for example, has avoided paying taxes on contracts in Iraq by using shell companies in the Cayman Islands that exist only as a name in a computer file. By technically hiring more than 21,000 of its employees via two Cayman subsidiaries, the company was able to avoid paying Social Security, Medicare, and Texas unemployment taxes.[48]

KBR officials claim that the practice saved the military money by allowing it to perform work more cheaply. But a *Boston Globe* investigation noted that the maneuver "results in a significantly greater loss in revenue to the government as a whole" while giving KBR a competitive advantage over companies that are not using the loophole.[49] The use of shell companies not only lowered KBR's contributions to the Social Security and Medicare trust funds, but also meant that its employees could not receive unemployment benefits if they lost their jobs because they were technically employed by a foreign corporation. Robert McIntyre, the director of the advocacy group Citizens for Tax Justice, told the *Globe*, "The argument that by not paying taxes they are saving the government money is just absurd."[50]

Similarly, when Halliburton spun off KBR as a separate company in 2007, the move of its corporate headquarters to Dubai was probably not unconnected to Dubai's lack of a corporate income tax and taxes on employee income. (Halliburton already had seventeen foreign subsidiaries in tax haven countries.) Although the company has remained legally incorporated in the United States, moving top executives to Dubai likely allowed Halliburton to avoid some employee payroll taxes and to reduce its corporate taxes by arguing that a portion of its global profits is attributable to work performed outside the United States.[51]

In general, under U.S. tax law, a U.S. firm with overseas operations can indefinitely postpone paying U.S. corporate tax on its foreign income by conducting its foreign operations through a foreign-chartered subsidiary. As long as the company's foreign earnings remain under the control of the subsidiary and are reinvested abroad, U.S. corporate income taxes are "deferred." The firm pays U.S. taxes on the overseas earnings of the subsidiary only when the parent company "repatriates" the earnings from the foreign subsidiary as intrafirm dividends or other income.[52] According to a 2012 J. P. Morgan study, U.S. multinational firms have over $1.7 trillion in foreign earnings "parked" overseas in this manner and thus shielded from U.S taxes.[53]

During a Government Accountability Office investigation, major military contractors admitted that "the use of offshore subsidiaries in foreign jurisdictions helps them lower their U.S. taxes. For example, one defense contractor's offshore subsidiary structure decreased its effective U.S. tax rate by approximately 1 percent, equaling millions of dollars in tax savings." Foreign subsidiaries also help protect companies from some legal liabilities and potential lawsuits.[54]

Because U.S. corporations are taxed only when they repatriate such foreign earnings, the current tax system encourages companies to earn and then keep their income overseas.[55] This congressionally enacted structural incentive applies to all industries, not just military contractors. However, in the case of contractors doing work on U.S. bases overseas, its significance extends far beyond lost tax revenues. Given equivalent contracts to provide services on a base in Texas and a base in the United Arab Emirates, for example, the base in the UAE offers significantly more options for indefinitely reducing U.S. taxes. In short, the U.S. tax code actually encourages contractors to support the stationing of bases and troops abroad rather than at home.

A SELF-LICKING ICE CREAM CONE

As the FOB2012 conference neared its end, I asked another conference participant (who requested that I not use his name) whether during his wartime deployments in Iraq he had seen the problem Major Elliott had described—a base with private security guards doing nothing but protecting privately contracted cooks who were doing nothing but cooking for those same private security guards.

"A lot," he replied. It's the "self-licking ice cream cone"—by which he meant a self-perpetuating system with no purpose or function except to keep itself going.

"I sat with my ice cream and my prime rib on Sundays" in Iraq, he continued. It's been this way since 2001, maybe even since Kosovo. There's been lots of waste and inefficiency. Maybe, he said of the logisticians who coordinate all the amenities, it would be better "to fire the lot and start over."

In one of the conference's final conversations, contractor and military representatives discussed fears about the military market drying up as U.S. and European governments cut defense budgets. Many agreed that contractors would increasingly move to build, supply, and maintain bases for UN and other international peacekeepers, as well as for oil and mining companies, whose extraction facilities often look like military bases already.

Peter Eberle, a representative from General Dynamics (which just missed making my list of the top twenty-five overseas contract recipients), asked: "What if we have peace break out" after the United States and NATO withdraw from Afghanistan?

"God forbid!" replied Major Elliott.

Caserma Dal Molin (now known as Caserma Del Din) under construction at an old airport in Vicenza, Italy. Although the base's main tenant is an airborne brigade, the construction destroyed the airport's sole existing runway; its remnants can be seen at bottom right.

13

The MilCon Con

The Army calls them "enduring communities." After the Bush administration announced its global base realignment plan, the Army said that in Europe it would largely consolidate its forces at seven such communities, each of which would include multiple bases. Five enduring communities were to be in Germany, one was in the Belgium/Netherlands/Luxembourg region, and one was in Vicenza, Italy. As part of the consolidation, in 2006, the Army asked Congress for $610 million in military construction—"MilCon"—funds to build a new base in Vicenza, at an old airport called Dal Molin. The Army said an elite rapid reaction brigade, the 173rd Airborne, was divided between Vicenza and two bases slated to close in Germany. The Army needed to build a new base to unite these forces. Other bases in Vicenza, Army officials said, were, "for the most part, oversubscribed."[1]

Texas Republican senator Kay Bailey Hutchison was one of only a few congressmembers to question the request at the time. During the hearings, she asked why an *airborne* brigade would consolidate on a base lacking an airfield or any means of getting aloft. (In fact, the planned construction at Dal Molin would destroy the existing runway that had served small numbers of U.S. aircraft since the mid-1950s.) To deploy, soldiers would have to travel two to three hours northeast from Vicenza to Aviano Air Base. Why, Hutchison asked, would a "rapid reaction" brigade be placed in such an unfavorable location? Why was the 173rd not consolidating around Aviano?

"My question is," Hutchison said to Army representatives, "have you thought this through?"

"We have thought it through greatly," Assistant Secretary of the Army Keith Eastin insisted. He said land acquisition costs at Aviano and other locations were prohibitive, while Dal Molin would come gratis. (Most, if not all, of the land for bases in Italy comes free of charge from the Italian government.)

"Ever since Hannibal, I do not think it has been particularly good to have part of your force on one side of the Alps and the other part on the other," Eastin said, referring to Vicenza and the two German bases. "So the intention is to bring it all in one place, that place being south of the Alps, which operationally I am told . . . significantly eases the ability to deploy from having to get only one clearance for airspace from one country rather than several, which would happen up in Germany."

Offering few other questions, Congress soon approved the Army's funding request. But seven years later, in the spring of 2013, the Army made a surprising announcement. With most of the $610 million allocated for the Vicenza construction already spent, and just weeks after it had started moving into the nearly completed base, the Army said it wouldn't be putting the entire 173rd brigade in Vicenza after all. Although consolidating the brigade in one location had been the justification for building the base in the first place, the plan was now to have two of the brigade's six battalions stay in Germany, moving to another base there. Only about one thousand troops and an equal number of family members—roughly half what had been planned—would relocate to Vicenza.

Not long after the announcement, a Senate Appropriations Committee report expressed pointed "concern" about the change in plans: "This decision is in direct contravention of the [consolidation's] original purpose."[2]

A CONSTELLATION OF BASES

Most tourists think of Italy as the land of Venetian canals, Roman ruins, Florentine palaces, and, of course, pizza, pasta, and wine. With little or no mention of bases in the tourist guidebooks, few think of Italy as a land of U.S. bases. But Italy's fifty "base sites" give it more American base locations than any country in the world except Japan, Germany, and South Korea.

Located near the foothills of the Southern Alps in Italy's affluent Veneto region, Vicenza really has no equivalent today in the United States. The city remains both wealthy and an industrial center. Vicenza's factories produce gold jewelry, high-end bicycle components, and even roller coasters and other rides for amusement parks like Brooklyn's Coney Island. The city revolves around a Renaissance-era center dominated by the architecture of Andrea Palladio, Vicenza's most famous son. Influenced by ancient Rome, Palladio's work has shaped architecture from Constantinople to London to Thomas Jefferson's Monticello.[3]

Today, Vicenza has a golden hue, especially at night when its streetlights glow on three- and four-story Renaissance-era buildings painted in tones of amber, cream, peach, and canary yellow. In the city's historical center, the narrow streets and alleyways are mostly still paved with cobblestones. The stones fit loosely together in cascading arcs emanating from the Corso Palladio, the city's main street. Dominated by walkers and bicyclists, it is framed by arcade-covered sidewalks lined with chic cafés and gelaterias, fancy chocolate and perfume shops, and the window displays of high-end boutiques.

It is a stark contrast to the way Vicenza looked during World War II, when hunger was so bad the city's inhabitants earned a reputation for eating cats. During their occupation of Italy, German troops turned Vicenza, including the Italian Air Force's Dal Molin airfield, into a major logistics hub. The city and the airfield experienced heavy Allied bombing for months. As German troops retreated, Vicenza saw fierce house-to-house fighting. Allied forces finally pushed the German army out of Vicenza on April 28, 1945. A day later, the German forces in Italy signed their surrender.

Following Italy's signing of a peace treaty in 1947, U.S. troops withdrew from Italy to Austria. But they soon returned: after Italy joined NATO, the 1951 NATO Status of Forces Agreement allowed U.S. troops to occupy Italian bases in Naples, Verona, and elsewhere. Still suffering from the war and unable to defend itself as Cold War tensions deepened, Italy also gave the U.S. military the rights to operate communication lines across the country and to occupy a large plot of coastal land near Pisa known as Camp Darby. By the mid-1950s, U.S. troops were also relocating to bases in the Italian northeast, including Caserma Ederle, the main base in Vicenza.[4]

Former army officer Fred Glenn remembered arriving in Vicenza in 1955 and finding sections of the city with bomb damage still visible. "You could still see the ravages of the war that had been visited upon them," he told me. Caserma Ederle was only two months old, and the officer recalled it being "rather primitive" at that point. "In the sun, it was a dust bowl. In the rain, it was a mud pie." But engineers quickly went to work, gutting entire buildings, pouring millions into new construction, and upgrading "in every way possible."

Eventually, there were ten thousand army troops spread between Camp Darby, Caserma Ederle, and nearby bases in Italy's north. The troops became the Southern European Task Force, primarily a logistical force prepared to receive massive reinforcements to protect Italy in case of an Eastern Bloc invasion from the northeast.[5]

Today, arriving at the Venice International Airport, one finds a small nondescript office labeled, in English, vicenza community. The office serves the ten thousand or so English speakers in the Vicenza area, a number equal to almost 10 percent of the city's population. These are the military personnel, family members, and civilians living and working on and around a constellation of bases scattered throughout the city. Even before Dal Molin's construction, the installations included a major headquarters, an underground weapons storage facility (which housed nuclear weapons during the Cold War), another underground base, depots, and a large gated housing development known as the Villaggio della Pace, the American Peace Village.

FINAL PREPARATIONS

A few months after the Army announced its decision to abandon the full consolidation of the 173rd brigade in Vicenza, I went on a tour of the newly operational base. Officially, the base was now called "Caserma Del Din," after Italian officials rebranded it in 2012—seemingly to distance the project from the vibrant "No Dal Molin" opposition movement that had garnered support across Italy. On base, fire trucks were still labeled dal molin, and many people still used the old name.

From afar, the place resembled a giant hospital complex or university campus. The long, narrow installation is a patchwork of thirty-one boxy peach- and cream-colored buildings with light red rooftops and rows of rectangular windows. A chain-link fence topped by razor wire surrounds the perimeter, with green mesh screens obscuring ground-level views inside. In scope, the base dwarfs everything in Vicenza, dominating the local horizon. It is far bigger than the city's largest green space.

When I arrived at the entrance gate, carabinieri and private security guards were positioned around six lanes for entering and exiting the base. I found the visitor center next to the community bank. Out front were two Bank of America ATMs—one still wrapped in shipping plastic, another advertising dollars and euros available. By their side sat two empty Rolling Rock and Red Stripe beer bottles.

After my guides signed me on to the base, they took me to the roof of one of the new (and nearly full) six-story parking garages. From the top, you could see the length of the garrison's 145 acres from north to south. Below, Italian workers were still installing street signs, in English, and finishing the final stages of construction on a few buildings. A bulldozer was flattening dirt for a baseball and softball field.

Near the parking lots sit the large brigade headquarters, two six-hundred-soldier barracks, the fire station, a fitness center, a multimedia entertainment facility and heated swimming pool, and a large cafeteria. Next to the small PX there's a minimart, a Subway, and an Italian-style coffee bar. Elsewhere on base, there are rows of buildings for various brigade units, rehabbed buildings from the old Italian Air Force base, a motor pool, an indoor shooting range, and a natural-gas-powered energy plant. Designed as a "walking base," rather than a sprawling Little America where frequent driving is required to get from one building on base to another, the installation was quiet and had little vehicle traffic in the middle of the workday. (The cars in the nearly full parking garages belonged to people commuting to work on the base.) According to the Army, Dal Molin was the first base campus to receive LEED Green Building certification.[6] The Army expects that it will eventually receive LEED Gold.

Unlike many U.S. bases, which resemble extravagant imitations of suburbia abroad, Dal Molin is quite utilitarian. There will be no families living on this base—just single soldiers. The new hospital, two new schools, and other amenities for family members are across town at the Caserma Ederle and the American Village. Beyond the estimated $610 million in construction across Vicenza, the Army was also planning to lease up to 240 made-to-order homes being built in surrounding communities—a plan to house troops and families suddenly called into question by the Army's decision to leave one third of the 173rd brigade in Germany.

CURIOUSER AND CURIOUSER

Given the strategic interest in consolidating south of the Alps, the decision to keep the 173rd brigade divided between Italy and Germany is perplexing on purely military grounds. The 173rd is supposed to be designed for rapid reaction to military emergencies. As the Army's Keith Eastin explained to Congress in 2006, keeping the brigade divided between bases in the two countries means the two battalions staying in Germany would almost surely face significantly longer deployment times than the four battalions in Vicenza.

The original consolidation idea becomes even more curious militarily given that Dal Molin and other bases in Vicenza do not have significant training areas. When I visited Vicenza, a military official (who asked not to be identified because he was not authorized to speak publicly) told me training opportunities are "extremely limited" at Dal Molin and the Caserma Ederle. Some training, he said, takes place on Italian bases near Aviano, but "most of the training areas are in Germany."

It's a well-known problem that the 173rd in Vicenza "has inadequate training areas in its immediate area and must conduct most of its high-intensity training six hours north in Germany," a 2012 article in the *Armed Forces Journal* explains.[7] In fact, the only place in Italy for the 173rd to train as a brigade would be on the island of Sardinia, off Italy's west coast, which is even farther from Vicenza than the German training areas.

This raises the question: Why would the Army want to move soldiers from Germany to Italy, only to send them back to Germany on a regular basis for training? Even if the new decision to maintain a split basing arrangement means that only four battalions will be making the nearly nine-hundred-mile round-trip to get to the training areas, transporting two thirds of the 173rd brigade to Germany on a regular basis clearly adds to the new base's effective total cost.

I contacted Bruce Anderson, a spokesperson for U.S. Army Europe, and asked him why the Army had decided to keep the brigade split between Italy and Germany given that consolidating the 173rd was the explicit justification for creating the base. Anderson replied in an email that European troop reductions had opened unexpected space in Germany. Moving two of the 173rd's battalions within Germany rather than to Italy, he said, means the Army will save on moving costs, on transportation costs when the battalions need to conduct regular training in Germany, and on closing costs for the two bases being vacated in Germany.

I repeatedly asked Anderson and other Army public affairs officials by telephone and email whether the Army had performed a cost analysis supporting these claims. I asked whether such an analysis had been shared with Congress, and if I could see the cost data. I received no response.

In Anderson's initial email, another detail caught my eye. "Experience over the last six years," he wrote, "has shown that, while full consolidation is optimal, the Brigade functions quite well and benefits from training with other units in Germany." Apparently being "split based" wasn't such a problem after all.

I mentioned to another U.S. military official in Italy that a cynic might say the Army never intended to consolidate the 173rd brigade in Vicenza in the first place and had merely used the idea of consolidation as a pretext to secure congressional funding for the new base at Dal Molin.

"I don't disagree that that optic is there," that official (who also asked to not be named) replied. He suggested, though, that the change in plans may have been motivated by a desire to hang on to the Army's "crown jewel" in Europe, the more than 57,000-acre Grafenwoehr training area.[8] New troop reductions at Grafenwoehr meant that there was going to be a lot of extra room there, and perhaps the Army felt a need to make conspicuous use of that space, especially since Congress had invested more than $700 million there since 2000. Placing part of the 173rd brigade in Grafenwoehr accomplished that goal.

Even if the consolidation idea wasn't a cynical way to win congressional funds, it seems that the decision not to consolidate was, at the very least, a cynical way to avoid possibly losing a prized base and to cover up the embarrassment of spending hundreds of millions on unnecessary and underutilized facilities. Either way, military necessity does not seem like the primary motive.

And it gets worse. Remember that the Pentagon's insistence on spending more than half a billion dollars on new construction in Vicenza hung on the idea that a new base would solve the problem of having the 173rd brigade divided between Italy and Germany. As I looked further, I realized that this "problem" was entirely of the Army's own making. The 173rd brigade had been deactivated after the Vietnam War, and reactivated in 2000. After that reactivation, the 173rd spent about six years being based entirely in Vicenza—meaning that for the first half decade or more of its most recent life, there was no split-basing problem at all.

Several sources, including State Department cables released by Wikileaks, show that the Army first asked the Italian government about building at Dal Molin in 2002 or 2003, if not before.[9] (This broke a promise made to Italian officials in 2000 to respect established troop limits in Vicenza and "build up and not out.")[10] In April 2005, the Italian government gave permission to build at Dal Molin. And it was only in 2006, around the time that the Pentagon sent Congress its first Dal Molin funding request, that the Army expanded the 173rd by adding four separate battalions in Germany to the two in Vicenza, thus creating the split-basing problem for the first time.[11]

In other words, the split basing of the 173rd appears to be a "problem" created by the Army itself, years into the planning for a new base, and just when the Army needed a justification for funding.

SYSTEMIC PROBLEMS

The money that taxpayers have poured into the Dal Molin base reflects broad and long-standing problems in the military construction system overseas. These problems include providing Congress with incomplete, misleading, and at times even fictional information to create budget justifications most likely to secure congressional funding.[12]

When the Navy was asking Congress for money to build a base on Diego Garcia in the late 1960s and early 1970s, for example, officials tried different justifications over the course of more than half a decade until finally securing Congress's agreement to provide MilCon funds. After suffering repeated congressional defeats, Secretary of Defense Melvin Laird gave the Navy simple instructions to downsize its initial funding request: "Make it a communications facility." Obligingly, the Navy soon submitted to Congress a proposal for a $17.8 million "communications facility."[13] However, a closer examination of the Navy's budget shows that half the cost of the "communications station" was for dredging Diego Garcia's lagoon and building an eight-thousand-foot airstrip at a facility that featured a mere $800,000 worth of communications equipment. The officially "austere" project featured the construction of a seventeen-mile road network, a small nightclub, a movie theater, and a gym.[14]

Under the guise of a communications station, in other words, the Navy was asking for the nucleus of a much larger base, with a design that allowed for ready restoration of previously envisioned base elements.[15] Although the Navy usually characterized the base as "limited" or "modest," officials always had grander visions for a large harbor, an airfield, and a coordination center for submarines patrolling the Indian Ocean. As one Navy official put it, "The communications requirements cited as justification are fiction."[16] Before Diego Garcia was even operational, officials were already planning to ask Congress for more money to expand. And expand it did, as Diego Garcia became a billion-dollar base within a decade.[17] At other base locations, too, once the military overcomes initial congressional opposition, the first round of MilCon funding often becomes a slippery slope to much larger expenditures.

An April 2013 Senate Armed Services Committee report also revealed other systemic problems. For example, upon returning bases to host countries, the Pentagon negotiates payments for the "residual value" of the returned facilities. Since 1991, the U.S. government has received more than $920 million in such payments. Legally, the Pentagon is required to get these as cash settlements, and is allowed to accept payments via in-kind contributions only as a last resort if cash negotiations fail. Yet more than 95 percent of these settlements, and all of them since 1997, have in fact come as in-kind payments. Despite the law, the military's negotiators now don't even discuss possible cash settlements. The law also requires the Pentagon to notify Congress before beginning in-kind negotiations; the Senate Committee found that the Pentagon simply "does not comply with that requirement."[18]

What's more, if in-kind contributions are to be used, the law also requires the secretary of defense to certify that these contributions replace future funding requests—in other words, that if it were not for the availability of in-kind payments, the military would have asked for future MilCon money for the project. But after reviewing twelve MilCon projects for which in-kind payments were used, the Senate Committee found that *none* had been considered for future funding requests. In other words, the military was specifically directing in-kind payments toward projects "unlikely to be included" on a list of funding priorities for Congress. As a result, the committee found, in-kind funding has gone to "questionable projects," including a $6 million furniture warehouse and $200,000 in sunroom additions for senior officers' homes.[19]

Perhaps most egregiously, the Pentagon has—without notifying Congress—asked for and accepted $60 million worth of *advance* in-kind payments from the German government for facilities the military plans to return to Germany in the future. The Senate Committee concluded, "There are serious questions as to whether the solicitation and expenditure of an advance is consistent with fiscal law."[20]

In South Korea, U.S. forces have similarly used Korean in-kind payments for construction without the authorization or notification of Congress, and with limited or no review by the Army, the Pacific Command, or the Pentagon. Among the projects planned by U.S. Forces Korea is a $10.4 million museum for the Army's 2nd Infantry Division. Officials described the museum as a "command requirement."[21] Elsewhere in South Korea, the Army has proposed a lease-build housing plan that would likely cost $755 million more than standard overseas housing allowances. Again, the Senate Committee had "questions about the legality of the plan."[22]

"A LIFE OF ITS OWN"

"Once an American overseas base is established, it takes on a life of its own," concluded a rare congressional investigation into the little-noticed expansion of bases abroad since World War II. "Original missions may become outdated, but new missions are developed, not only with the intent of keeping the facility going, but often to actually enlarge it."[23]

These words describe well what's happened in Vicenza, at Soto Cano in Honduras, and at many other bases around the globe. The words are more than four decades old. For eight months in 1969 and 1970, Walter Pincus—now a Pulitzer Prize–winning *Washington Post* columnist who writes about military, intelligence, and foreign policy issues—traveled the globe on behalf of the Senate Subcommittee on U.S. Security Agreements and Commitments Abroad, compiling a remarkable look at the sprawling base nation that was already taking shape.

If central casting called for an old-school reporter, they would have to look no farther than Brooklyn-born Pincus. When I met him for coffee near the *Washington Post* headquarters, he was wearing gray flannel trousers, a tie, and a slightly frayed white-striped shirt with its collar splayed open past the lapels of a blue blazer. His hair was stark white, his eyebrows bushy. When he walked, he teetered back and forth due to a damaged right leg.

Pincus's research took him to twenty-five countries hosting U.S. troops in Europe, Asia, and Africa. The subcommittee's hearings ran for thirty-eight days. All were closed to the public. The hearing transcripts and the subcommittee's final published report, which Pincus helped write, totaled 2,442 pages—not counting deletions requested by the Pentagon and State Department.

"We took away that we had bases all over the place," Pincus told me. He saw how the leaders of undemocratic governments like having American bases because they help keep local regimes in power. As Pincus saw it, overseas bases have a "commitment side" and a "corrupt side." The commitment side meant the United States would defend you. But the corrupt side, Pincus said, meant "we will also defend the regime that got us in there," because the regime's removal would threaten a base's existence.

Pincus said his time in General Francisco Franco's Spain was particularly telling. "I kept asking, 'Why do we keep Morón [Air Base]?'" The
answer, he was told, was that it was a "key base" for exercises.

"So what the hell are we exercising with Spain?" he asked. He discovered that the yearly exercises practiced saving the dictatorial government
from insurgents. Pincus also realized that the exercises were, not coin-
cidentally, timed to end around the start of one of Spain's biggest festi-
vals, the Feria de Sevilla. The good weather in southern Spain also didn't
hurt. This, Pincus said, was the "perk side" of overseas bases.

Spain also taught Pincus about the perks of the PX system, where one
can buy cheap tax-free goods. Overseas, Pincus saw that the military
isn't the only one to benefit from the PXs. The Air Force was flying its
jets directly over the Spanish capital, Madrid, but they got away with it
because high-ranking Spanish officers were allowed to use the PX and
the Officers Club. State Department Foreign Service officers shop at
the PXs, too, and, Pincus said, it "corrupts them" just as it does local
leaders. For many, the PX becomes another reason not to look criti-
cally at the need for a base. (To this day, Foreign Service officers and
their family members in Luxembourg, for example, drive hours to and
from Germany to get better deals at the PXs on bases there.)

"The Pentagon also takes care of Congress," Pincus added. When
members of Congress visit overseas bases, the military organizes everything, including a light schedule of three meetings a day plus "dinner and
shopping and all that shit." These are the people who "are supposed to be
doing oversight," he said. "And it's infectious." During Pincus's own
investigation, he had to break away from his handlers and set up his
own meetings by calling around the base. Eventually, the military
stopped providing him with base telephone directories.

The result of all this, according to the final subcommittee report that
Pincus helped author, is that "within the government departments most
directly concerned—State and Defense—we found little initiative to
reduce or eliminate any of these overseas facilities."[24] What's more, for
State Department and Pentagon officials, closing a base is hardly a way
to boost a career. "It is only to be expected that those in embassies abroad,
and also at overseas military facilities, would seek to justify continued

operations in their particular areas," explained the subcommittee report. "Otherwise, they recommend a reduction in their own position."[25]

The result has often been a series of rotating rationales to justify a base's continued existence and, often, expansion. A large number of decades-old bases have remained open, often with vague or dubious justifications. "Arguments can always be raised to justify keeping almost any facility open," the subcommittee concluded. "To the military, a contingency use can always be found. To the diplomat, a base closing or reduction can always be at the wrong time in terms of relations with the host country and other nations."[26] (At a psychological level, too, we can understand that few people would want to see something they've worked on declared "superfluous.")

These perpetual tendencies toward inertia and expansion have also meant there's every incentive for base officials to always suggest that their base needs more money. In the Pentagon, like most other bureaucracies, those controlling budgets generally try to spend every cent allocated to them, for fear of losing funding in the next fiscal year. One former Army cost analyst described to me what he called a "pathology" of unnecessary spending. "There was never a question of saving any money," said Bill Witherington (a pseudonym). "I had it said [explicitly], 'If we don't spend it . . . we won't get any more next year.'"

The Pentagon generally keeps any unspent funds at the end of the fiscal year, he said. So "commanders would say, 'Well, gee. We've got some money. What could we spend it on and then ask for more next year?'"

"If you didn't spend the money," I asked, "what would have happened?"

"That never happened," Witherington replied. "There was a wink-wink, nudge-nudge that the money will be committed and there will still be [unfunded] 'requirements'" left over. There was "never an instance" when money was left over, he said. "That would have been a career ender."

"INCONSISTENCIES, GAPS, AND CALCULATION ERRORS"

Despite the tendency of bases to take on lives of their own, the global transformation plans launched by the Bush administration and carried out by Andy Hoehn and others succeeded in closing more bases than were shuttered at any time since the first four years after the end of the Cold War. Many of the closures have been in Europe, where more than a hundred fifty bases have closed since 2001 and tens of thousands of troops have been withdrawn, mostly from Germany and Britain.

And yet, at the same time the military has been closing so many bases and returning them to host nations, there has simultaneously been an enormous construction boom on American bases around the globe.[27] "The largest military construction budget since World War II will buy some of the largest facilities in the Army's inventory and some of the most modern anywhere," noted a 2008 article in *Soldiers* magazine.[28]

While the Global Defense Posture Review envisioned billions in construction and other spending to carry out the transformation it recommended, it's hard to account for all the MilCon expenditures by looking at those realignment plans alone. The expansion of total MilCon funding worldwide has been breathtaking, almost tripling in constant dollar terms from $13.6 billion in fiscal year 2002 to $33.6 billion in fiscal year 2009, and reaching highs not seen since World War II.[29] That $33.6 billion, which doesn't even include almost $1 billion in additional MilCon funding in the military's separate war budget,[30] is almost double the previous postwar high, reached during the military buildup in Vietnam in 1966.[31] Since the start of the war on terror, the Pentagon has engaged in major construction in South Korea, Japan, Guam, Australia, and elsewhere in Asia; in the Marshall Islands; in Afghanistan and elsewhere in Central Asia; in Iraq and every other Persian Gulf nation except Iran; in eastern Europe; and increasingly in Africa and Latin America. In total, between 2002 and 2013, the military has received more than $30 billion in MilCon funding at bases overseas, with another $92.6 billion going to "unspecified locations" domestic and abroad.[32]

The MilCon spending in Europe is particularly striking given all the base closures taking place on the continent. In Italy, in addition to Vicenza, the Pentagon has spent almost $300 million since fiscal year 2001 on construction at the Sigonella Naval Air Station in Sicily. In Germany, in addition to Grafenwoehr, the Army is now spending around $500 million to move its European headquarters from Heidelberg to Wiesbaden. A Government Accountability Office report found that the Army's estimate of money saved by this move was inflated by almost double, and that construction delays have further eaten into any potential savings. "The original analyses," the GAO added, "were poorly documented, limited in scope and based on questionable assumptions."[33] This at a time when more and more critics are questioning why the Army is in Germany and Europe at all.

Adjacent to Ramstein Air Base in Germany, at the Rhine Ordnance Barracks, the Army is building a new $1 billion hospital to replace the Landstuhl Regional Medical Center as the military's main European medical facility. The Army said the hospital, which opened in 1953, had reached the end of its life span and could not be renovated to modern standards. Again, the GAO criticized the planning for the hospital, reporting that the Pentagon was unable to offer basic documentation for how it came up with its original funding request of $1.2 billion. The GAO found that the Pentagon's request was replete with "inconsistencies, gaps and calculation errors in planning documentation."[34]

Curious about why the Army wanted to replace what was still a world-class medical facility, I asked a Landstuhl surgeon who had been working there for a decade about the condition of the current hospital and whether there was any need for a replacement. The surgeon, who spoke on condition of anonymity, said he couldn't comment. Trying another tack, I asked him to tell me about the existing facility. The doctor said it was "top notch" and rated a Level 1 trauma center—the highest possible grade. There aren't many like it in the world, he said. (Other Level 1 hospitals include the elite Cedars-Sinai Medical Center in Los Angeles and Massachusetts General in Boston.) Landstuhl has since lost the status because, with U.S. involvement in Afghanistan declining, it is now seeing too few patients to qualify.

"Is the hospital deficient or suboptimal in any way?" I asked.

"No," the surgeon replied. If it were deficient in any way, he explained, it would have had to be repaired immediately to maintain the hospital's Level 1 status.[35]

Another justification given for the new facility is decreasing the transit time between the runway at Ramstein and the hospital. So I asked whether, medically speaking, there are any problems transporting people over the fifteen-to-twenty-minute drive between Ramstein and Landstuhl. "No," the surgeon said, "because they are very close." In his time at the hospital, he told me, he had seen "no adverse incidents," and he believed there had never been any such incidents in transit. (Others at the hospital reported the same.) After a seven-to-eight-hour flight from Afghanistan, he said, nothing's going to go wrong over such a short drive.

As of late 2014, the new hospital was scheduled to open in 2022. The Army estimates that it will take "about 15 minutes" to get there from Ramstein—in other words, little if at all faster than the current transit time.[36]

I asked Walter Pincus what he made of the billion-plus dollars being spent on the new hospital. He replied, "It implies we're going to keep fighting."

A WILLFUL DISREGARD FOR COSTS

While sometimes you need to spend money to save money, it's hard not to question the logic of spending billions on new and expanded European bases when the military is vacating so much space, downsizing its troop presence so dramatically, and shrinking the size of the entire military by tens of thousands, leaving plenty of excess space at domestic bases, too.[37]

Some of the bases being closed in Europe actually enjoyed significant construction and upgrades shortly before closure. For example, the garrison in Bamberg, Germany—whose closure Pentagon officials revealed no later than 2006—saw $87.6 million invested in barracks, a fitness center, and a child development center between 2000 and 2003. Over the same period, the Army invested $67.7 million at the base in Mannheim, where closure began in 2007.[38]

In 2013, the Pentagon was conducting a review of its European bases with the aim of further consolidation. And yet, before the review was even completed, the military had already asked for more than three quarters of a billion dollars in new European MilCon funding for the next fiscal year alone. The Senate Appropriations Committee questioned "the rationale for funding these projects before DOD has determined whether any missions can be consolidated or relocated, or any installations can be returned to the host nation." The committee was struck, for instance, by $328 million in requested funding for five schools in Germany and

Britain, given that "consolidation of missions could change base populations, which in turn could affect the required size or location of schools."[39] Since fiscal year 2008, budget documents show that the Pentagon has already received more than $320 million in funding for school construction in Germany alone. In 2012, the Pentagon opened a new school in Schweinfurt, a base set to close within three years (which indeed closed in 2014).[40] When the Pentagon finally announced the results of its European base review in 2014, it said twenty-one facilities would close across the continent. However, none of these was a major installation; most were superfluous recreation areas, depots, small training ranges, radio stations, and water well sites.[41]

Two recent GAO reports show that both the European and Pacific Commands were making major changes to their basing structures "without the benefit of comprehensive cost information or an analysis of alternatives." The Pentagon admitted that its combatant commanders, who are responsible for positioning bases and troops and determining the missions of component forces, do not even have access to comprehensive cost data.[42] For some of the most powerful people in the U.S. military and the entire U.S. government (their power often exceeds that of ambassadors and other high-ranking State Department officials), costs simply aren't part of the decision-making process.

A telling illustration of that indifference to financial matters is the Pentagon's 2013 decision to keep the headquarters for the Africa Command in Stuttgart despite its own analysis showing that moving the headquarters to the United States would save between $60 million and $70 million a year and create up to 4,300 jobs, with an annual economic impact in the United States of $350 million to $450 million. The Pentagon said Africom's commander decided keeping the headquarters in Germany was more operationally effective. The GAO pointed out that the Pentagon's evaluation was "not supported by a comprehensive and well-documented analysis" and did "not fully meet key principles for an economic analysis." The Pentagon agreed in part with the outside evaluation but stuck to its decision, saying it was based primarily on "military judgment, which is not easily quantifiable."

"We recognize that military judgment is not easily quantifiable," the GAO responded. "However, we continue to believe that an accurate and reliable analysis should provide a more complete explanation of how operational benefits and costs were weighed, especially in light of the potential cost savings that DOD is deciding to forgo."[43]

Repeatedly, one sees the Pentagon making decisions to spend hundreds of millions of taxpayer dollars based on incomplete data, shoddy math, little or no attempt to consider cheaper alternatives, and cost analyses that appear to be either incompetent or intentionally manipulated. A long, regular stream of GAO reports provides abundant evidence of the problems. Unfortunately, each report appears in isolation, and they generally portray the problems as unrelated incidents. Rarely does anyone point out the larger pattern: the Pentagon, the armed services, and many of their component parts are spending many, many billions of MilCon dollars with what frequently appears to be a willful disregard for costs and the law and little or no oversight by Congress.

These are, of course, symptoms of the rampant and shameless profligacy in the military budget as a whole and in the entire military-industrial complex that President Eisenhower warned us about. But it's time someone said it specifically: MilCon is totally and completely out of control.

"A BUREAUCRATIC MACHINE"

Encouragingly, cuts to the Pentagon budget brought about by Congress's sequestration process have reined in the out-of-control nature of recent MilCon spending. For fiscal year 2014, overseas MilCon expenditures amounted to around $1.5 billion, with another $2.8 billion at unspecified worldwide locations. Globally, the total reached $10.2 billion.[44] While this pales compared to funding for military pay, weapons procurement, and research and development, more money went to military construction around the world in 2014 than to each of the Department of Commerce, the Environmental Protection Agency, the National Science Foundation, the Small Business Administration, and the Corporation for National and Community Service.

To get another perspective on why the military has been building so many bases while it's in the process of vacating so many others in Europe, I talked to the conservative scholar Edward N. Luttwak, who had expressed public support for the new base at Dal Molin and once called any opponent of the base "a dirty commie" who is "purely ideological and negativist."[45]

"You could argue," Luttwak told me, "that instead of new bases you could consolidate" at some of the other bases being vacated. But MilCon for the Pentagon, he continued, is "a bureaucratic machine needing to be stopped by someone in Congress. To say, 'That's it . . . We don't want to spend money on bases. Goodbye!'"

That would work, he said. "Congress could do it." But in a system where it "takes enormous energy to get anything done," he explained, inertia is a powerful force. Once a project is started, officials are "extremely reluctant to stop for anything." For now, Luttwak said of members of Congress and military leaders alike, "They continue on like blind animals burrowing underground."

"So did we need a half-billion-dollar base in Vicenza?" I asked.

"No," he replied, "we didn't." In fact, he said, "There's no need to have troops in Italy. So, yeah, you could close it."

• •

PART V

CHOICES

The world's most dangerous base" is what many Okinawans call Marine Corps Air Station Futenma. The base is encircled by Ginowan City, Okinawa, Japan.

"The world's most dangerous base" is what many Okinawans call Marine Corps Air Station Futenma. The base is encircled by Ginowan City, Okinawa, Japan.

14

"Masters of Extortion"

In late 2010, to help prepare a group of students learning about U.S. bases for a study trip to Okinawa, I arranged a meeting with Kevin Maher at the State Department's Foggy Bottom headquarters. Maher had been a diplomat for thirty years. For eighteen of those, he had held various diplomatic posts in Japan before becoming director of the State Department's Japan desk.[1] With his crisp shirt and tie, polished leather shoes, perfectly parted red hair, and small, carefully trimmed red mustache, he was the very picture of a seasoned official in the national security bureaucracy.

Although the Okinawa prefecture makes up just 0.6 percent of Japan's land area, it is home to around 75 percent of all the military installations in Japan set aside for exclusive U.S. use—more than thirty bases altogether. American bases take up almost 20 percent of the main Okinawa island, in addition to expansive sea and airspace the military uses for training. And ever since the 1995 gang-rape of a twelve-year-old Okinawan girl, it has been among the most controversial and hotly protested base locations worldwide.[2]

"Look at the map," Maher told our group, explaining why so much of Okinawa was taken up by U.S. forces. Okinawa is closer to North Korea and China than to Tokyo, he pointed out, so in a way, Okinawans are "victims of geography," with a military presence there critical for guaranteeing regional security. Plus, Maher added, we get "friendly and great facilities," in a place that's a great location for Americans.

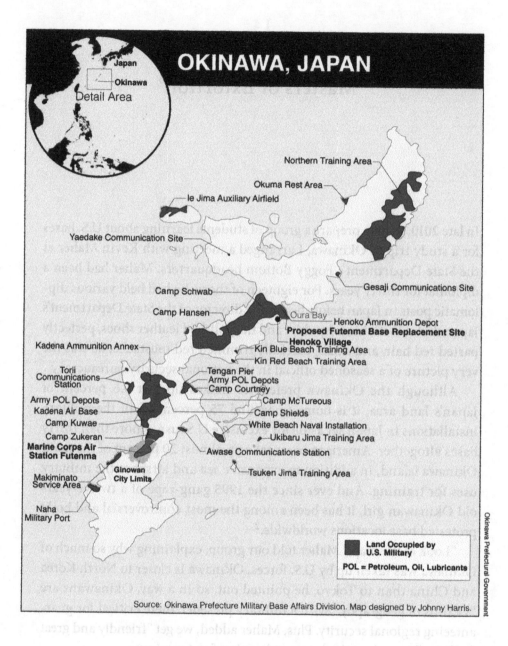

OKINAWA, JAPAN

Japan

Okinawa

Detail Area

Northern Training Area

Okuma Rest Area

Ie Jima Auxiliary Airfield

Yaedake Communication Site

Gesaji Communications Site

Camp Schwab

Camp Hansen

Oura Bay

Henoko Ammunition Depot

Proposed Futenma Base Replacement Site

Henoko Village

Kadena Ammunition Annex

Kin Blue Beach Training Area

Kin Red Beach Training Area

Torii
Communications
Station

Tengan Pier

Army POL Depots

Camp Courtney

Army POL Depots

Camp McTureous

Kadena Air Base

Camp Shields

Camp Kuwae

White Beach Naval Installation

Camp Zukeran

Ukibaru Jima Training Area

**Marine Corps Air
Station Futenma**

Awase Communications Station

**Ginowan
City Limits**

Tsuken Jima Training Area

Makiminato
Service Area

Naha
Military Port

Okinawa Prefectural Government

Land Occupied by
U.S. Military

POL = Petroleum, Oil, Lubricants

Source: Okinawa Prefecture Military Base Affairs Division. Map designed by Johnny Harris.

Then Maher expounded a bit on the island's history. Okinawa was colonized by Japan in 1879, he said, and a lot of the American bases there stem from the U.S. occupation of Japan after World War II. So Okinawa sits in an "interesting triangular relationship" with Japan and the United States. "This is not a politically correct way to say it," Maher added, "but, as a man in Okinawa told me, it's the Puerto Rico of Japan." Like Puerto Ricans, he said, Okinawans have "darker skin," are "shorter," and have an "accent."

This was not the briefing we had expected from someone with a job description involving diplomacy.

Okinawans, Maher continued, are "masters in extorting Tokyo for money." Most of the bases sit on private land leased by the Japanese government for the United States. When the leases come up for renewal, he said, you see a lot of Okinawan politicians and others calling for the removal of bases, but he didn't think they really wanted the bases to leave. "That's how you jack up the price on the rent."

Plus, Maher explained, Tokyo pays Okinawa compensation in the form of construction contracts. These mostly go to politicians' relatives, he said. You always hear that "Japanese culture" is so "group oriented" and focused on "consensus building"—but "that's such bullshit," he told us. "The 'group' is me and my buddies here." Maher said that payoffs were common in Japanese culture. "Okinawans are masters at this," at getting Tokyo's money and using "guilt" about Okinawans' suffering during World War II to do it.

Despite the construction contracts, Maher said, Okinawa is still the poorest prefecture in Japan. He said it was "partially because it was occupied until 1972" by the United States and wasn't integrated into the Japanese economy. But "you've got this island mentality," he added. That mentality traditionally involved planting sugarcane and *goya* (a bright green cucumber-shaped bitter melon iconic in Okinawa), and then just waiting around until cutting it down. And nowadays, Maher said, "They are too lazy [even] to grow it."[3] Before finishing the briefing, Maher attributed Okinawans' high rates of divorce, drunk driving, domestic violence, and childbearing to their taste for Okinawan rice liquor.

After Maher's briefing, our astonished group convened in a nearby café. Almost everyone was shocked by his characterizations. A student with Okinawan grandparents was so stunned he couldn't speak.

Several days later, at the suggestion of a Japanese graduate student in our group, a few students decided that when our study trip was done, they would share what we had heard with a Japanese journalist. I said I would back them up if anyone challenged their account; the meeting hadn't been recorded, but I had taken detailed notes. None of us had any idea of the uproar that would follow.

In March 2011, two months after our student group returned to Washington, the Japanese news agency Kyodo News published an article about Kevin Maher's pretrip briefing. The article used quotes from Maher's talk that the students had provided to the journalist Eiichiro Ishiyama. Okinawans and others were outraged, particularly with Maher's description of the Okinawan people as "extortionists" and "lazy." The article became front-page news in Japan, and Maher's comments were reprinted worldwide. Within three days, Assistant Secretary of State Kurt Campbell was issuing official apologies in Tokyo, and the State Department was removing Maher from his post.[4]

The "Maher Affair" was supplanted on the front pages in Japan only by the earthquake and tsunami that triggered the Fukushima Daiichi nuclear disaster. During the disaster, Maher reportedly played an important role in the U.S. government's humanitarian response. The next month he retired from the State Department. He commented on the uproar for the first time in a video interview with the *Wall Street Journal*. In the interview, Maher denied ever making the statements attributed to him, calling them "a kind of fabrication." He said the comments had been invented by the students.[5]

Outraged, I wrote a letter to the editor confirming the accuracy of the students' report. I also noted that, contrary to the *Wall Street Journal*'s description, neither Maher nor any State Department employee had told us at any time that the meeting was "off the record."[6]

Many expressed little surprise that Maher had made the derogatory comments. Former Okinawa governor Masahide Ota wrote that Maher had "a track record of making such verbal gaffes—statements that undoubtedly represent his true feelings."[7] When Maher was consul general in Okinawa, he was so disliked that he earned the nickname

"High Commissioner," a reference to the U.S. high commissioners who ruled Okinawa until 1972. A longtime U.S. reporter and analyst of U.S.-Japan relations, Peter Ennis, pointed out that no State Department or Japanese government officials rushed to Maher's defense. There were "no comments to the effect: 'Kevin, I can't believe they distorted your comments so much,' or 'Don't worry, everyone knows you didn't say those things.'"[8] Instead, Ennis quoted a senior Japanese reporter in Washington: "We had heard Kevin say things like this in the past."[9]

Maher's comments inflicted widespread hurt in Okinawa and Japan. His characterization of Okinawans as "lazy" and possessing an "island mentality," and his disparaging comparison of Okinawans to Puerto Ricans—successfully offending not one but two groups of people—are so offensive in deploying racial stereotypes that they speak for themselves. (The comments about "lazy" Okinawans are especially remarkable given that thousands of Okinawan employees help keep U.S. bases running.) On the other hand, linking the Puerto Ricans and Okinawans was inadvertently apt. Both cases sadly illustrate how an occupation by U.S. bases and troops works as part of a larger colonial relationship, impoverishing the occupied land and shaping many of the very real social problems found on both islands.

Despite the hurt Maher caused, many were pleased his views were aired. For many, far from looking like an aberration, the incident exposed some of the attitudes long underlying U.S. basing policy in Okinawa. An *Okinawa Times* newspaper editorial said Maher's comments showed that U.S. officials "seem, deep in their hearts, to despise Okinawa and make light of the base problem."[10] Okinawa's other major daily, the *Ryukyu Shimpo*, wrote that Maher had provided, "unintentionally, a revelation of real U.S. thinking."[11]

THE BATTLE OF OKINAWA

Okinawa feels more removed from Tokyo than the two-and-a-half-hour flight would suggest. For centuries, the archipelago existed as the independent Ryukyu Kingdom, best known for forsaking weapons and inventing karate. After Japan colonized the islands, it used them as a military outpost for further imperial incursions into Asia. The government banned

the use of the Okinawan language in public and enforced other discrim-
inatory policies against ethnic Okinawans.[12] Tokyo restaurants once
displayed signs saying no okinawans allowed.

Okinawa Island is about the size of New York City, and most of the
population lives in the island's southernmost third, which is almost
entirely one unbroken, paved urban area. Satellite images show the stark
divide: lush green on top, gray below. Outside the shiny capital, many of
the cities and towns look like run-down strip-mall American suburbia—
roads clogged with cars and lined with car dealerships, fast food joints,
small casino parlors, and 100 yen stores (the Japanese version of dollar
stores). Almost every one of the densely packed buildings dates from after
World War II, because almost every town and village on the island was
bombed, burned, or razed during the 1945 Battle of Okinawa.

Little remembered in the United States, the three-month battle was
the Pacific war's largest and deadliest. American strategists wanted to
capture Okinawa for use as the main launching point for an invasion of
Japan, while the Japanese military hoped to bog down the Americans on
Okinawa for as long as possible to build up the main islands' defenses
and negotiate an advantageous end to the war. U.S and allied naval vessels bombarded Okinawa with around forty thousand shells in what
became known as the "typhoon of steel."[13] Between 100,000 and 140,000
Okinawans—one quarter to one third of Okinawa's population—likely
died during the fighting. Warned by Japanese leaders about savage American soldiers, some committed suicide by throwing themselves off the
jagged cliffs along the coast. Others used hand grenades provided by Japanese troops. Some were forced to kill family members. A total of 1,202
cases of forced mass suicide have been documented.[14] Including the
12,520 U.S. troops and the more than 90,000 Japanese troops and Okinawan conscripts killed in action, as many people may have died during
the Battle of Okinawa as in the atomic bombings of Hiroshima and Nagasaki combined.[15]

At the time of the Battle of Okinawa, Masahide Ota, the prefecture's
future governor, was a teenager. The Japanese army conscripted him along
with the rest of his high school. Only 37 of 125 classmates survived; Ota
himself nearly died but was captured and sent to a prisoner of war
camp. In a meeting with our student group, Ota said that initially,

"Okinawan people's attitudes were so thankful to American soldiers." Whereas Japanese soldiers abandoned and killed hundreds of Okinawans, Americans "saved lives" during the battle. But in the early 1950s, Ota said, the Americans "confiscated Okinawan people's lands by force . . . Ever since, people's attitudes have changed."

Many Okinawans had lost their lands during the battle itself, when they were forced to flee for safety. Thousands of Okinawans like Ota spent months in displaced persons' camps and were barred from returning home. In many cases, there was little to go home to. Most everything had been flattened by the Allied bombardment. Ninety percent of the capital, Naha, was destroyed.[16] U.S. forces immediately began building bases atop villages and fields for the planned invasion of Japan. Within a year, the United States had seized forty thousand acres—equal to 20 percent of the island's arable land.[17]

When a *Time* magazine reporter visited in 1949, he found that "the battle of Okinawa completely wrecked the island's simple farming and fishing economy: in a matter of minutes, U.S. bulldozers smashed the terraced fields which Okinawans had painstakingly laid out for more than a century." Four years later, Okinawa had become a neglected place. "More than 15,000 U.S. troops, whose morale and discipline have probably been worse than that of any U.S. force in the world, have policed 600,000 natives who live in hopeless poverty."[18]

During the postwar occupation of Japan, U.S. negotiators insisted on retaining full control of Okinawa after nominally returning it to Japan.[19] Thus, when the occupation of Japan ended in 1952, the United States continued to rule Okinawa and smaller islands like Iwo Jima. American officials described Japan as maintaining "residual sovereignty" over these islands, but the U.S. government retained the right to establish military facilities on them, and effectively to govern them as it wished.[20] This arrangement was politically palatable to Japanese leaders because concentrating U.S. bases and troops in a colonized part of Japan meant reducing the U.S. military's impact elsewhere.[21]

In Okinawa, neither the new (U.S.-imposed) constitution of Japan nor the constitution of the United States applied. The occupation government required Okinawans to obtain a U.S-issued travel pass to visit Japan and controlled the movement of Japanese visitors to Okinawa. With U.S.

troops back at war in Korea, the military began a major base buildup. By the mid-1950s, the military had displaced nearly half the population and appropriated almost half of Okinawa's farmland by negotiation or force.[22]

More than 80 percent of Okinawans were farmers, Ota explained, so without their land, "they had no way to make a living." The appropriation of land also "disturbed the development of towns and cities" because "the most important areas" were occupied by bases. (Today, Okinawan families must get special permission to visit the tombs of their ancestors that lie within bases' fenced-off boundaries.) It's unfair that Okinawa was occupied when Japan regained its sovereignty, Ota said, "because we didn't start the war."

"INCIDENTS AND ACCIDENTS"

Starting with the first months after the war, there were scattered protests in Okinawa against the occupation, the land seizures, and the often heavy-handed U.S. occupation officials. Protests intensified in the 1950s and 1960s, partly due to opposition to the Vietnam War, during which Okinawan bases played an important role. The outcry was also fueled by a series of deadly jet crashes and vehicle accidents, as well as the dozens of rapes, murders, and other crimes involving GIs.[23]

Okinawans have long taken note of what they call "incidents and accidents" involving U.S. troops. In 1951, for instance, an Air Force fighter dropped a fuel tank on an Okinawan house, burning it to the ground and killing six residents. Eight years later, an Air Force jet crashed into an elementary school, killing seventeen students and teachers and injuring more than one hundred. Between 1959 and 1964, at least four Okinawans were shot and killed as the result of what military officials said were hunting accidents or stray bullets from training. Between 1962 and 1968, there were at least four more crashes and accidents involving military aircraft, leaving at least eight dead and twelve injured. At least fourteen people died after being hit by U.S. military vehicles, including a four-year-old killed by a crane.[24]

Not all the deaths were accidental. In 1955, a court convicted a U.S. sergeant of abducting, raping, and killing a six-year-old girl. During the Vietnam War, reports suggest that U.S. military personnel deployed to

Okinawa or on leave there killed seventeen women. Eleven of them had been working as bar hostesses or sauna attendants.[25]

In 1962, the Okinawan legislature passed a unanimous resolution condemning the United States for engaging in colonial rule, and by 1968, 85 percent of Okinawan and Japanese survey respondents favored the immediate return of Okinawa.[26] Eventually, Prime Minister Eisaku Sato and President Richard Nixon negotiated the return of Okinawa to Japanese rule by 1972. However, the actual base land to be returned was minimal. The proportion of U.S. bases in Okinawa as opposed to the rest of Japan would actually increase. The agreement failed to mollify many Okinawans.

Only after the 1995 schoolgirl rape and the uproar it provoked did Kevin Maher and other U.S. and Japanese officials finally negotiate to reduce Okinawa's base burden. In a 1996 agreement, U.S. officials pledged to return 12,361 acres of Okinawan land. It also promised to implement noise reduction mechanisms and changes to training procedures to reduce friction with neighboring communities.

Most important, the military also agreed to close the controversial Marine Corps Air Station Futenma. Built atop five villages destroyed during World War II, Futenma is now surrounded by Ginowan, a densely populated city of almost a hundred thousand. The airfield is only a few hundred yards from numerous schools, child care facilities, apartment buildings, and hospitals. In some cases, houses and playgrounds are just a matter of feet from the base's fences. Low-flying helicopters and planes are a nearly constant visual and aural presence. At Okinawa International University, just a few hundred yards from the airfield, our tour group witnessed students and faculty forced to close the windows in an extremely hot and humid, un-air-conditioned building because they couldn't hear one another talking above the helicopter noise. Even more seriously, there are no safety "clear zones" beyond Futenma's runways, as the law requires at U.S. military and civilian airfields. Airports worldwide are often situated in urban areas, but Futenma is so surrounded by Ginowan that it looks as if someone dug a 1,188-acre hole in the middle of the city.

"In the United States, a base with encroachment this severe," writes the retired Air Force officer Mark Gillem, "is a base that would find itself on the closure list."[27] Okinawans frequently invoke a phrase attributed to former secretary of defense Donald Rumsfeld calling Futenma "the World's Most Dangerous Base."

But when the U.S. and Japanese governments signed their 1996 agreement, there was a catch: the military wouldn't close Futenma until the Japanese government built the Marines a new base. And although most Okinawans expected the replacement would be outside their prefecture, the two governments selected a site on Okinawa's east coast, near an existing base called Camp Schwab.

Initially, Japanese officials proposed having the new base float on water. This idea came under intense criticism. Military officials were concerned about its technical feasibility. The General Accounting Office pointed out that the estimated annual operating costs were seventy times those at Futenma. Many were worried about the safety of plans to store ammunition under the runway. Environmentalists were concerned that the new base would seriously damage the maritime environment. Because of possible threats to the endangered dugong, a relative of the manatee, they filed a suit against the Pentagon and won a temporary block to construction. Voters in the proposed host city, Nago, have repeatedly opposed the new base.[28]

In 2005, the two governments finally agreed to change the plan. They announced that the base would be built at Camp Schwab, on a runway extending into Nago's Oura Bay. But environmentalists and others again expressed concerns about the impact of the new proposal on coral reefs and on marine life such as the dugong. Some in Nago's Henoko village risked their lives by taking their protest into the water to block construction. One protester told our group, "I will keep fighting even after I'm dead." By 2014, the Henoko village activists and their supporters marked a decade of sit-ins protesting the new base.[29]

THE STATUS OF FORCES

Deadly accidents, violent crime, and local anger have been a constant almost everywhere there are bases. Across the globe, it's clear that the impunity and power felt by troops can lead to theft, assault, rape, and murder. While only a minority of troops is involved, the effects of these attacks are profound not only for the victims, but for the broader local populations, who rarely regard crimes committed by the armed foreigners occupying their land as isolated events.

Some military leaders "will unhelpfully explain that soldiers commit fewer crimes per capita than residents of the host nation," notes Gillem. "Other officers recognize that numbers do not matter; any crime committed by U.S. soldiers is automatically an international event." As a former public affairs officer for U.S. Forces Japan explains, the crimes are seen "as an additive thing. They don't look at it as a rate—crimes per thousand or crimes per 100,000. It's just one more crime on top of a long history of earlier misconduct."[30]

In Germany, crimes committed by GIs during the Vietnam era helped sour many on the golden years of American occupation. As the war dragged on, the Army stationed some of its least well-trained troops in Germany. Base conditions deteriorated, and dissension and disorder grew accordingly. What's more, the value of the dollar against the mark had declined dramatically, and GIs suddenly felt and looked poor in the eyes of many Germans. Drug use was rife. Reports of mugging, robbery, assault, rape, and arson by GIs became common. In 1971, there was outright "insurrection," with soldiers in Wiesbaden refusing to participate in an exercise. vietnam has poisoned the u.s. army in germany, read one West German newspaper headline. Another declared, american terror as never before. The paper explained, "They are supposed to protect us. But they rob, murder, and rape. American soldiers in Germany arouse naked fears." With racial tensions in the military also exploding into view, in 1972 a newspaper described a clash in Stuttgart between African American GIs and German police as "the bloodiest pitched battle on the streets . . . since World War II."[31]

The cumulative result of these various problems—economic strain, crime, drugs, and racial conflict—was, as the historian Daniel Nelson says, that "a process of long-term atrophy in bedrock support for NATO and the American presence was set in motion in Germany." It would be a support that "could never be reproduced."[32]

In the Philippines, GI crimes similarly helped energize the movement that forced the U.S. military to leave the country in the early 1990s. More recently, a marine, who is among the hundreds of U.S. troops to return to the Philippines since 2002, was charged with murdering a transgender

Filipina, who was found with a broken neck on a hotel room toilet.[33] In South Korea, support for U.S. troops—long credited with protecting the South from communist invasion—was profoundly shaken when an armored vehicle killed two teenaged girls during a training exercise in 2002. The largest-ever protests against the U.S. presence followed.

The situation is only made worse by status of forces agreements (SOFAs) that often allow U.S. troops to escape prosecution by host nations for the crimes they commit. Little known in the United States, SOFAs govern the presence of U.S. troops in most countries abroad, covering everything from taxation to driving permits to what happens if a GI breaks the host country's laws. Each SOFA is different. Base expert Joseph Gerson once told me the length of a SOFA usually bears an inverse relationship to the power differential between the United States and the host country: the greater the power of the United States relative to the host, the shorter the SOFA, placing fewer restrictions on the military and its personnel.

When a Marine jet flying too low and too fast in Italy in 1998 severed a gondola cable, killing twenty skiers, many Italians were outraged when the pilot avoided Italian prosecution and then received a not guilty verdict in a North Carolina court-martial. Similarly, a U.S. military court once acquitted a sergeant who shot and killed a fifty-five-year-old Okinawan woman after he claimed he mistook her for a wild boar.[34] And in the aftermath of the 1995 schoolgirl rape, Okinawans were incensed by provisions in the U.S.-Japan SOFA that allowed the military to deny the Japanese police access to the rape suspects until the issuance of a formal indictment.[35]

INERTIA

It's been nearly two decades since the 1995 rape and the 1996 agreement to replace Futenma. In many ways, very little has happened. The military has returned some land, but many of the bases scheduled for return remain in operation. Futenma is still open and set to remain open until at least 2021. Construction of a replacement in Nago still faces intense protest and is moving very slowly, despite a new promise of $2.9 billion a year in Japanese government subsidies for the prefecture. Protests have grown and expanded islandwide. In Takae, a richly forested area in northern Okinawa that's the site of the Marines' Jungle Warfare Training Center, locals and their supporters have been protesting since 2007 against construction of six new helipads.[36]

Meanwhile, Okinawans have watched as military personnel continue to be involved in crimes and accidents on the island they are theoretically protecting. In the first sixteen years after the 1995 rape, there were reports of at least twenty-three more rapes and sexual assaults committed by U.S. military personnel in Okinawa.[37] In 2000, for example, a drunk nineteen-year-old marine sneaked into an apartment and sexually assaulted a fourteen-year-old girl.[38] In total, between 1972 (when Okinawa was returned to Japan) and 2011, the Okinawan prefectural government has documented 5,747 criminal cases involving GIs, including more than a thousand violent offenses. Over the same period, the prefecture documented 1,609 "incidents and accidents" ranging from speeding tickets to damage from military exercises, and more than a thousand aircraft-related accidents and forest fires. Between 1981 and 2011, the prefecture counted 2,764 traffic accidents, many related to drunk driving.[39] The nongovernmental organization Okinawa Women Act Against Military Violence has compiled a list of around 350 documented rapes, sexual assaults, and other crimes against women between 1945 and 2011. Since sexual assaults are especially prone to underreporting, there have likely been more crimes and accidents not included in the statistics.[40]

Crimes committed elsewhere in Japan have only further damaged the reputation of the military that's ostensibly protecting all Japanese citizens. In 2002, the aircraft carrier USS *Kitty Hawk* returned to the Yokosuka Navy base, south of Tokyo, after a deployment to support the war in Afghanistan. Within days, police forces arrested one sailor for assault and robbery, another for carjacking, and a third for drug smuggling.[41]

In 2012, the Marine Corps generated yet more opposition when it announced plans to move about two dozen MV-22 Osprey aircraft to Futenma. The hybrid plane/helicopter has a much-publicized accident record, leading to a demonstration that may have exceeded even the size of 1995's protests, estimated at 85,000 people. A *New York Times* editorial described the deployment as "rubbing salt into an old wound."[42] Just days after the first Ospreys arrived, two sailors were arrested and later convicted for raping and robbing an Okinawan woman in a parking lot. Military officials imposed an 11:00 p.m. curfew and "core values training," only for a series of new arrests to follow.[43]

In the face of continued Okinawan resistance, the Obama administration finally appeared to soften its position in 2012. Rather than demanding a replacement base before it would close Futenma, the administration announced it would move some nine thousand marines and around the same number of family members off Okinawa, whether the military had a replacement base or not. About five thousand marines would move to Guam; the other four thousand or so would disperse to bases in Hawaii, Australia, and Southeast Asia.[44] Japan agreed to provide $3.1 billion of the moving costs.[45] At the same time, though, the Marine Corps announced that it would actually *increase* its forces in Okinawa to nineteen thousand ahead of the planned withdrawal.[46]

While little has happened in terms of closing Futenma and moving marines off Okinawa, what has happened under the 1996 agreement is a lot of new base construction. Specifically, Japan had already agreed to fund $2 billion in new housing as part of a plan to replace 1,473 homes at Kadena Air Base and 1,777 units at Camp Foster. (On top of this, U.S. taxpayers funded a $95 million project to renovate 560 multifamily homes and expand parking to a very high 2.5 spaces per unit at Kadena.) "So what started out as a response to a rape ended up being a major housing construction program, providing new homes at no cost" to the United States, notes Mark Gillem.[47]

Government officials and military personnel in the United States, Japan, and Okinawa frequently express frustration at the slow pace of closing Futenma and moving marines off the island. Then again, for many of them, the status quo hasn't been so bad. The military still has its bases and lots of new housing. Japanese officials have shelled out billions of Japanese taxpayer dollars, but much of it has gone to Tokyo construction firms and other Japanese companies. Landowners, politicians, a few thousand base employees, and some businesses in Okinawa continue to benefit. Kevin Maher is gone, but bureaucrats like him on all sides have steady employment discussing the Okinawa issue. As my student group reached the end of our two-week exploration of bases, I increasingly wondered if many are more than content just to keep things as they are.

QUID PRO QUO

The uneven distribution of local benefits helps explain the complex politics of the base issue in many host communities. While almost all Okinawans want to see Futenma removed, for instance, opposition to other bases on the island is far from universal. Most of the landowners to whom the Japanese government pays rent support an ongoing U.S. presence,[48] and many business owners who benefit from sales to U.S. personnel are also supportive. A union that represents base employees likewise favors the bases, though other labor unions in Okinawa make up an important segment of the protest movement.

During my first visit to the prefecture, Okinawa International Professor of Politics Manabu Sato told our student group that Okinawa ultimately accepts the bases because, given the island's isolation, small size, and lack of natural resources, it needs the government aid they bring. The Japanese government has thus been pouring tens of millions into Okinawa as a "bribe" to make them accept the Futenma replacement, he explained.

The base expert Alexander Cooley details how the system works. "After reversion in 1972, Tokyo increased the rent it paid to the more than 30,000 private U.S. base landowners by 600 percent," easily exceeding market value. Then, writes Cooley, "construction companies and their subcontractors colluded with the prefecture and Tokyo to apportion and undertake hundreds of . . . new public works and development projects." "This quid pro quo" of economic investment in exchange for local acquiescence to the U.S. presence "has since become institutionalized," says Cooley, "and remains a hallmark of Okinawa's relations with the Japanese mainland."[49] When the Japanese government agreed to U.S. requests in 1978 to begin paying the salaries of thousands of Japanese civilians working on U.S. bases through what became known as the "sympathy budget," it further solidified Okinawan support at a time when bases' direct economic impact was declining.

Since the growth of antibase protest following the 1995 rape, the system has only expanded. The "militancy and opposition to the bases," explains Cooley, "have driven Tokyo to develop and institutionalize a comprehensive system of fiscal transfers, public works funds, and targeted payments to key island actors." With the help of a "permanent and well-funded state bureaucracy" in Tokyo, "these sizable transfers have established a political economy of base-related compensation that ultimately assures that a slight political majority in Okinawa continues to support the U.S. presence, albeit tacitly."[50]

At the same time, many acknowledge that much of the aid has gone toward building what Sato called "useless public facilities," such as little-used recreation centers and unnecessary monuments. Okinawan politicians accept the money because it means construction jobs, Sato said. But then Okinawa is stuck with the maintenance costs for the facilities. Meanwhile, much of the money ends up back in Tokyo, he added, because it's the big Tokyo construction firms that get most of the contracts.[51]

While Japan has spent an estimated $70 billion to raise Okinawa's level of development to Japanese standards since the end of the U.S. occupation in 1972, per capita income there remains the lowest among Japan's 47 prefectures, at around 70 percent of the national average. The unemployment rate remains the highest nationwide, at 7.5 percent.[52] People are realizing "this money is not to build a sustainable economy," said Sato. In rural northern communities of Okinawa, where most of the U.S. training bases are found, government spending is creating a "serious dependency problem."

HIDDEN COSTS

The immense amounts spent by Japan on the "sympathy budget" and other support for U.S. bases make it particularly ironic that Kevin Maher described Okinawans as "extortionists": U.S. negotiators themselves have long pressed the Japanese government for ever larger subsidies to the U.S. military presence in East Asia. Since at least 1972, Japan has generally paid more than any other host country to support the U.S. base and troop presence. Over time, those payments have added up to many tens of billions of dollars.

Although the 1972 deal that returned Okinawa to Japan was widely dubbed "reversion," Japan secretly agreed as part of the negotiations to abide by quotas on textile exports to the United States and to pay as much as $685 million for Okinawa's return. The payments included the cost of buildings and utilities returned to Japan and the expense of removing nuclear weapons from the island. (Another secret agreement allowed the reintroduction of nuclear weapons in emergencies.) The Japanese government also agreed to help prop up the weakening value of the dollar by depositing $112 million in New York's Federal Reserve Bank for twenty-five years, interest free. And the government paid another $250 million over five years for base maintenance and Okinawan defense costs. As Gavan McCormack, an expert on U.S.-Japan relations, puts it, "the 'return' of 1972 was actually a purchase, and Japan has continued ever since to pay huge amounts." These are "in effect a reverse rental fee, by which the Japanese landlord pays its American tenant."[53]

Today, Japanese sympathy payments subsidize the U.S. presence at an annual level of around $150,000 per service member.[54] For 2011 alone, Japanese taxpayers provided $7.1 billion, or around three quarters of total basing costs.[55] In addition to agreeing to pay $6.09 billion to help close Futenma and move marines off Okinawa, the Japanese government agreed to contribute around $15.9 billion toward a larger set of transformations involving bases in Okinawa, Guam, the Commonwealth of the Northern Mariana Islands, and Iwakuni, Japan.[56] As in 1972, Japan is effectively paying to get its land back.

Japanese taxpayers have also spent nearly $1 billion to soundproof civilian homes near noisy U.S. air bases in Okinawa, and millions more in damages assessed in noise pollution lawsuits. Because of favorable basing agreements, the U.S. military generally doesn't have to pay for environmental cleanup in Japan, South Korea, or elsewhere. These costs also come from citizens' taxes, further reducing the net value of any local benefits. Most U.S. and conservative Japanese officials would say that Japan has simply been paying the United States to provide security. While this argument may have been plausible during the Cold War, it seems harder to sustain today. Although there is real public fear of China, especially over tensions in the East China Sea, China's military power still does not rival that of the United States. Japan's so-called Self-Defense Forces are also one of the world's most powerful militaries, even though Japan's U.S.-drafted constitution renounces war and insists that armed forces "will never be maintained." The country regularly ranks among the world's top military spenders (fifth in 2012, eighth in 2013).[57] Since 2001, Japan has provided both financial contributions and "boots on the ground" in Afghanistan and Iraq. And Japan apparently feels secure enough in its self-defense to have a foreign military base of its own in Djibouti, the country's first since World War II.

"WE DON'T NEED MARINES IN OKINAWA"

Gradually, a growing number of military analysts have started to question the U.S. base presence in Okinawa—not on political or social grounds, but on purely military ones. The growing range and accuracy of Chinese and North Korean missiles have led many to conclude that bases so close to the Asian continent are so vulnerable to attack as to be of little value.[58]

More profoundly, analysts across the political spectrum are increasingly beginning to question the underlying justifications and rationale for the bases. As long as the United States has had bases in Okinawa and Japan, the primary justification for their existence has been that they ensure security for the United States, Japan, and the region. Initially, it was said that the bases helped contain and deter Soviet expansionist desires. Since the end of the Cold War, many have simply substituted China and North Korea for the USSR in the containment/deterrence framework. But North Korea is a small, impoverished nation, possibly on the verge of collapse. And while China's military power has grown in recent years, it doesn't approach that of the Soviet Union during the Cold War. What's more, placing bases and troops on another country's doorstep can be seen as an aggression in its own right, triggering exactly the kind of military response the strategy is supposedly designed to prevent.

Even within the context of containment and deterrence, the U.S. presence in Okinawa hardly looks like an optimal setup. Many now agree, for example, that the Marines' presence in Okinawa—including the controversial Futenma base and its debated replacement—likely has little deterrent effect. Barry Posen, who was a Pentagon official in the Bush administration, has said that with the large Air Force and Navy forces at Okinawa's Kadena Air Base and on mainland Japan, the withdrawal of the marines would see "no change in deterrence." Posen added that he "cannot see what role the Marine Corps might play in military actions" that conceivably might take place in the region.[59] Former Democratic House representative Barney Frank agreed, saying, "15,000 Marines aren't going to land on the Chinese mainland and confront millions of Chinese soldiers. We don't need Marines in Okinawa. They're a hangover from a war that ended 65 years ago."[60]

And there often haven't even been fifteen thousand marines in Okinawa, the number frequently cited by proponents of the status quo. During the wars in Afghanistan and Iraq, thousands of them deployed from Okinawa, decreasing troop levels by one quarter to one third from prewar averages.[61] If Okinawa-based Marines are so critical to deterrence, how could the military afford to let them leave?

Marines in Okinawa also don't have the transportation necessary to get involved in significant numbers during an emergency. To deploy, marines rely on Navy transportation vessels harbored in Sasebo, Japan. During a 2013 drill simulating a response to China's seizing contested territory, such as the Senkaku/Diaoyu islands, marines relied on a vessel based in San Diego to transport troops and weaponry.[62] The Marines' controversial Osprey tilt-rotor aircraft doesn't have the range to transport troops to the Senkaku/Diaoyus without in-air refueling; and with just twenty-four Ospreys in Okinawa, the Marines can send fewer than six hundred troops at most in a single deployment.[63] If the Marines can't operate independently and speedily from Okinawa, what kind of regional deterrent force are they?

The fact is that, in many ways, the Marines' entire presence in Okinawa has little to do with military strategy or security. Partly, they are attached to the island because it provides a great place to train. (When not deployed at war, much of what troops *do* is train.) The Marines don't want to relinquish facilities like Okinawa's huge Jungle Warfare Training Center, which was, until recently, the only jungle training center in the military. The Marine Corps' institutional attachment to the island also plays a significant role. Given the high casualties suffered in the Pacific War's deadliest battle, Okinawa has a hallowed place in the history of the Corps, so the Marines have long considered the territory to be "theirs." They simply don't want to give it up.

The Marine Corps also hasn't wanted to give up Okinawa because in recent years many marines have feared for the service's very existence.

During the wars in Afghanistan and Iraq, the Marine Corps has fought much like the Army. The Marines' last amphibious landing was more than half a century ago, in the Korean War, leading many to question why the military has an amphibious armed service that's effectively a second army. Giving up bases in Okinawa, and with them the idea that the Marines are necessary to maintain peace in East Asia, would mean the Marine Corps could lose one of its three main combat divisions.[64] "The Marines are so afraid because if the decision is made to move them," explained the former Pentagon official Ray DuBois, the next decision may be "that those marines will disappear." Losing some of the total marine troop strength would mean losing money in the Pentagon budget, raising more questions about whether the service needs to exist at all. Even the idea proposed by some senators of relocating marines from Futenma to available space at the Air Force's Kadena Air Base is anathema to the Marine Corps, given that such a move would cede power to another of the armed services.

More broadly, U.S. officials see removing bases and troops from Okinawa as weakening the U.S.-Japanese military alliance, whereas successive presidential administrations have been trying to deepen bilateral military cooperation. Some suggest that U.S. officials have been trying to turn Japan into something of the "Great Britain of Asia"— and that many Japanese officials are more than happy to assume that role, given the power and financial benefits it has brought Britain.[65] U.S. officials would like to use Japan's military as a subordinate force within a global military architecture that's increasingly relying on the incorporation of allied armies into a U.S.-controlled system. In the process, U.S. leaders hope to keep Japan locked into its position as a Cold War–era client state during a new era when the rationale for maintaining Cold War alliances has disappeared, when Japan could potentially assert more independence, and when U.S. political, economic, and military control in East Asia is being challenged by China and other rising powers. Holding on to bases in Okinawa becomes a way to try to hold on to a Japanese puppet and, with it, U.S. political-economic dominance.

Temporarily putting aside questions about the wisdom, efficacy, and morality of this strategy, its financial costs alone should raise serious doubts. Remember that despite large sums contributed by the Japanese government, U.S. taxpayers are likely paying $150 million to $225 million more per year to keep around fifteen thousand marines in Okinawa compared to basing them in the United States. Basing U.S. Army, Navy, and Air Force personnel in Okinawa and elsewhere in Japan is even more expensive for the U.S. government compared to domestic basing.[66] The total additional cost to U.S. taxpayers to maintain 113 base sites and more than fifty thousand troops in Japan could easily top one billion dollars a year. Ironically enough, in addition to those being extorted in Okinawa and Japan, Americans are being extorted too.

"No Dal Molin" protest against the construction of a new U.S. Army base in Vicenza, Italy.

15

"It's Enough"

Vroom, vroom, vroooom. A soldier loudly revved the engine on his Dodge Charger muscle car as he waited at the traffic light at the Katterbach Kaserne's exit gate, seemingly annoyed at the dozen activists standing a few yards away. It was the summer of 2010, and the protesters were taking part in a weekly demonstration outside Katterbach, one of several large bases in Ansbach, Germany. Most were members of a local citizen's initiative or another activist group called Etz Langt's, whose name in local Franconian means "It's Enough." Many wore white T-shirts with the symbol of their movement: a helicopter inside a red-slash "no" sign. One carried a rainbow peace flag. Others carried posters in German and English with phrases like stop the helicopter noise, helicopters to wind turbines, and, simply, you can get out.

Fierce resistance to military bases has never been an issue in Okinawa alone. Around the world, the construction of new U.S. bases and the operation of existing ones have increasingly become the subject of protest. This is now true even in countries such as Germany and Italy, which have long been regarded as some of the friendliest and most stable base locations abroad.

Ansbach, a small Bavarian city of about forty thousand, has been a typically supportive home for a significant U.S. presence since World War II. When the Pentagon announced its base transformation plans for Europe, it named Ansbach one of the Army's seven "enduring communities" in Europe. Since then, the Army's five major *kasernes* around Ansbach and surrounding towns have seen a string of major new construction projects. These have included a new town house development, a shopping center, and tens of millions spent on family housing renovations, recreational facilities, and fitness centers.[1]

At the protest, I asked a social worker, Ann Klose, why she was there. "The noise, first," she replied. The city's primary military occupant is one of the Army's largest aviation brigades, and it flies numerous helicopters, including Apaches, Black Hawks, and large dual-rotor Chinooks.[2] One man described living less than five hundred yards from the fence surrounding the Katterbach Kaserne and awaking at night with the sound of helicopters in his ears. "You can't sleep," he said. The vibration of the helicopters' blades makes his kitchen plates rattle. "*Whoomp, whoomp, whoomp, whoomp,*" he said, imitating the sound. It's so bad, he added, that many people in his neighborhood have thought of selling their homes. Even though they're living outside the fences, the helicopters are so loud that sometimes they feel as if they're living inside the base.

The majority of people in the movement are involved because of the noise, said Klose (a pseudonym). When the helicopters are in Ansbach and training, she explained, many more people come to the protests. When most of the soldiers and helicopters are deployed, as they were during my visit, the protests were smaller. On the curb, a pile of protest signs lay unused.

Klose told me she was also protesting because she believed the local Ansbach administration knew about the Army's buildup plans but tried to keep them secret from citizens. There was "a kind of conspiracy of silence" between politicians and the media, she said.

And there was more to it, too. Klose was carrying a sign that read no more war from germany, and she readily acknowledged that her opposition to the base went beyond the helicopter noise and the secrecy around the expansion's planning. For her, as for others, opposition to the U.S. base presence was rooted to varying degrees in the fact that the United States had invaded Iraq and was waging war from their lands. In Ansbach, Klose and others told me, some of their discomfort comes not so much from the noise itself as from what it represents. The *whoomp-whoomp* of the whirling blades symbolizes the wars that those helicopters have helped wage, and hosting the helicopters in their city makes the locals feel complicit. For some, there is a painful irony in the garrison's motto, "We are all part of the fight."

SIMMERING RESENTMENTS

The army garrison in Vicenza, Italy, is another place where vehement antibase protests have surprised many. Opposition in Italy had long been restricted to small, scattered protests in places such as Naples and Pisa, and a movement against a missile base in Sicily in the 1980s. U.S. officials had long thought of Italy's wealthy and strongly conservative northeast as a particularly supportive host. But the plans to build a new base at Vicenza's Dal Molin airport unexpectedly provoked a widespread surge of protest. Equally surprising, the opposition movement was remarkably diverse: it joined self-identified housewives and businessmen, former 1960s radicals and young anarchists, university students and religious organizations, pacifists and disaffected members of the openly racist anti-immigrant Northern League. They formed a sometimes rocky but effective and unusually creative coalition.

While historically Vicenza saw little of the protest found in other communities hosting U.S. bases, there were some long-standing tensions that were largely suppressed until opposition built against Dal Molin. Army officer Fred Glenn remembers that when he arrived in Vicenza shortly after the return of U.S. forces in 1955, most Americans were "standoffish." Few wanted to live off base, and other than some Italian Americans, "very few bothered to learn the language." From time to time, Glenn was the officer in charge of payroll for the local workers. When handing cash to the waiting Italians, "We were required to have a pistol highly, highly visible," he says. "In fact, on the pay table." He thought the rule was "outrageous."

As at many other locations, the military presence around Vicenza also distorted the local housing market. When Vicenza native Enzo Ciscato and U.S.-born Annetta Reams started looking for a home as newlyweds in the 1980s, Ciscato remembers, the preference for renting to soldiers' families was so great that they had trouble finding an apartment. Eventually, a friend introduced them to someone in the housing office of Vicenza's main base, Caserma Ederle. When the staffer learned that

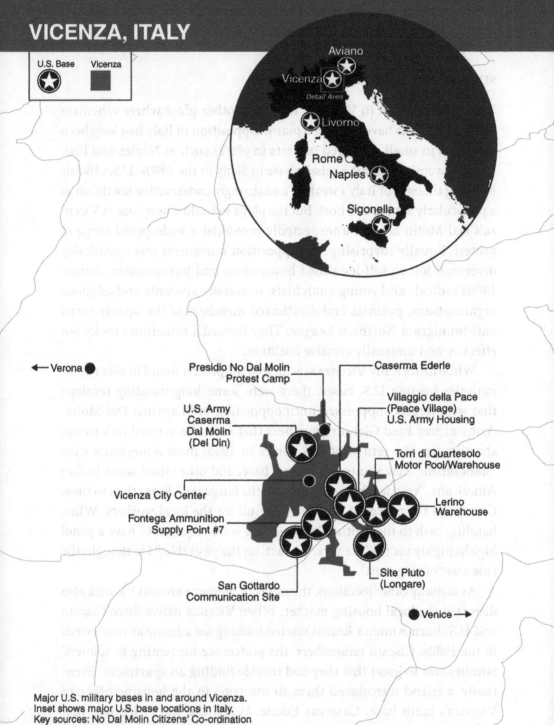

VICENZA, ITALY

U.S. Base   Vicenza

Aviano
Vicenza
Detail Area
Livorno
Rome
Naples
Sigonella

← Verona

Presidio No Dal Molin
Protest Camp

Caserma Ederle

U.S. Army
Caserma
Dal Molin
(Del Din)

Villaggio della Pace
(Peace Village)
U.S. Army Housing

Torri di Quartesolo
Motor Pool/Warehouse

Vicenza City Center

Lerino
Warehouse

Fontega Ammunition
Supply Point #7

San Gottardo
Communication Site

Site Pluto
(Longare)

Venice →

Major U.S. military bases in and around Vicenza.
Inset shows major U.S. base locations in Italy.
Key sources: No Dal Molin Citizens' Co-ordination
Committees of the City of Vicenza map, 2007;
U.S. Army Garrison Vicenza.

Reams was an American, he said, "Oh that's great!" Then he told Ciscato to "shut up" when visiting apartments. "Act like a couple of Americans, because if they know you are Italian, they will not rent to you."

"You can think how great" that felt, Ciscato told me. "As a person born in this town, to go to look for a house in this town, acting [like] an American soldier to be able to have a house."

Another Vicenza local recalled growing up near the Caserma Ederle during the Cold War and seeing American soldiers all around in the streets and the shops. "It was normal to wake up in the morning when they practiced" their marching cadences, she told me. "We were angry and annoyed," she said, but people felt they just had to "tolerate it, to be patient . . . What can you do?"

With such resentment already simmering under the surface, the buildup to the 2003 U.S. invasion of Iraq was a major point of motivation for antibase activists in Vicenza, just as it was in Ansbach and many other parts of the world. Several hundred gathered for protests and marches around the Caserma Ederle. Some attempted to block trains moving military matériel for Ederle-based battalions deploying to Iraq.[3]

Guido Lanaro was one of the activists involved, and he remembers first hearing rumors about a new base around the same time, in 2003 or 2004. Enzo Ciscato, for his part, first heard alarming talk about the old Dal Molin airport when he was a member of his local neighborhood governing committee. A city council member told the committee there were rumors about "something happening with the Americans." It was then, Ciscato said, that it "started to smell strange. Because after mentioning something, everything was kept secret."

NO DAL MOLIN

In May 2006, around the time the Army was asking Congress for Dal Molin construction funding, a Vicenza city official and U.S. military representatives finally presented a detailed plan for the new base to the city council. The presentation came complete with PowerPoint slides, documents, maps, and pictorial renderings, and for many it confirmed suspicions that the mayor and the city council had known about the project for some time. Many believed that it was "deliberately hidden from the citizenry," Lanaro said.[4]

Reams remembers the same feeling: people felt that "their rights were being taken away" by the politicians and secret agreements. "They say, 'Here is a present for you. And what you have to say doesn't matter. Take it whether you like it or not.' "

Beyond feeling excluded from the decision-making process, many in Vicenza grew increasingly concerned as details about the base emerged. The new base was set to take over 135 acres at the Dal Molin airport and a large adjacent grassy field; many feared it would destroy one of Vicenza's last areas of green space. Environmental scientists and engineers showed that the military's plan to drive hundreds of pylons into the ground to support the buildings' foundations risked puncturing the city's aquifer and its main source of drinking water, in addition to causing other environmental damage. Many were afraid that the base would harm the internationally famous architectural and cultural fabric of the city while increasing traffic in an already congested town by bringing in thousands of new soldiers and family members. Given the critical role the 173rd brigade played in the fighting in Afghanistan and Iraq, people also worried that returning soldiers would bring the trauma of war back to Vicenza; many pointed to the case of a soldier who brutally raped a sex worker after returning from an Iraq deployment and successfully gained a reduction in his sentence because of the "prolonged psychological stress" he had experienced at war.[5]

Ciscato points out that the nature of the U.S. presence in Vicenza has changed since the Cold War. In those days, he says, the Italian bases were strategically positioned to defend "against Russian invaders," but now "it is an operative site. People from here—they don't stay here . . . They go to war and come back. They bring their damages back. They rest. They go to war again." Now, he said, "We're talking about combat units being here. It's a bit different."

The official announcement of the plan for Dal Molin led to increasingly large protests against the base. A little more than a month after the city council presentation, hundreds blocked the airport's entrance for hours. Later that summer, thousands peacefully occupied the Basilica Palladiana, one of Vicenza's central landmarks, for twenty-four hours, talking through the night on its steps and draping no dal molin banners and giant peace flags from the arched balconies. It was a struggle "for dignity," one of the protesters said to me. "Not to be part of a city where soldiers live to go around the world and kill people. I don't like this . . . When someone asks me, 'Where do you live?' I want to be proud to say, 'I live in Vicenza: a beautiful city.'" She paused. "But now, I'm not so proud. Because [when] everybody speaks of Vicenza, of the military base—it's not good for our image in the world."

Soon, the No Dal Molin activists also built their own base, which they called the Presidio—a headquarters for the movement, adjacent to the Dal Molin construction site.[6] Beginning as a trailer parked in a cornfield, over time it grew to include two large tents and three shipping containers, with a full-scale kitchen, storage, and toilets. Starting in 2007, No Dal Molin members occupied the Presidio around the clock for more than two years, making a permanent encampment and permanent protest against the base. The Presidio became a kind of community center, a common ground where people could meet and connect with people from diverse political and social backgrounds. The Presidio was more than a movement headquarters. It became, as Guido Lanaro put it, "like a second home."

Thanks to the Presidio's creation and continuing protests, the largest of which drew an estimated hundred thousand people in a city with just 115,000 inhabitants, No Dal Molin gained national and international attention.[7] "We felt so powerful," Marco Palma, a No Dal Molin spokesperson, told me. "We felt it was impossible that the base could be built. Because when you have so much energy from so many people, we felt like we could do anything in the world."

BASE ECONOMICS

In communities like Ansbach and Vicenza, public opinion about the base presence is often divided. When the Dal Molin plan went before the Vicenza City Council, twenty-one center-right allies of Prime Minister Silvio Berlusconi's party overcame the votes of seventeen center-left coalition members. Around this time, the city's major newspaper—whose controlling interest belongs to the equivalent of the city's Chamber of Commerce—began running stories suggesting that the U.S. military would close the Caserma Ederle if prevented from building at Dal Molin. from ederle a desperate sos: "save our jobs," read one headline. The reports fueled fears that rejecting the base would damage the local economy.

To support the base plan, one Italian Caserma Ederle employee, Roberto Cattaneo, formed the Yes to Dal Molin Committee. The new base, the Yes Committee's website said, was "offering with it an opportunity for economic and occupational development for the city and for all the surrounding areas." The committee cited total economic benefits of more than €1.5 billion from construction at Dal Molin.[8]

The suggestion from base supporters in Vicenza that rejecting construction at Dal Molin would damage the local economy is a frequent theme in debates over U.S. bases. When I was watching the protest outside the Katterbach Kaserne in Ansbach, I struck up a conversation with two of the gate guards. Both lived locally and worked for a company contracted to provide security for Army bases in Bavaria. One of the guards acknowledged that the noise is indeed loud and helicopters fly very low over the neighborhood. But Ansbach depends on the bases economically, he said.

This is a common perception. In Germany and other countries around the world, bases are widely regarded as an economic boon, just as they are in communities in the United States. And, indeed, bases do enrich some local communities.* The "golden years" in places like Baumholder show us as much. After all, U.S. taxpayers spend tens of billions of dollars every year to maintain bases and troops overseas. All that money has to go somewhere.

However, research about the economic effects of bases in Germany, the United States, and elsewhere consistently shows that the economic benefits of bases are less significant than one might expect. The benefits are enjoyed disproportionately by relatively few individuals and industries, and people tend to ignore a variety of costs associated with bases that significantly decrease their net economic impact. Moreover, bases

---

*The one clear exception is Guantánamo Bay, where the local economic impact is almost entirely negative. The base is entirely self-sufficient, and there is no economic activity connecting the base and Guantánamo city or other surrounding communities.

are an inefficient form of economic investment; often, they actually inhibit more productive and profitable forms of economic activity. Okinawa, for example, remains Japan's poorest prefecture. The causes of that poverty are complex, but the period of formal U.S. occupation of Okinawa that lasted until 1972 clearly inhibited economic growth. In recent years, as the base presence has declined, Okinawa's economy has expanded and diversified around tourism, IT, call centers, and logistics.[9]

Baumholder also shows how the golden years often fade. As the dollar weakened relative to the mark, soldiers' economic impact declined. Meanwhile, with the West German "economic miracle" taking off in the late 1950s, better jobs—especially for women—appeared than those available on and around the bases. Often, most on-base jobs available to locals are relatively low-skill, low-wage positions, such as janitorial and landscaping staff. Other off-base employment supported in part by a base presence appears in the service sector or the construction and industrial trades, but the vast majority of higher-skill, higher-wage jobs go to U.S. military personnel and U.S. civilians. From the perspective of the local community, most of the people working on foreign bases are, of course, foreigners—so bases offer far fewer jobs than their sprawling size might suggest.[10]

Bases also tend to occupy valuable land that could be used in other ways. This has been especially true in German cities such as Heidelberg, Würzburg, and Berlin, in densely urbanized Japan, and in the middle of downtown Seoul. Bases also occupy thousands of acres of precious beachfront property in places such as Okinawa, Guam, and Diego Garcia.

In recent decades, the economic impact of U.S. bases has also declined as bases have become increasingly self-sufficient and isolated from local economies. Bases like Ramstein, with their plentiful food outlets, entertainment, and shopping, mean that troops and their families almost never have to leave base. In turn, this means most of their money never reaches the local economy.

Spending by troops is only part of the story, of course. As we have seen, most U.S. taxpayer money goes to construction, the procurement of goods, and the daily operation, maintenance, and repair of bases. In Germany, some of these U.S. contracts go to German companies—but many do not. Instead, they often go to U.S.-based firms. (For fiscal year 2015,

Congress placed significant restrictions on awarding large contracts to foreign companies.)[11] Sometimes U.S. firms subcontract to local businesses, but in either case, the vast majority of contract dollars goes to large corporations. As we have seen, out of an estimated $385 billion the Pentagon paid between 2001 and 2013 to private companies for work done abroad, about one third went to the top ten recipients— companies like former Halliburton subsidiary KBR and other major military contractors such as DynCorp, ITT/Exelis, and the oil giant BP. This means that much of the money generated by bases flows out of local communities to company headquarters (and, not infrequently, to various offshore banking havens). The trend is particularly pronounced in Okinawa, where much of the money flowing from the U.S. presence has gone to Tokyo-based construction companies rather than Okinawan businesses.

Among locals who do benefit from foreign bases' presence, some of the most advantaged are those involved in real estate. The Pentagon pays for the housing of U.S. military personnel, and it pays generously—often well above market rates. Property owners, real estate developers, land speculators, real estate agents, and construction companies often enjoy large profits as a result. An Italian base employee described in a letter how military housing allowances are "in most cases significantly more than locals can spend on rent," which makes Americans "a most welcome and cherished community on the demand side of the real estate market." The employee noted that since Americans pay higher rents, landlords "have, in the course of time, started to plan and build houses and homes specifically designed for Americans . . . In some communities entire streets or new construction projects are leased out to Americans." As a result, local renters can find themselves priced out of their own communities.[12] Locals also don't come with the financial security of the U.S. government paying their bills. As the Vicenza-based anthropologist Guido Lanaro explained, it's "very convenient to rent to the Americans because you are one hundred percent sure that the rent will be paid."

Smaller amounts of base money tend to flow into local service industries such as restaurants, bars, and taxis. The German base expert Elsa Rassbach pointed out to me that taxi drivers have been very supportive of U.S. bases in places like Ansbach because the military often pays for expensive rides between towns in the area. I asked Rassbach if she thought this was deliberate. "Absolutely," she replied. "It's community relations."

When locals focus on bases' perceived economic benefits, they also often overlook bases' costs, which can be less visible. For instance, host countries usually provide land without requiring the United States to pay rent or taxes on it. Whether people know it or not, that's a subsidy provided by local governments and their citizens. Host countries have also financially supported U.S. bases for decades through "burden-sharing," "sympathy payments," and, increasingly, through in-kind contributions. (These include the provision of security in Germany and other countries; base construction in several Persian Gulf nations; and the free use of buildings and training ranges in Italy.) In 2004, the Pentagon calculated host countries' in-kind contributions at $4.3 billion, in addition to billions more in direct burden-sharing payments.[13]

WHEN BASES CLOSE

The most illuminating perspective on the economic impact of bases comes from studies of what happens when bases close. In communities threatened with base closures, locals often fear dire consequences. Andy Hoehn, one of the senior U.S. officials sent to Germany to discuss a "very significant drawdown" of forces as part of the Bush administration's global base realignment, recalls local politicians in Rheinland-Pfalz, Bavaria, and other states with large base concentrations pleading that their areas be spared the cuts. Hoehn was somewhat surprised to note "their appeals to us were really . . . of culture and economy, and not of security. They were not there to make an argument that there were security reasons for a large number of troops to remain in Germany in 2004." Instead, the politicians simply insisted that "our local economies depend upon the presence of these troops."

"And not only were they appealing to us," Hoehn explained, "but they were positioning among each other. So it was, 'At least don't leave my region . . . If you've got to do it over there, that's okay. But just don't leave *here*.'" He added, "It was emotional. It was a plea. They were pleading. This was a plea to us not to leave."

Given the politicized nature of base closures, it's not surprising that some of the early research into the effects of U.S. base closures was often politicized as well.[14] But more recent research from around the globe is coming to a clear conclusion: while communities often anticipate that base closures will cause catastrophic economic damage, generally the impact is relatively limited and in some cases actually positive. In the cases where communities do suffer intense economic harm, most tend to rebound within a few years' time.

In Germany, the Bonn International Center for Conversion conducted an authoritative study of U.S. base closings after the Cold War, primarily using the Pentagon's own data. It showed that between 1991 and 1995, the U.S. military returned around a hundred thousand acres of base land to the German government and withdrew 75 percent of its forces, or almost two hundred thousand troops.[15] Annual U.S. military spending in Germany dropped by around $3 billion. Because most U.S. troops have been concentrated in Rheinland-Pfalz, Bavaria, and three other states in southern Germany, some regions and communities where U.S. troops were based were "seriously impacted" by the drawdown. Across the country, although 34,500 Germans lost civilian jobs, representing about 0.04 percent of the country's population and 1 percent of the labor force, the study found, the closures and reductions had no "significant effect on Germany's economy as a whole."[16]

A more recent study of the German military's own base closures in 298 communities in Germany between 2003 and 2007 showed that "negative impacts of base closures" were "non-existent." Specifically, there was "no significant impact on the economic development of the communities around a base as measured by household income, regional output, the unemployment rate, and revenues from the value-added tax (VAT) and income tax." While U.S. bases in both Germany and the United States tend to be larger and more integrated into local communities than German bases are, these results are striking. The authors hypothesize that the speed with which local communities converted former bases into other uses such as hospitals and tourist attractions may have helped to offset any negative effects.[17] German communities facing the closure of U.S. bases have undertaken similar conversion efforts, creating schools, housing, offices, and retail space. In Ansbach, for example, after the Army returned the Hindenburg Kaserne, the city transformed the base into the Ansbach University of Applied Sciences, plus a shopping mall and office space.[18]

In the United States, research on the impact of base closures has produced similar findings. A review of sophisticated broad-based econometric studies showed an "unambiguous" conclusion: "Base closures had either no significant regional impact or a small impact that quickly vanishes with time."[19] The result was corroborated by a study of the effects of the Swedish military's closure of bases in Sweden.[20]

Focusing more specifically on the jobs question, a Government Accountability Office study showed that the majority of communities affected by closures did not experience rising unemployment.[21] A Congressional Research Service study actually found a *drop* in unemployment rates in communities where bases closed compared to the national average. A 1998 Pentagon study found that only 14 percent of federally employed civilians eligible to claim unemployment insurance following a base closure actually claimed it, suggesting they found other jobs or left the workforce. A study of 3,092 counties and 963 domestic base sites over twenty years also contradicted "doom and gloom" predictions about job losses. It showed instead that closure had a positive impact on employment after only two years, perhaps because of government conversion assistance and "community optimism (following apprehension)." In short, the study concluded, the long-run impacts of base job reductions are "overall positive."[22]

The experience in Okinawa further confirms much of the research. The closure of an Army base, for example, provided seaside land for the creation of an entertainment and shopping area, which now employs about three thousand people and attracts around a million visitors annually. A 2007 study found that the area's impact on the local economy was about 215 times that of the base. Another study has shown that a shopping mall and office complex in the Okinawan capital, Naha, has sixteen times the economic benefit of the military housing formerly occupying the site.[23]

Such findings should not be surprising: "bases are not corporations that accumulate capital and contribute to the growth of the local economy," explains the Okinawa International University economist Moritake Tomikawa. Having land resources occupied by U.S. bases, he says, "is a huge economic loss for the prefecture." With the military gradually returning base land, economists expect Okinawa's diversifying economy to grow faster than that of any of Japan's other prefectures.[24]

TRUE DEMOCRACY?

Such positive statistics are often little known, and in Vicenza most local base supporters, along with U.S. military officials, tended to portray the No Dal Molin movement as a small minority in town. The No Dal Molin activists tended to say the same about the size of the Yes movement, while acknowledging the power of the business interests, politicians, and government officials supporting the base. An October 2006 survey by a prominent Italian political scientist found that 61 percent of Vicenza residents opposed the base, while 85 percent supported a referendum to decide the plan's fate.[25] In 2008, it appeared this wish would come true: in response to a lawsuit brought by base opponents, a regional court ordered work on the base suspended and decreed a local referendum to decide Dal Molin's fate.[26] The court found the government's approval of the plan on the basis of nothing more than a verbal agreement to be "absolutely incompatible" with the law.[27]

Italian courts are notoriously slow. Across Italy, there are around nine million cases awaiting appeal.[28] And yet, in the Dal Molin case, the Berlusconi government appealed the regional court's ruling directly to Italy's highest court and won a judgment within forty days. Invoking the secret 1954 bilateral agreement with the United States and a Mussolini-era law from 1924, the justices said the lower court lacked jurisdiction over decisions about a base, since such decisions are essentially a political question.[29] On the basis of the ruling, another Italian court suspended the local referendum four days before the vote.

In a show of defiance, however, local volunteers held their own referendum. With the help of Vicenza mayor Achile Variati and strictly following election rules, almost 25,000 participated. Ninety-five percent voted against the base.[30] Buoyed by the results, protests continued. In early 2009, hundreds of protesters cut through the fence to Dal Molin and created a "Peace Park" there, occupying part of the construction site for three bitterly cold and snowy days in January.

Days later, the Italian and U.S. governments announced final approval for the base. In the months that followed, more than a dozen construction cranes rose around the site, visible from miles around.

When I toured the mostly completed Dal Molin base in 2013, an Italian civilian working for the Army said, "I loved this project from the very beginning." She and a U.S. colleague, both of whom asked not to be named, had little interest in the protesters. She described the Presidio as a "gypsy camp," while he saw the protesters' actions as mostly "vandalism." (At one point, when No Dal Molin activists discovered new fiber optic cables laid without proper authorization near Dal Molin, around a hundred people dressed as utility workers gathered on the street and sealed the access points to the cables with concrete.[31]) "They tried all the protests they could try," the American said, but he thought the majority of the community didn't care. Anyway, he added, "a local protest won't change the direction of national policy."

Traditional political science would typically agree with this assessment. Many political scientists would say that local protest should generally be irrelevant in such a situation. Even if a majority of Vicenza residents opposed the base, even if a newly elected mayor and city council rejected the plan (as they did in late 2008), decisions about military matters and other issues of foreign policy should be made not by local authorities but by nationally elected politicians. And in this case, the Italian government approved the base.[32] Many would suggest that this was democracy at work. Some might point to the U.S. base in Manta, Ecuador, as a telling comparison: in that case, the majority of locals supported the base, but the national government opposed it, and the base was eventually removed.[33]

Still, many in Vicenza ask how democratic the decision to build the Dal Molin base really was if the presence of U.S. bases in Italy rests on a secret 1954 agreement approved without the consent of the Italian parliament or the U.S. Congress. They ask whether the decision was really democratic if Italian and U.S. officials carried out their Dal Molin negotiations in secret, preventing any public debate at either the national or local level until after they had made an initial agreement. They ask whether a real democratic decision would violate Italian and European contract bidding regulations, as a regional court found. They ask whether a democratic decision would bypass an environmental impact assessment planned by the Ministry of the Environment, which the court also determined was required under national law. (In a leaked letter, a special commissioner responsible for overseeing the project acknowledged the environmental danger posed by the base and discussed ways to circumvent the environmental assessment because of its potential to "put the final decision in jeopardy."[34]) And how truly democratic was it, many in Vicenza ask, if a foreign power—the United States—exerted what appears to be significant pressure on the Italian government to follow through with the agreement, regardless of what Italians really wanted?[35]

A DIVERSITY OF MOVEMENTS

Though the No Dal Molin movement failed to stop the construction of the new base in Vicenza, it did win a concession. The U.S. military agreed to move the base from its originally planned location at the civilian airport on the east side of the Dal Molin site to a former Italian Air Force base on the site's west side. The mayor declared the eastern half would be a permanent "Peace Park," although the city hasn't decided yet what it will look like. The antibase activists themselves are divided about what this park represents. Several neighborhood associations, who see the entire Dal Molin site as space stolen from Vicenza's people, regard the park as a reminder of the movement's defeat. Others see it as a tangible victory, a "beautiful space," and "a peaceful provocation" to the new base—a way of constantly reminding the soldiers that there is another way to live, one that does not revolve around making war.

Enzo Ciscato was among those skeptical of the park. It couldn't be a site "where you go to relax," he said. Watching the base's construction and knowing it was causing "irreversible" damage had made him "feel sick." At best, Ciscato said, he hoped the Peace Park could become a center for learning about militarization and the harms of war, a place where people go to transform anger about the base into something positive for the community.

Guido Lanaro agreed that building a "documentation center" about militarization and military bases would be "the best way to keep alive the spirit of the Presidio." Perhaps, he said, the park could be home to a new kind of Presidio that might help other movements stop bases from being built elsewhere.

For some in the No Dal Molin movement, perhaps there was a small consolation when the Army announced in 2013 that—contrary to the stated reason for the base construction—it was not going to consolidate the 173rd Airborne Brigade at Dal Molin after all. Ultimately, the movement was right: there was little need for the new base.

Like No Dal Molin, movements worldwide have achieved mixed results in their efforts to stop the construction of new bases, to close existing bases, or to change how bases and troops affect their countries and communities. The victories and defeats are not always clear-cut. In Okinawa, for example, protesters have failed to remove the Futenma base, but they have dramatically slowed the creation of a new Marine Corps base in Henoko, which now may never get built.

Elsewhere, movements led by ordinary citizens and politicians alike have closed or blocked bases or won significant concessions from U.S. forces over the decades. In the aftermath of World War II, U.S. troops (along with Soviet and other foreign forces) were forced to withdraw from bases in Austria as part of the declaration of Austrian neutrality, which included a constitutional ban on foreign bases. Newly independent, decolonized nations such as Morocco, Trinidad, and Libya forced the closure of bases during the 1960s. In 1966, Charles de Gaulle ended most of France's involvement in NATO and ordered the removal of U.S. bases within a year's time. American bases were the source of major controversy in Turkey throughout the 1960s and 1970s, prompting major protests, strikes by base employees, and bombings and kidnappings by extremists; in 1975, U.S. troops withdrew from all but two bases there.[36] Elsewhere during these turbulent decades, the military was forced to vacate some of its bases in Japan, Taiwan, Ethiopia, and Iran.

Following the 1986 overthrow of the U.S.-backed regime of Ferdinand Marcos and the creation of a new constitution banning foreign bases, the Philippines famously refused to renew the lease on U.S. bases in the country. Not long after the volcanic eruption of Mount Pinatubo badly damaged Clark Air Base in 1991, U.S. bases and troops were gone.[37] By decade's end, the military also vacated its bases in Panama as part of the termination of the Panama Canal Zone Treaty.

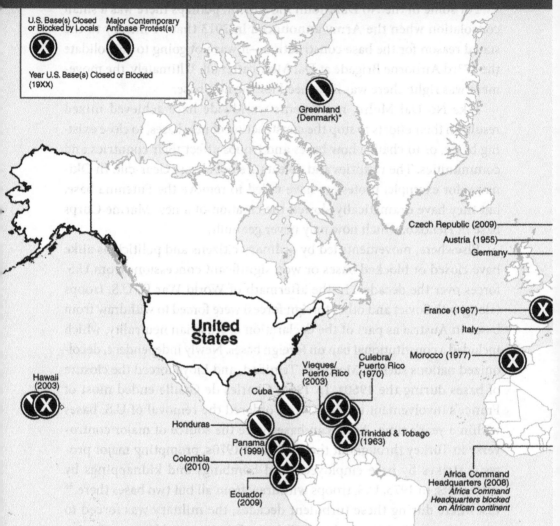

ANTIBASE PROTEST AND OPPOSITION, 1945–2015

U.S. Base(s) Closed or Blocked by Locals

Major Contemporary Antibase Protest(s)

Year U.S. Base(s) Closed or Blocked (19XX)

Greenland (Denmark)*

Czech Republic (2009)

Austria (1955)

Germany

France (1967)

Italy

Morocco (1977)

United States

Hawaii (2003)

Cuba

Honduras

Vieques/ Puerto Rico (2003)

Culebra/ Puerto Rico (1970)

Trinidad & Tobago (1963)

Panama (1999)

Colombia (2010)

Ecuador (2009)

Africa Command Headquarters (2008)
Africa Command Headquarters blocked on African continent

Local social movements and national governments have forced the closure or blocked the creation of U.S. bases worldwide. There are surely additional cases. The antibase protests here represent particularly large and prominent contemporary examples. Complaints, protest, and opposition appear at virtually every U.S. base overseas.
Key sources: Robert E. Harkavy, *Strategic Basing and the Great Powers, 1200–2000*; Catherine Lutz, *The Bases of Empire*; Joseph Gerson and Bruce Birchard, *The Sun Never Sets*; Alexander Cooley, *Base Politics*.

*Movement by displaced people demanding the right of return but not necessarily base closure.

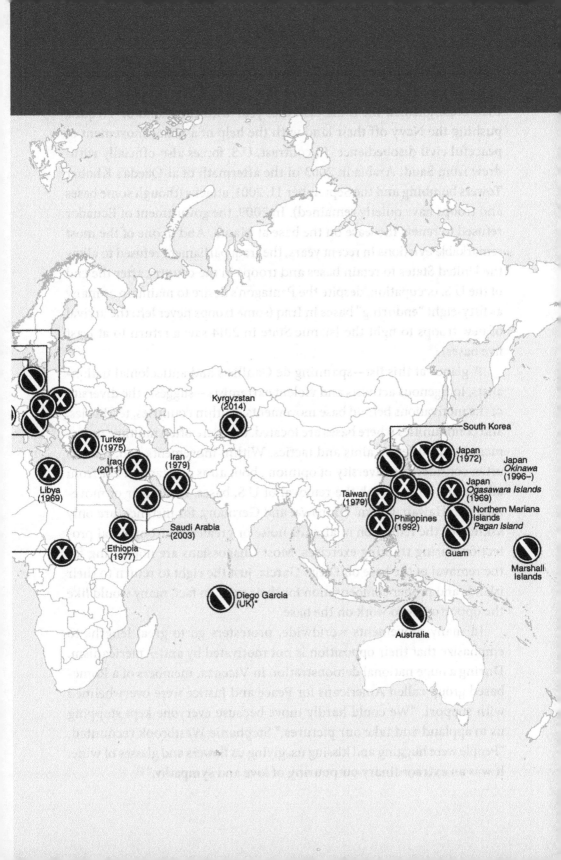

Kyrgyzstan
(2014)

South Korea

Japan
(1972)

Japan
Okinawa
(1996–)

Turkey
(1975)

Iraq
(2011)

Iran
(1979)

Japan
Ogasawara Islands
(1969)

Libya
(1969)

Taiwan
(1979)

Northern Mariana
Islands
Pagan Island

Saudi Arabia
(2003)

Philippines
(1992)

Guam

Ethiopia
(1977)

Marshall
Islands

Diego Garcia
(UK)*

Australia

In 2003, Hawaii persuaded the Navy to return Kahoolawe Island, home to important sacred sites for native Hawaiians.[38] The people of Puerto Rico accomplished the same task that year with the island of Vieques, pushing the Navy off their land with the help of a major movement of peaceful civil disobedience. In contrast, U.S. forces also officially withdrew from Saudi Arabia in 2003 in the aftermath of al-Qaeda's Khobar Towers bombing and the September 11, 2001, attacks (though some bases and troops have quietly remained). In 2009, the government of Ecuador refused to renew the lease on the base at Manta. And in one of the most remarkable evictions in recent years, the Iraqi parliament refused to allow the United States to retain bases and troops in the country after the end of the U.S. occupation, despite the Pentagon's desire to maintain as many as fifty-eight "enduring" bases in Iraq (some troops never left; the arrival of new troops to fight the Islamic State in 2014 saw a return to at least five bases).[39]

A glance at this list—spanning de Gaullists and anticolonial nationalists, indigenous activists and violent extremists—suggests the diversity of the motivations behind base movements. Within countries, territories, and communities where bases are located, there are often multiple movements with different aims and tactics. Within movements, too, there is often considerable diversity of opinion about aims and tactics. Far from all the movements seek the removal of U.S. bases. A number of movements in Hawaii, Guam, Okinawa, and Germany, for instance, are only asking for the reduction of aircraft noise or greater environmental protection during training exercises. Most Chagossians are not calling for the removal of the base on Diego Garcia, just the right to return to their islands and proper compensation for their exile; in fact, many would like the opportunity to work on the base.

In many movements worldwide, protesters go to great lengths to emphasize that their opposition is not motivated by anti-Americanism. During a huge national demonstration in Vicenza, members of a Rome-based group called Americans for Peace and Justice were overwhelmed with support. "We could hardly move because everyone kept stopping us to applaud and take our pictures," Stephanie Westbrook recounted. "People were hugging and kissing us, giving us flowers and glasses of wine. It was an extraordinary outpouring of love and sympathy."[40]

After the demonstration, Gina Masi, a local seventeen-year-old dressed like a punk in black and spiked metal, approached one Yankee who had joined the protest. Masi was in tears. "Please tell your people that we are not anti-American!" she said. "Look at me. My clothes are American, the music I love is American. Even my boots are American Eagle. But we want to relate to Americans through culture and music, not military bases and war."[41]

Desert training outside Camp Lemonnier, Djibouti.

16

The Lily Pad Strategy

Since at least the decolonization era of the 1950s, U.S. officials have feared the kind of protest increasingly seen in places such as Vicenza, Vieques, and Okinawa. Planners covet safe, worry-free bases insulated from opposition, military constraints, and the risk of eviction. They want bases free of the kinds of restrictions the military faced during the Arab-Israeli wars of the 1970s, when several European allies prevented the use of their bases and airspace to support Israel, and again in the lead-up to the second invasion of Iraq in 2003, when Turkey and other European countries limited the use of U.S. bases on their soil. A Pentagon official explained in a 2009 presentation that the new aim is to "lighten U.S. foreign footprints to reduce friction with host nations" and avoid offending "host nation and regional sensitivities."[1] Avoidance of local populations, publicity, and potential opposition is the goal. And to achieve it, the Pentagon is increasingly turning to small, covert sites scattered around the globe—the "cooperative security locations" frequently referred to simply as "lily pads."

Some of the attractiveness of the lily pad strategy, with its relative shift from large bases to smaller ones, has clearly been the lower costs involved, especially in the face of Pentagon budget cuts. Most lily pads are located in economically and politically weak countries that are more easily influenced by the economic benefits and political payoffs promised by bases, and where labor and other operating costs are lower than in more powerful countries such as Germany, Italy, and Japan. Poorer countries' less stringent environmental regulations also make operations cheaper and easier.

Thanks to lily pads' low costs, many military planners also like the idea of building new bases in as many nations as possible—what the Pentagon calls "redundant capabilities and access."[2] With a big collection of small bases joining a smaller number of main operating bases like Ramstein and Camp Humphreys in South Korea, planners hope "to respond rapidly to crises and contingencies anywhere in the world" by turning from one country to another if a host denies use of a U.S. base in wartime (as Turkey and other European countries did to varying degrees in the lead-up to the second invasion of Iraq in 2003).[3] Maintaining larger numbers of bases also increases the challenge for any potential adversary who wants to target American bases in wartime. And the relatively low costs of lily pads mean that if a host country ever evicts one, the financial damage is far smaller than the losses at bases like Clark and Subic Bay.

Lily pads have also grown in popularity as some military planners, on both the right and left of the political spectrum, have challenged one of the traditional rationales for maintaining large numbers of bases overseas: deployment speed. According to a Bush administration study, for example, because of technological advancements in airlift and sealift, deploying troops to a conflict from most overseas bases saves little if any time compared to deploying from domestic bases.[4] More and more military analysts are thus concluding that maintaining stores of weapons and supplies overseas—what the military calls "pre-positioning"—is more important than having tens of thousands of troops there, with the attendant costs to support them and their families. Most lily pads can serve this pre-positioning function while also offering, like somewhat bigger forward operating sites, "surge capacity" to expand easily and rapidly in order to accommodate much larger numbers of troops and weaponry in a crisis. A 2005 exercise, for example, showed how hundreds of U.S. troops from Illinois could deploy to a lily pad in Bulgaria run by KBR and local contractors.[5]

More broadly, the lily pad strategy is a critical part of what many are calling a "new way of war" for the United States, aimed at maintaining U.S. global dominance amid growing economic and geopolitical competition from China, the European Union, and rising powers such as Russia and India. The days of hundreds of bases and hundreds of thousands of U.S. forces occupying Iraq and Afghanistan may be over, but the development of lily pad bases in places such as Honduras, the Philippines, and Niger is a warning that—whether we realize it or not—the military is increasingly inserting itself into new areas of the world and into new conflicts, with potentially disastrous consequences.

"PRESENCE"

Of all the U.S. military personnel I met during my travels, Army Lieutenant Colonel Frank Duffy may have been the only one to suggest a meal at a restaurant that was not a U.S. chain. Instead, he recommended we meet for *pupusas*, the corn-and-cheese-based Salvadoran specialty popular among Hondurans. ("Frank Duffy" is a pseudonym; like other military personnel in Honduras, he asked me not to use his real name.)

As we ate during the summer of 2011, I asked Duffy about reports of "new U.S. bases" in the country. The Pentagon had recently invested around $4 million in small military facilities, including forward operating locations, a counternarcotics facility, a safe house, and a team room and range.[6] The Pentagon had also bought more than $48 million in fuel for "various military locations" in Honduras.[7] Although the money invested is tiny compared to the overall military budget, many have been asking what the military is once again doing in the jungles of Central America. The suspicion is that the "Honduran" bases the U.S. military is helping to upgrade or create in remote parts of the country are actually new American lily pads.

Duffy told me matter-of-factly that Southern Command has been providing the Honduran military with funding for some time. And, he said, it continues to fund "bases that have missions in our best interest."

"What's that mean?" Duffy continued. Switching into the monotone register often used to utter official bureaucratic phrases, he said that these are missions to "detect, monitor, and interdict as much illicit [material] as possible." The aim is to "disrupt trafficking" by building up the Honduran navy and its bases, "some in remote areas along the coast."

Is there a U.S. presence at these bases? I probed.

THE GLOBAL PROLIFERATION OF LILY PAD BASES

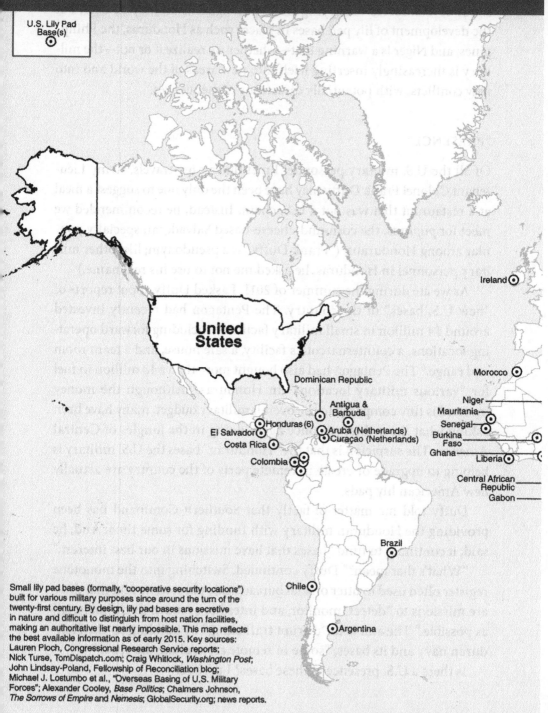

U.S. Lily Pad Base(s)

Ireland

United States

Morocco

Dominican Republic

Antigua & Barbuda

Niger
Mauritania
Senegal
Burkina Faso
Ghana
Liberia

El Salvador
Honduras (6)
Aruba (Netherlands)
Curaçao (Netherlands)
Costa Rica

Colombia

Central African Republic
Gabon

Brazil

Chile

Argentina

Small lily pad bases (formally, "cooperative security locations")
built for various military purposes since around the turn of the
twenty-first century. By design, lily pad bases are secretive
in nature and difficult to distinguish from host nation facilities,
making an authoritative list nearly impossible. This map reflects
the best available information as of early 2015. Key sources:
Lauren Ploch, Congressional Research Service reports;
Nick Turse, TomDispatch.com; Craig Whitlock, Washington Post;
John Lindsay-Poland, Fellowship of Reconciliation blog;
Michael J. Lostumbo et al., "Overseas Basing of U.S. Military
Forces"; Alexander Cooley, Base Politics; Chalmers Johnson,
The Sorrows of Empire and Nemesis; GlobalSecurity.org; news reports.

Poland

Hungary

Romania (5)

Bulgaria (4)

Georgia

Iraq
Israel (9)

Egypt

Saudi
Arabia

Yemen

Chad

Djibouti

Ethiopia

South Sudan

Kenya

Uganda

Burundi

Mozambique

Pakistan

Thailand

Cambodia

Singapore

Philippines (7)

Northern Mariana
Islands

Seychelles

Australia

Wiping his mouth with a napkin, Duffy paused. We "investigate the safety and efficiency of the people operating these facilities," he replied in the same exaggerated monotone. Then, looking straight into my eyes, he asked, "Does it sound like I'm being too careful?"

I didn't know what to say. Duffy broke the silence by adding that it's a "pretty insignificant amount of money in the scheme of things." The Honduran armed forces doesn't even have enough gas to patrol its waterways or food to feed its troops, he explained. So what we're funding is the construction of basic things like docks, barracks, spare parts.

Are there agreements outlining what access U.S. forces have to the facilities? I asked.

"The answer to your question is yes," Duffy said. "End use monitoring. There's always a requirement to allow end use monitoring" to ensure facilities are being used properly.

But do U.S. military personnel use or have access to these bases?

What you need to do, Duffy said, in what initially felt like a non sequitur, is go back to the 1980s to look at the bases the United States provided for Honduras. Or look at the city of Trujillo, he said. It has a U.S. Navy hospital from World War II. That's "cool," he added with emphasis.

So is there a U.S. presence at these facilities the way there was in the eighties? I asked.

"There's *no* U.S. presence," Duffy said abruptly, seeming to bristle at the word "presence," which for the military often implies permanence. "And let's be clear, there are *no U.S. bases* in Honduras," he added. Then he leaned forward over the table and stared at me, unblinking, for several long seconds, until I finally looked away.

TRAINING GROUNDS

The next time I met Duffy, we had breakfast at a local McDonald's. Given that it was the Fourth of July, he thought it appropriate enough.

"Let me ask a . . . direct question," I said hesitatingly, looking for a way around the Pentagon's linguistic façade. "There are no U.S. military bases in Honduras. But are there any U.S. military facilities or installations in Honduras?"

"No," Duffy replied curtly, looking down, his eyes locked to the table.

"Is there a U.S. presence at any of the Honduran bases?" I asked.

"We have teams that are very limited—I shouldn't say 'limited.' It's on a case by case basis," he demurred. "Three, four, five weeks at a time." For example, an Air Force team might be there for "six weeks . . . living and working with" the Hondurans, he said.

There are "no other troops that are permanently" there, Duffy said. Though, he added, there are some "special ops cases" where they're on site for "four to six months."

In April 2012, Southcom revealed to the *New York Times* more or less what Duffy couldn't (or wouldn't) say to me the previous summer. The *Times* revealed that the military had built at least three remote "forward operating bases," including one at a former Contra base.[8] U.S. officials said the new lily pads are officially "under Honduran command." They said the bases allow Honduran and U.S. forces to combat drug traffickers more effectively in isolated, unpopulated parts of the country.[9] "Each site supports two-week rotations for 55 people," the *Times* reported, with "spartan but comfortable barracks," fuel supplies, and gas and solar generators. Most of the personnel appear to be Honduran troops and U.S. special operations trainers.[10]

In total, the military now has regular access to at least twelve bases, training ranges, and other military facilities in Honduras. Unlike in almost every other country where the United States has bases and troops, there is no status of forces agreement in Honduras governing the American military presence. Instead, under the 1982 bilateral agreement, the U.S. military has nearly unrestricted access to *all* of Honduras's military facilities.

Many of these facilities have been built or upgraded without public notice. At least one facility has been built via "exercise related construction," recalling methods used to evade congressional authority over base construction in the 1980s. In one sense, there's little news here: the Pentagon has been building infrastructure, as well as providing weaponry and equipment, for the poorly resourced Honduran military since at least the 1930s.[11] What is new, however, is the presence of U.S. troops at a growing number of bases in isolated parts of the country on a de facto permanent basis. Duffy said there is "no U.S. presence," but he later acknowledged that teams of U.S. forces—some "limited" in size and

others larger—are spending weeks or months at a time at the bases to provide training. He later told me there were more than one hundred training events in fiscal year 2011 alone. Another military official in Honduras
explained, "We almost always have a few trainers in the country. But it's
not really by design." They're simply cycling in and out "for different
needs," he said.

Except that it's precisely by design that there's a constant rotation of
mobile training teams and advisers at the new bases and other facilities.
Since at least 2008, the Pentagon has acknowledged its attempts to create
"permanent" deployments of special operations forces worldwide.[12] In
Honduras, the frequent training rotations, often by special operations
forces, mean the U.S. military has an increasing presence in a growing
swath of the country. The need to conduct "end use monitoring" for new
bases, and for the new equipment and weapons provided to the Honduran military and police, similarly justifies the widespread deployment
of U.S. forces.[13] A 2009 U.S. embassy cable released by Wikileaks details
how international exercises and frequent medical missions and other
"humanitarian" events have also done much the same. In La Moskitia,
the isolated Atlantic coast region that has become a major drug transit
point, for example, the United States has used such activities as an excuse
to establish "military presence," collect intelligence, and conduct surveillance.[14]

When troops deploy for a humanitarian activity such as providing
dental care or vaccinations, "its primary purpose is not to treat poor
people," Duffy explained to me when we met in Washington, D.C., in
2013. "It's not to train host nation medical people. It's not to train host
nation military people. The primary purpose is for U.S. personnel to practice, to get training in preparing for deployment." Pentagon budget documents tell a similar story, explaining that humanitarian operations help
"maintain a robust overseas presence" and provide "access to regions
important to U.S. interests."[15]

Of course, Duffy said, diplomacy goes on so Hondurans don't think
you're coming to take advantage of them. You need to show them "your
people are going to get benefits. Your doctors are going to get benefits.
Your local politicians are going to get benefits," in the form of donated
equipment or construction.

But from the viewpoint of the U.S. military, much of what troops need to do with their time is deploy to conduct training in realistic scenarios. "That's why the U.S. has been so good at wars," Duffy said. "To be able to do it, you've got to practice it." And Honduras provides a good place to practice. So you take units from the States, explained Duffy, you "deploy, build something"—whether a military facility or a school—and when you leave it behind, "it's a sign of goodwill on our part."

"But again, you don't advertise that to the host nation. You say the primary purpose is to work together."

REPLACING SUBIC AND CLARK

A similar mixture of lily pads, training, and exercises has also allowed the military to make a remarkable return to the Philippines, within barely a decade of the eviction of U.S. bases from the country.

As a prelude to the lily pads to come, U.S. negotiators first signed a "visiting forces agreement" with the Philippines in 1996 that allowed U.S. troops back into the country for a variety of military exercises and training. The Philippines Senate ratified the agreement in 1999. By 2003, the U.S. military was participating in eighteen such exercises a year; U.S. troops outnumbered Filipino troops in the largest exercise. Soon, there were more than thirty exercises per year. By 2006 there were 5,500 U.S. troops involved, almost twice as many as in the 2,800-person Filipino contingent. By 2008, the 6,000 Americans were three times the number of Filipinos.[16] Relatively quickly, the exercises had become a way to hide the near-permanent deployment of large numbers of U.S. troops involved in counterinsurgency operations. The journalist Robert D. Kaplan reports hearing that top Pentagon civilians "hated the fact that they had to hide such troop insertions under the cover of annual exercises."[17]

The Filipino security analyst Herbert Docena explains, "U.S. military strategists consider these training exercises as a way of securing on-again, off-again, but continuous access to the country where they are training." He quotes former Pacific Command commander Admiral Thomas Fargo as saying, "Access over time can develop into habitual use of certain facilities by deployed U.S. forces with the eventual goal of being guaranteed use in a crisis, or permission to pre-position logistics stocks and other critical material in strategic forward locations." Indeed, a separate 2002 Mutual Logistics Support Agreement gave U.S. forces the right to pre-position weapons and equipment, build structures, and organize full logistical services in the country. A 2001 agreement also provided access to Philippines airspace, airfields, sea lanes, and harbors; U.S. naval vessels now make near constant port visits. As in Honduras, medical and humanitarian activities have offered additional opportunities to train U.S. troops in regions where they might one day be involved in combat, while at the same time winning locals' trust and creating local intelligence networks.[18]

Soon, U.S. troops had regained access to Subic Bay and Clark. A 2014 agreement allows a still larger U.S. presence. Negotiators have released few details, but talks appear to have revolved around the question of Fili-pino access to "temporary" facilities built by U.S. troops on Philippines soil. Both governments insist the agreement will respect Philippines sov-ereignty and create no U.S. "bases." Still, some Filipinos are challenging that assessment and asking whether the plan violates the country's con-stitutional ban on foreign military bases.[19] Military facilities in the Phil-ippines that Filipino troops might not be able to visit certainly sounds like foreign bases, raising doubts about Pentagon official Ray DuBois's earlier promises of "no flag, no forward presence, no families."

Together, this complex of lily pads, exercises, port visits, medical activ-ities, and access agreements means, as Docena says, that the U.S. mili-tary now has "everything—and arguably more—than it had in Subic and Clark." Only now, it has this broad presence "without the economic and political costs of maintaining large garrison-like bases that can serve as visible symbols for the opposition."[20]

A CONTINENT OF LILY PADS

Nowhere has the arrival of lily pads been more striking than in Africa. There, the same developments going on in Honduras and the Philippines are happening on a continental scale.

Until recently, the Pentagon had paid little attention to Africa. Before the creation of an Africa Command (Africom) in 2007, there was no com-mand strictly responsible for Africa. The continent was essentially an afterthought overseen by the European Command. The largest U.S. military involvement in Africa came in the early 1990s, when the Pentagon deployed more than twenty-five thousand troops as part of UN humanitarian operations in Somalia. After U.S. soldiers took heavy casualties in Mogadishu in 1993, there was a rapid retreat from the country and from any thought of sending U.S. troops into African combat.

However, nine days after the attacks of September 11, 2001, U.S. officials began inquiring about creating a base in Djibouti. It would be near the strategic entrance to the Persian Gulf and within striking distance of the Middle East and much of Africa. A little more than a year later, hundreds of troops started arriving at Camp Lemonnier, a base adjacent to a French installation dating to French colonial rule. The cost: just $30 million a year and a Voice of America radio transmitter.[21] Within a few years, there were more than four thousand troops at the six-hundred-acre base and hundreds of millions of dollars in construction and annual spending.[22]

The pace of military activities in Africa accelerated further after President George W. Bush established Africom. He said Africom "will enhance our efforts to bring peace and security to the people of Africa and promote our common goals of development, health, education, democracy, and economic growth."[23]

Many in Africa, and elsewhere, were less enthusiastic. No fewer than seventeen countries, including the continental powers South Africa and Nigeria, expressed explicit opposition to Africom. With the exception of Liberia, no country offered to host the command. Given the criticism from other nations and civil society organizations, its headquarters remained in Stuttgart, Germany. Many saw Africom as little more than nineteenth-century Western colonialism rebooted—a plan for the domination of African oil and other resources, cloaked in the language of humanitarianism. Many U.S. critics also feared that the command represented the militarization of foreign policy and development aid, with Africom set to usurp many of the roles played by the State Department and the U.S. Agency for International Development.[24]

Since then, Africom has downsized some of its planned diplomatic and humanitarian roles. With the command headquarters still in Germany, Africom representatives have insisted to me and others that Camp

Lemonnier is the only U.S. base on the continent. They say any other facility is "temporary." An Africom representative declined to provide a list of facilities occupied by U.S. forces, citing "operational security and force protection reasons" and "the request of our host nation partners."[25]

While the command's secrecy makes getting a full picture difficult, evidence suggests that Africom's on-the-ground expansion has been rapid and broad. A 2014 article in the U.S. Army's magazine *Army Sustainment* identified nine forward operating locations in the Horn of Africa alone.[26] Likewise, a series of *Washington Post* reports have shown that since 2007, the Pentagon has quietly created "about a dozen air bases" in countries including Niger, Chad, Ethiopia, and the Seychelles for drones and surveillance operations over Africa and the Arabian Peninsula.[27] In Burkina Faso, special operations forces are using part of the Ouagadougou international airport for "high-risk activities" in Africa's Sahel. In Mauritania, the military has used a forward operating base to conduct periodic surveillance operations of Tuareg rebels in nearby Mali. The military also had a lily pad in Mali until a 2012 coup forced a withdrawal.[28]

In Mombasa, the military is using at least six buildings at two Kenyan bases, while the Navy has spent at least $10 million to upgrade a small base in Manda Bay.[29] There are special operations outposts in South Sudan and the Democratic Republic of the Congo and two in the Central African Republic.[30] In 2013, the investigative journalist Nick Turse reported U.S. deployments at six "austere locations" and seven classified cooperative security locations on the continent, including one in Entebbe, Uganda, used to track Joseph Kony and his Lord's Resistance Army. Around one hundred U.S. special operations forces had been deployed since 2012 as part of the hunt for Kony.[31]

In Burundi and outside Kampala, Uganda, at the Singo Training School, U.S. contractors and military advisers have been training African soldiers as part of a more than $500 million U.S. effort to train and equip African Union troops fighting in Somalia.[32] Africom has also deployed around two dozen military advisers directly into Somalia to lead efforts to defeat the country's al-Qaeda-linked group, al-Shabab. The military has pursued a covert war in the country and launched raids to

THE U.S. MILITARY'S GROWING INTEREST IN AFRICA

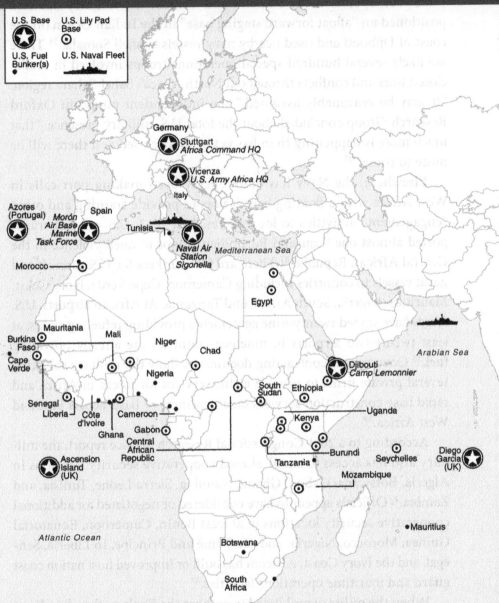

The U.S. military presence in Africa is especially difficult to determine given the secrecy and lack of transparency involved in U.S. Africa Command operations. This map reflects the best available information. Fuel bunkers are indicated only in countries without a confirmed base presence; most countries hosting U.S. lily pads also host U.S. fuel bunkers. The U.S. military also has access agreements for military facilities in the following countries, although there is no confirmed base presence: Algeria, Botswana, Ghana, Namibia, Sierra Leone, Tunisia, Zambia. Key sources: Lauren Ploch, Congressional Research Service reports; Nick Turse, TomDispatch.com; Craig Whitlock, *Washington Post*; Richard Reeve and Zoë Pelter, "From New Frontier to New Normal"; Alexander Cooley, *Base Politics*; Chalmers Johnson, *Nemesis*; news reports.

capture and extradite at least two al-Shabab fighters to the United States.[33] The CIA has secretly had a permanent presence for several years. For operations in Somalia and Yemen, the military has also positioned an "afloat forward staging base" in the Indian Ocean off the coast of Djibouti and used nearby navy vessels to shell Somalia.[34] There are likely several hundred special operations troops involved in undisclosed wars and conflicts throughout North Africa's Sahel-Sahara region. "It may be reasonably assumed," the independent nonprofit Oxford Research Group concluded about the total U.S. military presence, "that much more is happening than has yet been disclosed and there will be more to come."[35]

Elsewhere, the Navy has quite openly been making port calls in West Africa with a floating base it uses to provide training and other "engagement" activities to local forces.[36] In 2013, U.S. aircraft transported almost one thousand Burundian troops to quell violence in the Central African Republic.[37] There are fuel bunkers for U.S. aircraft and naval vessels in countries including Cameroon, Cape Verde, Ivory Coast, Mauritius, Nigeria, South Africa, and Tanzania. At African airports, U.S. forces have signed twenty-nine agreements providing refueling rights; at least twenty-two airports in nineteen countries are already providing fuel.[38] Government contracting documents show the military soliciting several private firms to provide airlift services for forces in Africa and rapid base construction services on a contingency basis across East and West Africa.[39]

According to a 2011 Congressional Research Service report, the military also has access to small, shared cooperative security locations in Algeria, Botswana, Gabon, Ghana, Namibia, Sierra Leone, Tunisia, and Zambia.[40] Officials appear to have considered or negotiated for additional cooperative security locations in at least Benin, Cameroon, Equatorial Guinea, Morocco, Nigeria, and São Tomé and Príncipe. In Liberia, Senegal, and the Ivory Coast, Africom has built or improved host nation coast guard and maritime operations facilities.[41]

When the military mobilized to combat the Ebola outbreak in West Africa in the fall of 2014, it began building a network of health and military logistics facilities.[42] They included seventeen one-hundred-bed "Ebola treatment units" and a field hospital in Monrovia, Liberia, and an "intermediate staging base" in Dakar, Senegal. While many portrayed the military's reaction to Ebola as pure altruism, months before the Ebola deployment, the Pentagon already had plans to build three to five new bases on the continent as well as an intermediate staging base in West Africa—that is, like the one now under construction in Dakar, Senegal.[43] When I asked an Africom spokesperson if the command will seek another intermediate staging base in West Africa, Benjamin Benson replied in an email that the command "is exploring options at several locations that would allow for staging in the event of crisis."[44]

In total, since late 2001, the military has spent around $30 billion or more on a growing military infrastructure as well as other military aid and programs in Africa. This infrastructure includes nineteen lily pads in around seventeen countries; access to an additional eight or more "cooperative security locations" without any permanent U.S. presence; jet and naval fuel storage at twenty-eight or more locations in at least twenty countries; the construction or upgrading of scores of host country military facilities; and the expansion of several large bases in Europe to support operations in Africa. Since 2001, the military's presence on the continent has grown from a few hundred to what is now, on any day, likely between seven thousand and eleven thousand U.S. troops.[45] While the military's power in Europe, East Asia, and the Middle East significantly exceeds that in Africa, the Pentagon's presence on the continent now tops that in Latin America and the Caribbean—long declared by U.S. leaders to be "America's backyard."[46] The military is now operating in at least forty-nine of the fifty-four African countries. It may be operating in every single one.[47]

STOCKPILING LILY PADS

One African lily pad location that has been under consideration appears to be São Tomé and Príncipe, the tiny island nation off the oil-rich west coast of West Africa. Around 2002, high-ranking military officials and U.S. senators suddenly started visiting São Tomé. General Charles Wald, then deputy commander of the U.S. European Command, said publicly that São Tomé could become "another Diego Garcia." Other U.S.

officials said there was neither the time nor the budget to carry out such a grand plan amid two wars. But, they said, São Tomé might make a good location for a lily pad.[48]

Fradique de Menezes, the president of São Tomé at the time, told Portuguese television that he "received a call from the Pentagon to tell me that the issue [was] being studied." What he described sounded a lot like a lily pad: "It is not really a military base on our territory, but rather a support port for aircraft, warships, and patrol ships."[49]

The sudden interest in one of the smallest and poorest countries in the world stems from the petroleum found beneath the Gulf of Guinea and elsewhere in West Africa. Since the turn of the century, the region has become an increasingly important source of global energy supplies, and it may have even larger undiscovered reserves. Several U.S. companies, including ExxonMobil and Noble Energy, have won oil exploration concessions in the Gulf. Although recent U.S. oil production has caused a drop in imports from West Africa, a few years ago, the Council on Foreign Relations was suggesting that sub-Saharan Africa was "likely to become as important a source of U.S. energy imports as the Middle East."[50]

In addition to the prospective West African oil riches, East Africa is also growing in importance as a source of oil and gas, and North Africa continues to be a large supplier. (And beyond its natural resources, Africa represents a vast and largely untapped consumer market—one of the few remaining over which corporations can compete.) Unsurprisingly, in the eyes of many a "new scramble for Africa" has begun, with the United States, China, the EU, Russia, and others all eager to secure their access to the continent.

Amid the scramble, Africa appears to be following the basing trajectory of the Middle East and, more recently, the Caspian Sea region, where the U.S. military has also tried to create a base infrastructure.[51] The difference is that because of political and financial constraints, the Pentagon can't build major new bases in Africa, the way it has done at Diego Garcia or in many of the Persian Gulf states. Without this freedom, the Pentagon is using a growing collection of lily pads and other forms of military presence in its bid for regional control.

A NEW WAY OF WAR

Far beyond Africa, the nineteenth-century scramble for the continent has now gone global. Indeed, as the United States and rising powers such as China, Russia, and Brazil find themselves locked in an increasingly intense competition, the struggle for economic and geopolitical supremacy has spread to resource-rich lands in South and East Asia, in Central and South America, and beyond.

The Chinese government has generally pursued this competition and the challenge of securing oil, resources, and markets by using its economic might—that is, by dotting the globe with strategic investments and development projects, such as a planned canal through Nicaragua that would rival the Panama Canal.[52] The U.S. government, by contrast, has focused relentlessly on using military might as its trump card regionally and globally—that is, by dotting the planet with lily pads, troops, and other forms of military power.

"Forget full-scale invasions and large-footprint occupations on the Eurasian mainland," Nick Turse has written of the strategy that many are calling America's "new way of war." "Instead, think: special operations forces working on their own but also training or fighting beside allied militaries (if not outright proxy armies) . . . the militarization of spying and intelligence, the use of drone aircraft, the launching of cyber-attacks, and joint Pentagon operations with increasingly militarized 'civilian' government agencies."[53]

We can add to this list nominally humanitarian missions that clearly serve military intelligence, patrol, and "hearts and minds" functions; the rotating deployment of U.S. forces around the globe coupled with port visits and other long-standing "showing the flag" demonstrations of U.S. military might; expansion of joint military exercises; the growing use of military contractors; and regular training provided by permanently deployed special operations forces, who give the military de facto "presence" worldwide.

Plus lots and lots of lily pads.

Indeed, lily pads and other bases are in many ways at the heart of this new way of war. In the wake of September 11, 2001, many military strategists have come to believe the neoconservative mantra that "the whole world is a battlefield."[54] They anticipate a future of endless small-scale interventions in which a large, geographically dispersed collection of bases will always be primed for instant operational access. Pentagon officials dream of nearly limitless flexibility, the ability to react with remarkable rapidity to developments anywhere on earth, and thus something approaching complete military control over the entire planet.

DEEPENING TIES

Lily pads are about more than military dominance alone. They are also a kind of back door to introduce into host countries a range of military tools and activities whose ultimate ends are as much political and economic as they are martial. Because of the contact and negotiations that lily pads generally require, they provide an opportunity to deepen ties between the U.S. and foreign militaries. A lily pad can lead to increased training and humanitarian assistance activities, which can lead to military exercises, which can lead to arms sales and much more. Southcom commander General Charles Wilhelm admitted as much when he talked with a top Salvadoran general about creating a new lily pad air base. "We realize, in a diplomatic sense, this plan is for counterdrug only," Wilhelm said. "As a practical matter, all of us know that this agreement will give us a superb opportunity to increase the contact with all our armed forces in a variety of ways."[55]

One result is the growing incorporation of foreign military leaders and foreign militaries into the U.S. military structure. Military officials talk in terms of "interoperability," but the hierarchical nature of these relationships is clear enough. Foreign militaries eventually become, if not proxy armies, at least functional adjuncts or extensions of the U.S. military.[56] Indeed, the aim is increasingly to get "them" to do most of the fighting, and lily pads have become one of several tools to push other militaries in that direction.

Importantly, these deepening military ties involve highly unequal relationships, in which U.S. leaders can offer their counterparts various "gifts"—including, for example, sophisticated and expensive equipment and weapons, or prestigious training opportunities in the United States.

To militaries like that of Honduras, which is almost completely dependent on international donors for its equipment, such gifts are deeply significant.[57] But like most gifts, these come with obligations and a certain degree of expected loyalty. The obligation-laden relationships can later bear fruit for U.S. military leaders—when, for example, they want to gain valuable intelligence from their high-ranking counterparts, or to shape decisions about another country's arms purchases or military policy. "You identify officers and senior NCOs [noncommissioned officers]," the former Bush administration official Ray DuBois explained to me, "and you make friends with them when they are sergeants and captains . . . so when they are colonels and generals you have relationships with them." These relationships, DuBois continued, "are sources of information," and "you may be able to influence the country's procurement policies so they will buy U.S. equipment."

The anthropologist Lesley Gill describes how the training of Latin American military leaders at the infamous School of the Americas has "secured their collusion" in U.S. military and geopolitical strategy "to a considerable degree." By building relationships with military leaders and exposing them to U.S. doctrine and U.S. power, the school "bound them closer to the United States, opened them to greater manipulation . . . and preempted military assistance from other states that might challenge U.S. dominance."[58] Relationships built around lily pads and other military activities do much the same, offering possibilities to sway foreign governmental decisions on matters far beyond things military alone.

Much like the patrol bases that helped "open" China to trade in the nineteenth century, lily pads can thus help advance U.S. business interests. They provide privileged U.S. access to overseas markets, resources, and investment opportunities. They create stability for the regular working of capitalism. And they solidify political alliances. A lily pad "has an influence by virtue of its presence," DuBois said. "A political impact." Through these intertwined and growing political, economic, and military ties, the U.S. military ultimately helps to deepen the dependence of countries such as Honduras on the United States.

For the first time in the post–Cold War era, in places like Central and South America, U.S. political and economic dominance is being called into question as a growing number of countries are asserting their independence or gravitating toward China and other rising powers. In response, U.S. officials hope that the relationships built by lily pads and other military activities will bind entire governments as closely as possible to the U.S. military and the rest of the United States—and so to continued U.S. political-economic hegemony.

DANGEROUS LILIES

Relying on smaller bases may at first sound smarter and more cost-effective than maintaining huge bases that have often caused anger in places like Okinawa, Vicenza, and the Philippines. But the "lily pad" language can be misleading. By design or otherwise, small bases can quickly grow into behemoths. As we have seen, the Navy presented Diego Garcia to Congress as an "austere communications facility," but it has grown into a multibillion-dollar base.[59] Similarly, the 2002 Philippines deployment has grown into multiple lily pads, pier and airfield construction, and a return to Clark and Subic Bay.[60] By 2006, Robert D. Kaplan found that at least one lily pad had transformed from a "grim, spartan camp . . . with an air of impermanence" into one "with proper walkways and creature comforts that befit a more hardened, permanent arrangement."[61] Because lily pads are generally designed for rapid expansion, they often offer a nucleus from which larger bases can easily grow, with costs tending to snowball accordingly. Like other bases, as Walter Pincus's Vietnam War–era Senate investigation found, lily pads can take on lives of their own through bureaucratic tendencies toward inertia and expansion.[62]

This is especially dangerous because the strategy of building small bases in as many nations as possible also guarantees collaboration with a significant number of despotic, corrupt, and murderous regimes. As we have seen, bases small and large have tended to provide legitimacy for and help prop up undemocratic regimes while interfering with efforts to encourage political and democratic reform. (Opponents may also use the bases to rally nationalist sentiment and violent opposition against ruling regimes and the United States.) As the U.S. military cooperates with local militaries to create lily pads, it becomes increasingly likely that Americans will become involved in local conflicts and political struggles

about which U.S. leaders know little and whose victims are often inno-
cent civilians. In Africa and other poorer parts of the globe, where struggles over resources have often led to corruption, repression, and violence,
strengthening local militaries can also encourage ruling regimes to use
them against opponents. It likewise can encourage opponents to see military force as the only way to claim a share of a country's wealth and
political power, increasing the possibility of coups and instability.[63] Notably, the 2012 coup in Mali was carried out by a soldier who had received
extensive U.S. training.

Although lily pads seem to promise insulation from local opposition,
over time even small bases have harmed local communities and have
often led to anger and protest movements. Crashes at drone bases in Djibouti and the Seychelles have already caused local apprehension and
opposition. Military personnel operating from a lily pad in Colombia
have committed rape. In Ecuador, U.S. Coast Guard counternarcotics
operations sank several fishing vessels and may have been responsible for
the deaths of fishers aboard at least one boat. And in Australia's Cocos
Islands, where U.S. officials have considered a lily pad, some locals fear
they might suffer the same fate that befell the Chagossians exiled from
Diego Garcia.[64]

Finally, a proliferation of lily pads only accelerates the militarization
of large swaths of the globe. Like real lily pads, which are actually aquatic
weeds, bases have a way of reproducing uncontrollably.[65] Bases can beget
bases and spur "base races" with other nations, heightening military
tensions and discouraging diplomatic solutions to conflicts.[66] In Africa,
where China has provided some military aid and weaponry, U.S. lily pads
may encourage China to build lily pads of its own. This could increase
regional tensions and the danger of a clash between the two powers or
their proxies.[67] If the proliferation of lily pads continues, the United States
runs an increasing risk of being drawn into new conflicts and new wars.

Lily pads near the borders of China and Russia are especially dangerous. If China, Russia, or Iran were to build even a single lily pad near
U.S. borders, many would surely call for a military response. If lily pads
keep multiplying as part of this dangerous new American way of war,
the country risks generating unknown and deadly forms of blowback
for years to come.

After the U.S. Army returned the Hindenburg Kaserne to Germany in 1992, the city of Ansbach transformed the former base into the Ansbach University of Applied Sciences.

17

True Security

During one of my research trips to Vicenza, I heard about the death of Private First Class Russell Madden, a member of the 173rd Airborne brigade that's split between Vicenza and Germany. Madden had died in Afghanistan just a few days earlier, on June 23, 2010, from blast injuries sustained when a rocket-propelled grenade tore through his vehicle.

I regularly followed the deaths of troops at war in Afghanistan and Iraq, but when I learned more about Madden's life his death struck me as particularly poignant. He grew up in Bellevue, Kentucky, a town of six thousand, where he was a high school football star. At twenty-nine, he enlisted in the Army because he needed health insurance to cover treatment for his four-year-old son's cystic fibrosis. "He joined because he knew that Parker would be taken care of no matter what," Madden's sister told the *Cincinnati Enquirer*.

For several years I hoped to speak with a member of Russell Madden's family. Finally, I found his mother, Peggy Madden Davitt. She told me that Russell had signed up for the Army soon after his son was turned away by the Mayo Clinic, where the family had hoped to get treatment. "No one will ever send my son away again," she remembers Russell saying.

After Russell's death, Peggy received a standard condolence letter from President Obama. "I am deeply saddened to learn of the loss of your son," the letter said. "Our Nation will not forget his sacrifice, and we can never repay our debt to your family." Turning over the presidential stationery,

Peggy addressed a response to President Obama. "If my son had found a decent employer and sufficient health insurance in this great land of ours," she wrote, "my son would not have had to sacrifice his life for his son." Peggy sent the letter back to the White House. She did not receive a reply.

Russell Madden's story is a reminder of the life-and-death significance of the choices connected to our base nation. Unlike virtually all of the wealthy industrialized countries in which the United States maintains bases—Germany, Japan, South Korea, Britain, Spain, Italy, Portugal, Norway, and Belgium among them—the United States does not guarantee health care for all its citizens. The idea of doing so is often dismissed as too expensive. Meanwhile, the nation spends immense sums every year supporting a global base infrastructure largely born of a world war and a cold war that ended decades ago.

Health care, of course, is not the only area in which we have made a questionable trade-off. During my travels, I was struck by the impressive public transportation systems found in some of the countries hosting our bases, such as Germany, Japan, and South Korea. Even in Italy, where many often criticize the train system and the public sector, the speed and efficiency of public transportation options are far superior to those in the United States. Initially, I included this observation in my notes as an aside, distinct from the subject of my research. It was only later that I realized the interrelated nature of the two phenomena—the U.S. overseas base infrastructure and host countries' public transportation infrastructures. While countries such as Germany, Japan, South Korea, and Italy have spent large amounts supporting U.S. bases on their soil, their military spending has been accompanied by impressive investments to improve their citizens' lives. Meanwhile, U.S. investments in bases have come at the cost of decades of neglecting transportation, health, education, housing, infrastructure, and other human necessities. Think about what just half of the $70 billion or more going into the base world every year could do to improve the lives of Americans.

MAINSTREAM DEBATE

When I began this book almost six years ago, the issue of overseas bases was on the margins of political discourse. Today, it is increasingly moving toward the center of debates about the Pentagon budget and the shape and function of the U.S. military in the twenty-first century. The tremendous costs of maintaining such an unparalleled collection of bases abroad have made closing foreign bases one of the rare ideas that draw support from across the political spectrum, including liberals, conservatives, libertarians, far-right Tea Party members and far-left Occupiers, and moderates in both parties.

In recent years, for example, conservative Republican senator Tom Coburn and the liberal Center for American Progress proposed cutting troop deployments in Europe and Asia by a third to save $70 billion by 2021.[1] Others, like Democratic senator Jon Tester and retired Republican Texas senator Kay Bailey Hutchison, have called for moving overseas bases and military spending back home. Hutchison proposed a "Build in America" policy to protect "the future security posture of U.S. military forces and . . . the fiscal health of our nation."[2]

The libertarian Ron Paul made the closure of overseas bases a major platform of his 2012 presidential campaign. "We have to have a strong national defense, but we don't get strength by diluting ourselves in 900 bases in 130 countries," he said in a Republican debate. "I want to bring the troops home."[3]

Still others, like the New York Times columnist Nicholas Kristof, argue that investing in disease research, education, and diplomacy would do more to protect U.S. citizens than bases in Germany. "Do we fear," he asked in 2011, "that if we pull our bases from Germany, Russia might invade?"[4] (Russia's recent annexation of the nearly defenseless Crimea doesn't make this far-fetched scenario any more likely; Germany, by itself, has nearly as many high-quality tanks as Russia, to say nothing of the rest of NATO.)

The once wonkish topic of overseas bases has even become material for prime-time comedy. "Europeans get full health care coverage, a generous pension, day care, long paid vacations, maternity leave, free college, and public transportation that doesn't smell like pee," Bill Maher has joked on his HBO show Real Time. "Whereas our tax dollars go towards military bases in Germany, subsidies to oil companies, building bridges to nowhere, wars, and putting half of Cheech and Chong in prison."[5]

Even within the military, growing numbers are questioning whether the country can afford hundreds of bases abroad. "We've got too many daggone bases," the former commander of U.S. Air Forces in Europe General Roger Brady has said publicly. "There's big money to be saved by closing them."[6]

At the same time, more base experts of all political persuasions are concluding that the days of maintaining lots of overseas bases—especially sprawling "Little Americas"—are numbered. They see that technological advancements in the air and at sea now allow the rapid movement of military forces and power directly from the United States, decreasing any strategic value for permanent foreign bases. The former Pentagon official Ray DuBois and others in the George W. Bush administration have pointed to a Joint Chiefs of Staff study showing that, in most cases, the time difference between deploying troops to potential war zones from bases in Europe and deploying them from the east coast of the United States is either insignificant or completely nonexistent.[7] A RAND study explains, "Ground forces based in Europe do not provide a significant deployment benefit to other theaters . . . If a situation is time-sensitive, lighter units can be airlifted from [the United States] in a time span comparable to those for European-based units."[8] A congressionally mandated National Defense Panel has suggested maintaining forces based in the United States ready to "project significant power" overseas "within hours or days, rather than months."[9]

Sustaining large numbers of forces in any lengthy war or peace-keeping operation far from the United States would still require significant basing facilities, most likely in allied nations. But as far as quickly sending military forces abroad in an emergency is concerned, overseas installations are simply not necessary. Thanks to fast airlift and sealift, long-range bombers, in-air refueling capabilities, eleven aircraft carriers, a large submarine fleet, other elements of the world's most powerful naval and air forces, and large numbers of domestic bases, the U.S. military already has the capability—even without any bases abroad—to deploy more military power faster and over longer distances than any other military on earth, by far. The nation's current basing network and its broader military strategy are not the only option.

DETERRENCE?

The primary argument in favor of maintaining bases and troops overseas has long been that they keep the peace and make the United States and the world safer and more secure. After six years of working on this book and fourteen years studying the issue, I have a simple response to that assertion: prove it.

For decades, supporters of the overseas status quo have simply proclaimed the security benefits as a self-evident truth. Rarely has anyone forced them to support their claims. Scholarly debates about the effectiveness of various strategies of military deterrence—the threat to use force to prevent another power from using force—have raged for decades without end. Considerable research has led to what one review summarized as "widely different results and little or no consensus on a set of variables that predict [effective] deterrence."[10] Others are even more critical, concluding, for example, that "deterrence emerges as a shabby parody of a scientific theory. Its fundamental behavioral assumptions are wrong. Its basic terms are ill defined. It is used in inconsistent and contradictory ways. Commonly cited examples of effective deterrence are often based on flawed assumptions of history, sometimes reflecting ignorance, sometimes deliberate misrepresentation."[11]

Some analysts ardently support the validity and continued relevance of deterrence theory.[12] But almost all of their research analyzes deterrence in the face of immediate threats (like troops massed at a border, ready to invade). There has been little investigation of the effectiveness of long-term deterrence, of the kind supposedly provided by U.S. bases overseas.[13]

This is not to say that overseas bases never contribute to security. The intellectually honest truth is that evaluating the effect overseas bases have on security is extremely difficult. Often, if not always, people come down on one side or another based not on evidence but on a set of underlying beliefs and assumptions about military force and foreign policy.

The major assumption underlying a belief in the value of overseas bases and foreign military presence is the idea that if France and Britain and the United States had aggressively confronted Hitler in the 1930s rather than pursuing a policy of "appeasement," World War II could have been averted. Many treat this counterfactual scenario as *the* lesson of

World War II. But given that history doesn't allow for do-overs or scientific controls, there's no way to prove conclusively whether that assumption is true or false.

Many have made similarly questionable arguments in stating that the outcome of the Cold War proves the effectiveness of deterrence. Demolishing such conclusions, the international relations scholar Steve Chan writes:

> Was the U.S. deterrence against the USSR effective? That Moscow did not attack Western Europe might have been because of the effectiveness of this U.S. deterrence. It could also be that Moscow never had any intention of launching such an attack, or that it might have been dissuaded from carrying out such an attack by its economic weakness, dissension among its leaders, concern for a challenge from China, or some other reason. Thus, one needs to guard against spurious inferences, giving credit to deterrence for keeping peace and stability when this policy does not quite deserve such credit.[14]

Even if the assumptions about pre–World War II history or about the Cold War were hypothetically correct, these singular cases would not come close to providing conclusive evidence that overseas bases ensure security across time and place. One could make an equally emotionally resonant argument that if the United States had not occupied the Muslim holy land of Saudi Arabia with military bases and troops after the first Gulf War, al-Qaeda's attacks on the United States on September 11, 2001, could have been averted. Like the Hitler appeasement argument, this may be true, but it is equally unknowable.

The confrontation between North and South Korea is another helpful case. Proponents of a large overseas U.S. military presence often argue that U.S. forces in South Korea and in other parts of Asia have deterred North Korea from invading South Korea and kept the peace in East Asia. That may be so. But there may be an equally strong, if not stronger, case to be made that the presence of U.S. troops in South Korea has prolonged the conflict and a war that has never technically ended. From North Korea's perspective, having the world's most powerful military on its doorstep seems like good reason to build up its military power—and a nuclear capability—rather than working to de-escalate the conflict. For China, there's similarly good reason to prop up North Korea, given that the dissolution of the North and reunification of Korea could put tens of thousands of U.S. forces—already on the Asian mainland—onto the Chinese border.

Rather than keeping the peace and making the Korean peninsula safer, U.S. bases may be contributing to a state of heightened tension that has made the outbreak of war more likely and peace more difficult to achieve. In fact, there's a reasonable argument that it's been in the interest (conscious or unconscious) of some U.S. officials to maintain a state of war, to have a justification for maintaining troops and bases in Korea and thus on the Asian mainland.

HARM

While there is no evidence to say conclusively that overseas bases make the United States or the world safer in a military sense, we have seen abundant evidence that bases abroad are harming the safety, security, and well-being of millions of people—ranging from the locals living near bases to the military personnel, family members, and civilians living and working on them. It's also indisputable that U.S. bases and troops abroad have consistently generated opposition and anger. In some extreme but far from isolated cases, bases and troops have either spawned violence against Americans or provided convenient targets, as in attacks on marines in Lebanon in 1983 and on the USS *Cole* in Yemen in 2000. The U.S. occupation of Saudi Arabia was a major recruiting tool for al-Qaeda and part of Osama bin Laden's professed motivation for the 9/11 attacks.[15] Research has shown that U.S. bases and troops in the Middle East have been "major catalysts for anti-Americanism and radicalization" and that there has been a strong correlation between a U.S. basing presence and al-Qaeda recruitment.[16]

The rapid spread of lily pad bases today risks arousing more opposition, despite their small size. Intimately linked with the deployment of special operations forces to nearly every nation on earth, the lily pad strategy and the new way of war that it represents appear to be part of a troubling and dangerous expansion of the Cold War–era "forward strategy."[17]

ENABLING WARS
IN THE MIDDLE EAST, 1980–2015

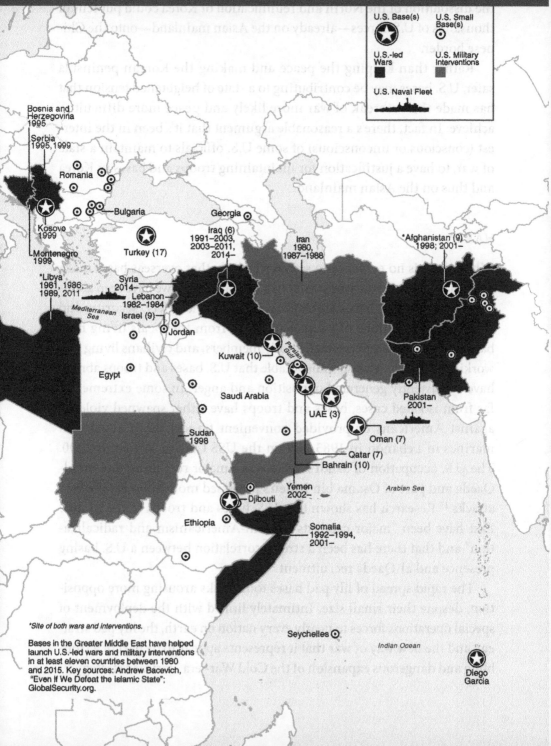

U.S. Base(s)

U.S. Small Base(s)

U.S.-led Wars

U.S. Military Interventions

U.S. Naval Fleet

Bosnia and Herzegovina 1995

Serbia 1995, 1999

Romania

Kosovo 1999

Bulgaria

Georgia

Montenegro 1999

Turkey (17)

Iraq (6) 1991–2003, 2003–2011, 2014–

Iran 1980, 1987–1988

*Afghanistan (9) 1998; 2001–

*Libya 1981, 1986, 1989, 2011

Syria 2014–

Lebanon 1982–1984

Mediterranean Sea

Israel (9)

Jordan

Kuwait (10)

Persian Gulf

Pakistan 2001–

Egypt

Saudi Arabia

UAE (3)

Oman (7)

Sudan 1998

Qatar (7)

Bahrain (10)

Yemen 2002–

Arabian Sea

Djibouti

Ethiopia

Somalia 1992–1994, 2001–

*Site of both wars and interventions.

Bases in the Greater Middle East have helped launch U.S.-led wars and military interventions in at least eleven countries between 1980 and 2015. Key sources: Andrew Bacevich, "Even If We Defeat the Islamic State"; GlobalSecurity.org.

Seychelles

Indian Ocean

Diego Garcia

After World War II, the forward strategy transformed U.S. ideas about security, defense, and threats to the United States. As the base expert Catherine Lutz put it, the United States moved from being "a nation suspicious of standing armies to one whose military patrols the globe in all of its corners, twenty-four hours each day."[18] Lutz wrote those words shortly before 2001; since then, thanks to the global "war on terror," the military's reach has grown even further, with troops and U.S. military facilities located in almost every country in the world.

As the journalist Robert D. Kaplan has said, the U.S. military now stands ready "to flood the most obscure areas of [the earth] with troops at a moment's notice." When Kaplan visited U.S. troops at lily pad bases and other obscure and remote locations around the globe, he heard a consistent refrain: "Welcome to Injun Country."[19] These words, and the frequent descriptions of lily pads as "frontier forts" hosting a "global cavalry," are deeply troubling—for their racial overtones, for their invocation of a Manifest Destiny–like "civilizing" mission, and for the suggestion of ever-expanding military operations. One doesn't go to "Injun Country" just for the scenery. One goes looking for Injuns.

On Independence Day in 1821, John Quincy Adams, then the secretary of state, warned of the dangers of looking for enemies abroad. America, he said, "goes not abroad in search of monsters to destroy." If it were to do so, Adams cautioned, the country "would involve herself, beyond the power of extrication, in all the wars of interest and intrigue, of individual avarice, envy, and ambition, which assume the colors and usurp the standard of freedom."[20]

For Adams, this did not mean neglecting other nations and the causes of freedom and independence. Rather, he said, America should support those causes, but through "the countenance of her voice, and the benignant sympathy of her example" rather than military power. If the country did involve itself in foreign wars, Adams said,

> The fundamental maxims of her policy would insensibly change from liberty to force. The frontlet upon her brows would no longer beam with the ineffable splendor of freedom and independence; but in its stead would soon be substituted an imperial diadem, flashing in false and tarnished lustre the murky radiance of dominion and power. She might

become the dictatress of the world: she would be no longer the ruler of her own spirit.[21]

For almost two hundred years, the United States has increasingly failed to heed this advice. Force has become one of America's fundamental policy maxims. As Eisenhower would explain 140 years after Adams, military power has become a key organizing principle for the country's political and economic systems. And as Adams suggested, the luster of global domination and power has proved false and self-defeating.

It is not too late for the country to heed Adams's words. And beyond words, the country would do well to note the agenda Adams laid out as president. In contrast to the expansionist visions of Presidents James Monroe and Andrew Jackson, who preceded and followed him, Adams proposed broad improvements to the nation's infrastructure of roads and canals; investments to support science, invention, and enterprise; and global efforts toward "the common improvement of the species." He also refused to sign a treaty that would have dispossessed the Creek nation of its lands in Georgia. Unfortunately, Adams's political instincts never matched his ideas and his ideals, and much of his agenda was never implemented. But we still have a chance today to make the investments in transportation, science, education, entrepreneurship, energy, and housing that have been neglected while trillions of dollars have been poured into unnecessary wars and military bases abroad.[22]

LOOKING FOR FIRES

Since the end of the Cold War, part of the problem has been that, lacking a superpower rival, the U.S. military has gone looking for new monsters and new enemies. This resembles what some call the "firefighter problem": in an era when there are fewer and fewer fires for firefighters to deal with, they have tended to look for other things to do. Most firefighters today spend little of their time actually fighting fires, while their help in medical emergencies and other work often comes at great and inefficient expense.

That the military, too, has looked for new things to do is in many ways understandable. Few of us have the vision and strength, whether as indi-

viduals or as part of larger institutions, to say that we are not needed or
that our roles should be reduced or eliminated. (The March of Dimes had
a similar problem after the eradication of polio, the disease the organization was founded to combat.) But this understandable inertia does not
justify the massive waste and suffering that overseas bases inflict.

The global basing transformation initiated in the early days of the
Bush administration was supposed to reduce the collection of bases and
move the remaining ones into more strategic positions. Instead, thanks
to the wars in Afghanistan and Iraq and the boom in base construction
around the world, our base presence abroad has resembled a game of
Whac-A-Mole: every time a base has been closed down, another base (or
millions in new MilCon spending) has tended to pop up somewhere else.

In even more complicated ways than major weapons systems, overseas military bases are the true incarnation of President Eisenhower's
worst nightmares about the military-industrial complex.[23] The establishment of overseas bases has created entire social worlds, with thousands
of people and corporations that have become economically, socially,
bureaucratically, psychologically, and, as Eisenhower said, even spiritu-
ally dependent on the continued operation of those worlds—just like fire
departments but on a much larger scale. Even worse, these bases tend to
entrench themselves in local communities and host nations, creating yet
more dependence around the world.

As the Senate's Vietnam-era investigation of overseas bases showed
decades ago, once overseas bases are established, they become difficult
to close whether they're needed or not. Indeed, the base world is a perfect,
if horrifying, symbol of how the military-industrial complex is like
Frankenstein's monster, taking on a life of its own and gaining "unwar-
ranted" influence[24] thanks to the spending it commands. This has been
true since the days of Eisenhower, but it's become even more the case since
the start of the wars in Afghanistan and Iraq. In the decade after September 2001, Pentagon budgets roughly doubled. Military spending
reached levels not seen since the height of the Cold War, nearly equaling
the rest of the world's military spending combined[25]—despite the absence
of another superpower and facing an al-Qaeda threat numbering only
in the thousands of militants and with very limited ability to attack the
United States. Given such profligacy, there should be little surprise that

bases in Afghanistan and Iraq became so luxurious and laden with "ice cream" they made some soldiers cringe. There should be little surprise that they became the sites for tens of billions of dollars lost to waste, fraud, and abuse.

The danger of bases taking on lives of their own of course extends beyond the wasted money and national resources. Unlike firefighters, when bases abroad look for things to do, the consequences extend far beyond potential waste and inefficiency. In many ways, instead of providing security, overseas bases are often helping to make the world a more dangerous place. In South Korea, for example, military leaders are planning for troops' housing needs a decade or more in advance,[26] with seemingly no thought that the Korean conflict might end and make these bases unnecessary. One wonders whether such ingrained assumptions have limited U.S. peacemaking efforts and the prospects for peace between the Koreas. Likewise, U.S. officials may say that building new bases in East Asia (on top of hundreds of existing ones in the region) is defensive and will help ensure the peace. But how do those bases look from China's perspective? A base that's reassuring for one power can look like a threat to another.

Whatever the rhetoric of ensuring peace and spreading democracy, overseas bases are meant to threaten. They are designed to demonstrate power and dominance. But it's far from clear that demonstrating power and dominance makes the United States or the world any safer or more secure. Remember how the Kennedy administration reacted when the Soviet Union began installing nuclear weapons in Cuba—its only base in the Western hemisphere—at a time when the United States and its allies already had hundreds of bases, many stocked with nuclear weapons, surrounding the Soviet Union. The world then came closer to a nuclear conflict than at any other point during the Cold War.

Recently, Russia publicly announced its intention to build four new overseas bases—in the Seychelles, Singapore, Nicaragua, and Venezuela— to complement the nine foreign bases it already possesses. "We need bases for refueling [our aircraft] near the equator, and in other places," said Defense Minister Sergei Shoigu in February 2014. He also announced Russia's intention to sign agreements in the four countries to allow for increased port visits and the use of airfields. Additionally, Russia is in the process of increasing the size of its presence at bases in Tajikistan, Belarus, and Kyrgyzstan.[27]

As Russia's plans show, the creation of U.S. bases overseas risks encouraging other nations to boost their own military spending and build their own foreign bases in what could become escalating "base races."[28] Given Russia's professed desire to increase its influence and stature worldwide, building new Russian bases abroad would be an unsurprising move, especially given recent U.S. attempts to use base construction, training, exercises, and other military activities to deepen its influence in Africa, Latin America, eastern Europe, and East Asia. China seems likely to try to follow suit, in Africa and the Indian Ocean in particular.[29]

Bases near the borders of China and Russia are especially dangerous as they threaten to fuel new cold wars. (Some say these are already under way.) Quite in contrast to the claim that overseas bases increase global security, we can see how they lead to growing international tensions and a greater risk of military confrontation.

For the United States, overseas bases have appeared to provide protection, safety, and security. They have appeared to hold out the promise of never having to fight a world war again. Instead, these bases have in many ways damaged national security. By making it simpler to wage foreign wars, they have made military action an even more attractive option among the foreign policy tools available to American policymakers, and they have made war more likely. (The rise of lily pad bases only deepens this problem, since a major part of their appeal for military officials is the flexibility they provide in applying military force without restriction.) The disastrous outcomes of the wars in Afghanistan and Iraq have created widespread public opposition to large-scale U.S. intervention and warfare—but as others have pointed out, when all you have in your foreign policy toolbox is hammers, everything starts looking like a nail.[30]

CHANGE

Today, there are some encouraging signs that the base nation is shrinking, thanks in part to Pentagon-wide budget cuts. While it remains unclear whether the military will fully withdraw its bases and troops from

Afghanistan and Iraq, the withdrawal of most U.S. forces has been a positive development, albeit amid continuing devastation and violence in both countries. The closure of large numbers of Cold War–era bases and the removal of tens of thousands of troops from Europe and, to a lesser extent, East Asia since the George W. Bush administration initiated its Global Posture Review have continued a much-needed drawdown begun after the dissolution of the Soviet Union but halted prematurely in the mid-1990s. The Pentagon is currently undertaking a "European Infrastructure Consolidation Review" to eliminate unnecessary facilities as part of plans to cut forces by a further 15 percent in Europe by 2023.[31] European Command commander General Philip Breedlove has said, "There is infrastructure I believe we can still divest."[32]

Among the armed services, the Navy has acknowledged having unnecessary bases and the Air Force has said it has "a lot of excess infrastructure" worldwide, according to its deputy chief of staff for logistics, installations, and mission support. The Air Force has a "20/20" program to eliminate 20 percent of its global infrastructure footprint by 2020 and says it is more than halfway to its goal. General Judith Fedder has said the service "could make better use of [its total] infrastructure if we could close installations."[33]

The Army estimates having 10 to 15 percent excess base capacity in Europe and 18 percent worldwide. Assistant Secretary of the Army Katherine G. Hammack has said, "In today's fiscally constrained environment, the Army cannot afford to keep and maintain excess infrastructure and overhead."[34] The Army's highest-ranking officials have told Congress that a failure to close unnecessary facilities is an "empty space tax" wasting "hundreds of millions of dollars per year."[35]

As Army officials acknowledge, the Pentagon's plans to continue cutting the total size of the armed forces should make closing superfluous bases all the more important.[36] And with so much extra domestic infrastructure—the Army and Air Force both have around 20 percent excess base capacity in the United States[37]—there's plenty of room to bring troops home.

Closing Cold War bases built for a much larger military would lead to both immediate and long-term savings. The possibility of canceling billions in base construction, operations, and maintenance contracts is a good reminder that there are immediate savings available by reducing troop deployments and bases abroad. As we have seen, bringing troops and base spending back to the United States will mean stemming the leakage of money out of the U.S. economy and ensuring that economic spillover effects remain at home. In many cases, too, host nations will actually pay us for infrastructure we vacate. When we leave, we should assist in the work of cleaning up the environmental damage we caused; beyond that, we should properly consider residual value payments a peace dividend, rather than money to be funneled back into the base nation or the larger military budget.

The Cold War bases in Europe should be an obvious place to start with closures continuing progress the military has already made. The construction of new bases in Germany, such as the Army's new billion-dollar hospital and half-billion-dollar European headquarters, is unnecessary and should be halted immediately. Bases in Latin America should have been among the first to be closed decades ago at the end of the Cold War. Closing Futenma and other bases in Okinawa and scrapping the ill-conceived and dangerous buildup on Guam and across the Asia-Pacific region are other important places to start; marines and other departing troops can and should move to bases with excess capacity on the west coast of the United States. Halting the construction of all new lily pads, no matter how small, is also critical.

Closing these and other bases may seem like a daunting task. Powerful institutional forces within the military, in the State Department, and among U.S. and local politicians and businesses will often align to block such change and maintain the status quo. On the other hand, compared to the challenge of closing domestic bases, closing overseas installations should be relatively easy. After all, U.S. politicians have few constituents abroad to whom they need be beholden. Prioritizing the interests of the country, its citizens, and the military itself by shutting down unnecessary bases is a realistic goal.

Closing bases overseas also offers a range of transformation opportunities. There are numerous models: former bases in Germany, Japan, and the United States have been turned into schools, public parks, housing developments, shopping malls, offices, business incubators, airports, and tourist destinations. Rather than simply handing over bases to host nations and leaving, Americans could collaborate with former base hosts, investing money and expertise in mutually beneficial ways. Throughout such transformation efforts, hiring preferences could be given to local base employees and veterans, helping them transition out of military life in the wake of base closures and military downsizing and making use of their skills and experience.

Beyond a onetime list of base closures, the Pentagon and Congress should create a regular review process to assess the need to maintain every base site overseas. The Pentagon should internally scrutinize every site on at least a yearly basis, and Congress should provide a second layer of scrutiny and oversight. Congress could also create incentives for the military to identify and carry out base closures abroad by ensuring that a proportion of these cuts would remain in each service's budget rather than being ceded completely. Congress and the president should also change the tax code to ensure that contracts abroad do not offer tax advantages over contracts at domestic bases, thus eliminating a reason for contractors to favor keeping bases overseas.

Another encouraging sign has been the significant reduction in the size of military construction budgets in recent years. Still, the military and Congress can go farther when billions of dollars are still going to build new base infrastructure such as the new Army hospital and headquarters in Germany or to expand in places from Africa to Southeast Asia. Ending the profligacy of overseas MilCon would be an easy way to save money immediately in a time of budget cuts. Canceling contracts and declaring a moratorium on all new construction (except in cases where unsafe housing or workplace conditions might endanger lives) would provide immediate savings. Again, compared to the political difficulty of cuts and closures at domestic bases, these changes should be relatively easy to accomplish.

In the budget for fiscal year 2015, Congress took several critical steps to assert much-needed control over the MilCon process and Pentagon spending. Most important of all, Congress is attempting to prevent the military from building overseas without proper oversight. "None of the funds," reads the year's MilCon spending bill, "may be used to initiate a new installation overseas without prior notification to the Committees on Appropriations of both Houses of Congress." Another provision of the law requires the Pentagon to alert Congress to any MilCon of more than $100,000 planned for military exercises, which has long been a way to build without congressional approval. To prevent military officials from wastefully spending MilCon money at the end of the fiscal year, Congress also prohibited the use of more than 20 percent of funding in the fiscal year's last two months.[38]

Congress should make each of these provisions permanent, and there is more to be done. Congress should extend the Leahy Law, which cuts off aid to governments found to abuse their citizens' human rights, in order to ensure that bases are not opened or maintained in undemocratic nations. Silencing criticism of human rights abuses as we maintain bases in countries like Bahrain makes the United States complicit in these states' crimes. Maintaining bases in other undemocratic countries is equally counterproductive and makes a mockery of legitimate U.S. efforts to spread democracy and improve the well-being of people around the world. American bases have no business propping up repressive regimes.

Even in the most democratic of countries, the agreements that form the legal and political foundation for maintaining our bases are almost always secret, in whole or in part. In the interest of transparency and democracy, Congress should require that every status of forces agreement and base agreement on the books be published in its entirety. Many basing agreements are secret because they have been created as executive agreements not subject to congressional oversight. But base agreements are effectively treaties, and they should be subject to Congress's approval.

Given the danger of foreign base races, the United States would be wise to use its current position of relative strength to propose and negotiate an international ban on foreign bases except under the strictest of circumstances and under the most transparent of conditions. Forgoing such a proposal now runs the risk of other countries' acquiring bases in larger numbers and far closer to U.S. borders. A bases ban would need to allow for the creation of alliances and the establishment of foreign bases by explicit and transparent invitation when a country is under attack or facing a direct, credible threat. It could also make allowances for pre-positioning sites that could be monitored by UN inspectors and allow for the storage of military matériel around the world to be used only in UN-sanctioned peacekeeping operations.

A succession of empires and world powers through the centuries have amassed and subsequently lost most if not all of their foreign bases, either by force or divestment. Following in the footsteps of Portugal, Holland, Spain, and France, Britain had to shutter most of its foreign bases in the midst of an economic crisis in the 1960s and 1970s. The United States is headed in that same direction. The only questions are when and whether the country will close its bases and downsize its global mission by choice, or whether it will follow Britain's path as a fading power forced to give up its bases from a position of weakness.

This is a large and politically challenging list of proposals. But proclaiming that things can never change is a self-fulfilling prophecy. Not making such proposals, not developing alternatives to the existing base nation, is the surest way to guarantee the continuation of a status quo that has hurt us all.

AUTHOR'S NOTE

No one is objective. Like the anthropologist David Graeber, I tend to think that if anyone tells you she or he is objective, that person is probably trying to sell you something.[1] Still, I believe we can and must strive for objectivity, even if it's an unattainable goal. In this book, I have tried to be fair and to consider as many perspectives as possible on every issue I examined. As my ideas and conclusions took shape, I particularly tried to consider points of view opposite my own.

I think a good measure of fairness is whether, before publication, one can share one's writing with interviewees with whom one might disagree. To that end, I showed drafts of sections and chapters to as many people involved in the research as possible and gave them opportunities to offer feedback, suggestions, and corrections. I am thankful for the openness with which so many people read my writing, especially when they dissented from my perspectives, and the helpful corrections that they offered.

In any work of research or writing, one's background inevitably shapes the investigation and analysis. In the interests of transparency, here are some relevant parts of mine: I have been reporting and writing about U.S. military bases for more than thirteen years. I came to the subject in 2001, after lawyers representing the exiled people of Diego Garcia asked me to document the effects of the Chagossians' expulsion on their lives. Over the next seven years, I conducted research with the exiled people in Mauritius, the Seychelles, and the United Kingdom. I then coupled that work with extensive archival research and with interviews in the United States, talking to some of the military and diplomatic officials who had helped create the base on Diego Garcia. Almost to a man (and all the officials involved were men), they expressed regret about the way the Chagossians were treated. My work culminated in the 2009 publication of *Island of Shame: The Secret History of the U.S. Military Base on Diego Garcia*.

I also helped produce *The Counter-Counterinsurgency Manual*, a critical analysis of counterinsurgency strategy, war, and militarization. I coauthored the book with other members of the Network of Concerned Anthropologists. The NCA is a group that sought, on both ethical and military grounds, to oppose the Army's attempts to recruit anthropologists as embedded and sometimes armed members of combat brigades in the Bush administration's war on terror. On the other hand, in January 2012, I published an opinion piece in *Defense News* that was coauthored with Ray DuBois, the former Bush administration Pentagon official whom I quote in the present work.

I conducted research for this book between 2009 and 2015 with the help of a grant from the Stewart R. Mott Foundation's Fund for Constitutional Government and with faculty research support from American University and its College of Arts and Sciences. Otherwise, I funded my travels with savings, frequent flier miles, and the generosity of many who hosted me in their homes and assisted my work in so many ways. I will donate all proceeds from the book's royalties to nonprofit organizations serving military veterans, their families, and other victims of war and violence.

NOTES

INTRODUCTION

1. Phil Stewart, "Ecuador Wants a Military Base in Miami," UK.Reuters.com, October 22, 2007, http://uk.reuters.com/article/2007/10/22/ecuador-base -idUKADD25267520071022.
2. Nick Turse, "Afghanistan's Base Bonanza: Total Tops Iraq at That War's Height," *TomDispatch*, September 4, 2012, http://www.tomdispatch.com/blog/175588/. My other source for Afghanistan is David de Jong, email to author, February 4, 2014, quoting a press officer for the secretary of defense: "Using October 2011 as a bench-mark, we had about 800 facilities—ranging from very small checkpoints that have maybe a squad or platoon of ISAF forces on it to bases that have several hundred to as many as a thousand ISAF members on them."
3. U.S. Department of Defense, "Base Structure Report—Fiscal Year 2014 Baseline: A Summary of the Real Property Inventory," report, Washington, DC, 2014. The Pentagon generally considers U.S. territories including American Samoa, the Commonwealth of the Northern Mariana Islands, Guam, Puerto Rico, and the U.S. Virgin Islands "overseas." Given that they lack full democratic incorporation into the United States, I also count them as overseas. The District of Columbia also lacks full democratic rights, but given that it is the nation's capital and is not overseas, I consider D.C. bases domestic. For counting purposes, it makes sense to follow the lead of the Pentagon, which uses the term "base site." In some cases, this means that an installation generally referred to as a single base—like Aviano Air Base in Italy—actually consists of multiple base sites—in Aviano's case, at least eight. Counting each base site makes sense because sites with the same name are often in geographically disparate locations. Generally, too, each base site reflects distinct congressional appropriations of taxpayer funds. (See the first pages of the above annual report.) To come up with my estimate of eight hundred base sites and to compile the maps in this book, I compiled a database of bases from the "Base Structure Report" and scholarship and news sources.
4. Department of Defense, "Base Structure Report Fiscal Year 2014 Baseline (A Summary of DoD's Real Property Inventory)," report, Washington, DC, 2014; Nick

Turse, "Empire of Bases 2.0: Does the Pentagon Really Have 1,180 Foreign Bases?" *TomDispatch.com*, January 9, 2011, http://www.tomdispatch.com/blog/175338/. Turse has documented the Pentagon's difficulty in tracking the number of bases and facilities in Iraq and Afghanistan alone.

5. Department of Defense, "Base Structure Report 2014." The Army generally uses *post*, *camp*, and *fort*; the Navy and Marine Corps mostly prefer *installation, camp, base*, and *station*; the Air Force likes *base*. When it comes to foreign bases, terminology often reflects political, legal, and public relations calculations more than analytic accuracy: using the terms *military facility* or *forward operating location*, for example, helps minimize perceptions of a base's size and significance and the idea that an occupying military has usurped another nation's sovereignty. Ensuring that base ownership officially remains with the "host" country and that the United States is officially a "guest" is likewise one way to try to reduce local opposition and political furor. In reality, the degree to which a host exercises effective sovereign control over its territory varies widely and generally reflects broader power relations between the United States and a host (another term that can be something of a misnomer depending on the degree of control a country actually has over its U.S. guests). Despite the use of "America" in the book's title, I have tried to use the technically inaccurate "America," "American," and "Americans" as sparingly as possible when United States, U.S., and U.S. Americans are meant.

6. Building off the definition of former Pentagon official James Blaker, "Installations Routinely Used by Military Forces," in Catherine Lutz, ed., *The Bases of Empire: The Global Struggle Against U.S. Military Posts* (New York: New York University Press, 2009), 4.

7. See Robert E. Harkavy, *Strategic Basing and the Great Powers, 1200–2000* (London: Routledge, 2007), 14; Robert E. Harkavy, *Bases Abroad: The Global Foreign Military Presence* (Oxford: Oxford University Press/SIPRI, 1989), 17. On golf, see Dave Gilson, "Don't Tread on Me," *Mother Jones*, January/February 2014, 28.

8. U.S. Department of Defense, "Operations and Maintenance Overview: Fiscal Year 2015 Budget Requests," Washington, DC, March 2014, 117; U.S. Department of Defense, "Department of Defense Base Structure Report: Fiscal Year 2012 Baseline (A Summary of DoD's Real Property Inventory)," Washington, DC, 2012, 23.

9. U.S. Department of Defense, "2013 Demographics: Profile of the Military Community," report, Washington, DC, 2014, 185.

10. Joel Wuthnow, *The Impact of Missile Threats on the Reliability of U.S. Overseas Bases: A Framework for Analysis* (Carlisle, PA: Strategic Studies Institute, 2005), 1.

11. George Stambuk, *American Military Forces Abroad: Their Impact on the Western State System* (Columbus: Ohio State University Press, 1963), 13.

12. George W. Bush, "National Security Strategy of the United States of America," Washington, DC, September 2002, 29.

13. U.S. Department of Defense, "Quadrennial Defense Review Report," Washington DC, February 2010, 63–64.

14. Lutz, ed., *Bases of Empire*, 27.

1: THE BIRTH OF BASE NATION

1. C. T. Sandars, *America's Overseas Garrisons: The Leasehold Empire* (New York: Oxford University Press, 2000), 3; Department of the Navy, *Building the Navy's*

Bases in World War II: History of the Bureau of Yards and Docks and the Civil Engineer Corps 1940–1946, vol. II, part III, *The Advance Bases* (Washington, DC: Government Printing Office, 1947). Available at http://www.history.navy.mil /library/online/buildbaseswwii/bbwwii2.htm.

2. Blaker, "Installations," 9; Robert E. Harkavy, *Great Power Competition for Overseas Bases: The Geopolitics of Access Diplomacy* (Elmsford, NY: Pergamon Press, 1982).

3. Martin H. Brice, *Stronghold: A History of Military Architecture* (New York: Schocken Books, 1985), 13–45.

4. Ibid., 48–55, 13–4.

5. Washington Irving, *Life and Voyages of Christopher Columbus and the Voyages and Discoveries of the Companions of Columbus* (New York: Thomas Y. Crowell, 1892?), 136–46.

6. Historic Jamestown, "Jamestown Fort: The First English Settlement," webpage, n.d., accessed July 5, 2013, http://apva.org/rediscovery/page.php?page_id=178.

7. Stacie L. Pettyjohn, *U.S. Global Defense Posture, 1783–2011* (Santa Monica, CA: RAND Corporation, 2012), 16, 16n3.

8. Reginald Horsman, *Expansion and American Indian Policy, 1783–1812* (East Lansing: Michigan State University Press, 1967), 141,157.

9. Anni P. Baker, *American Soldiers Overseas: The Global Military Presence* (Westport, CT: Praeger, 2004), 4. Some of this history is also recounted in David Vine, *Island of Shame: The Secret History of the U.S. Military Base on Diego Garcia* (Princeton, NJ: Princeton University Press, 2009).

10. Francis P. Prucha, *A Guide to the Military Posts of the United States, 1789–1895* (Madison: State Historical Society of Wisconsin, 1964), 23.

11. Ibid., 34; Robert M. Utley, *The Indian Frontier: 1860–1890* (Albuquerque: University of New Mexico Press, 1984), 92.

12. Pettyjohn, *U.S. Global Defense Posture*, 17–18.

13. Andrew Krepinevich and Robert O. Work, *New US Global Defense Posture for the Transoceanic Era* (Washington, DC: Center for Strategic and Budgetary Assessments, 2007), 41–42.

14. Ibid.

15. Ibid., 43.

16. Chris Ames, "Crossfire Couples: Marginality and Agency Among Okinawan Women in Relationships with U.S. Military Men," in *Over There: Living with the U.S. Military Empire from World War Two to the Present*, edited by Maria Höhn and Seungsook Moon (Durham, NC: Duke University Press, 2010), 199n5.

17. A. M. Jackson, memorandum for the Chief of Naval Operations, December 7, 1964, Naval Historical Center: 00 Files, 1965, Box 26, 11000/1B, 2.

18. Joint Base Elmendorf-Richardson, "Military History in Alaska, 1867–2000," fact sheet, November 13, 2006, http://www.jber.af.mil/library/factsheets/factsheet.asp ?id=5304.

19. Pettyjohn, *U.S. Global Defense Posture*, 27n6; Stephen A. Kinzer, *Overthrow: America's Century of Regime Change from Hawaii to Iraq* (New York: Times Books, 2006), 18–19.

20. Jana K. Lipman, *Guantánamo: A Working-Class History Between Empire and Revolution* (Berkeley: University of California Press, 2008), 21; Stephen I. M. Schwab, *Guantánamo, USA: The Untold Story of America's Cuban Outpost* (Lawrence: University Press of Kansas, 2009), 36–60.

21. Schwab, *Guantánamo, USA*, 60.

22. Lipman, *Guantánamo*, 23.

23. Ibid., 23–24; Schwab, *Guantánamo, USA*.

24. Lipman, *Guantánamo*, 27–28. The text read: "So long as the United States of America shall not abandon the said naval station of Guantánamo or the two Governments shall not agree to a modification of its present limits, the station shall continue to have the territorial area that it now has."

25. Krepinevich and Work, *New US Global Defense Posture*, 49.

26. Kinzer, *Overthrow*, 33.

27. Ibid., 86–87; Krepinevich and Work, *New US Global Defense Posture*, 47–48, 50; Hall M. Friedman, *Creating an American Lake: United States Imperialism and Strategic Security in the Pacific Basin, 1945–1947* (Westport, CT: Greenwood Press, 2001), 3.

28. Carolyn Hall and Héctor Pérez Brignoli, *Historical Atlas of Central America*, cartographer John V. Cotter (Norman: University of Oklahoma Press, 2003), 228; John Lindsay-Poland, *Emperors in the Jungle: The Hidden History of the U.S. in Panama* (Durham, NC: Duke University Press, 2003), 27.

29. Sandars, *America's Overseas Garrisons*, 140.

30. William Earl Weeks, *Building the Continental Empire: American Expansion from the Revolution to the Civil War* (Chicago: Ivan R. Dee, 1996), 140–43; Hall and Pérez Brignoli, *Historical Atlas*, 184–85, 209; Lindsay-Poland, *Emperors in the Jungle*, 16–17.

31. Hall and Pérez Brignoli, *Historical Atlas*, 228.

32. Michael S. Sherry, *In the Shadow of War: The United States Since the 1930s* (New Haven, CT: Yale University Press, 1995), 30–31; Sandars, *America's Overseas Garrisons*, 3–6.

33. Elliott V. Converse III, *Circling the Earth: United States Plans for a Postwar Overseas Military Base System, 1942–1948* (Maxwell Air Force Base, AL: Air University Press, 2005), 1; Sandars, *America's Overseas Garrison*, 5–6.

34. Michael C. Desch, *When the Third World Matters: Latin American and United States Grand Strategy* (Baltimore: Johns Hopkins University Press, 1993), 183 n123; Lindsay-Poland, *Emperors in the Jungle*, 45; Krepinevich and Work, *New US Global Defense Posture*, 66–69.

35. Blaker, "Installations," 23, 9.

36. Converse, *Circling the Earth*, xv.

37. Ibid., 15.

38. Pettyjohn, *U.S. Global Defense Posture*, 45–46.

39. Converse, *Circling the Earth*, 1–10, 38–39.

40. Sandars, *America's Overseas Garrisons*, 5.

41. Converse, *Circling the Earth*, xv.

42. Ibid., 89.

43. *Monthly Review*, "U.S. Military Bases and Empire," March 2002, http://www.monthlyreview.org/0302editr.htm.

44. Peter Hayes, Lyuba Zarsky, and Walden Bello, *American Lake: Nuclear Peril in the Pacific* (Victoria, Australia: Penguin Books, 1986), 23–24.

45. Donald F. McHenry, *Micronesia: Trust Betrayed* (New York: Carnegie Endowment for International Peace, 1975), 67, 66.

46. Friedman, *Creating an American Lake*, 1–2.

47. Hayes et al., *American Lake*, 28.

48. Blaker, "Installations," 32.

49. Stambuk, *American Military Forces Abroad*, 9.

50. Catherine Lutz, "Introduction: Bases, Empire, and Global Response," in Lutz, ed., *Bases of Empire*, 14–15.

51. See e.g. Duncan Campbell, *The Unsinkable Aircraft Carrier: American Military Power in Britain* (London: Paladin Books, 1986).

52. Catherine Lutz, *Homefront: A Military City and the American Twentieth Century* (Boston: Beacon, 2001), 47–48.

53. Sherry, *In the Shadow of War*, 33.

54. Ibid., 30–44.

55. Lutz, *Homefront*, 86.

56. Department of the Navy, "Strategic Concepts of the U.S. Navy, NWP 1 (Rev. A)," Washington, DC, May 1978.

57. See my *Island of Shame*, 183–91.

58. Neil Smith, *American Empire: Roosevelt's Geographer and the Prelude to Globalization* (Berkeley: University of California Press, 2003), 2, 14–16, 21.

59. Ibid.; Chalmers Johnson, *Blowback: The Costs and Consequences of U.S. Empire* (New York: Metropolitan/Owl, 2004[2000]); Chalmers Johnson, "America's Empire of Bases," *TomDispatch*, January 15, 2004, available at http://www.tomdispatch.com /index.mhtml?pid1181; *Monthly Review*, "U.S. Military Bases and Empire."

60. United States Senate Subcommittee on United States Security Agreements and Commitments Abroad, Committee on Foreign Relations, "United States Security Agreements and Commitments Abroad," 91st Congress, Washington, DC, 1971, vol. 2, 2417.

61. Smith, *American Empire*, 349, 360.

62. Blaker, "Installations," 32.

63. United States Senate Subcommittee on United States Security Agreements and Commitments Abroad, "United States Security Agreements and Commitments Abroad," 2417.

64. Jimmy Carter, "State of the Union Address 1980," Washington, DC, January 23, 1980.

65. This section draws in part on my "The Bases of War in the Middle East: From Carter to the Islamic State, 35 Years of Building Bases and Sowing Disaster," *TomDispatch*, November 13, 2014, http://www.tomdispatch.com/blog/175922/. See also Nick Turse, "America Begins Nation-Building at Home (Provided Your Home Is the Middle East)," *TomDispatch*, November 15, 2012, http://www.tomdispatch.com /blog/175617/; Vytautas B. Bandjunis, *Diego Garcia: Creation of the Indian Ocean Base* (San Jose: Writer's Showcase, 2001).

66. AFP, "In Detail: The US Military Strength in the Middle East," *Australian*, September 23, 2014, http://www.theaustralian.com.au/news/world/in-detail-the-us -military-strength-in-the-middle-east/story-e6frg6so-1227068027888?nk=8377e e0d489781c9ee1ce50d431c0d45; Ben Piven, "Map: US Bases Encircle Iran," *Al Jazeera.com*, May 1, 2012, http://www.aljazeera.com/indepth/interactive/2012/04 /2012417131242767298.html.

67. Justin Elliott, "No, the U.S. Is Not Leaving Iraq," *Salon*, December 17, 2011, http:// www.salon.com/2011/12/17/no_the_u_s_is_not_leaving_iraq/.

68. Craig Whitlock, "U.S. Relies on Persian Gulf Bases for Airstrikes in Iraq," *Washington Post*, August 26, 2014, http://www.washingtonpost.com/world/national

-security/us-relies-on-persian-gulf-bases-for-airstrikes-in-iraq/2014/08/25
/517dcde0-2c7a-11e4-9b98-848790384093_story.html.

69. Michael Klare, *Blood and Oil: The Dangers and Consequences of America's Grow-ing Dependency on Imported Petroleum* (New York: Owl Books, 2004).

70. Chalmers Johnson, *The Sorrows of Empire: Militarism, Secrecy, and the End of the Republic* (New York: Holt Paperbacks, 2004), 253.

2: FROM LITTLE AMERICAS TO LILY PADS

1. GlobalSecurity.org, "Ramstein Air Base," n.d., accessed December 11, 2014, http://www.globalsecurity.org/military/facility/ramstein.htm.

2. 86th Air Wing Public Affairs Office, fiscal year 2011 data.

3. Elsa Rassbach, "Protesting U.S. Military Bases in Germany," *Peace Review* 22, no. 2 (2010): 123.

4. Gregory D. Kutz, Bruce A. Causseaux, and Terrell G. Dorn, "Military Construc-tion: Kaiserslautern Military Community Center Project Continues to Experience Problems," Testimony Before the Committee on Oversight and Government Reform, House of Representatives (GAO-08-923T), Washington, DC, Government Accountability Office, June 25, 2008; Mark Abramson, "Oft-delayed KMCC Set to Open Early 2009," *Stars and Stripes*, November 3, 2008. www.ramstein.af.mil /library/factsheets/factsheet.asp?id=15548.

5. Army and Air Force Exchange Service, "Annual Report 2009," Dallas, TX, 2010, 4.

6. John Spanier, quoted in Daniel J. Nelson, *A History of U.S. Military Forces in Germany* (Boulder, CO: Westview Press, 1987), 186–87.

7. John Willoughby, *Remaking the Conquering Heroes: The Postwar American Occu-pation of Germany* (London: Palgrave Macmillan, 2001), 25–28.

8. Maria Höhn, " 'You Can't Pin Sergeant's Stripes on an Archangel': Soldiering, Sexuality, and U.S. Army Policies in Germany," in Höhn and Moon, eds., *Over There*, 118.

9. Höhn, "You Can't Pin," 118.

10. Quoted in Willoughby, *Conquering Heroes*, 138–39.

11. Willoughby, *Conquering Heroes*, 138–39, 46–49, 137, 140–41.

12. Anni Baker, *Life in the U.S. Armed Forces: (Not) Just Another Job* (Westport, CT: Praeger Security International, 2008), 118–19; A. Baker, *American Soldiers Over-seas*, 15.

13. Quoted in Willoughby, *Conquering Heroes*, 118.

14. Willoughby, *Conquering Heroes*, 118–21.

15. Nelson, *Forces in Germany*, 40–45, 81; Tim Kane, "U.S. Troop Deployment Data-set," Excel file, Heritage Foundation, Washington, DC, March 1, 2006.

16. A. Baker, *American Soldiers Overseas*, 53–54.

17. Donna Alvah, "U.S. Military Families Abroad in the Post-Cold War Era and the 'New Global Posture,'" in Höhn and Moon, eds., *Over There*, 151.

18. Maria H. Höhn, *GIs and Fräuleins: The German-American Encounter in 1950s West Germany* (Chapel Hill: University of North Carolina Press, 2002), 6, 31, 52.

19. A. Baker, *American Soldiers Overseas*, 54.

20. Höhn, *GIs and Fräuleins*, 4.

21. Willoughby, *Conquering Heroes*, 150; Nelson, *Forces in Germany*, 55–56. The pres-

ence of families and the comforts of Little Americas normalized the peacetime deployment of U.S. troops abroad and the long-term occupation of sovereign countries in Western Europe and Japan for Americans and people in the occupied countries alike.

22. Willoughby, *Conquering Heroes*, 150.

23. Ibid.

24. Department of Defense, "Strengthening U.S. Global Defense Posture, Report to Congress," Washington, DC, September 17, 2004, 5.

25. Keith B. Cunningham and Andreas Klemmer, "Restructuring the US Military Bases in Germany: Scope, Impacts, and Opportunities," Bonn International Center for Conversion, report 4, Bonn, Germany, June 1995, 13, 20. There is a discrepancy in this report, which cites more than 92,000 acres (37,260 hectares) returned by the United States in total and more than 100,000 (40,500 hectares) returned by the U.S. Army alone.

26. George W. Bush, "Statement on the Ongoing Review of the Overseas Force Posture," November 25, 2003, American Presidency Project, http://www.presidency.ucsb.edu/ws/?pid=64105.

27. Mark L. Gillem, *America Town: Building the Outposts of Empire* (Minneapolis: University of Minnesota Press), 160, xv–xvi.

28. Lawrence L. Knutson, "U.S. Troop Presence in Honduras Called Temporary but Indefinite," *Associated Press*, April 6, 1987.

29. John Lindsay-Poland, "Honduras and the U.S. Military," report, Nyack, NY, Fellowship of Reconciliation, September 2011, 2; General Accounting Office, "Honduras: Continuing U.S. Military Presence at Soto Cano Base Is Not Critical" (GAO/NSIAD-95-39), Washington, DC, February 1995, 10.

30. General Accounting Office, "Honduras," 2.

31. General Accounting Office, "Honduras: U.S. Military Presence at Soto Cano Air Base" (GAO/NSIAD-89-107BR), Washington, DC, March 1989, 1.

32. Lindsay-Poland, "Honduras and the U.S. Military"; A. Louis Arana-Barradas and Megan Schafer, "Changes Make Soto Cano More Permanent," *Airman*, July 2005, 42.

33. Lindsay-Poland, "Honduras and the U.S. Military."

34. Captain David McCain, email to author, August 24, 2011.

35. Gillem, *America Town*, 272; Alexander Cooley, *Base Politics: Democratic Change and the U.S. Military Overseas* (Ithaca, NY: Cornell University Press, 2008), 236; John T. Bennett, "U.S. Military Envisions More Bases Like Djibouti Facility," *DOT-MIL* blog, January 30, 2012, http://www.usnews.com/news/blogs/dotmil/2012/01/30/us-military-envisions-more-bases-like-djibouti-facility.

36. Thomas Donnolly and Vance Serchuk, "Toward a Global Cavalry: Overseas Rebasing and Defense Transformation," report, Washington, DC, American Enterprise Institute, July 1, 2003, available at http://www.aei.org/article/foreign-and-defense-policy/toward-a-global-cavalry/.

37. Office of the Undersecretary of Defense (Policy), "Global Defense Posture and International Agreements Overview," slide presentation, Department of Defense, April 27, 2009, 6, 9–10.

38. Chris Woods, "Drone Strikes in Pakistan: CIA Drones Quit One Pakistan Site—But US Keeps Access to Other Airbases," Bureau of Investigative Journalism, December 15, 2011, http://www.thebureauinvestigates.com/2011/12/15/cia-drones-quit-pakistan-site-but-us-keeps-access-to-other-airbases/.

39. Robert D. Kaplan, *Hog Pilots, Blue Water Grunts: The American Military in the Air, at Sea, and on the Ground* (New York: Vintage Departures, 2007), 79–80.

40. Eric G. John, cable to U.S. Secretary of Defense, Bangkok, Thailand, May 23, 2008, http://wikileaks.org/cable/2008/05/08BANGKOK1611.html; Kaplan, *Hog Pilots,* 79–82.

41. Craig Whitlock, "U.S. Seeks Return to SE Asian Bases," *Washington Post,* June 22, 2012, http://www.washingtonpost.com/world/national-security/us-seeks-return-to -se-asian-bases/2012/06/22/gJQAKP83vV_story.html.

42. Robert D. Kaplan, "What Rumsfeld Got Right: How Donald Rumsfeld Remade the U.S. Military for a More Uncertain World," *Atlantic,* July 1, 2008, http://www .theatlantic.com/magazine/archive/2008/07/what-rumsfeld-got-right/306870/.

43. Robert D. Kaplan, *Imperial Grunts: On the Ground with the American Military* (New York: Vintage Departures, 2005),151, 131–84. See also e.g. Carlo Muñoz, "The Philippines Re-opens Military Bases to US Forces," June 6, 2012, http://thehill.com /blogs/defcon-hill/operations/231257-philippines-re-opens-military-bases-to-us -forces-.

44. Kaplan, "What Rumsfeld Got Right."

3: THE DISPLACED

1. U.S. Embassy London, telegram to Secretary of State, February 27, 1964, Naval History and Heritage Command Archives: 00 Files, 1964, Box 20, 11000/1B, 1–2. Parts of this chapter stem from my *Island of Shame* and "Forty Years of Heartbreak: Let the People of Diego Garcia Return to Their Homeland," *Huffington Post,* May 28, 2013, http://www.huffingtonpost.com/david-vine/forty-years-of-heartbreak_b _3344190.html. I began my research about Diego Garcia and the Chagossians when lawyers for the Chagossians invited me in 2001 to conduct research for lawsuits they were bringing against the U.S. and British governments. I wrote three expert reports based on this research. I was never employed by the lawyers but had some of my research expenses reimbursed during 2001–2004.

2. Horacio Rivero, enclosure to memorandum to Chief of Naval Operations, May 21, 1960, Naval History and Heritage Command Archives: 00 Files, 1960, Box 8, 5710, 2. Rivero credited Barber with doing most of the writing for the Long Range Objectives Group, which produced this document.

3. Rivero, enclosure, May 21, 1960, 2.

4. Horacio Rivero, enclosure to memorandum to Chief of Naval Operations, July 11, 1960, Naval History and Heritage Command Archives: 00 Files, 1960, Box 8, 5710; Rivero, "Long Range Requirements."

5. Rivero, enclosure, July 11, 1960.

6. Ibid.

7. U.S. Embassy London, telegram to RUEHCR/Secretary of State, May 10, 1965, Lyndon B. Johnson Presidential Library: NSF, Country File, Box 207, UK Memos vol. IV 5/65–6/65.

8. United Kingdom of Great Britain and Northern Ireland, "Availability of Certain Indian Ocean Islands for Defense Purposes," exchange of notes, December 30, 1966, 1–2.

9. Alun A. G. J. Chalfont, letter to David K. E. Bruce, December 30, 1966, National

Archives and Records Administration: RG 59/150/64–65, Subject-Numeric Files 1964–1966, Box 1552.

10. Roy L. Johnson, memorandum for Deputy Chief of Naval Operations (Plans and Policy), July 21, 1958, Naval History and Heritage Command Archives: 00 Files, 1958, Box 4, A4-2 Status of Shore Stations, 2–3. See also, Vine, *Island of Shame*, introduction, chapter 3.

11. CIA Board of National Estimates, "Strategic and Political Interests in the Western Indian Ocean," special memorandum, April 11, 1967, Lyndon B. Johnson Presidential Library: NSF, Country File, India, Box 133, India, Indian Ocean Task Force, vol. II; Horacio Rivero, "Assuring a Future Base Structure in the African-Indian Ocean Area," enclosure, memorandum to Chief of Naval Operations, July 11, 1960, Naval History and Heritage Command Archives: 00 Files, 1960, Box 8, 5710.

12. Foreign Relations of the United States, 1969–1976, vol. XXIV, Middle East Region and Arabian Peninsula, 1969–1972; Jordan, September 1970, Document 39, Paper Prepared in the Office of the Chief of Naval Operations (Moorer), Washington, DC, February 11, 1970.

13. Stuart B. Barber, letter to Paul B. Ryan, April 26, 1982, 3. My thanks to Richard Barber for providing this and other invaluable documents.

14. John Pilger, *Freedom Next Time: Resisting the Empire* (New York: Nation Books, 2007), 25.

15. Rob Evans and Richard Norton-Taylor, "WikiLeaks: Foreign Office Accused of Misleading Public over Diego Garcia," *Guardian*, December 3, 2010, http://www .theguardian.com/politics/2010/dec/03/wikileaks-cables-diego-garcia-uk.

16. Robert A. Frosch, memorandum for the Deputy Secretary of Defense, February 27, 1970, Naval History and Heritage Command Archives: 00 Files, 1970, Box 111, 11000; John H. Chafee, memorandum for the Secretary of Defense, January 31, 1970, Naval History and Heritage Command Archives: 00 Files, 1970, Box 111, 11000.

17. Attachment to E. L. Cochrane Jr., memorandum for the Deputy Chief of Naval Operations (Plans and Policy), March 24, 1971, NHC: 00 Files, 1971, Box 174, 11000, 2.

18. See e.g. *Stealing a Nation: A Special Report by John Pilger*, directed by John Pilger and Christopher Martin (2004; London: Granada Television); Pilger, *Freedom Next Time*, 28.

19. David Ottaway, "Islanders Were Evicted for U.S. Base," *Washington Post*, September 9, 1975, A1; *Washington Post*, "The Diego Garcians," editorial, September 11, 1975.

20. Jonathan Weisgall, *Operation Crossroads: The Atomic Tests at Bikini Atoll* (Annapolis, MD: Naval Institute Press, 1994), 32.

21. Ibid., 106–7.

22. Ibid., 107–8.

23. Ibid., 308–9.

24. Ibid., 309–14.

25. See e.g. Barbara Rose Johnston and Holly M. Barker, *The Consequential Damages of Nuclear War: The Rongelap Report* (Walnut Creek, CA: Left Coast Press, 2008); Holly M. Barker, *Bravo for the Marshallese: Regaining Control in a Post-Nuclear, Post-Colonial World*, 2nd ed. (Independence, KY: Cengage Learning, 2012).

26. U.S. Naval Institute, "Reminiscences of Admiral Horacio Rivero, Jr.," 302–3.

27. Cheryl Lewis, "Kahoʻolawe and the Military," ICE case study, Washington, DC, Spring 2001, http://www.american.edu/ted/ice/hawaiibombs.htm.

28. Lindsay-Poland, *Emperors in the Jungle*, 28–29, 42–43, 193.

29. Katherine T. McCaffrey, *Military Power and Popular Protest: The U.S. Navy in Vieques, Puerto Rico* (New Brunswick, NJ: Rutgers University Press, 2002), 9.

30. Congressional Research Service, "Bill Summary and Status, 100th Congress (1987–1988), H.R.442," CRS Summary, 1987.

31. Leevin Camacho, "Resisting the Proposed Military Buildup on Guam," in Daniel Broudy, Peter Simpson, and Makoto Arakaki, eds., *Under Occupation: Resistance and Struggle in a Militarised Asia-Pacific* (Newcastle upon Tyne, UK: Cambridge Scholars Publishing, 2013), 186. Some quote a figure as high as 82 percent. See LisaLinda Natividad and Victoria Lola Leon-Guerrero, "The Explosive Growth of U.S. Military Power on Guam Confronts People Power: Experience of an Island People Under Spanish, Japanese and American Colonial Rule," *Asia-Pacific Journal* 49, issue 3, no. 10 (2010).

32. C. Johnson, *Sorrows of Empire*, 50–53, 200; C. Johnson, *Blowback*, 11; Kensei Yoshida, *Democracy Betrayed: Okinawa Under U.S. Occupation* (Bellingham, WA: Western Washington University, n.d. [2001]); Kozy K. Amemiya, "The Bolivian Connection: U.S. Bases and Okinawan Emigration," in *Okinawa: Cold War Island*, edited by Chalmers Johnson (n.p.: Japan Policy Research Institute, 1999), 63.

33. Quoted in Michiyo Yonamine, "Economic Crisis Shakes US Forces Overseas: The Price of Base Expansion in Okinawa and Guam," *Asia-Pacific Journal* 9, no. 9/2 (2011).

34. Eiichiro Azuma, "Brief Historical Overview of Japanese Emigration, 1868–1998," Japanese American National Museum, http://www.janm.org/projects/inrp/english/overview.htm.

35. C. Johnson, *Sorrows of Empire*, 50–53, 200; C. Johnson, *Blowback*, 11; Yoshida, *Democracy Betrayed*; Amemiya, "The Bolivian Connection, 63; Cooley, *Base Politics*, 146.

36. Aqqaluk Lynge, *The Right to Return: Fifty Years of Struggle by Relocated Inughuit in Greenland* (n.p: Atuagkat Publishers, 2002); D. L. Brown, "Trail of Frozen Tears," *Washington Post*, October 22, 2002, C1; J. M. Olsen, "US Agrees to Return to Denmark Unused Area near Greenland Military Base," Associated Press Worldstream, September 24, 2002.

37. Lynge, *Right to Return*, 10, 27, 32–36.

38. David Hanlon, *Remaking Micronesia: Discourses over Development in a Pacific Territory 1944–1982* (Honolulu: University of Hawaiʻi Press, 1998), 189–91, 201–2.

39. Ibid., 193; Peter Marks, "Paradise Lost; The Americanization of the Pacific," *Newsday*, January 12, 1986, 10.

40. PCRC, "The Kwajalein Atoll and the New Arms Race: The US Anti-Ballistic Weapons System and Consequences for the Marshall Islands of the Pacific," *Indigenous Affairs* 2 (2001): 38–43; City Mayors, "The Largest Cities in the World," n.d., accessed December 18, 2014, http://www.citymayors.com/statistics/largest-cities-density-125.html; Republic of the Marshall Islands Economic Policy, Planning, and Statistics Office, "Census of Population and Housing: Summary and Highlights Only," report, February 14, 2012, 7.

41. Hanlon, *Remaking Micronesia*, 201.

42. Robert C. Kiste, *The Bikinians: A Study in Forced Migration* (Menlo Park, CA: Cummings Publishing, 1974), 198.

43. McCaffrey, *Military Power*, 9–10.

44. Gillem, *America Town*, 37.

45. Catherine Lutz, "A U.S. 'Invasion' of Korea," *Boston Globe*, October 8, 2006; KCTP English News, "When You Grow Up, You Must Take the Village Back," http://www.antigizi.or.kr/zboard/zboard.php?id=english_news& page=1&sn1= &divpage=1&sn=off&ss=on&sc=on&select_arrange=headnum&desc=asc &no=204.

46. Anders Riel Müller, "One Island Village's Struggle for Land, Life and Peace," Save Jeju Now, blog, April 19, 2011, http://savejejunow.org/history; Christine Ahn, "Naval Base Tears Apart Korean Village," Foreign Policy in Focus, blog, August 19, 2011, http://fpif.org/naval_base_tears_apart_korean_village.

47. Anthropologists have shown that race is not biologically real and that it is not a valid or useful biological concept even if it is a very real social phenomenon having powerful social effects on people's lives and life chances.

48. A. M. Jackson, memorandum for the Chief of Naval Operations, December 7, 1964, Naval History and Heritage Command Archives: 00 Files, 1965, Box 26, 11000/1B, 3<n->4.

49. Ibid.

50. See e.g. John Madeley, "Diego Garcia: A Contrast to the Falklands," Minority Rights Group Report 54 (1985); Vine, *Island of Shame*.

51. See Laura Jeffery's writing, esp. *Chagos Islanders in Mauritius and the UK* (Manchester: Manchester University Press, 2011).

52. Barber, unpublished letter to the editor of the *Washington Post*, March 9, 1991.

53. Barber, letter to Senator Ted Stevens, October 3, 1975.

4: THE COLONIAL PRESENT

1. Cooley, *Base Politics*, 65–66. The title for this chapter stems from Derek Gregory, *The Colonial Present: Afghanistan, Palestine, Iraq* (Malden, MA: Blackwell Publishing, 2004).

2. Many in the military called for complete incorporation of some or all of the islands, including Guam and the other Marianas, into the United States as part of Hawaii or as a new state.

3. Stanley de Smith, quoted in Roy H. Smith, *The Nuclear Free and Independent Pacific Movement: After Mururoa* (London: I. B. Tauris, 1997), 42.

4. See Sandars, *America's Overseas Garrisons*, 36.

5. See e.g. ibid.

6. Kaplan, *Hog Pilots*, 60–61.

7. City of Norfolk, "Norfolk 2030: The General Plan of Norfolk," report, March 26, 2013, 2–1.

8. Shirley A. Kan, "Guam: U.S. Defense Deployments," Congressional Research Service, report, Washington, DC, April 11, 2013, 2–3.

9. Michael L. Bevacqua, *Chamorros, Ghosts, Non-voting Delegates: GUAM! Where the Production of America's Sovereignty Begins* (PhD dissertation, University of California, San Diego, 2010), 1, 8.

10. *Dan Rather Reports*, "Goin' to Guam," October 5, 2010.

11. LisaLinda Natividad and Gwyn Kirk, "Fortress Guam: Resistance to US Military Mega-Buildup," *Asia-Pacific Journal* 19, no. 1 (2010); Hermon Farahi, "A Holistic Approach to Understanding the Military Buildup of Guam (*Guahan*)," unpublished paper, George Washington University, n.d.

12. Natividad and Kirk, "Fortress Guam." See also *Insular Nation*, directed by Vanessa Warheit (Blooming Grove, NY: New Day Films, 2010).

13. Miyumi Tanji, "Japanese Wartime Occupation, War Reparation and Guam's Chamorro Self-Determination," in Broudy et al., *Under Occupation*, 162–67. Thanks to James Oelke, War in the Pacific National Monument, National Parks Service, for his help with the details of the World War II history.

14. Timothy P. Maga, *Defending Paradise: The United States and Guam 1898–1950* (New York: Garland Publishing, 1988), 173–75.

15. National Park Service, "War in the Pacific National Historical Park Guam," guide, n.d.

16. National Park Service, "War in the Pacific"; James Oelke, personal correspondence, March 17, 2014.

17. Maga, *Defending Paradise*, 193.

18. My thanks to John Calvo, Guam Fishermen's Cooperative Association, for helping to clarify this for me.

19. Maga, *Defending Paradise*, 203–7.

20. Department of the Interior Office of Insular Affairs, "Definitions of Insular Area Political Organizations," n.d., http://www.doi.gov/oia/islands/politicatypes.cfm.

21. Guam Department of Labor, "The Unemployment Situation on Guam: March 2013," March 27, 2013; Mar-Vic Cagurangan, "Guam's Poverty Rate Up, Income Gap Wide," *Marianas Variety*, December 4, 2013.

22. Camacho, "Resisting," 185. The Pentagon later revised the 79,000 figure to 59,000.

23. E.g. Joint Guam Program Office, "Guam/CNMI Military Relocation Opportunities for a Growing Community," fact sheet, Guam, n.d.

24. GuamBaseBuildup.com, email, "Opportunity of a Lifetime!" September 17, 2011.

25. Guam Chamber of Commerce Armed Forces Committee, "Guam and the CNMI: America's ONLY Sovereign Assets in Asia (100 Years and Counting)," white paper, June 2011.

26. Camacho, "Resisting," 185–86; Department of the Navy, "Guam and CNMI Military Relocation Relocating Marines from Okinawa, Visiting Aircraft Carrier Berthing, and Army Air and Missile Defense Task Force," Final Environmental Impact Assessment Reader's Guide, Pearl Harbor, HI, July 2010, 2-58, 2-61–62.

27. Natividad and Kirk, "Fortress Guam"; Blaine Harden, "Guam's Support for Military Has Its Limits," *Washington Post*, March 22, 2010, A1, A7.

28. Quoted in *Dan Rather Reports*.

29. Cara Flores-Mays, "The truth about the military," email, October 21, 2010. The quotations that follow come from the email except the single line about the Chamorro man's teeth, which comes from an interview with Flores-Mays in October 2011.

30. Camacho, "Resisting," 187.

31. Ibid., 184–89.

32. Government Accountability Office, "Defense Management: More Reliable Cost Estimates and Further Planning Needed to Inform the Marine Corps Realignment in the Pacific," report to Congress, June 2013. The Pentagon submitted a plan in 2014.

33. See e.g. Kan, "Guam."

5: BEFRIENDING DICTATORS

1. Associated Press, "U.S. Military Expands Its Drug War in Latin America," February 3, 2013; John Lindsay-Poland, "Pentagon Continues Contracting U.S. Companies in Latin America," Fellowship of Reconciliation blog, January 31, 2013, http://forusa.org/blogs/john-lindsay-poland/pentagon-continues-contracting-us -companies-latin-america/11782.

2. Parts of this chapter stem from my "When a Country Becomes a Military Base: Blowback and Insecurity in Honduras, the World's Most Dangerous Place," in *Bioinsecurity and Vulnerability*, edited by Lesley Sharp and Nancy Chen (Santa Fe, NM: School for Advanced Research Press, 2014), 25–44.

3. Eduardo Galeano, *Open Veins of Latin America: Five Centuries of the Pillage of a Continent* (New York: Monthly Review Press, 1973), 121.

4. Lindsay-Poland, *Emperors in the Jungle*, 16–17; Hall and Pérez Brignoli, *Historical Atlas*, 209.

5. Greg Grandin, *Empire's Workshop: Latin America, the United States, and the Rise of the New Imperialism* (New York: Metropolitan Books, 2006), 3, 20.

6. Lester D. Langley and Thomas Schoonover, *The Banana Men: American Mercenaries and Entrepreneurs in Central America, 1880–1930* (Lexington: University of Kentucky Press, 1995), 38–39; John Farley, *Bilharzi: A History of Tropical Medicine* (Cambridge: University of Cambridge Press, 1991), 155.

7. Walter LaFeber, *Inevitable Revolutions: The United States in Central America* (New York: W. W. Norton), 1983, 42, 42–46; Langley and Schoonover, *Banana Men*, 40–41.

8. LaFeber, *Inevitable Revolutions*, 44–45; Grandin, *Empire's Workshop*, 19.

9. LaFeber, *Inevitable Revolutions*, 42; Langley and Schoonover, *Banana Men*, 38–39; Farley, *Bilharzi*, 155.

10. LaFeber, *Inevitable Revolutions*, 45.

11. Ibid., 43.

12. Ibid., 9, 184; Tim Merrill, ed., *Honduras: A Country Study* (Washington, DC: Government Printing Office, 1995).

13. LaFeber, *Inevitable Revolutions*, 9.

14. Ibid., 44–45.

15. William M. LeoGrande, *Our Own Backyard: The United States in Central America, 1977–1992* (Chapel Hill: University of North Carolina Press, 1998), 116–18.

16. Ibid., 117–18.

17. Todd Greentree, *Crossroads of Intervention: Insurgency and Counterinsurgency Lessons from Central America* (Westport, CT: Praeger Security International, 2008), 117; LeoGrande, *Our Own Backyard*, 150, 297.

18. LeoGrande, *Our Own Backyard*, 150, 297.

19. Greentree, *Crossroads*, 121, 162.

20. Ibid., 121–22, 162.

21. William R. Meara, *Contra Cross: Insurgency and Tyranny in Central America, 1979–1989* (Annapolis, MD: Naval Institute Press, 2006), 28–29.

22. LeoGrande, *Our Own Backyard*, 150; Phillip E. Wheaton, *Inside Honduras: Regional Counterinsurgency Base* (Washington, DC: EPICA Task Force, 1982), 40.

23. Glenn Garvin, *Everybody Had His Own Gringo: The CIA and the Contras* (Washington, DC: Brassey's, 1992), 40–41; LeoGrande, *Our Own Backyard*, 395.

24. Government of Honduras, "Annex to the Bilateral Military Assistance Agreement between the Government of Honduras and the Government of the United States of America Dated May 20, 1954," Tegucigalpa, Washington, DC, May 7, 1982, sect. 1.

25. For more detail, see my "When a Country Becomes a Military Base." See also Problemas Internacionales, "Honduras: Enclave contra Nicaragua," report, Madrid: Instituto de Estudios Politicos para América Latina y Africa, 1982; Dieter Eich and Carlos Rincón, *The Contras: Interviews with Anti-Sandinistas* (San Francisco: Synthesis Publishers, 1984); Garvin, *Own Gringo*, 111; Wheaton, *Inside Honduras*; Eric L. Haney, "Inside Delta Force," in *American Soldier: Stories of Special Forces from Iraq to Afghanistan*, edited by Clint Willis (New York: Adrenaline, 2002), 27–36; LeoGrande, *Our Own Backyard*, 311, 115, 117, 436, 478, 391, 384–85, 491; Meara, *Contra Cross*, 89–91; Trevor Paglen, *Blank Spots on the Map: The Dark Geography of the Pentagon's Secret World* (New York: Dalton, 2009), 231–33.

26. LeoGrande, *Our Own Backyard*, 587.

27. Ibid., 317; see also Greentree, *Crossroads*, 37.

28. National Security Archive, *Chronology: The Documented Day-by-Day Account of the Secret Military Assistance to Iran and the Contras* (New York: Warner Books, 1987), 52–53.

29. Haney, "Inside Delta Force," 28; Greentree, *Crossroads*, 116.

30. See e.g. Tom Hayden, *Street Wars: Gangs and the Future of Violence* (New York: New Press, 2004), 57; LeoGrande, *Our Own Backyard*, 699nn119–20.

31. LeoGrande, *Our Own Backyard*, 299.

32. Trial transcript. *Reyes et al. v. Grijalba*, United States District Court Southern District of Florida, March 6, 2006.

33. Greentree, *Crossroads*, 7.

34. General Accounting Office, "Honduras: Continuing US Military Presence at Soto Cano Base Is Not Critical," GAO/NSIAD-95-39, Washington, DC, February 8, 1995, 1.

35. Ibid., 4, 1.

36. Ibid., 8.

37. Scott M. Hines, "Joint Task Force–Bravo: The U.S. Military Presence in Honduras; U.S. Policy for an Evolving Region," master's thesis, University of Maryland and National Defense University, 1994.

38. Meara, *Contra Cross*, 32, 155.

39. Dana Priest, *The Mission: Waging Wars and Keeping Peace with America's Military* (New York: W. W. Norton, 2003), 199.

40. Ibid., 200–3.

41. Ibid., 203, 205, 199.

42. Ibid., 206, 77.

43. Associated Press, "Honduran Govt Cooperating with US Human Rights Probe, Foreign Aid Maintained," *Washington Post*, August 13, 2012.

44. United Nations Office on Drugs and Crime, "Global Study on Homicide 2013: Trends, Contexts, Data," report, Vienna, March 2014, 24, 126.

45. *Vívelo Hoy*, "Niños Hondureños Parten Hacia EEUU para Evitar el Reclutamiento de las Pandillas," October 9, 2014, http://www.vivelohoy.com/noticias/8419803/ninos-hondurenos-parten-hacia-eeuu-para-evitar-el-reclutamiento-de-las-pandillas.

46. Alberto Arce, "Honduras Police Accused of Death Squad Killings," Associated Press, March 17, 2013.

47. Adrienne Pine, "Where Will the Children Play? Neoliberal Militarization in Pre-Election Honduras," *Upside Down World*, blog, November 5, 2013, http://upsidedownworld.org/main/index.php?option=com_content&view=article&id=4542:where-will-the-children-play-neoliberal-militarization-in-pre-election-honduras&catid=23:honduras&Itemid=46.

48. Pine, "Where Will the Children Play?"

49. Michael A. Allen, *Military Basing Abroad: Bargaining, Expectations, and Deployment*, Ph.D. dissertation, State University of New York, Binghamton, 2011, 35.

50. See e.g. Cooley, *Base Politics*, 208–9.

51. Human Rights Watch, *World Report 2014* (New York: Human Rights Watch, 2014), 526–30.

52. Ibid., 532–38.

53. Adam Taylor and Anup Kaphle, "Thailand's Army Just Announced a Coup. Here Are 11 Other Thai Coups since 1932," *Washington Post*, March 22, 2014.

54. Kent E. Calder, *Embattled Garrisons: Comparative Base Politics and American Globalism* (Princeton, NJ: Princeton University Press, 2007), 76, 115–16.

55. Cooley, *Base Politics*, 105–13.

56. Ibid., 250.

57. Ibid., 249–51.

58. Thanks and credit to Joe Masco for suggesting this line of analysis.

59. C. Johnson, *Blowback*, xi.

60. Adrienne Pine, *Working Hard, Drinking Hard: On Violence and Survival in Honduras* (Berkeley: University of California Press, 2008), 35–38; T. W. Ward, *Gangsters Without Borders: An Ethnography of a Salvadoran Street Gang* (Oxford: Oxford University Press, 2012).

61. Paglen, *Blank Spots*, 237, 211.

62. Thom Shanker, "Lessons of Iraq Help U.S. Fight a Drug War in Honduras," *New York Times*, May 5, 2012, 1.

63. United Nations Office on Drugs and Crime.

6: IN BED WITH THE MOB

1. Earlier versions of this chapter were published as "Married to the Mob? Uncovering the Relationship between the U.S. Military and the Mafia in Southern Italy," in *Anthropology Now* 4, no. 2: 54–69; and "Yankee City in the Heart of the Camorra: The U.S. Military in Campania," in *Meridione: Sud e Nord nel Mondo: La Napoli degli Americani dalla Liberazione alle basi Nato* [Southern Italy: South and North in the World: Americans in Naples from Liberation to NATO Bases], no. 4 (2011), edited by Chiara Ingrosso and Luca Molinari, 243–64.

2. Roberto Saviano, *Gomorrah: A Personal Journey into the Violent International Empire of Naples' Organized Crime System*, translated by V. Jewiss (New York: Picador, 2007), 161.

3. Carlo Alfiero, "Criminal Organisations in Southern Continental Italy: Camorra, 'Ndrangheta, Sacra Corona Unita," in *Rivista papers of the 1st European Meeting 'Falcon One' on Organised Crime*," Rome, April 26–28, 1995, http://www.sisde.it/sito/supplemento.nsf/stampe/10.

4. David Lane, *Into the Heart of the Mafia* (New York: Thomas Dunne Books, 2002), 187.

5. Saviano, *Gomorrah*, 46–47, 63–67, 120.

6. Ibid., 161.

7. Reuters, "EU Sends Italy Back to Court Over Naples Trash Epidemic," Reuters.com, June 20, 2013, http://www.reuters.com/article/2013/06/20/italy-garbage-eu -idUSL5N0EW2KY20130620.

8. Edna Buchanan, "Lucky Luciano: Criminal Mastermind," *Time*, December 7, 1998, http://www.time.com/time/magazine/article/0,9171,989779-1,00.html.

9. Rodney Campbell, *The Luciano Project: The Secret Wartime Collaboration of the Mafia and the U.S. Navy* (New York: McGraw-Hill, 1977), 1–2.

10. Salvatore Lupo, *History of the Mafia*, translated by Anthony Shugaar (New York: Columbia University Press, 2009), 187.

11. R. Campbell, *Luciano Project*, vii; Tom Behan, *See Naples and Die: The Camorra and Organized Crime* (London: Taurus Parke Paperbacks), 50–51; Tim Newark, *Lucky Luciano: The Real and the Fake Gangster* (New York: Thomas Dunne Books, 2010), 164; Lupo, *History of the Mafia*, 187; Salvatore Lupo, "The Allies and the Mafia," *Journal of Modern Italian Studies* 2, no. 1 (1997): 21–33.

12. Tom Behan, *Defiance: The Story of One Man Who Stood Up to the Sicilian Mafia* (London: I. B. Taurus, 2008), 4–5.

13. Lupo, "Allies," 29.

14. Behan, *See Naples*, 53. See also Alexander Cockburn and Jeffrey St. Clair, *Whiteout: The CIA, Drugs, and the Press* (London: Verso, 1998), 127–29.

15. Cockburn and St. Clair, *Whiteout*, 128.

16. Norman Lewis, *Naples '44: A World War II Diary of Occupied Italy* (New York: Carroll and Graf Publishers, 2005[1978]), 125. See also Gigi di Fiore, *Controstoria della Liberazione* (Milan: Rizzoli, 2012). My thanks to a friend who passed along the reference.

17. Lewis, *Naples '44*, 69–70.

18. On Sicily, see esp. Lupo, "Allies," 26.

19. Lewis, *Naples '44*, 109.

20. Ibid., 123.

21. Lane, *Into the Heart*, 189, 192; Behan, *See Naples*, 46.

22. Lewis, *Naples '44*, 109–10.

23. Cockburn and St. Clair, *Whiteout*, 128.

24. Behan, *See Naples*, 54–56.

25. Cooley, *Base Politics*, 199, 199nn88–89. A subsequent treaty signed in 1995 adds to but does not invalidate the BIA.

26. Daniele Gánser, *NATO's Secret Armies: Operation GLADIO and Terrorism in Western Europe* (New York: Frank Cass, 2005), 63.

27. See A. Zecca, "Basi e Intallazioni Militari in Campania," in *Napoli Chiama Vicenza: Disarme i Territori, Costruire la Pace*, edited by Angelica Romano (Pisa: Quaderni Satyagraha, 2008), 46.

28. Lewis, *Naples '44*, 141.

29. Behan, *See Naples*, 57–58.

30. Ibid.; J. Patrick Truhn, "Organized Crime in Italy II: How Organized Crime Distorts Markets and Limits Italy's Growth," cable to Secretary of State, 08NAPLES37, 6 June 2006, Wikileaks.

31. R. Campbell, *Luciano Project*, 1–2.

32. Francesco Erbani, "La Città degli Abusi," *La Repubblica*, July 9, 2002.

33. Saviano, *Gomorrah*, 187–88.
34. Ibid., 168; Erbani, "La Città."
35. Paolo Spiga, "Famiglia Cristiana, Grandi Dinasty Mattonare—i Coppola," *La Voce della Voci*, October 2010, 21.
36. Erbani, "La Città."
37. Felia Allum, *Camorristi, Politicians, and Businessmen: The Transformation of Organized Crime in Post-War Naples* (Leeds: Northern Universities Press, 2006), 162, xvi, 172.
38. Sue Palumbo, "Agnano Seamen to Stay in Barracks," *Stars and Stripes*, May 16, 1997, 3.
39. Spiga, "Famiglia Cristiana," 21; Erbani, "La Città."
40. U.S. Undersecretary of Defense John McGovern wrote, "Congressman Ron Dellums will be the chairman of the House Armed Services Committee. Tom Foglietta has assumed a new role in the appropriations subcommittee on military construction, which provides funds for the projects. These two friends are in a powerful position to ensure the authorization and the appropriation of the project in Naples." See Spiga, "Famiglia Cristiana," 21.
41. F. Geremicca, "Invece di una Nuova Pompei il Villaggio della US Navy," *Diario*, September 21/27, 2001, http://dust.it/articolo-diario/invece-di-una-nuova-pompei-il-villaggio-della-us-navy.
42. Andrea Cinquegrani, "Farano un Deserto e lo Chiameranno NATO," *La Voce della Campania*, April 6-9, 2001, 7.
43. Geremicca, "Nuova Pompei"; ibid.
44. Ward Sanderson, "Mafia Linked to Navy Site: Developers Accused of Conspiracy," *Stars and Stripes*, July 18, 1999, 1, 4.
45. Ibid., 1, 4.
46. Geremicca "Nuova Pompei"; Spiga, "Famiglia Cristiana," 21.
47. Sanderson, "Mafia Linked," 1, 4.
48. Ibid., 4.
49. Ibid.
50. CNN, "Navy's Top Officer Dies of Gunshot, Apparently Self-Inflicted," CNN.com, May 16, 1996, available at http://www.cnn.com/US/9605/16/boorda.6p/.
51. Even a single shot to the chest is a relatively uncommon method of suicide. Veljko Strajina and Slobodan Nikolić, "Forensic Issues in Suicidal Single Gunshot Injuries to the Chest: An Autopsy Study," *American Journal of Forensic Medicine and Pathology* 33, no. 4 (2012): 373–76.
52. *New York Times*, "21 U.S. Sailors Seized in Italy in Drug Inquiry," May 29, 1996, A17; C. Stewart, "Admiral's Suicide Pre-empts Vietnam Medal Investigation," *Weekend Australian*, May 18, 1996; *Deutsche Presse-Agentur*, "Top U.S. Naval Officer Dies of Self-Inflicted Gunshot Wound," May 16, 1996.
53. Sanderson, "Mafia Linked," 4.
54. E.g. an anonymous blog comment: "I've worked in Naples, Italy for less than a year and the word about Admiral Boorda out here is he was the victim of a mafia hit by the commorah [sic]. He helped land a contract with a suspected member of the mafia in building a military base . . . All the Italians here claim he was murdered." http://news4a2.blogspot.com/2005/05/adm-jeremy-mike-boorda-may-16-1996-pt.html.
55. Lorenzo Cremonese, "NATO Commander Tells Government: Protect Our Men from Casalesi Clan," *Corriere della Sera*, translated by BBC Monitoring Europe,

November 6, 2008; Paola Totaro, "NATO Pours Rent Money into Mafia Coffers," *Sydney Morning Herald*, November 6, 2008; Paul Bompard, "Nato Officers Rent Villa Owned by Naples Mafia Boss," *Times* (London), October 27, 2008; U.S. Treasury, "Treasury Sanctions Members of the Camorra," press release, Washington, DC, August 1, 2012.

56. Totaro, "NATO Pours."

57. Cremonese, "NATO Commander."

58. Totaro, "NATO Pours."

59. Lisa M. Novak, "Italian Police Ask Navy for Records to 6 Naples Homes Court-Order Could Be Tied to Mafia Probe," *Stars and Stripes*, December 17, 2008.

60. Sandra Jontz, "Official Seeks Assurance for Naples' U.S. Renters," *Stars and Stripes*, November 27, 2008.

61. *Il Matino*, "Sanzioni ai Casalesi: Agli Americani È Vietato Entrare nelle Case dei Boss," August 3, 2012, http://www.ilmattino.it/articolo.php?id=212167&sez =CAMPANIA; Ermete Ferraro, "NATO' CERCA . . . CASALESI," *Ermete's Peacebook*, blog, August 4, 2012, http://ermeteferraro.wordpress.com/2012/08/04/nato -cerca-casalesi/.

62. Comptroller General of the United States, "Improved Procedures Needed for Obtaining Facilities for U.S. Naval Support Activity Naples, Italy by Lease-Construction Method," report, Washington, DC, January 4, 1970, 2, 16–17.

63. Roberto Saviano, *Beauty and the Inferno: Essays* (New York: Verso, 2012), 165.

64. Laura Simich, "The Corruption of a Community's Economic and Political Life: The Cruise Missile Base in Comiso," in Joseph Gerson and Bruce Birchard, eds., *The Sun Never Sets: Confronting the Network of Foreign U.S. Military Bases* (Philadelphia: American Friends Service Committee, 1991), 79, 85, 91, 82.

65. 238 F.3d 1324 (Fed. Cir. 2000), *Impresa Construzioni Geom. Domenico Garufi v. United States*, United States Court of Appeals for the Federal Circuit, January 3, 2001.

66. Quoted in Simich, "Corruption of a Community," 91.

67. Mazzeo, "Niscemi, la Mafia e il MUOS," Antonio Mazzeo Blog, November 19, 2012, http://antoniomazzeoblog.blogspot.com/2013/11/niscemi-la-mafia-e-il-muos.html.

68. Walter Mayr, "The Mafia's Deadly Garbage: Italy's Growing Toxic Waste Scandal," *Spiegel Online International*, January 16, 2014, http://www.spiegel.de/international /europe/anger-rises-in-italy-over-toxic-waste-dumps-from-the-mafia-a-943630 .html.

69. Ibid.; Steven Beardsley, "Naples Base Seeks to Assuage Fears Amid New Reports of Toxic Dumping," *Stars and Stripes*, November 22, 2013.

70. Fabrizio Bianchi, Pietro Comba, Marco Martuzzi, Raffaele Palombino, and Renato Pizzuti, "Italian 'Triangle of Death,'" *Lancet Oncology* 5, no. 12 (2004), 710; Kathryn Senior and Alfredo Mazza, "Italian 'Triangle of Death' Linked to Waste Crisis," *Lancet Oncology* 5, no. 9 (2004), http://www.uonna.it/lancet-journal-acerra.htm; Pietro Comba et al., "Cancer Mortality in an Area of Campania (Italy) Characterized by Multiple Toxic Dumping Sites," *Annals of the New York Academy of Sciences* 1076 (September 2006), 449–61; Marco Martuzzi et al., "Cancer Mortality and Congenital Anomalies in a Region of Italy with Intense Environmental Pressure Due to Waste," *Occupational Environmental Medicine* 66, no. 1 (2009), 725–32.

71. *Vice*, "Toxic: Napoli," Vice.com, 2009, http://www.vice.com/video/toxic-napoli-1 -of-2.

72. Naval Facilities Engineering Command Atlantic, *Final Phase I Environmental Test-*

ing Support Assessment Report Volume I Naval Support Activity Naples, April 2009; "Naples Water Buffalo Herds Are Quarantined," *Stars and Stripes*, March 22, 2008, http://www.stripes.com/news/naples-water-buffalo-herds-are-quarantined-1.76792.

7: TOXIC ENVIRONMENTS

1. *Saipan Tribune*, "Navy Granted Use of Farallon de Medinilla," May 23, 2002; DMZ Hawai'i Aloha 'Aina, "Navy to Conduct Live-fire Exercises on Farallon de Medinilla," October 10, 2009, blog, http://www.dmzhawaii.org/?tag=farallon-de-medinilla.

2. Robert F. Durant, *The Greening of the U.S. Military: Environmental Policy, National Security, and Organizational Change* (Washington, DC: Georgetown University Press, 2007), 6–8.

3. Ibid., 5.

4. Ibid., 5–9.

5. Ibid., 11.

6. U.S. Army Garrison Vicenza, "Del Din Green Building Education Tour," presentation slides, Vicenza, Italy, n.d. [2013].

7. Sharon Weiner, "Environmental Concerns at U.S. Overseas Military Installations," working paper, Defense and Army Control Studies Program, Center for International Studies, Massachusetts Institute of Technology, July 1992, 4.

8. Michael T. Klare, *The Race for What's Left: The Global Scramble for the World's Last Resources* (New York: Metropolitan Books, 2012), 13.

9. David S. Sorenson, *Military Base Closure: A Reference Handbook* (Westport, CT: Praeger Security International, 2007), 67.

10. Ibid., 69–70; John M. R. Bull, "The Deadliness Below: Weapons of Mass Destruction Thrown into the Sea Years Ago Present Danger Now—and the Army Doesn't Know Where They All Are," *Daily Press* (Hampton Roads, VA), October 30, 2005.

11. Durant, *Greening*, 77–79.

12. In the United States, the military won exemptions to parts of the Endangered Species and Marine Mammal Protection acts and has sought exemption from the Clean Air Act and other environmental laws. Congress provided an exemption to the Migratory Bird Treaty Act in 2003 in response to a court ruling that naval training on Farallon de Medinilla violated the act. Government Accountability Office, "Military Training: Compliance with Environmental Laws Affects Some Training Activities, but DOD Has Not Made a Sound Business Case for Additional Environmental Exemptions," GAO-08-407, March 2008.

13. Jon Mitchell, "Pollution Rife on Okinawa's U.S.-Returned Base Land," *Japan Times*, December 4, 2013.

14. Weiner, "Environmental Concerns," 24–25; Sorenson, *Base Closure*, 120.

15. Dina Fine Maron, "Toxic Burn Pits at U.S. Marine Base in Afghanistan Threaten Health," *Scientific American*, July 11, 2013, http://blogs.scientificamerican.com/observations/2013/07/11/toxic-burn-pits-at-u-s-marine-base-in-afghanistan-threaten-health/.

16. Spencer Ackerman, "Leaked Memo: Afghan 'Burn Pit' Could Wreck Troops' Hearts, Lungs," Danger Room blog, Wired.com, May 22, 2012, http://www.wired.com/dangerroom/2012/05/bagram-health-risk.

17. Sorenson, *Base Closure*, 69.

18. Peter H. Sand, *U.S. and the U.K. in Diego Garcia: The Future of a Controversial Base* (London: Palgrave Macmillan, 2009), 51–62; David Vine, S. Wojciech Sokolowski, and Philip Harvey, "*Dérasiné*: The Expulsion and Impoverishment of the Chagossian People [Diego Garcia]" (unpublished expert report, April 9, 2005), 183–90.

19. Ari Phillips, "Decades-Old Underground Jet Fuel Leak in New Mexico Still Decades from Being Cleaned Up," ThinkProgress.org, January 14, 2014, http://thinkprogress.org/climate/2014/01/14/3160291/kirtland-jet-fuel-leak-water-contaminated/#.

20. Environment News Service, "Residents Near U.S. Okinawa Air Base Sue over Noise," April 28, 2011, http://ens-newswire.com/2011/04/28/residents-near-u-s-okinawa-air-base-sue-over-noise-3/.

21. Office of the Special Inspector General for Afghanistan Reconstruction, "Observations on Solid Waste Disposal Methods in Use at Camp Leatherneck," alert, Department of Defense, Alexandria, VA, July 17, 2013.

22. Dina Fine Maron, "Pentagon Weighs Cleanups as It Plans Iraq Exit," *New York Times*, January 13, 2010.

23. Richard Albright, *Cleanup of Chemical and Explosive Munitions: Location, Identification and Environmental Remediation* (Oxford: William Andrew, 2008), 118, 122–23, 126–28; Charles Bermphol, "Spring Valley: At Risk from WWI Poisons?" *Current Supplement*, B10–11.

24. Albright, *Cleanup*, 123; Mark Leone, "How the Landscape of Fear Works in Spring Valley, a Washington, D.C. Neighborhood," *City and Society* 18, no. 1 (2006): 37.

25. Harry Jaffe, "Ground Zero," *Washingtonian*, December 1, 2000; Steve Vogel, "U.S. Ignored High Arsenic Level at NW Home in Mid-'90s," *Washington Post*, July 25, 2001, A1.

26. Harry Jaffe, "Eleanor Holmes Norton Wants Family Relocated from Spring Valley Superfund Site," *Washingtonian*, February 21, 2013, http://www.washingtonian.com/blogs/capitalcomment/local-news/eleanor-holmes-norton-wants-family-relocated-from-spring-valley-superfund-site.php; Jaffe, "Ground Zero."

27. Jaffe, "Ground Zero."

28. Jaffe, "Eleanor Holmes Norton"; Brady Holt, "Neighbors Back Plans for Glenbrook Road Cleanup," *Northwest Current*, November 2, 2011, 1, 29.

29. Jaffe, "Eleanor Holmes Norton."

30. Sorenson, *Base Closure*, 120.

31. Ashley Rowland, "U.S. Military: No Agent Orange at South Korea Base," *Stars and Stripes*, June 23, 2011.

32. Yonhap News, "Underground Water Near Seoul's U.S. Military Camp Contaminated," October 23, 2012, http://english.yonhapnews.co.kr/national/2012/10/23/27/0301000000AEN20121023007900315F.html.

33. Jason Strother, "Environmental Investigation Underway on US Base in S. Korea," *Voice of America News*, June 28, 2011, http://www.voanews.com/english/news/Environmental-Investigation-Underway-on-US-Base-in-South-Korea-124639199.html.

34. Tammy Leitner, "Valley Veteran Blows Whistle on Burial of Agent Orange; Steve House, 2 Others Say They Just Followed Orders in 1978," KPHO CBS 5 News, May 13, 2011, http://www.kpho.com/news/27892124/detail.html.

35. Christine Ahn and Gwyn Kirk, "Agent Orange in Korea," *Foreign Policy in Focus*, July 7, 2011, http://www.fpif.org/articles/agent_orange_in_Korea.

36. Strother, "Environmental Investigation Underway"; Environmental Protection

Agency, "An Introduction to Indoor Air Quality (IAQ): Formaldahyde," June 20, 2012, http://www.epa.gov/iaq/formaldehyde.html#Health_Effects; Gillem, 46–47.

37. Bandjunis, *Diego Garcia*, 47–49.

38. Peter H. Sand, email to author, October 19, 2009.

39. Cathal Milmo, "British Government under Fire for Pollution of Pristine Lagoon," *Independent*, March 28, 2014, http://www.independent.co.uk/news/world/americas /exclusive-british-government-under-fire-for-pollution-of-pristine-lagoon -9222170.html; Cathal Milmo, "Exclusive: World's Most Pristine Waters Are Polluted by US Navy Human Waste," *Independent*, March 15, 2014, http://www .independent.co.uk/news/uk/home-news/exclusive-worlds-most-pristine-waters -are-polluted-by-us-navy-human-waste-9193596.html.

40. Steve Goldstein, "They 'Punched Out' and Lived to Tell," *Edmonton Journal*, May 26, 2002, Sunday Reader, D6.

41. Jon Mitchell, "Fears Widen over Kadena Toxins," *Japan Times*, February 1, 2014.

42. Sorenson, *Base Closure*, 120.

43. Weiner, "Environmental Concerns."

44. John Lindsay-Poland, "U.S. Military Bases in Latin America and the Caribbean," in *Bases of Empire*, 87.

45. Katherine T. McCaffrey, "Environmental Struggle after the Cold War: New Forms of Resistance to the U.S. Military in Vieques, Puerto Rico," in *Bases of Empire*, 235– 37; McCaffrey, *Military Power*; Lindsay-Poland, "U.S. Military Bases," 87; see also Lindsay-Poland, *Emperors in the Jungle*.

46. David Beardon, "Vieques and Culebra Islands: An Analysis of Cleanup Status and Costs," Congressional Research Service, report, Washington, DC, July 7, 2005; McCaffrey, "Environmental Struggle," 218; Ben Fox, "Vieques Cleanup: Island at Odds with U.S. Government Declaration That 400-Acre Bomb Site Cleanup Is Complete," Associated Press, October 5, 2012, available at http://www .huffingtonpost.com/2012/10/05/vieques-cleanup-bomb-site_n_1942107.html.

47. National Park Service, American Memorial Park, Saipan, CNMI.

48. Nautilus Institute for Security and Sustainability, "Toxic Bases in the Pacific," APSNet Special Reports, November 25, 2005, http://nautilus.org/apsnet/toxic-bases -in-the-pacific.

49. Urban Niblo, memo to Chief of Ordnance, Pentagon, "Report of Bomb Disposal Activities, Marianas-Bonins Command," June 9, 1947.

50. Natividad and Kirk, "Fortress Guam."

51. Nic Maclellan, "Toxic Bases in the Pacific," *Pacific News Bulletin*, 2000; Natividad and Kirk, "Fortress Guam"; Saipan Tribune, "U.S. EPA Completes Water Sampling," May 25, 2000, http://www.saipantribune.com/index.php/95eba5ac-1dfb -11e4-aedf-250bc8c9958e/.

52. Government Accountability Office, "DOD Can Improve Its Response to Environmental Exposures on Military Installations," report to Congress, Washington, DC, May 2012, 28n54; Maclellan, "Toxic Bases"; Natividad and Kirk, "Fortress Guam"; Sorenson, *Base Closure*, 68; Jon Mitchell, " 'Deny, Deny Until All the Veterans Die'—Pentagon Investigation into Agent Orange on Okinawa," Truthout.com, June 13, 2013, http://truth-out.org/news/item/16945-deny-deny-until-all-the -veterans-die-pentagon-investigation-into-agent-orange-on-okinawa.

53. Robert Hicks, "Andersen AFB Saves $25 Million with Contamination Cleanup Concept," Air Force news, http://www.af.mil/news/story.asp?id=123339500.

54. Nicholas Duchesne, "Death from the Skies!" *Slate*, December 3, 2013, http://www
    .slate.com/blogs/wild_things/2013/12/04/poison_pill_mice_parachuted_onto
    _guam_fighting_brown_tree_snakes_with_tylenol.html.
55. Travis J. Tritten and Lisa Tourtelot, "US Wants to Expand Training Exercises in
    Western Pacific," *Stars and Stripes*, November 3, 2013, http://www.stripes.com
    /news/us-wants-to-expand-training-exercises-in-western-pacific-1.250588; Zoe
    Loftus-Farren, "US Plans to Expand War Games in Ecologically Rich Mariana
    Islands," *Earth Island Journal*, November 22, 2013, http://www.earthisland.org
    /journal/index.php/elist/eListRead/us_plans_to_expand_war_games_in
    _ecologically_rich_mariana_islands/. See also savepaganisland.org and http://
    www.cnmijointmilitarytrainingeis.com.
56. Natividad and Kirk, "Fortress Guam." Chamorros on Guam also suffer from diabe-
    tes at approximately five times the U.S. rate.
57. Government Accountability Office, "DOD Can Improve," 53–54.
58. McCaffrey, *Military Power*, 9–10.

8: EVERYONE SERVES

1. Bubbie Baker, "Life on a Military Base," MilitaryBases.com, March 8, 2012, http://
   militarybases.com/blog/life-on-a-military-base/.
2. Defense Finance and Accounting Service, Department of Defense, "Military Pay
   Table 2014," table, January 1, 2014, http://www.dfas.mil/militarymembers
   /payentitlements/militarypaytables.html; AFL-CIO, "CEO-to-Worker Pay Gap in
   the United States," Executive Paywatch, 2013, https://www.aflcio.org/Corporate
   -Watch/CEO-Pay-and-You/CEO-to-Worker-Pay-Gap-in-the-United-States.
3. Gillem, *America Town*, 113.
4. Sarah Stillman, "The Invisible Army," *New Yorker*, June 6, 2011.
5. Alvah, "U.S. Military Families," 151.
6. U.S. Department of Defense, "2013 Demographics: Profile of the Military Community," report, Washington, DC, 2014, 185.
7. Quoted in Willoughby, *Conquering Heroes*, 120.
8. See A. Baker, *Life in the U.S. Armed Forces*, 121.
9. A. Baker, *American Soldiers Overseas*, 57–58.
10. A. Baker, *Life in the U.S. Armed Forces*, 120–22.
11. Ibid., 117–18, 129.
12. Rod Powers, "Overseas Cost of Living Allowance (COLA)," About.com, Septem-
    ber 14, 2010, http://usmilitary.about.com/od/fy2008paycharts/a/ocola.htm; Defense
    Travel Management Office, "Overseas Cost of Living Allowances (COLA)," Depart-
    ment of Defense, http://www.defensetravel.dod.mil/site/cola.cfm.
13. In 2011, per-student spending in the military's school system was between $23,000
    and $33,000. U.S. Department of Defense, "Fiscal Year (FY) 2013 Budget Estimates:
    Department of Defense Dependents Education," DoDDE-360; National Center for
    Education Statistics, "Public School Expenditures," Institute of Education Sci-
    ences, U.S. Department of Education, April 2014, http://nces.ed.gov/programs
    /coe/indicator_cmb.asp.
14. Nicholas D. Kristof, "Our Lefty Military," *New York Times*, June 15, 2011.
15. A. Baker, *Life in the U.S. Armed Forces*, 126–27.
16. Lutz, *Homefront*, 188.

17. Pamela R. Frese, "Guardians of the Golden Age: Custodians of U.S. Military Culture," in *Anthropology and the United States Military: Coming of Age in the Twenty-first Century*, edited by Pamela R. Frese and Margaret C. Harrell (New York: Palgrave Macmillan, 2003), 57.
18. A. Baker, *Life in the U.S. Armed Forces*, 116.
19. John Ramsey, "Colonel's Wife Accused of Harassing Soldiers," *Fayetteville* (NC) *Observer*, June 11, 2010.
20. Lutz, *Homefront*, 187.
21. Gillem, *America Town*, 292n38.
22. Lutz, *Homefront*, 188.
23. A. Baker, *Life in the U.S. Armed Forces*, 116.
24. Mitzi Uehara Carter, "Nappy Routes and Tangled Tales: Critical Ethnography in a Militarised Okinawa," in Broudy et al., *Under Occupation*, 22.
25. See e.g. Ramsey, "Colonel's Wife."
26. David Abrams, *Fobbit* (New York: Black Cat, 2012), 2.
27. Greg Jaffe, "Facebook Brings the Afghan War to Fort Campbell," *Washington Post*, November 5, 2010.

9: SEX FOR SALE

1. Cynthia Enloe, *Bananas, Beaches and Bases: Making Feminist Sense of International Politics* (Berkeley: University of California Press, 1989), 72; Frese, "Guardians," 65, 45.
2. Nick Schwellenbach and Carol Leonnig, "U.S. Policy a Paper Tiger against Sex Trade in War Zones," July 18, 2010, A4; Rajiv Chandrasekaran, *Imperial Life in the Emerald City: Inside Iraq's Green Zone* (New York: Vintage Books, 2006), 64.
3. Seungsook Moon, "Regulating Desire, Managing the Empire: U.S. Military Prostitution in South Korea, 1945–1970," in Höhn and Moon, eds., *Over There*, 43–44.
4. Statistics from Women's Active Museum on War and Peace (Tokyo, Japan, 2010); S. Moon, "Regulating Desire," 45.
5. S. Moon, "Regulating Desire," 42–43.
6. Quoted in and translated by S. Moon, "Regulating Desire," 51.
7. S. Moon, "Regulating Desire," 53–54.
8. Gillem, *America Town*, 51–53.
9. Quoted in S. Moon, "Regulating Desire," 66, 58–67.
10. S. Moon, "Regulating Desire," 76n90; Katherine Moon, *Sex Among Allies: Military Prostitution in U.S.-Korea Relations* (New York: Columbia University Press, 1997), 37.
11. Sang-hun Choe, "Ex-Prostitutes Say South Korea and U.S. Enabled Sex Trade Near Bases," *New York Times*, January 7, 2009.
12. Rick Mercier, "Way Off Base: The Shameful History of Military Rape in Okinawa," *On the Issues*, Winter 1997, http://www.ontheissuesmagazine.com/1997winter/w97 _Mercier.php.
13. A. Baker, *Life in the Armed Forces*, 106–8.
14. Gillem, *America Town*, 49.
15. Choe, "Ex-Prostitutes."
16. Ibid.

17. Durebang / My Sister's Place, "Durebang Report: Concerning Migrant Women Involved with U.S. Bases: From 2002–2009," report, Uijeongbu, South Korea, n.d. [2010], 40.
18. Seungsook Moon, "Camptown Prostitution and the Imperial SOFA: Abuse and Violence Against Transnational Camptown Women in South Korea," in Höhn and Moon, eds., Over There, 342–43, 348.
19. "Durebang Report"; S. Moon, "Camptown Prostitution."
20. "Durebang Report," 89.
21. Reed Irvine and Cliff Kincaid, "The Pentagon's Dirty Secret," Media Monitor, August 7, 2002, http://www.aim.org/publications/media_monitor/2002/08/07.html.
22. Barbara Demick, "Off-Base Behavior in Korea," Los Angeles Times, September 26, 2002.
23. Irvine and Kincaid, "Pentagon's Dirty Secret"; S. Moon, "Camptown Prostitution," 346; Gillem, America Town, 67.
24. Donna M. Hughes, Katherine Y. Chon, and Derek P. Ellerman, "Modern-Day Comfort Women: The U.S. Military, Transnational Crime, and the Trafficking of Women," Violence Against Women 13, no. 9 (2007), 918.
25. Irvine and Kincaid, "Pentagon's Dirty Secret."
26. GI Korea, "Stars and Stripes Exposes Prostitution in South Korea's Juicy Bars," ROKDrop.net, September 8, 2009.
27. Gillem, America Town, 54.
28. Demick, "Off-Base Behavior."
29. Ibid.
30. S. Moon, "Camptown Prostitution," 352–53; "Durebang Report."
31. Hughes, Chon, and Ellerman, "Modern-Day Comfort Women," 910, 919; Timothy C. Lim and Karam Yoo, "The Dynamics of Trafficking, Smuggling and Prostitution: An Analysis of Korean Women in the U.S. Commercial Sex Industry," report, Bombit Women's Foundation, Seoul, South Korea, n.d., 19.
32. K. Moon, Sex Among Allies, 35.
33. Calvin Sims, "A Hard Life for Amerasian Children," New York Times, July 23, 2000.
34. Höhn, "'You Can't Pin Sergeant's Stripes on an Archangel,'" 124.
35. See e.g. Toshio Suzuki, "From Dooley to Jones, Bases in Germany Feed US Soccer Team's Multicultural Success," Stars and Stripes, December 13, 2013.
36. Jon Rabiroff and Hwang Hae-rym, "'Juicy Bars' Said to Be Havens for Prostitution Aimed at U.S. Military," Stars and Stripes, September 9, 2009.
37. Jon Rabiroff, "Inside the Juicy Bars: Drinks, Conversation and . . ." Stars and Stripes, April 24, 2010.
38. Irvine and Kincaid, "Pentagon's Dirty Secret."
39. Enloe, Bananas, Beaches, and Bases, 165. See also an estimate of 25,000–30,000 around bases nationwide, in A. Baker, American Soldiers Overseas, 119.
40. Women Who Built the House on the Street, directed by Durebang (South Korea: Durebang / My Sister's Place, 2007).
41. Kelly Patricia O'Meara, "US: DynCorp Disgrace," Insight Magazine, January 14, 2002.
42. Ibid.
43. Human Rights Watch, "Hopes Betrayed: Trafficking of Women and Girls to Post-

Conflict Bosnia and Herzegovina for Forced Prostitution," *Bosnia and Herzegovina* 14, no. 9 (D) (November 2002): 64.

44. *Diane Rehm Show*, "Kathryn Bolkovac: 'The Whistleblower,'" transcript, January 11, 2011, http://thedianerehmshow.org/shows/2011-01-11/kathryn-bolkovac -whistleblower.

45. O'Meara, "DynCorp Disgrace."

46. Ibid.; *Diane Rehm*, "Kathryn Bolkovac."

47. The transcript is quoted in O'Meara, DynCorp Disgrace."

48. Cynthia Enloe, "Bananas, Bases, and Patriarchy," in *Women, Militarism, and War: Essays in History, Politics, and Social Theory*, edited by Jean B. Elshtain and Sheila Tobias (Savage, MD: Rowman and Littlefield Publishers, 1990), 200.

49. See e.g. Aïssata Maïga and Sol Torres, "Legal Prostitution in Europe: The Shady Facade of Human Trafficking," Open Security blog, September 17, 2014, https:// www.opendemocracy.net/opensecurity/a%C3%AFssata-ma%C3%AFga-sol -torres/legal-prostitution-in-europe-shady-facade-of-human-trafficking.

10: MILITARIZED MASCULINITY

1. GI Korea, "The Off Limits Game," ROK Drop, February 3, 2007, http://rokdrop.net /2007/02/03/the-off-limits-game/#sthash.OovTDj11.dpuf.

2. GI Korea, "It's the Ville Stupid!" ROK Drop, February 7, 2007, http://rokdrop.net /2007/02/07/its-the-ville-stupid.

3. K. Moon, *Sex Among Allies*, 37.

4. Cynthia Enloe, "Beyond 'Rambo': Women and the Varieties of Militarized Masculinity," *Women and the Military System*, edited by Eva Isaakson (New York: St. Martin's Press, 1988), 71–93.

5. GI Korea, "What Is Really Happening in Regards to GI Crime," ROKDrop, July 17, 2005, http://rokdrop.net/2005/07/17/what-is-really-happening/#sthash.OH32cBga .dpuf.

6. As the Korean anthropologist Joowon Park explained to me, there is a direct connection between the militarized masculinity bred in the camptowns and the frequent bar fights in popular Seoul nightspots between GIs and local Korean men stemming from feelings of the "racial superiority of the American."

7. Anu Bhagwati, quoted in David Crary, "Military's Sex Assault Problem Has Deep Roots," Military.com, June 3, 2013, http://www.military.com/daily-news/2013/06 /03/militarys-sex-assault-problem-has-deep-roots.html.

8. The name is a pseudonym used in the film *Living Along the Fenceline*, Lina Hoshino, Women for Genuine Security, 2011. Thanks go to Women for Genuine Security, Gwyn Kirk, Deborah Lee, and Lina Hoshina for their help with this section.

9. Okinawa Women Act Against Military Violence, "Postwar U.S. Military Crimes Against Women in Okinawa," report, October 1, 2011; Mercier, "Way off Base"; Okinawa Prefectural Government, "US Military Base Issues in Okinawa," Regional Security Policy Division, September 2011, 4; Okinawa Prefectural Government, "US Military Base Issues in Okinawa," Military Base Affairs Division, n.d. [2011], 15; Kozue Akibayashi and Suzuyo Takazato, "Okinawa: Women's Struggle for Demilitarization," in Lutz, *Bases of Empire*, 252, 260.

10. Linda Isakao Angst, "The Rape of a Schoolgirl: Discourses of Power and Gendered

National Identity in Okinawa," in *Islands of Discontent: Okinawan Responses to Japanese and American Power,* edited by Laura Heig and Mark Selden (Lanham, MD: Rowman and Littlefield, 2003), 135–37; A. Baker, *American Soldiers Overseas,* 136–37.

11. Irvin Molotsky, "Admiral Has to Quit over His Comments on Okinawa Rape," *New York Times,* November 18, 1995.

12. David Allen, "Former Marine Who Sparked Okinawa Furor Is Dead in Suspected Murder-Suicide," *Stars and Stripes,* August 25, 2006, http://www.stripes.com/news/former-marine-who-sparked-okinawa-furor-is-dead-in-suspected-murder-suicide-1.53269.

13. Martin Kasindorf and Steven Komarow, "USO Cheers Troops, But Iraq Gigs Tough to Book," *USAToday,* December 22, 2005.

14. H. Patricia Hynes, "The Battlefield and the Barracks: Two War Fronts for Women Soldiers," *Truthout,* five-part series, January 11–February 15, 2012, http://www.truth-out.org/women-battlefield-and-barracks-five-part-series-two-war-fronts-women-soldiers/1326230543.

15. H. Patricia Hynes, "Reforming a Recalcitrant Military," *Truthout,* February 15, 2012, http://www.truth-out.org/news/item/6713:reforming-a-recalcitrant-military.

16. H. Patricia Hynes, "Military Sexual Abuse: A Greater Menace than Combat," *Truthout,* January 26, 2012, http://truth-out.org/opinion/item/6299.

17. Hynes, "Battlefield and the Barracks."

18. Hynes, "Military Sexual Abuse"; H. Patricia Hynes, "Picking Up the Pieces from Military Sexual Assault," *Truthout,* February 8, 2012, http://www.truth-out.org/news/item/6515-picking-up-the-pieces-from-military-sexual-assault.

19. Hynes, "Battlefield and the Barracks."

20. Department of Defense, "Department of Defense (DOD) Annual Report on Sexual Assault in the Military, Fiscal Year 2012," report, Washington, DC, January 18, 2013, II: 142.

21. Hynes, "Military Sexual Abuse."

22. U.S. Department of Defense, "Report to the President of the United States on Sexual Assault Prevention and Response 2014," report, Washington, DC, November 25, 2014, Appendix A, 12, 5.

23. SAPRO report 2013, Enclosures 2–4. The percentages overseas ranged from 22 percent in the Marines to 36 percent in the Army, with the Air Force and Navy reporting 26 and 27 percent respectively. The percentages should be treated as approximations, given inconsistencies and omissions in the data provided by the services.

24. See also Gillem, *America Town,* 49.

25. Service Women's Action Network, "Rape, Sexual Assault and Sexual Harassment in the Military: Quick Facts," July 2012; "Briefing Paper: Department of Defense (DOD) Annual Report on Sexual Assault in the Military, Fiscal Year (FY) 2011," brief, n.d.[2012].

26. Hynes, "Military Sexual Abuse"; Hynes, "Picking Up the Pieces"; James Risen, "Hagel to Open Review of Sexual Assault Case," *New York Times,* March 11, 2013; Brittany L. Stalsburg, "Military Sexual Trauma: The Facts," fact sheet, Service Women's Action Network, New York, n.d. [2010].

27. Anna Mulrine, "After Sex Scandal, Air Force Mulls Using Only Women to Train Female Recruits," *Christian Science Monitor,* June 28, 2012, http://www.csmonitor

.com/USA/Military/2012/0628/After-sex-scandal-Air-Force-mulls-using-only
-women-to-train-female-recruits.

28. H. Patricia Hynes, "The Military and the Church: Bedfellows in Sexual Assault,"
    Truthout, February 1, 2012, http://www.truth-out.org/news/item/6420-the-military
    -and-the-church-bedfellows-in-sexual-assault2012.

29. Hayes Brown, "More Men than Women Were Victims of Sexual Assault in Mili-
    tary, Report Finds," *Think Progress*, May 1, 2014, http://thinkprogress.org/world
    /2014/05/01/3433055/dod-men-mst/.

30. Aaron Belkin, *Bring Me Men: Military Masculinity and the Benign Facade of Amer-
    ican Empire, 1898–2001* (New York: Columbia University Press, 2012), 79.

31. Ibid., 79–80.

32. Ibid., 83–86.

33. Dahr Jamail, "Rape Rampant in US Military," *Veterans Today*, December 23,
    2010, http://www.veteranstoday.com/2010/12/23/rape-rampant-in-us-military
    -drill-instructors-indoctrinate-new-recruits-into-it-at-the-outset-by-routinely
    -referring-to-women-as-%E2%80%9Cgirl%E2%80%9D-%E2%80%9Cpussy%E2
    %80%9D-%E2%80%9Cbitch/.

34. Hynes, "Reforming a Recalcitrant Military."

35. Penny Coleman, "Does Military Service Turn Young Men into Sexual Predators?"
    AlterNet, October 21, 2009, http://www.alternet.org/story/142942/does_military
    _service_turn_young_men_into_sexual_predators?paging=off&current_page
    =1#bookmark.

36. H. Patricia Hynes, "Why Do Soldiers Rape?" *Truthout*, January 18, 2012, http://
    www.truth-out.org/news/item/6041:why-do-soldiers-rape.

37. A. Baker, *Life in the U.S. Armed Forces*, 134.

38. Hynes, "Why Do Soldiers Rape?"

39. Institute of Medicine of the National Academies, "Substance Use Disorders in
    the U.S. Armed Forces," report brief, September 2012, 2, 1.

11: THE BILL

1. Michael J. Lostumbo et al., "Overseas Basing of U.S. Military Forces: An Assessment of Relative Costs and Strategic Benefits," report, RAND Corporation, Santa
   Monica, CA, April 29, 2013, xxv.

2. RAND Corporation, "U.S. Overseas Military Posture: Relative Costs and Strategic Benefits," research brief, Santa Monica, CA, April 29, 2013.

3. Ibid.

4. Lostumbo et al., "Overseas Basing of U.S. Military Forces," 280–82.

5. See 10 U.S.C. 2634.

6. Based on approximately 166,000 troops outside the fifty states as of March 31,
   2014. U.S. Department of Defense, "Total Military Personnel and Dependent End
   Strength as of March 31, 2014," Washington, DC, n.d. [2014].

7. Mike Fitzgerald, "DOD, Where's My Car? Transcom Searches for Missing Vehicles," *Belleville News-Democrat*, August 16, 2014.

8. 37 U.S.C. 406.

9. Ibid.

10. Parts of this chapter stem from and are a revised version of my article "Picking Up
    a $170 Billion Tab: How U.S. Taxpayers Are Paying the Pentagon to Occupy the

Planet," *TomDispatch*, December 11, 2012, http://www.tomdispatch.com/blog /175627/. See also davidvine.net for a more detailed paper.

11. U.S. Department of Defense, "Operations and Maintenance Overview Fiscal Year 2014 Budget Estimates," Washington, DC, April 2013, 204–7. The requirement appears in Section 8125 of the fiscal year 1989 Department of Defense Appropriations Act (P.L. 100–463). See also 10 U.S.C. 113.

12. Ibid., 205.

13. U.S. Office of Management and Budget, "The Budget of the United States Government, Fiscal Year 2013," Washington, DC, 2012.

14. Anita Dancs and Miriam Pemberton, eds., "The Cost of the Global U.S. Military Presence," *Foreign Policy in Focus*, July 2, 2009, http://fpif.org/the_cost_of_the _global_us_military_presence/.

15. R. Jeffrey Smith, "Pentagon's Accounting Shambles May Cost an Additional $1 Billion," *Center for Public Integrity*, October 13, 2011, updated March 23, 2012; Barbara Lee, "Audit the Pentagon," *Daily Kos* blog, October 25, 2012, http://www .dailykos.com/story/2012/10/25/1150275/-Audit-the-Pentagon#.

16. Dave Gilson, "Don't Tread on Me," *Mother Jones*, January/February 2014, 31.

17. R. Jeffrey Smith, "Accounting Shambles."

18. See Section 8125 of the fiscal year 1989 Department of Defense Appropriations Act (P.L. 100–463); 10 U.S.C. 113.

19. Turse, "Afghanistan's Base Bonanza."

20. U.S. Department of Defense, "Fiscal Year 2013 (FY) President's Budget: Justification for Component Base Contingency Operations and the Overseas Contingency Operation Transfer Fund (OCOTF)," Washington, DC, March 2012.

21. The figures listed in each section will not always match the subtotals provided because of rounding. The table provided offers precise figures.

22. U.S. Census Bureau, "Puerto Rico and the Island Areas," in *Statistical Abstract of the United States: 2012* (Washington, DC: Government Printing Office, 2012), 815–22.

23. Spending figures for the territories are difficult to acquire. The best estimates available come from 2004. See *Statemaster*, "Guam: Military," http://www.statemaster .com/red/state/GU-guam/mil-military&all=1; Governor of Guam, "One Guam Buildup," Guam Realignment Annual Report, Hagåtña, Guam, 2012; Interagency Coordination Group of Inspectors General for Guam Realignment, "Annual Report 2013," Washington, DC, February 1, 2013, 10–11; Bureau of Statistics and Plans, "Guam's Facts and Figures at a Glance," Office of the Governor, Hagåtña, Guam, 2011. Below, I subtract Japanese spending for the move to Guam.

24. Spending figures come from 2004 data available at www.statemaster.com. Spending for Puerto Rico is estimated at $1.175 billion. Spending for the Commonwealth of the Northern Mariana Islands and for Wake Island, for which I could not locate data, is estimated as equivalent to spending in American Samoa ($12 million), which has a similar military presence.

25. See Sandars, *America's Overseas Garrisons*, 36; Justin Nobel, "A Micronesian Paradise—for U.S. Military Recruiters," *Time*, December 31, 2009.

26. U.S. Department of Defense, "Financial Summary Tables, Department of Defense Budget for Fiscal Year 2013, FAD 792," Washington, DC, February 2012, 2.

27. U.S. Department of Defense, "Operations and Maintenance Overview, Fiscal Year 2013," 134–36. The total includes an additional $3 million in Navy funding for its Offshore Petroleum Discharge System and for exercises abroad (conservatively esti-

mated as 17 percent of total exercise spending using the same percentage of total Navy and Marine Corps forces afloat and abroad).

28. Elizabeth Robbins email to author, Office of the Assistant Secretary of Defense for Public Affairs, December 6, 2012.

29. U.S. Department of Defense, "Financial Summary Tables, Fiscal Year 2013," 5; U.S Office of Management and Budget, "Object Class Analysis: Budget of the U.S. Government Fiscal Year 2013," Washington, DC, 2012, 3; U.S. Department of Defense, "Operations and Maintenance Overview, Fiscal Year 2013," 136.

30. Department of Defense, "Financial Summary Tables, Fiscal Year 2013," 10. The Pentagon comptroller prepares the Overseas Cost Summary, at the instruction of Congress, by compiling individual cost reports submitted by each of the armed forces. Thus, the summary appears to omit most "Defense-wide" spending.

31. It is possible that some of this spending was reported in the OCS; however, the conservative nature of all my other estimates more than makes up for any potential double counting here. U.S. Department of Defense, "Fiscal Year 2014 Budget: Construction Programs (C-1)," Washington, DC, April 2013, 15."

32. Gillem, America Town, 88–89.

33. See "Financial Statements" in Army and Air Force Exchange Service, "Annual Report 2012," n.p., 2013, 12; NEXCOM, "NEXCOM Annual Report 2012," Virginia Beach, VA, n.d. [2012], 15. I was unable to locate a Marine Corps Exchange annual report or data on its annual subsidies. Therefore, I calculated the percentage of total sales that the AAFES subsidy represents (3.4 percent) to estimate the 2012 subsidy for the MCX on sales of $1,038.3 million. William C. Dillon, "Statement of William C. Dillon, Director, Semper Fit & Exchange Services Division, Manpower & Reserve Affairs, United States Marine Corps Before the Subcommittee on Military Personnel of the House Armed Services Committee on Military Resale," Washington, DC, November 20, 2013, 6. All of these figures do not include subsidies and reimbursements for retail operations in Afghanistan and other war zones, which I assume are funded in war appropriations.

34. U.S. Department of Defense, "Operations and Maintenance Overview, Fiscal Year 2014," 160.

35. Calder, Embattled Garrisons, 200.

36. Ibid., 201.

37. Ibid., 200–6.

38. Blaker, "Installations," 107–9.

39. U.S. Department of State, "Executive Budget Summary: Function 150 and Other International Programs Fiscal Year 2014," Washington, DC, April 10, 2013, 1–4.

40. U.S. Office of Management and Budget, "The Budget for Fiscal Year 2013," Washington, DC, February 2012, 277, 324.

41. A RAND study calculated $2.3 billion in direct and in-kind contributions between Japan and South Korea in 2012 and $830 million from Germany in 2009. Lostumbo et al., "Overseas Basing of U.S. Military Forces," 409–12.

42. U.S. Office of Management and Budget, "Budget for Fiscal Year 2013," 304.

43. U.S. Department of Defense, "Fiscal Year (FY) 2013 Budget Estimates," 732.

44. Army budget information states, "Support of Other Nations funds the Department's contribution to the North Atlantic Treaty Organization (NATO) and directed missions to other nations." U.S. Department of Defense, "Operations and Maintenance, Fiscal Year (FY) 2013," 252, 274, 292.

45. Department of Defense, *Financial Summary Tables*, FAD-769, 6.
46. Andrew Feickert, "The Unified Command Plan and Combatant Commands: Background and Issues for Congress," Congressional Research Service, report, Washington, DC, July 17, 2012, 12. Earlier versions of this calculation used slightly different assumptions that resulted in a higher estimate. I have revised the assumptions out of an abundance of caution because even the commands headquartered outside the United States spend some of their money domestically.
47. Ibid., 12.
48. In addition to the Combatant Commands' budgets, this conservatively includes half of the $764,755,000 in the Combatant Commander's Exercise Engagement and Training Transformation program. U.S. Department of Defense, "Fiscal Year (FY) 2013 Budget Estimates," 704–7, 733.
49. Robbins email to author.
50. U.S. Department of Defense, "Operations and Maintenance, Fiscal Year (FY) 2014," 69–72.
51. See Defense Environmental International Cooperation program. U.S. Department of Defense, "Fiscal Year (FY) 2013 Budget Estimates," 731; "Fiscal Year (FY) 2013 Budget Estimates, Justification for FY 2013, Operation and Maintenance, Defense-Wide," vol. 2, Washington, DC, February 2012, 224, 229, 236, 237.
52. U.S. Department of Defense Threat Reduction Agency, "Fiscal Year (FY) 2013 Budget Estimates; Cooperative Threat Reduction Program," Washington, DC, February 2012, 75–76, 84.
53. Robert Beckhusen and Noah Shachtman, "See for Yourself: The Pentagon's $51 Billion 'Black' Budget," *Wired*, February 15, 2012, http://www.wired.com/dangerroom /2012/02/pentagons-black-budget/.
54. Department of Defense, "2013 DOD Black Budget," https://docs.google.com /spreadsheet/ccc?key=0Anb82yNPJZc0dDVadWM1c0xTZXlfVjRGZUlRQ3pja0 E#gid=3.
55. Federation of American Scientists, "Intelligence Budget Data," www.fas.org, 2014, http://www.fas.org/irp/budget/index.html.
56. Tom Engelhardt and Nick Turse, "The Shadow War Making Sense of the New CIA Battlefield in Afghanistan," *TomDispatch*, January 10, 2010, http://www.tomdispatch .com/blog/175188/tomgram:_engelhardt_and_turse,_the_cia_surges/.
57. Ben Armbruster, "Republicans Reveal Location of Secret CIA Base During House Hearing on Libya Attacks," *ThinkProgress*, October 11, 2012, http://thinkprogress .org/security/2012/10/11/991231/republicans-reveal-cia-base-libya/; Jeremy Scahill, "The CIA's Secret Sites in Somalia," *Nation*, July 12, 2011; Mark Mazzetti, "C.I.A. Building Base for Strikes in Yemen," *New York Times*, June 14, 2011.
58. Barton Gellman and Greg Miller, "U.S. Spy Network's Successes, Failures and Objectives Detailed in 'Black Budget' Summary," *Washington Post*, August 26, 2013; *Washington Post*, "The Black Budget," August 29, 2013, http://www.washingtonpost.com /wp-srv/special/national/black-budget/. This may be an underestimate: GlobalSecurity.com director John Pike told me that covert operations may account for as much as a third of the CIA's total budget currently. Fiscal year 2012 CIA spending was about $1 billion higher than for 2013, so using the later figures should again, if anything, be an underestimate, especially given the declining use of drone strikes.
59. The OCS says it accounts for "all" the costs of supporting the children of military

personnel and civilian employees. My repeated inquiries to the Pentagon went unanswered. The more than $1.3 billion includes $1.24 billion for DoDDS schools in fiscal year 2012. The Department of Defense Educational Activity considers schools in Guam and Puerto Rico to be domestic schools, so there would be additional costs from the Department of Defense Domestic Dependent Elementary and Secondary Schools' $504.7 million budget as well as funding for schooling at non-DOD schools in Canada, Mexico, and the Americas. See U.S. Department of Defense Educational Activity, "Budget Book Fiscal Year 2012," Washington, DC, n.d. [2011].

60. See Amy Belasco, "The Cost of Iraq, Afghanistan, and Other Global War on Terror Operations Since 9/11," Congressional Research Service report, Washington, DC, March 29, 2011, 17, 33–34.

61. U.S. Department of Defense, "United States Department of Defense Fiscal Year 2015 Budget Amendment: Overview Overseas Contingency Operations," Washington, DC, June 2014, 6.

62. Neta C. Crawford, "U.S. Costs of Wars Through 2013: $3.1 Trillion and Counting: Summary of Costs for the U.S. Wars in Iraq, Afghanistan and Pakistan," Costs of War project, March 13, 2013, http://www.usf-iraq.com/wp-content/uploads/2013/03/Us_Costs_of_Wars.pdf. I reached my figure by summing Crawford's costs beyond direct war funding for fiscal years 2001–2013 and dividing that figure by thirteen to approximate the funding for a single year.

63. Office of the Secretary of Defense (Personnel and Readiness) budget, Department of Defense, Fiscal Year (FY) 2013 Budget Estimates, 733.

64. The almost $2 billion in "rental" costs is based on around $11 billion in total aid found in State Department war appropriations less USAID funding (Department of State, Congressional Budget Justification: Foreign Assistance Summary Tables Fiscal Year 2013 [Washington, DC, February 2012], 6–7). See also U.S. Department of Defense, "United States Department of Defense Fiscal Year 2015 Budget Amendment: Overview Overseas Contingency Operations," Washington, DC, June 2014, 6.

65. U.S. Department of Defense, "United States Department of Defense Fiscal Year (FY) 2015 Budget Request: Overview Overseas Contingency Operations Budget Amendment," Washington, DC, November 2014, 3.

66. U.S. Office of Management and Budget "The Budget for Fiscal Year (FY) 2015," Washington, DC, 2014, 203.

67. Senator Kay Bailey Hutchison, "Build Bases in America," *Politico*, July 13, 2010, http://www.politico.com/news/stories/0710/39625.html.

68. Robert Pollin and Heidi Garrett-Peltier, "The U.S. Employment Effects of Military and Domestic Spending Priorities: 2011 Update," report, Political Economy Research Institute, University of Massachusetts, Amherst, December 2011, 1–3.

69. James Heintz, "Military Assets and Public Investment," manuscript, CostsofWar .org, February 2, 2011.

70. Dwight D. Eisenhower, "The Chance for Peace," speech, Washington, DC, April 16, 1953.

71. National Priorities Project, "Cost of War: Taxpayers in the US and Department of Defense in FY2014," http://nationalpriorities.org/tradeoffs/041713/.

72. Gillem, *America Town*.

12: "WE'RE PROFITEERS"

1. IQPC, "Forward Operating Bases 2012," conference website, http://www.iqpc .com/Event.aspx?id=678548; IQPC, "Sponsorship Opportunities," "Forward Operating Bases 2012," conference website, http://www.iqpc.com/Event.aspx?id =655810.

2. Parts of this chapter stem from my articles "'We're Profiteers': How Military Contractors Reap Billions from U.S. Military Bases Overseas," *Monthly Review* 66(3); and "Where Has All the Money Gone? How Contractors Raked in $385 Billion to Build and Support Bases Abroad Since 2001," *TomDispatch*, May 14, 2013, http:// www.tomdispatch.com/blog/175699/david_vine_baseworld_profiteering. Special thanks for this chapter go to Michael Tigar, John Mage, Tom Engelhardt, Clifford Rosky, Laura Jung, all those who generously offered their time and insights during interviews, and many, many others for their help with the work involved.

3. Commission on Wartime Contracting in Iraq and Afghanistan, "Transforming Wartime Contracting: Controlling Costs, Reducing Risks," final report to Congress, August 2011.

4. David Cay Johnston, "The U.S. Government Is Paying Through the Nose for Private Contractors," *Newsweek*, December 12, 2012, http://www.newsweek.com/us -government-paying-through-nose-private-contractors-224370.

5. Pratap Chatterjee, *Halliburton's Army: How a Well-Connected Texas Oil Company Revolutionized the Way America Makes War* (New York: Nation Books, 2009), 24–27, 18–20.

6. P. W. Singer, *Corporate Warriors: The Rise of the Privatized Military Industry* (Ithaca: Cornell University Press, 2003), 80.

7. Chatterjee, *Halliburton's Army*, 61–62.

8. Ibid., 214.

9. Commission on Wartime Contracting in Iraq and Afghanistan, 208–10.

10. Switzerland would have been number five on the list, given 116,527 contracts listing the place of performance as Switzerland. However, the vast majority of these contracts are for delivering food to troops in Afghanistan and, to a lesser extent, at bases in countries worldwide other than Switzerland. The explanation is that one of the major companies providing food, an arm of Supreme Group, is based in Switzerland. Canada and Saudi Arabia would also have made the top ten. Those contracts are also for the most part unrelated to the limited U.S. military presence in the two countries. Thus I exclude those three countries from this list.

11. Linda Bilmes, "Who Profited from the Iraq War?" *EPS Quarterly* 24, no. 1 (March 2012), 6. The Federal Procurement Data System that's supposed to track government contracts "often contains inaccurate data," according to the Government Accountability Office ("Federal Contracting: Observations on the Government's Contracting Data Systems," report, GAO-09-1032T, Washington, DC, September 29, 2009). For example, my research showed hundreds of thousands of contracts with no "place of performance" listed. On the other hand, some of the contacts included in the list are unrelated to the provision of goods and services for overseas bases; however, the simultaneous omission of base-related contracts means this methodology provides a useful portrait of where contracts and taxpayer dollars are going overseas. Still, the totals listed should be treated as rough estimates.

12. See e.g. *Washington Post*, "Black Budget"; Beckhusen and Shachtman, "See for Yourself."

13. Or various iterations of the same term.

14. Commission on Wartime Contracting in Iraq and Afghanistan, 209.

15. Chatterjee, *Halliburton's Army*, 49.

16. Ibid., 9.

17. Sharon Weinberger, "Military Logistics: The $37 Billion (Non)Competition," *Wired*, August 30, 2011, http://www.wired.com/2011/08/military-logistics-the-37 -billion-noncompetition/.

18. Valerie B. Grosso, "Defense Contracting in Iraq: Issues and Options for Congress," Congressional Research Service, report, Washington, DC, June 18, 2008.

19. United States House of Representatives Committee on Oversight and Government Reform, "It's Your Money: Iraq Reconstruction," n.d. [2006], http://oversight-archive .waxman.house.gov.

20. Ellen Nakashima, "KBR Connected to Alleged Fraud, Pentagon Auditor Says," *Washington Post*, May 5, 2009.

21. Dana Hedgpeth, "Audit of KBR Iraq Contract Faults Records for Fuel, Food," *Washington Post*, June 25, 2007; U.S. Department of Justice Office of Public Affairs, "United States Sues Houston-based KBR and Kuwaiti Subcontractor for False Claims on Contracts to House American Troops in Iraq," press release, November 19, 2012, http://www.justice.gov/opa/pr; Walter Pincus, "U.S. Files Civil Suit Against Defense Contractor KBR," *Washington Post*, April 2, 2010.

22. Chatterjee, *Halliburton's Army*, 63–64.

23. *Defense Industry Daily*, "LOGCAP 4: Billions of Dollars Awarded for Army Logistics Support," August 3, 2011, http://www.defenseindustrydaily.com/Billions-of -Dollars-Awarded-Under-LOGCAP-4-to-Supply-US-Troops-in-Afghanistan -05595/.

24. U.S. Department of Justice Office of Public Affairs.

25. The best source for this section is David de Jong, "Supreme Owner Made a Billionaire Feeding U.S. War Machine," *Bloomberg*, October 7, 2013, http://www.bloom berg.com/news/2013-10-06/supreme-owner-made-a-billionaire-feeding-u-s-war -machine.html.

26. Andrew Zajac, "Supreme Foodservice Sues Over U.S., Afghan Food Contract," *Bloomberg*, April 8, 2013, http://www.bloomberg.com/news/2013-04-08/supreme -foodservice-sues-over-u-s-afghan-food-contract.html. See also *Supreme Foodservice, GmbH v. United States*, no. 13-245 C (September 18, 2013).

27. Walter Pincus, "Agency Extends Afghan Food-Supply Contract for Firm that Hired Former Director," *Washington Post*, January 4, 2011.

28. Neil Gordon, "Pentagon Ordered to Lift Suspension of Kuwaiti Contractor's Affiliates," *POGO Blog*, July 3, 2012, http://pogoblog.typepad.com/pogo/2012 /07/pentagon-ordered-to-lift-suspension-of-kuwaiti-contractors-affiliates .html.

29. David Beasley, "Agility Prosecutors Probing 'Potential New Charges' in U.S., Judge Writes," *Bloomberg*, July 27, 2011, http://www.bloomberg.com/news/2011 -07-27/agility-prosecutors-probing-potential-new-charges-u-s-judge-writes .html.

30. Neil Gordon, "POGO Obtains Second Helping of 'Compelling Reason' Memos,"

POGO Blog, October 9, 2013, http://www.pogo.org/blog/2013/07/20130709-pogo-obtains-second-helping-of-compelling-reason-memos.html.

31. Project on Government Oversight (POGO), "Fluor Corporation," Federal Contractor Misconduct Database, n.d. [2014], http://www.contractormisconduct.org/index.cfm/1,73,222,html?CaseID=1780; Transparency International UK, "Defence Companies Anti-Corruption Index 2012," report, London, October 2012.

32. Project on Government Oversight (POGO), "Top 100 Contractors," Federal Contractor Misconduct Database, n.d. [2014], http://www.contractormisconduct.org http://www.contractormisconduct.org/index.cfm?sort=4.

33. U.S. Department of Defense, "Department of Defense Annual Energy Management Report Fiscal Year 2011," report, Washington, DC, September 2012; U.S. Energy Information Administration, "Countries," n.d.[2013], http://www.eia.gov/countries/index.cfm?view=consumption.

34. Johnston, "U.S. Government Is Paying."

35. American Society of Military Comptrollers, "Service Support Contractors: One of the FY 2012 Budget Efficiencies," PowerPoint presentation, Arlington, VA, October 2011, http://www.asmconline.org/wp-content/uploads/2011/10/ASMCBreakfastServiceSupportContractors.pptx.

36. Belasco, "Cost of Iraq," 38.

37. Lolita C. Baldor, "Top Army General Accused of Lavish Spending," *Boston Globe*, August 18, 2012.

38. Center for Responsive Politics, "Defense," n.d. [2014], http://www.opensecrets.org/industries/indus.php?Ind=D.

39. Center for Responsive Politics, "DynCorp International, Expenditures," n.d. [2014], http://www.opensecrets.org/pacs/expenditures.php?cycle=2012&cmte=C00409979; "DynCorp International, Recipients," n.d. [2014], http://www.opensecrets.org/pacs/pacgot.php?cmte=C00409979&cycle=2012.

40. Center for Responsive Politics, "Halliburton Co, Summary," n.d. [2014], http://www.opensecrets.org/lobby/clientsum.php?id=D000000281&year=2012.

41. Government Accountability Office, "Decision in the Matter of Kellogg Brown & Root Services, Inc.," File: B-400787.2, B-400861, Washington, DC, February 23, 2009.

42. Center for Responsive Politics, "Supreme Group USA, Summary," n.d. [2014], http://www.opensecrets.org/lobby/clientsum.php?id=D000065800&year=2012.

43. Center for Responsive Politics, "Agility Public Warehousing Co, Summary," n.d. [2014], http://www.opensecrets.org/lobby/clientsum.php?id=D000065284&year=2011.

44. Center for Responsive Politics, "Fluor Corp, Summary," n.d. [2014], http://www.opensecrets.org/lobby/clientsum.php?id=D000000277&year=2014.

45. David Isenberg, *Shadow Force: Private Security Contractors in Iraq* (Westport, CT: Praeger Security International, 2009), 65.

46. Robert S. McIntyre et al., "Corporate Taxpayers & Corporate Tax Dodgers 2008–10," report, Institute on Taxation and Economic Policy, Providence, RI, November 2011, 8; U.S. Government Accountability Office, "Corporate Income Tax: Effective Tax Rates Can Differ Significantly from the Statutory Rate," report to Congress, GAO-13-520, Washington, DC, May 2013.

47. Robert D. Hershey Jr., "Tax Questions for Military's Contractors," *New York Times*, February 12, 2004.

48. Farah Stockman, "Top Iraq Contractor Skirts U.S. Taxes with Offshore Shell Companies," *Boston Globe*, March 9, 2008, E7.
49. Ibid.
50. Ibid. A 2008 change in U.S. tax law closed the loophole that allowed companies to avoid paying Social Security and Medicare taxes but left the loophole intact for unemployment taxes, meaning that former employees remain ineligible for unemployment insurance. Government Accountability Office, "Defense Contracting: Recent Law Has Impacted Contractor Use of Offshore Subsidiaries to Avoid Certain Payroll Taxes," Highlights of GAO-10-327, Washington, DC, January 2010.
51. Chatterjee, *Halliburton's Army*, 210–11; Laura Mandaro, "Halliburton's Dubai Move Raises Issue of Expat Taxes," *MarketWatch*, March 13, 2007, http://www.marketwatch.com/story/halliburton-dubai-move-revives-foreign-tax-controversy.
52. Congressional Research Service, "Tax Exemption for Repatriated Foreign Earnings: Proposals and Analysis," report, Washington, DC, April 27, 2006.
53. Senate Republican Policy Committee, "Territorial vs. Worldwide Taxation," September 19, 2012, http://www.rpc.senate.gov/policy-papers/territorial-vs-worldwide-taxation; Emily Chasan, "At Big U.S. Companies, 60% of Cash Sits Offshore: J. P. Morgan," *Wall Street Journal*, May 17, 2012.
54. U.S. Government Accountability Office, "Defense Contracting: Recent Law."
55. Senate Republican Policy Committee, "Territorial vs. Worldwide Taxation."

13: THE MILCON CON

1. The following exchange comes from United States Senate Committee on Appropriations, Hearings before a Subcommittee of the Committee on Appropriations, 109th Congress, 2nd session, Military Construction and Veterans Affairs, and Related Agencies Appropriations for Fiscal Year 2007, part 7, 117–18.
2. United States Senate Committee on Appropriations, Senate Report 113-048, Military Construction and Veterans Affairs, and Related Agencies Appropriation Bill, 2014, 113th Congress, 1st session, June 27, 2013.
3. Nicolai Ouroussoff, "He Made Antiquity Modern," *New York Times*, April 9, 2010, C21; Elisabetta Povoledo, "Coney Island Getting a $30 Million Italian Makeover," *New York Times*, April 23, 2010.
4. GlobalSecurity.org, "United States Army Africa (USARAF); Southern European Task Force (SETAF)," http://www.globalsecurity.org/military/agency/army/sertaf.htm.
5. GlobalSecurity.org, "United States Army Africa (USARAF)."
6. U.S. Army Garrison Vicenza, "Del Din Green Building Education Tour."
7. Michael Wise, "Head East," *Armed Forces Journal*, December 3, 2012, 22.
8. U.S. Army Garrison Bavaria, "A Leader's Guide to the Bavaria Military Community," website, accessed January 3, 2015, http://www.grafenwoehr.army.mil/smartcard.asp.
9. Sembler cable to Bloomfield, U.S. Embassy Rome, 04ROME2248, June 14, 2004, http://wikileaks.org/cable/2004/06/04ROME2248.html; Andrew Yeo, *Activists, Alliances, and Anti-U.S. Base Protests* (New York: Cambridge University Press, 2011), 102.
10. Sembler cable to Department of State, U.S. Embassy Rome, 03ROME4736, October 16, 2003, http://wikileaks.org/cable/2003/10/03ROME4736.html.

11. United States Committee on Armed Services, Hearings on S. 2766, 109th Congress, 2nd Session, Department of Defense Authorization for Appropriations for Fiscal Year 2007, part 3, February 7, March 2, 15, April 5, 2006.

12. Parts of this section stem from my *Island of Shame*, chapter 6.

13. Tazewell Shepard, memorandum for Harry D. Train, January 26, 1970, Naval History and Heritage Command: 00 Files, 1970, Box 111, 11000.

14. Robert A. Frosch, memorandum for the Deputy Secretary of Defense, February 27, 1970, Naval History and Heritage Command: 00 Files, 1970, Box 111, 11000; John H. Chafee, memorandum for the Secretary of Defense, January 31, 1970, Naval History and Heritage Command: 00 Files, 1970, Box 111, 11000.

15. Bandjunis, *Diego Garcia*, 8–14; J. H. Gibbon et al., "Brief on UK/US London Discussions on United States Defence Interests in the Indian Ocean," memorandum, March 6, 1964, UK National Archives: CAB 21/5418, 81174, 1–2. See also Vine, *Island of Shame*, chapter 6.

16. See attachment, Op-605E4, "Proposed Naval Communications Facility on Diego Garcia," briefing sheet, [January] 1970, Naval History and Heritage Command: 00 Files, 1970, Box 111, 11000. For more detail, see my *Island of Shame*, chapter 6.

17. Vine, *Island of Shame*, chapter 6.

18. United States Senate Committee on Armed Services, "Inquiry into U.S. Costs and Allied Contributions to Support the U.S. Military Presence Overseas," report, Washington, DC, April 15, 2013, ii–iii; Senate Committee on Appropriations, Senate Report 113-048.

19. Senate Committee on Appropriations, Senate Report 113-048; Senate Committee on Armed Services, "Inquiry," ii–iii.

20. Committee on Appropriations, Senate Report 113-048; Senate Committee on Armed Services, "Inquiry," ii.

21. Senate Committee on Appropriations, Senate Report 113-048; Senate Committee on Armed Services, "Inquiry," iv.

22. Senate Committee on Armed Services, "Inquiry," iv.

23. United States Senate Subcommittee on United States Security Agreements and Commitments Abroad, "United States Security Agreements and Commitments Abroad," 2433–34.

24. Ibid.

25. Ibid., 2434.

26. Ibid.

27. Dorothy Robyn, Statement before the House Armed Services Committee Subcommittee on Readiness, Washington, DC, March 8, 2012.

28. Heike Hasenauer, "The Army's Building Boom," *Soldiers Magazine*, March 1, 2008.

29. U.S. Department of Defense, "National Defense Budget Estimates For FY 2014 [Green Book]," Washington, DC, May 2013, 146–48.

30. Belasco, "Cost of Iraq," 33.

31. U.S. Department of Defense, "National Defense Budget Estimates, FY 2014," 143.

32. Calculation from annual U.S. Department of Defense "Construction Program (C-1)" budget submissions and war spending through for fiscal years 2004–2011 in Belasco, "Cost of Iraq," 33.

33. Seth Robbins, "Army Missteps in Basing Troops in Europe Could Cost Taxpayers Billions, GAO Report Finds," *Stars and Stripes*, September 14, 2010.

34. Thom Shanker, "Pentagon and Congress Argue over Hospital for Troops," *New York Times*, June 10, 2012.

35. Matt Millham, "Landstuhl Hospital's Trauma Status on the Line as Afghan War Winds Down," *Stars and Stripes*, May 3, 2013, http://www.stripes.com/news /landstuhl-hospital-s-trauma-status-on-the-line-as-afghan-war-winds-down-1 .219529.

36. Chuck Roberts, "Groundbreaking Ceremony Marks Beginning of Construction of New Medical Center," *Army.mil*, October 27, 2014, http://www.army.mil/article /136938/Groundbreaking_ceremony_marks_beginning_of_construction_of _new_medical_center/.

37. Loren Thompson, "Congress Wastes More Money on Unneeded Military Bases than Belgium, Sweden or Switzerland Spend on Defense," *Forbes*, May 16, 2014.

38. See U.S. Department of Defense, "Construction Program (C-1)" budget submissions for fiscal years 2002–2006.

39. United States Senate Committee on Appropriations, Senate Report 113-048.

40. Department of Defense Dependents Education, "Operations and Maintenance Fiscal Year (FY) 2013 Budget Estimates," Washington, DC, 2012, 388.

41. John Vandiver, "DOD to Save $60M by Dropping Recreational, Excess Sites in Europe," *Stars and Stripes*, May 23, 2014.

42. Government Accountability Office, "Force Structure: Improved Cost Information and Analysis Needed to Guide Overseas Military Posture Decisions," report, Washington, DC, June 2012, 8, 19. A Senate committee report recently described a $2.5 billion Marine Corps estimate for the costs of moving troops from Okinawa to Hawaii as "highly speculative." United States Senate Committee on Armed Services, "Inquiry," vi.

43. Government Accountability Office, "Defense Headquarters: DOD Needs to Reassess Options for Permanent Location of U.S. Africa Command," Report to Congressional Committees, Washington, DC, September 2013.

44. U.S. Department of Defense "Department of Defense Budget Fiscal Year 2015: Construction Program (C-1)," March 2014, 24, 35.

45. *Standing Army*, directed by Thomas Fazi and Enrico Parenti (Italy: Effendemfilm and Takae Films, 2010).

14: "MASTERS OF EXTORTION"

1. NMV Consulting, "Kevin K. Maher," biography, http://nmvconsulting.com/NMV _Consulting/Maher.html.

2. Japan Ministry of Defense, "Defense of Japan 2013," white paper, Tokyo, 2013, 156–57.

3. The last sentence draws on Sayo Saruta, "The Meeting at the Department of State, December 3, 2010, 4pm, at the State Department," notes, n.d. [2010]. All of the other quotations come from my own notes. I present quotations from Maher exactly as he spoke them and exactly as I recorded them during the briefing. I have not paraphrased or changed Maher's words, and I use quotation marks only when I am certain that I captured his exact speech. Any discrepancies between my notes and those compiled by Saruta from other students' notes reflect trivial differences in our recording of Maher's remarks. See also Satoko Norimatsu, "Anger Spreads over Kevin Maher's Derogatory Comments on Okinawans," Peace Philosophy Centre

blog, March 8, 2011, http://peacephilosophy.blogspot.com/2011/03/anger-spreads -over-kevin-mahers.html.

4. Travis J. Tritten, "State Dept. Official in Japan Fired over Alleged Derogatory Remarks," *Stars and Stripes*, March 9, 2011, http://www.stripes.com/news/pacific /japan/state-dept-official-in-japan-fired-over-alleged-derogatory-remarks-1 .137181; Martin Fackler, "U.S. Apologizes for Japan Remark," *New York Times*, March 10, 2011, A6.

5. *Wall Street Journal*, "U.S.'s Ex-Japan Head," blog, April 14, 2011, http://blogs.wsj .com/japanrealtime/2011/04/14/exclusive-video-u-s-s-ex-japan-head.

6. David Vine, "Smearing Japan," *Foreign Policy in Focus*, April 20, 2011. See also David Vine, "The Session Was Not Off-the-Record," letter to the editor, *Wall Street Journal*, March 21, 2011.

7. Masahide Ota, "Former Governor of Okinawa Masahide Ota: Maher's Remarks Represent His True Feelings," translated by T&CT, Mark Ealey, *Ryukyu Shimpo*, March 12, 2011, http://english.ryukyushimpo.jp/2011/03/12/99/.

8. Peter Ennis, "The Roots of the Kevin Maher–Okinawa Commotion," *Dispatch Japan*, blog, March 10, 2011, http://www.dispatchjapan.com/blog/2011/03/the-roots -of-the-kevin-maher-okinawa-commotion.html.

9. Ibid.

10. Gavan McCormack and Satoko Oka Norimatsu, *Resistant Islands: Okinawa Confronts Japan and the United States* (Lanham, MD: Rowman and Littlefield, 2012), 196–97.

11. Ibid., 197.

12. Akibayashi and Takazato, "Okinawa," 247–48.

13. McCormack and Norimatsu, *Resistant Islands*, 17.

14. Ibid., 25–32, 47n60. My thanks to Satoko Norimatsu for her important help with these details and other sections about Okinawa.

15. Ibid., 17.

16. *Testimonies of the Battle of Okinawa*, directed by Keifuku Janamoto, 2005[?].

17. C. Johnson, *Sorrows of Empire*, 50–53, 200; C. Johnson, *Blowback*, 11; Yoshida, *Democracy Betrayed*; Amemiya, "The Bolivian Connection," 63.

18. Frank Gibney, "Forgotten Island," *Time*, November 28, 1949, 24.

19. C. Johnson, *Sorrows of Empire*, 201.

20. Roy H. Smith, *The Nuclear Free and Independent Pacific Movement: After Mururoa* (London: I. B. Tauris, 1997), 42.

21. My thanks to Joseph Gerson for pointing this out to me and for the expertise he generously shared in reviewing this chapter.

22. C. Johnson, *Sorrows of Empire*, 50–53, 200; C. Johnson, *Blowback*, 11; Yoshida, *Democracy Betrayed*; Amemiya, "The Bolivian Connection," 63.

23. See e.g. Cooley, *Base Politics*, 147; Okinawa Peace Network Los Angeles, "List of Main Crimes Committed and Incidents Concerning the U.S. Military on Okinawa—Excerpts," translated from *Okinawa Times*, October 12, 1995, http:// www.uchinanchu.org/history/list_of_crimes.htm.

24. Okinawa Peace Network Los Angeles.

25. Mercier, "Way Off Base."

26. Cooley, *Base Politics*, 147–48. Japan regained control of Iwo Jima and other islands in 1968.

27. Gillem, *America Town*, 242, 256–58.

28. Initially, the city council voted to accept the base when the Japanese government offered $95 million in "economic aid." Later, Nago's mayor and other politicians announced their opposition to the new base. Ibid., 256–61.

29. *Asahi Shimbun*, "Sit-In Against Relocation of Air Station Futenma Marks 10th Anniversary," April 20, 2014, http://ajw.asahi.com/article/behind_news/social _affairs/AJ201404200012.

30. Gillem, *America Town*, 48.

31. Daniel J. Nelson, *A History of U.S. Military Forces in Germany* (Boulder, CO: Westview Press, 1987), 104–8, 123.

32. Ibid., 127.

33. Floyd Whaley, "Murder Charge Is Recommended for U.S. Marine in Death of Transgender Filipino," *New York Times*, December 15, 2014, http://www.nytimes .com/2014/12/16/world/asia/murder-charge-is-recommended-for-us-marine-in -death-of-transgender-filipino.html.

34. Mercier, "Way Off Base."

35. Linda Isakao Angst, "The Rape of a Schoolgirl: Discourses of Power and Gendered National Identity in Okinawa," in *Islands of Discontent: Okinawan Responses to Japanese and American Power*, edited by Laura Heig and Mark Selden (Lanham, MD: Rowman and Littlefield, 2003), 137.

36. *U.S. Bases in Okinawa: Takae's Story*, website, accessed January 5, 2015, http:// okinawa-takae.org.

37. Okinawa Women Act Against Military Violence, "Postwar U.S. Military Crimes," 23–25.

38. Associated Press, "Friction Between Japan, U.S. Military," *Los Angeles Times*, February 11, 2001, http://articles.latimes.com/2001/feb/11/news/mn-24065.

39. Prior to 1972, local officials were powerless to arrest or investigate crimes. Okinawa Prefectural Government, "US Military Base Issues in Okinawa," Regional Security Policy Division, September 2011, 4; Okinawa Prefectural Government, "US Military Base Issues in Okinawa," Military Base Affairs Division, n.d. [2011], 15.

40. Mercier, "Way Off Base"; Okinawa Women Act Against Military Violence, "Postwar U.S. Military Crimes"; Akibayashi and Takazato, "Okinawa," 252, 260.

41. C. Johnson, *Sorrows of Empire*, 109–10.

42. *New York Times*, "Ospreys in Okinawa," editorial, September 12, 2012, A22.

43. Travis J. Tritten and Matthew M. Burke, "US Military in Japan Wrestles with Curfew's Ineffectiveness," *Stars and Stripes*, November 27, 2012, stripes.com/news/pacific /japan/us-military-in-japan-wrestles-with-curfew-s-ineffectiveness-1.198539.

44. Kan, "Guam," 2.

45. Ibid.

46. Travis J. Tritten, "US to Beef Up Marine Presence on Okinawa Before Drawdown," *Stars and Stripes*, June 12, 2012, http://www.stripes.com/news/us-to-beef-up -marine-presence-on-okinawa-before-drawdown-1.180172.

47. Gillem, *America Town*, 247.

48. Cooley, *Base Politics*, 151; Emma Chanlett-Avery and Ian E. Rinehart, "The U.S. Military Presence in Okinawa and the Futenma Base Controversy," Congressional Research Service, report, Washington, DC, August 14, 2014.

49. Cooley, *Base Politics*, 151.

50. Ibid., 143, 158–59.

51. Thanks to Joseph Gerson for pointing this out and for comments that were extremely helpful in drafting this chapter and avoiding error.

52. Gavan McCormack, *Client State: Japan in the American Embrace* (New York: Verso, 2007), 163; Statistics Japan, "Okinawa," Prefecture Comparisons, 2014, http://stats-japan.com/t/tdfk/okinawa; "Prefectural Income," Prefecture Comparisons, 2014, http://stats-japan.com/t/kiji/10714.

53. McCormack, *Client State*, 158–59.

54. Ibid., 83.

55. Lostumbo et al., "Overseas Basing of U.S. Military Forces," 146; Cooley, *Base Politics*, 195; Calder, *Embattled Garrisons*, 192–94.

56. Government Accountability Office, "Comprehensive Cost Information and Analysis of Alternatives Needed to Assess Military Posture in Asia," report, GAO-11-316, Washington, DC, May 2011.

57. Stockholm International Peace Research Institute, "Table 3.3: The 15 Countries with the Highest Military Expenditure in 2012," *Trends in World Military Expenditure, 2012*, Stockholm, April 15, 2013; Sam Perlo-Freeman and Carina Solmirano, "Trends in World Military Expenditure, 2013," fact sheet, Stockholm International Peace Research Institute, April 2014.

58. Lostumbo et al., "Overseas Basing of U.S. Military Forces," chapter 5.

59. Quoted in Yonamine, "Economic Crisis."

60. Ibid. See also John Feffer, "Pacific Pushback: Has the U.S. Empire Reached Its High-Water Mark?" *TomDispatch*, March 4, 2010, http:www.tomdispatch.com/blog/175214/.

61. Tritten, "US to Beef Up."

62. Manabu Sato, "The Marines Will Not Defend the Senkakus," *Asia-Pacific Journal* 11, no. 27/2 (July 8, 2013), http://japanfocus.org/-Sato-Manabu/3964.

63. According to the manufacturer, the combat radius of an Osprey with twenty-four troops is 390 nautical miles; the round-trip distance between Naha, Okinawa, and the the Senkaku/Diaoyus is 440 nautical miles. See http://www.boeing.com/boeing/rotorcraft/military/v22/.

64. Interviews with Andrew Hoehn, April 29 and July 2, 2012.

65. McCormack, *Client State*, 77–81.

66. Lostumbo et al., "Overseas Basing of U.S. Military Forces," 280–82.

15: "IT'S ENOUGH"

1. U.S. Army Garrison Ansbach, "Your Army Home, Community Guide," Ansbach, Germany, n.d., 1.

2. U.S. Army Garrison Ansbach, "USAG Ansbach History," n.d. [2013], available at http://www.ansbach.army.mil/USAGhistory.html.

3. Guido Lanaro, *Il Popolo delle Pignatte: Storia del Presidio Permanente No Dal Molin (2005–2009)* (Verona, Italy: Qui Edit di S.D.S., 2010), 15–17.

4. Ibid., 19n11.

5. Sandra Jontz, "Soldier Convicted of Vicenza Rape Will Be Free Pending Appeal," *Stars and Stripes*, March 10, 2006, http://www.stripes.com/news/soldier-convicted-of-vicenza-rape-will-be-free-pending-appeal-1.46062.

6. Lanaro, *Il Popolo*, 28.

7. The lowest of police estimates was 50,000 to 80,000. Organizers usually cite fig-

ures of 100,000 to 120,000. With the truth usually somewhere in the middle, the total probably reached six digits with ease.

8. Comitato del Si al Dal Molin, "Si Dal Molin," n.d. [2009], http://clubgiovani.it /sialdalmolin/category/Comitato-del-si.

9. Alexander Martin, "Okinawa's Reinvention Enters Next Phase; Prefecture Seeks to Exploit Location in New Ways and Move Beyond Military Bases," *Wall Street Journal*, November 13, 2014, http://www.wsj.com/articles/okinawas-reinvention -enters-next-phase-1415912139.

10. Keith B. Cunningham and Andreas Klemmer, "Restructuring the US Military Bases in Germany: Scope, Impacts, and Opportunities," Bonn International Center for Conversion, Bonn, report 4, June 1995, 6.

11. Consolidated and Further Continuing Appropriations Act, 2015, Pub. L. No. 113-235 (2014), secs. 108–12.

12. Lutz, "Introduction," in *Bases of Empire*, 32–33.

13. U.S. Department of Defense, "2004 Statistical Compendium on Allied Contributions to the Common Defense," Washington, DC, 2004; Lostumbo et al., "Overseas Basing of U.S. Military Forces," 131–32.

14. Patrick E. Poppert and Werner W. Herzog Jr., "Force Reduction, Base Closure, and the Indirect Effects of Military Installations on Local Employment Growth," *Journal of Regional Science* 43, no. 3 (2003): 460–61.

15. Cunningham and Klemmer, "Restructuring the US Military Bases," 6, 13, 20. There is an apparent discrepancy in this report, which cites more than 92,000 acres returned by the United States in total (p. 6) and more than 100,000 (p. 20) returned by the U.S. Army alone.

16. Ibid., 22, 6–7. "Population Statistics from Organisation for Economic Co-operation and Development," *OECD Economic Surveys Germany 1991–1992* (Paris: OECD, 1992), 7.

17. Alfredo R. Paloyo, Colin Vance, and Matthias Vorrell, "The Regional Economic Effects of Military Base Realignment and Closures," *Defense and Peace Studies Journal* 21, nos. 5–6 (2010): 567–69.

18. U.S. Army in Germany, "U.S. Army Installations—Ansbach," website, accessed January 7, 2015, http://www.usarmygermany.com/Sont.htm?http&&&www .usarmygermany.com/USAREUR_City_Ansbach.htm.

19. Paloyo et al., "Regional Economic Effects," 568, 578–79.

20. Linda Andersson, Johan Lundbergb, and Magnus Sjöström, "Regional Effects of Military Base Closures: The Case of Sweden," *Defense and Peace Economics* 18, no. 1 (2007): 87–97.

21. Government Accountability Office, "Military Base Closures: Updated Status of Prior Base Realignments and Closures," report, GAO-05-138, Washington, DC, January 2005.

22. Poppert and Herzog, "Force Reduction," 479–80, 463–64.

23. Travis J. Tritten and Chiyomi Sumida, "Ready or Not, Okinawa Aims to Wean Itself Off of Military Dollars," *Stars and Stripes*, August 20, 2011, http://www.stripes.com /news/ready-or-not-okinawa-aims-to-wean-itself-off-of-military-dollars-1.152708.

24. A. Martin, "Okinawa's Reinvention."

25. Valerio Volpi, "An Airbase in Vicenza: How Italy Became a Launching Pad for the US Military," *Counterpunch*, October 4, 2007, http://www.counterpunch.org/2007 /10/04/how-italy-became-a-launching-pad-for-the-us-military/.

26. Stephanie Westbrook, "Italian Court Blocks Construction of U.S. Military Base," U.S. Citizens for Peace and Justice, blog, n.d. [2008], http://www.peaceand justice.it/vicenza-tar.php.

27. Ibid.; Stephanie Westbrook, "U.S. Military Interests Reign Supreme in Italy," U.S. Citizens for Peace and Justice, blog, July 30, 2008, http://www.peaceandjustice.it /vicenza-cds.php.

28. Barry Moody and Roberto Landucci, "Overloaded Justice System Ties Italy in Knots," Reuters, April 5, 2012. http://in.reuters.com/article/2012/04/05/italy-justice -idINDEE83406F20120405.

29. Westbrook, "U.S. Military Interests."

30. Ibid.; Lanaro, *Il Popolo*, 86–87.

31. Lanaro, *Il Popolo*, 76–79, 94.

32. Yeo, *Activists*, 112.

33. See e.g. Erin E. Fitz-Henry, "Municipalizing Sovereignty: The U.S. Air Force in Manta, Ecuador" (Ph.D. dissertation, Princeton University, 2009).

34. Westbrook, "U.S. Military Interests."

35. In January 2007, one week before center-left prime minister Romano Prodi approved the Dal Molin construction plan, U.S. ambassador to Italy Ronald Spogli visited Vicenza in an effort to pressure Prodi to accept the base. State Department cables released by Wikileaks illustrate more of the pressure U.S. officials brought to bear. One shows that five days before approving the base, Prodi tried to find a compromise to appease base opponents. Prodi offered Ambassador Spogli and Assistant Secretary of State Daniel Fried another site for the new base thirty miles from Aviano Air Base (i.e., closer to the deployment point for the 173rd Airborne Brigade). Spogli refused to consider the alternative. "We've been working on the project for two years and have spent $25 million on planning," the cable signed by Spogli reports him as saying. "Going somewhere else, like Aviano, loses the benefit of collocation of forces. Since we're so far down the road, at this point we either have expansion at Dal Molin or not at all." Spogli noted there would be "over a billion dollars invested" and that annual spending locally would rise by more than $130 million. He suggested that if the government didn't agree, the United States would "take the project to Germany." "This is not a threat," said the ambassador, "it's just a statement of fact." This casts at least some doubt on the Bush administration's claim that moving troops and spending to Italy was not a way to punish Germany for expressing opposition to an invasion of Iraq. Yeo, *Activists*, 112; Ronald Spogli cable to Department of State, "Fried Presses Prodi on Afghanistan, Dal Molin Base Decision," cable no. 07ROME96, U.S. Embassy Rome, January 17, 2007.

36. See Amy A. Holmes, *Social Unrest and American Military Bases in Turkey and Germany since 1945* (Cambridge: Cambridge University Press, 2014); Cooley, *Base Politics*.

37. For a brief summary, see Gina Apostol, "In the Philippines, Haunted by History," *New York Times*, April 28, 2012, http://www.nytimes.com/2012/04/29/opinion /sunday/in-the-philippines-haunted-by-history.html?_r=1.

38. Cheryl Lewis, "Kahoʻolawe and the Military," ICE case study, Washington, DC, Spring 2001, http://www.american.edu/ted/ice/hawaiibombs.htm.

39. Leila Fadel, "U.S. Seeking 58 Bases in Iraq, Shiite Lawmakers Say," *McClatchy DC*, June 9, 2008. http://www.mcclatchydc.com/2008/06/09/40372/us-seeking-58-bases -in-iraq-shiite.html.

40. Medea Benjamin, "Italian Women Lead Grassroots Campaign Against US Military Base," U.S. Citizens for Peace and Justice, blog, n.d. [February 2008], http://www.peaceandjustice.it/nodalmolin-post.php.
41. Ibid. Four days after the protest, Prodi resigned as prime minister over the lack of support for his foreign policy, including the Dal Molin base.

16: THE LILY PAD STRATEGY

1. U.S. Department of Defense, "Global Defense Posture and International Agreements Overview," slide presentation, April 27, 2009, 6.
2. Ibid., 9.
3. Ibid., 3. Two principles that have guided the acquisition and maintenance of large numbers of overseas bases since World War II still appear to be at work today. They are "redundancy"—the more bases, the safer the nation—and "strategic denial"—preventing supposed enemies from using a territory by denying them access—both of which hold that even if the military has little interest in using a base or a territory, it should acquire as many as possible for every possible contingency and almost never cede its acquisitions.
4. Cited by Raymond F. DuBois in Center for Strategic and International Studies, "2010 Global Security Forum: What Impact Would the Loss of Overseas Bases Have on U.S. Power Projection?" transcript, Federal News Service, May 13, 2010.
5. David C. Chandler Jr., "'Lily-pad Basing Concept Put to the Test," *Army Logistician*, March–April 2005, 11–13.
6. John Lindsay-Poland, "Pentagon Building Bases in Central America and Colombia Despite Constitutional Court Striking Down Base Agreement," Fellowship of Reconciliation, blog, January 27, 2011, http://forusa.org/blogs/john-lindsay-poland/pentagon-building-bases-central-america-colombia/8445; "Honduras and the U.S. Military," Fellowship of Reconciliation, blog, September 21, 2011, http://forusa.org/blogs/john-lindsay-poland/honduras-us-military/9943.
7. U.S. Department of Defense, Contract Announcement, Defense Logistics Agency, Washington, DC, April 25, 2009, http://www.defense.gov/Contracts/Contract.aspx?ContractID=2994; Contract Announcement, Defense Logistics Agency, Washington, DC, January 15, 2009, http://www.defense.gov/Contracts/Contract.aspx?ContractID=3944.
8. Thom Shanker, "Lessons of Iraq Help U.S. Fight a Drug War in Honduras," *New York Times*, May 5, 2012, A1, http://www.nytimes.com/2012/05/06/world/americas/us-turns-its-focus-on-drug-smuggling-in-honduras.html?pagewanted=all&_r=0.
9. Ibid., A1.
10. Ibid., A14.
11. Library of Congress, "Honduras: United States Military Assistance and Training," Country Studies Series, Federal Research Division, Washington, DC, http://www.country-data.com/cgi-bin/query/r-5731.html.
12. Kathleen H. Hicks, "Transitioning Defense Organizational Initiatives: An Assessment of Key 2001–2008 Defense Reforms," report, Center for Strategic and International Studies, November 2008, 13.
13. Thanks to John Lindsay-Poland for making this point.
14. The unpublicized multiagency campaign also outlined a "public-private partnership"

involving a major real estate development firm, General Electric, and humanitarian aid groups (including one directed by the son of Undersecretary of State Maria Otero). Hugo Llorens, "Mission Integrated Strategy to Fight Crime and Illicit Trafficking in La Mosquitia," cable no. 09TEGUCIGALPA353, Tegucigalpa, May 15, 2009, http://wikileaks.org/cable/2009/05/09TEGUCIGALPA353.html.

15. U.S. Department of Defense, "Operations and Maintenance, Fiscal Year (FY) 2014," 69–72.

16. Herbert Docena, "The US Base in the Philippines," *Inquirer.net*, February 20, 2012, http://opinion.inquirer.net/23405/the-us-base-in-the-philippines; Jane's Sentinel Security Assessment, "Philippines—Security and Foreign Forces," May 14, 2009.

17. Kaplan, *Hog Pilots*, 315.

18. Ibid., 154.

19. Carmela Fonbuena, "PH, US 'Close' to Signing Military Deal," *Rappler.com*, February 5, 2014, www.rappler.com/nation/49733-philippines-united-states-bases-access; "PH, US Bases Access Talks Reach 'Impasse,'" *Rappler.com*, November 6, 2013, http://www.rappler.com/nation/43025-bases-access-philippines-united-states -impasse.

20. Docena, "US Base in the Philippines."

21. Amedee Bollee, "Djibouti: From French Outpost to US Base," *Review of African Political Economy* 30, no. 97 (2003): 481–84.

22. Lauren Ploch, "Africa Command: U.S. Strategic Interests and the Role of the U.S. Military in Africa," Congressional Research Service, report, Washington, DC, July 22, 2011, 9, 13. On the four thousand figure: Benjamin A. Benson email to author, November 13, 2014.

23. George W. Bush, "President Bush Creates a Department of Defense Unified Combatant Command for Africa," press release, February 6, 2007, http://georgewbush -whitehouse.archives.gov/news/releases/2007/02/20070206-3.html.

24. Catherine Besteman, "Counter AFRICOM," in *The Counter-Counterinsurgency Manual, or Notes on the Militarization of America*, edited by the Network of Concerned Anthropologists Steering Committee (Chicago: Prickly Paradigm Press, 2009), 118–21.

25. Benson email to author. See also Nick Turse, "The Classic Military Runaround: Your Tax Dollars at Work Keeping You in the Dark," *TomDispatch*, July 7, 2013, www.tomdispatch.com/blog/175721.

26. Akil R. King, Zackary H. Moss, and Afi Y. Pittman, "Overcoming Logistics Challenges in East Africa," *Army Sustainment*, January-February 2014, 30.

27. Craig Whitlock, "U.S. Expands Secret Intelligence Operations in Africa," *Washington Post*, June 13, 2012, http://www.washingtonpost.com/world/national -security/us-expands-secret-intelligence-operations-in-africa/2012/06/13 /gJQAHyvAbV_story.html; Craig Whitlock and Greg Miller, "U.S. Building Secret Drone Bases in Africa, Arabian Peninsula, Officials Say," *Washington Post*, September 20, 2011, http://www.washingtonpost.com/world/national-security/us -building-secret-drone-bases-in-africa-arabian-peninsula-officials-say/2011/09 /20/gIQAJ8rOjK_story.html?wprss=rss_homepage; Craig Whitlock, "Contractors Run U.S. Spying Missions in Africa," *Washington Post*, June 14, 2012, http://www .washingtonpost.com/world/national-security/contractors-run-us-spying -missions-in-africa/2012/06/14/gJQAvC4RdV_story.html.

28. Whitlock, "U.S. Expands"; Craig Whitlock, "Mysterious Fatal Crash Provides Rare

Glimpse of U.S. Commandos in Mali," *Washington Post*, July 8, 2012, http://www
.washingtonpost.com/world/national-security/mysterious-fatal-crash-provides
-rare-glimpse-of-us-commandos-in-mali/2012/07/08/gJQAGO71WW_story
.html.

29. Shashank Bengali, "U.S. Military Investing Heavily in Africa," *Los Angeles Times*,
October 20, 2013. http://www.latimes.com/world/la-fg-usmilitary-africa-20131020
-story.html#page=1.

30. Nick Turse, "The Pivot to Africa," *TomDispatch*, September 5, 2013, www.tom
dispatch.com/blog/175743.

31. Craig Whitlock, "U.S. to Airlift African Troops to Central African Republic,"
Washington Post, December 9, 2013, http://www.washingtonpost.com/world
/national-security/us-to-airlift-african-troops-to-central-african-republic/2013
/12/09/abdd9c64-6107-11e3-bf45-61f69f54fc5f_story.html.

32. Craig Whitlock, "U.S. Trains African Soldiers for Somalia Mission," *Washington
Post*, May 13, 2012, http://www.washingtonpost.com/world/national-security/us
-trains-african-soldiers-for-somalia-mission/2012/05/13/gIQAJhsPNU_story
.html.

33. Bureau of Investigative Journalism, "Somalia: Reported US Covert Actions 2001–
2014," website, February 22, 2012, http://www.thebureauinvestigates.com/2012/02
/22/get-the-data-somalias-hidden-war/; Whitlock, "U.S. Trains African Soldiers"; Richard Reeve and Zoë Pelter, "From New Frontier to New Normal:
Counter-terrorism Operations in the Sahel-Sahara," London: Remote Control
Group/Oxford Research Group, August 2014, 25.

34. Jeremy Scahill, "The CIA's Secret Sites in Somalia," *Nation*, December 10, 2014
[August 1–8, 2011], http://www.thenation.com/article/161936/cias-secret-sites
-somalia; Reeve and Pelter, "New Frontier to New Normal," 25.

35. Reeve and Pelter, "New Frontier to New Normal," 2, 4.

36. Ploch, "Africa Command," 22–23.

37. Whitlock, "U.S. to Airlift African Troops."

38. Turse, "Pivot to Africa"; Reeve and Pelter, "New Frontier to New Normal," 22.

39. See e.g. Guy Martin, "AAR Awarded US Military African Airlift Contract," *Defence-
Web*, December 4, 2013, http://www.defenceweb.co.za/index.php?option=com
_content&view=article&id=32932:aar-awarded-us-military-african-airlift
-contract&catid=47:Logistics&Itemid=110; Lalit Wadha, "The Society of American Military Engineers," U.S. Army Corps of Engineers Europe District, Power-
Point presentation, April 12, 2013; see also Reeve and Pelter, "New Frontier to New
Normal," on contracts.

40. Ploch, "Africa Command," 10; C. Johnson, *Nemesis*, 147–48; Cooley, *Base Politics*,
238, 242.

41. Carter Ham, Statement of General Carter Ham, USA Commander United States
Africa Command, Before the Senate Armed Services Committee, March 7,
2013.

42. Brady Dennis and Missy Ryan, "Fewer U.S. Troops than Initially Planned Will Be
Deployed Against Ebola in West Africa," *Washington Post*, November 12, 2014,
http://www.washingtonpost.com/national/health-science/fewer-us-troops-than
-initially-planned-will-be-deployed-against-ebola-in-west-africa/2014/11/12
/74e37574-6a9a-11e4-a31c-77759fc1eacc_story.html.

43. Claudette Roulo, "DoD Brings Unique Capabilities to Ebola Response Mission,

Official Says," *DOD News*, November 12, 2014, http://www.defense.gov/news /newsarticle.aspx?id=123624; see also Reeve and Pelter, "New Frontier to New Normal."

44. Benson email to author.

45. Paul McLeary, "US Deployments to Africa Raise a Host of Issues," *Defense News*, May 3, 2014, http://www.defensenews.com/article/20140503/DEFREG04/305030020 /US-Deployments-Africa-Raise-Host-Issues, citing 5,000–8,000 plus the 3,000 Ebola additions. See also Rick Rozoff, "Pentagon's Last Frontier: Battle-Hardened Troops Headed to Africa," *Op-ed News*, June 12, 2012, http://www.opednews.com /articles/Pentagon-s-Last-Frontier--by-Rick-Rozoff-120612-54.html.

46. The total troop size at the two largest bases in Latin America, Guantánamo Bay and Soto Cano, totals around 2,500 to 4,000 at most. Small numbers of troops are deployed elsewhere in Latin America. U.S. Department of Defense, "Total Military Personnel and Dependent End Strength, as of: June 30, 2014."

47. Turse, "Pivot to Africa"; Oscar Nkala and Kim Helfrich, "US Army Looking to Contractors for African Operations," *DefenceWeb*, September 17, 2013, http:// www.defenceweb.co.za/index.php?option=com_content&view=article&id =31919:us-army-looking-to-contractors-for-african-operations&catid=56:diplo macy-a-peace&Itemid=111. Some members of Congress favor an even larger presence. In its fiscal year 2015 national defense bill, the House asked the Pentagon to increase the U.S. presence and "achieve the associated basing and access agreements to support such forces across the Continent of Africa."

48. Paul C. Wright, "U.S. Military Intervention in Africa: The New Blueprint for Global Domination," *Global Research*, August 20, 2010, http://www.globalresearch.ca /PrintArticle.php?articleId=20708; Voice of America, "Sao Tome Sparks American Military Interest," October 28, 2009, http://www.voanews.com/content/a-13-2004 -11-12-voa42-66870572/376603.html.

49. BBC News, "US Naval Base to Protect Sao Tome Oil," BBC, August 22, 2002, http:// news.bbc.co.uk/2/hi/business/2210571.stm.

50. James Bellamy Foster, "A Warning to Africa: The New U.S. Imperial Grand Strategy," *Monthly Review* 58, no. 2 (2006), http://www.monthlyreview.org/0606jbf.htm.

51. Michael Klare and Daniel Volman, "America, China and the Scramble for Africa's Oil," *Review of African Political Economy* 33, no. 108 (2006): 298–302.

52. Randal C. Archibold, "China Buys Inroads in the Caribbean, Catching U.S. Notice," *New York Times*, April 7, 2012, http://www.nytimes.com/2012/04/08/world/americas /us-alert-as-chinas-cash-buys-inroads-in-caribbean.html?pagewanted=all.

53. Nick Turse, "The New Obama Doctrine, A Six-Point Plan for Global War Special Ops, Drones, Spy Games, Civilian Soldiers, Proxy Fighters, and Cyber Warfare," *TomDispatch*, June 14, 2012, http://www.tomdispatch.com/archive/175557/nick _turse_the_changing_face_of_empire.

54. Jeremy Scahill, *Dirty Wars: The World Is a Battlefield* (New York: Nation Books, 2013), 4.

55. Priest, *Mission*, 206

56. Lesley Gill, *The School of the Americas: Military Training and Political Violence in the Americas* (Durham, NC: Duke University Press, 2004), 235–37.

57. Peter J. Meyer, "Honduras-U.S. Relations," Congressional Research Service, report, Washington, DC, February 5, 2013, 14.

58. Gill, *School of the Americas*, 235.

59. Vine, *Island of Shame*, chapter. 6.
60. Kaplan, *Imperial Grunts*, 167.
61. Kaplan, *Hog Pilots*, 319.
62. United States Senate Subcommittee on United States Security Agreements and Commitments Abroad, "United States Security Agreements and Commitments Abroad," 2433–34.
63. Klare and Volman, "America, China and the Scramble," 306; Sandra T. Barnes, "Global Flows: Terror, Oil, and Strategic Philanthropy," *African Studies Review* 48, no. 1 (2005): 11.
64. Samantha Hawley, "Cocos Islands: US Military Base, Not in Our Lifetime," *PM*, March 28, 2012, http://www.abc.net.au/pm/content/2012/s3465894.htm; Pauline Bunce, "The Riddle of the Islands: Australia's Oft Forgotten Indigenous Island Community," *Arena Magazine* 128 (2014): 36–38.
65. http://www.cdfa.ca.gov/plant/IPC/weedinfo/nymphaea.htm.
66. Harkavy, *Strategic Basing*, chapter 6.
67. Klare and Volman, "America, China and the Scramble," 307.

17: TRUE SECURITY

1. For this proposal and others, see Howard W. Hallman, "Deficit Reduction by Closing Overseas Bases," European Disarmament, blog, November 8, 2011, https://europeandisarmament.wordpress.com/2011/11/08/deficit-reduction-by-closing-overseas-bases/.
2. Sen. Kay Bailey Hutchison, "Build Bases in America," *Politico*, July 13, 2010, http://www.politico.com/news/stories/0710/39625.html; Sen. Jon Tester, "Tester to Defense Dept.: Close Overseas Military Bases, Not Facilities in the U.S.," press release, Washington, DC, February 29, 2012, http://www.tester.senate.gov/?p=press_release&id=2137.
3. Fox News, "Transcript: Fox News Channel & Wall Street Journal Debate in South Carolina," January 17, 2012, http://foxnewsinsider.com/2012/01/17/transcript-fox-news-channel-wall-street-journal-debate-in-south-carolina/.
4. Nicholas D. Kristof, "The Big (Military) Taboo," *New York Times*, December 25, 2010, http://www.nytimes.com/2010/12/26/opinion/26kristof.html.
5. "New Rules," *Real Time with Bill Maher*, HBO, episode 222, July 29, 2011, http://www.hbo.com/real-time-with-bill-maher/episodes/0/222-episode/article/new-rules.html#/.
6. *Reuters*, "Military Needs to Close More Bases: General," September 15, 2010, http://www.reuters.com/article/2010/09/15/us-pentagon-bases-idUSTRE68E6H420100915.
7. Center for Strategic and International Studies, "2010 Global Security Forum." See also Harkavy, *Strategic Basing*, 167–68.
8. Lostumbo et al., "Overseas Basing of U.S. Military Forces," 291.
9. Calder, *Embattled Garrisons*, 214.
10. Jeffery D. Berejikian, "A Cognitive Theory of Deterrence," *Journal of Peace Research* 39, no. 2 (2002): 169.
11. Baruch Fischhoff, "Do We Want a Better Theory of Deterrence?" *Journal of Social Issues* 43, no. 4 (1987): 73.
12. See e.g. Austin Long, "Deterrence from Cold War to Long War: Lessons from Six

Decades of RAND Deterrence Research" (Santa Monica, CA: RAND Corporation, 2008).

13. Paul K. Huth, "Deterrence and International Conflict: Empirical Findings and Theoretical Debates," *Annual Reviews of Political Science* 2 (1999): 27.

14. Steve Chan, "Extended Deterrence in the Taiwan Strait: Learning from Rationalist Explanations in International Relations," *World Affairs* 166, no. 2 (2003): 109–25.

15. Stephen Glain, "What Actually Motivated Osama bin Laden," *U.S. News & World Report*, May 3, 2011, http://www.usnews.com/opinion/blogs/stephen-glain/2011/05/03/what-actually-motivated-osama-bin-laden.

16. Bradley L. Bowman, "After Iraq: Future U.S. Military Posture in the Middle East," *Washington Quarterly* 31, no. 2 (2008): 85.

17. Nick Turse identified 134 countries in 2014, although Robert D. Kaplan cites 170 countries before 2001. Nick Turse, "The Special Ops Surge: America's Secret War in 134 Countries," *TomDispatch*, January 8, 2014, http://www.tomdispatch.com/blog/175794/tomgram%3A_nick_turse,_secret_wars_and_black_ops_blowback/; Kaplan, *Imperial Grunts*, 7.

18. Lutz, *Homefront*, 9.

19. Kaplan, *Imperial Grunts*, 1–2.

20. John Q. Adams, "She Goes Not Abroad in Search of Monsters to Destroy," *American Conservative*, July 4, 2013, http://www.theamericanconservative.com/repository/she-goes-not-abroad-in-search-of-monsters-to-destroy/.

21. Ibid.

22. National Park Service, "John Quincy Adams Biography," Adams National Historical Park, accessed January 7, 2015, http://www.nps.gov/adam/jqa-bio-page-3.htm.

23. Dwight D. Eisenhower, "Farewell Address," January 17, 1961, *OurDocuments.gov*, http://www.ourdocuments.gov/doc.php?flash=true&doc=90.

24. Ibid.

25. SIPRI 2009. Today, the United States still spends more than twice China's military budget and exceeds the military spending of the next seventeen countries (most of whom are allies) combined.

26. Gillem, *America Town*, 211.

27. *Moscow Times*, "Russia Has a Base in Syria Defense Ministry Seeking New Locations for Air Bases Abroad," February 27, 2014, http://www.themoscowtimes.com/news/article/defense-ministry-seeking-new-locations-for-air-bases-abroad/495332.html.

28. Harkavy, *Strategic Basing*, chapter 6.

29. Klare and Volman, "America, China and the Scramble," 307.

30. *Standing Army*, directed by Fazi and Parenti.

31. Mackenzie Eaglen, "Congress Ignores Pentagon's Drawdown Abroad to Stall Domestic Military Base Closures," *AEIdeas* blog, May 21, 2013.

32. Gordon Lubold, "U.S. Will Keep Cutting Its Bases in Europe, Top General Says," *ForeignPolicy* January 13, 2014, http://www.foreignpolicy.com/posts/2014/01/13/trim_bases_not_boots_why_this_air_force_four_star_thinks_the_us_should_stay_in_euro.

33. Courtney Albon, "USAF Consolidating Excess Infrastructure but Still Calling for Base Closures," *Inside the Air Force*, January 17, 2014.

34. Katherine G. Hammack, "2014 Green Book: The Costly Consequences of Excess Army Infrastructure and Overhead," *Army.mil*, September 30, 2014, http://www

.army.mil/article/134864/2014_Green_Book__The_costly_consequences_of _excess_Army_infrastructure_and_overhead.

35. "Posture of the United States Army Before the Committee on Armed Services," United States House of Representatives, 113th Congress, March 25, 2014, statement of John M. McHugh, Secretary of the Army, and Raymond T. Odierno, Chief of Staff United States Army, 30.

36. Hammack, "2014 Green Book."

37. Ibid.; Eaglen, "Congress Ignores Pentagon"; Albon, "USAF Consolidating Excess"; Lubold, "U.S. Will Keep Cutting."

38. "Consolidated and Further Continuing Appropriations Act, 2015," secs. 110–28.

AUTHOR'S NOTE

1. David Graeber, "Neoliberalism, or the Bureaucratization of the World," in *The Insecure American: How We Got Here and What We Should Do About It*, edited by Hugh Gusterson and Catherine Besteman (Berkeley: University of California Press, 2009), 79–96.

ONLINE RESOURCES

In addition to the books, articles, and other works cited in the notes, the following are some helpful websites for learning more about U.S. military bases overseas and their impacts. (This selection is focused mostly on English-language materials and is far from exhaustive.) Additional information, articles, and other resources are available at davidvine.net.

GENERAL RESOURCES

Base Structure Reports [Department of Defense]: www.acq.osd.mil/ie

GlobalSecurity.org

Militarism Watch: forusa.org/groups/services/militarism-watch

MilitaryBases.com

Military Installations [Department of Defense]: www.militaryinstallations
.dod.mil

"Mission Creep" investigation: www.motherjones.com/politics/2008/08/table
-contents

ROK Drop blog: www.rokdrop.net

Security Assistance Monitor: www.securityassistance.org

BASE CONVERSION AND ALTERNATIVES

Base Tuono, Italy: www.basetuono.it/en

Bonn International Center for Conversion: www.bicc.de

Department of Defense Office of Economic Adjustment: www.oea.gov

Institute for Policy Studies: www.ips-dc.org/projects/peace-economy
-transitions

Presidio of San Francisco Trust: www.presidio.gov

BASE SOCIAL MOVEMENTS

Overviews

Transnational Institute: www.tni.org/archives/act/17124 and www.tni.org
/primer/foreign-military-bases-and-global-campaign-close-them

Africa

America's Codebook: Africa: codebookafrica.wordpress.com

Chagos Refugees Group [Diego Garcia]: www.chagosrefugeesgroup.org

Lalit de Klas [Mauritius]: www.lalitmauritius.org

Resist Africom: org.salsalabs.com/o/1552/t/5734/content.jsp?content_KEY
=3855

UK Chagos Support Association [Diego Garcia]: www.chagossupport.org.uk

Asia

Anti-Bases Campaign Australia: www.anti-bases.org

Close the Base [Okinawa]: www.closethebase.org

Durebang (My Sister's Place) [South Korea]: www.durebang.org

National Campaign for Eradication of Crimes by U.S. Troops in Korea: www
.usacrime.or.kr

No Base Stories Korea: nobasestorieskorea.blogspot.com

Peace Philosophy Centre blog [Japan]: peacephilosophy.blogspot.com

Save Jeju [South Korea]: www.savejejunow.org

Save Life Center [Henoko, Okinawa]: www.geocities.jp/nobasehenoko

Solidarity for Peace and Reunification of Korea: www.spark946.org

Takae blog [Okinawa]: takae.ti-da.net

US for Okinawa: us-for-okinawa.blogspot.com

Working Group for Peace and Demilitarization in Asia and the Pacific: www
.asiapacificinitiative.org

Europe

Antonio Mazzeo's blog [Italy]:
  antoniomazzeoblog.blogspot.com

Bombspotting [Belgium]: www.vredesactie.be/en

Comitato Pace e Disarmo Campania [Naples, Italy]:
  www.pacedisarmo.org

Campaign for the Accountability of American Bases [UK]:
  www.caab.org.uk

DFG-VK [Germany]: www.dfg-vk.de

Etz Langt's [Ansbach, Germany]: www.etz-langts.de

GI Café Germany: www.gicafegermany.com

Global Peace and Justice Coalition [Turkey]:
  www.kureselbak.org

No Dal Molin [Vicenza, Italy]: www.nodalmolin.it

No MUOS [Sicily, Italy]: www.nomuos.org/en

Shannon Watch [Ireland]: www.shannonwatch.org

Latin America

Colombia No Bases Coalition: www.colombianobases.org

COPINH [Honduras]: www.copinh.org

School of the Americas Watch: www.soaw.org

Vieques Vive La Lucha Continua:
  facebook.com/viequesvive

United States

Carlton Meyer overseas base closure list:
  www.g2mil.com/OBCL.htm

DMZ Hawaii/Aloha 'Aina: www.dmzhawaii.org

Global Network Against Weapons and Nuclear Power in Space: www
  .space4peace.org

Guam Chamber of Commerce: www.guamchamber.com.gu/committees
  /armed-forces-committee

Save Pagan Island [Northern Mariana Islands]:
  savepaganisland.org

We Are Guåhan [Guam]: weareguahan.com

Women for Genuine Security: www.genuinesecurity.org

ENVIRONMENTAL DAMAGE

Agent Orange on Okinawa: www.jonmitchellinjapan.com/agent-orange-on
-okinawa.html

Center for Public Environmental Oversight: www.cpeo.org

FAMILY MEMBERS OF MILITARY PERSONNEL

Blue Star Families: www.bluestarfam.org

Department of Defense Military OneSource: www.militaryonesource.mil
/phases-family-life

National Military Families Association: www.militaryfamily.org

Military Families Speak Out: www.militaryfamiliesspeakout.com

Yellow Ribbon Support Foundation: www.yellowribbonsupport.com

FILM

The Insular Empire: America in the Mariana Islands: theinsularempire
.blogspot.com

Living Along the Fenceline: alongthefenceline.com

Occupy Turkey: Resistance in the Baseworld: amyaustinholmes.com/film

Restrepo: restrepothemovie.com

Standing Army: www.snagfilms.com/films/title/standing_army

Stealing a Nation [Diego Garcia]: johnpilger.com/videos/stealing-a-nation

GOVERNMENT RESOURCES

U.S. Air Force Historical Research Agency: www.afhra.af.mil

U.S. Army Center for Military History: www.history.army.mil

U.S. Army Corps of Engineers Office of History: www.usace.army.mil/About
/History.aspx

U.S. Marine Corps History Division: www.mcu.usmc.mil/historydivision
/SitePages/Home.aspx

U.S. Naval History and Heritage Command: www.history.navy.mil

MAPS, MUSEUMS, PHOTOGRAPHY

Civil Rights Struggle, African -American GIs, and Germany: www.aacvr -germany.org

"Fifty-One US Military Outposts": www.mishkahenner.com/filter/works/Fifty -One-US-Military-Outposts

Google Earth map of the world's foreign bases: www.tni.org/archives/act/17252

Guantánamo Public Memory Project: gitmomemory.org

"Limit Telephotography" [domestic U.S. bases]: www.paglen.com/?l=work&s =limit

Rendition Project: www.therenditionproject.org.uk

"Traces of the Soviet Empire" [former Soviet bases]: www.ericlusito.com

"United Bases of America" map: news.nationalpost.com/2011/10/28/graphic -mapping-a-superpower-sized-military

"U.S. Drone and Surveillance Flight Bases in Africa": publicintelligence.net/us -drones-in-africa

"U.S. Empire" map: www.radicalcartography.net/index.html?usempire

MILITARY SPENDING, CONTRACTING, AND CONTRACTOR ABUSE

Costs of National Security Trade-offs tool: www.nationalpriorities.org /interactive-data/trade-offs

Department of Defense Budget Materials: comptroller.defense.gov /BudgetMaterials.aspx

Department of Defense Contract Announcements: www.defense.gov /contracts

House Military Construction, Veterans Affairs, and Related Agencies Subcommittee: appropriations.house.gov/subcommittees/subcommittee/?IssueID =35986

MsSparky.com

Senate Military Construction, Veterans Affairs, and Related Agencies Subcommittee: www.appropriations.senate.gov/subcommittee/military-construction -veterans-affairs-and-related-agencies

Special Commission on Wartime Contracting: www.wartimecontracting.gov [archived]

Special Inspector General for Afghanistan Reconstruction: www.sigar.mil

Special Inspector General for Iraq Reconstruction: www.sigir.mil [archived]

SEXUAL ASSAULT

Department of Defense Safe Helpline: www.safehelpline.org

Department of Defense Sexual Assault Prevention and Response: www.sapr
.mil

RAINN: www.rainn.org/types-of-sexual-assault/military-sexual-trauma

Service Women's Action Network: www.servicewomen.org

U.S. VETERANS

Department of Labor Veterans' Employment and Training Service: www.dol
.gov/vets

Department of Veterans Affairs Resource Directory: www.ebenefits.va.gov
/ebenefits/nrd

Iraq and Afghanistan Veterans Association Referral Program: www.iava.org
/rrrp-contact-us

Iraq Veterans Against the War: www.ivaw.org

Veterans Crisis Line: www.veteranscrisisline.net

Service Members, Veterans, and Families Assistance Center: www.samhsa.gov
/smvf-ta-center

The Soldiers Project: www.thesoldiersproject.org

WAR AND ITS COSTS

American Friends Service Committee: www.afsc.org/key-issues/issue/peace
-policy-advocacy

Code Pink: www.codepink.org/bring_our_war_dollars_home

Costs of War project: www.costsofwar.org

Global Campaign on Military Spending: www.demilitarize.org

"Move the Money": www.peace-action.org/issues/move-the-money

War costs spending counters: www.nationalpriorities.org/cost-of

ACKNOWLEDGMENTS

I am profoundly grateful to everyone who helped me complete this book. Given the breadth of the book's subject matter and geographic scope, I could not have written it without the assistance and generosity of hundreds of people. Thank you especially to everyone who spoke with me about my research, who hosted me during my travels, and who helped arrange visits, tours, meetings, interviews, interpretation and translation, access to research materials, meals, lodging, transportation, and other critical pieces of the project. Authorship rightly belongs to all of us collectively.

With that in mind, I know there is no way to appropriately thank all the people and organizations who helped me. Even listing them all here has been a challenge, and I apologize in advance to anyone I accidentally overlooked. Because I promised anonymity to some of the people I met and interviewed, I cannot thank them by name but their contributions have been critical and I am grateful to them all. Readers should note that acknowledgment by name indicates neither that I used an individual's words or ideas in the text nor that an individual supports any of my conclusions.

For research about Diego Garcia, I will always be incredibly grateful to the Chagos Refugees Group, Chagos Committee (Seychelles), Chagos Football Association, Olivier Bancoult and the entire Bancoult family, Bernadette Dugasse, Richard Gifford, Phil Harvey, Sabrina Jean, Laura Jeffery, Robin Mardemootoo, Peter Sand, Wojtek Sokolowski, Dick Kwan

Tat, Maureen Tong, Andy Worthington, and many, many others. Thank you also to Michael and Jane Tigar, Ali Beydoun, and all the remarkable members, past and present, of the American University UNROW Human Rights Impact Litigation Clinic.

In Ecuador, my deepest thanks to Maria Amelia Viteri and David Barmettler for making all my research—and an unexpectedly extended stay—possible. Thanks also to Toby Bonilla, Alberto Chonillo, Cristina Camacho, Erin Fitz-Henry, Rafael Jacque, Gualdemar Jimenez, Laura Gonzalez, Marcos Martínez, Miguel Moran, Daniel Ponton, Edgar Rios, Fredy Rivera, and my hosts and friends in Manta. I owe a special acknowledgment to the widows and other family members of those who died on the *Jorge IV*. Thank you for sharing such a terrible and sad part of your lives. Although I could not write about the *Jorge IV* in this book, I will be sharing your story soon.

In Germany, thank you to Chris Capps-Schubert, Meike Capps, Barbara Danowski, Bärbel Felden, Flachi, Peter Gramm, Colonel Douglas Hammer, Thomas Leuerer, Maria Höhn, Boris-André Meyer, Elsa Rassbach, Katja Sipple, Rainer Stache, and many others in Ansbach who welcomed me so warmly, Tommy and Rike and all my biking friends with DFG-VK, and the public affairs offices at Ramstein Air Base and Landstuhl Regional Medical Center, including Major Elizabeth Aptekar, Sandra Archer, Kilian Bluemlein, Juan Melendez, Chuck Roberts, and Marie Shaw.

On Guam and in the Northern Mariana Islands, I am deeply grateful for the help of Julian Aguon, Major Aisha Bakkar, Michael Bevacqua, Leevin Camacho, Hope Cristobal Sr., Hope Cristobal Jr., the entire Cristobal family, Annette Donner, Cara Flores-Mayes, Angelique Gonzales, LisaLinda Natividad, James Oelke, Melvin Pat-Borja, Toni Ramirez, Scott Russell, Desiree Taimanglo, Vanessa Warheit, the wonderful couple identified in this book as "Miguel and Janice Mueller," as well as the Andersen Air Force Base public affairs office, attendees at Navy Base Guam Rosh Hashanah services, the Guam Chamber of Commerce and its armed services committee, MITT EIS representatives who graciously helped answer my questions, the University of Guam, Famoksaiyan, and We are Guåhan.

For my research in Guantánamo Bay, Cuba, thank you to Jana Lipman,

Mark Denbeaux, Anant Raut, and the public affairs offices and all those I met (but cannot name) at Naval Station Guantánamo Bay and Joint Task Force GTMO, whose help and friendship I greatly appreciate.

For my research in Honduras, a huge thanks to Jeremy Bigwood, Dario Euraque, Dana Frank, Adam Isaacson, Bertha Oliva and COFA-DEH, Adrienne, Lilia, Camille, Oscar, Simón, the public affairs office at Soto Cano Air Base, and many other Hondurans and U.S. military personnel and officials whom I cannot name for reasons of confidentiality.

In Italy, there are more people to thank than space allows. Please know that I will always treasure my experiences and all the people I met in Vicenza, Napoli, Pisa/Livorno, Roma, Genova, and beyond. Thanks to Laura Bettini, Michael Blim, Cinzia Bottene, Lenka Coufalíková, Manuel Falsarella, Giorgio Gallo, Lindsay Harris, Chiara Ingrosso, Olol Jackson, Francesco Lenci, Antonio Mazzeo, Fabio Mini, Marco Palma, Panificio Claretta, Francesco Pavin, Alberto Peruffo, Mario Pianta, Pizzeria da Michele, Gordon Poole, Kambiz Razzaghi, Susana Revolti, Angelica Romano, Philip Rushton, Sonia Salvini, carabinieri "Starksy and Hutch," Alix Tindall, Laura Testoni, Mayor Achille Variati, Stephanie West-brook, Katherine Wilson and Salvatore Avallone, Laura Zanardi, Giorgio Zanardi, and Berti, as well as many, many more in Vicenza, including Anna, Caterina, Delfino, Diletta, Emanuele, Fede, Grappa, Janis, Jimi, La Billo, Lorena, Marta, Martina, Massimo, Monica, Moran, Nicoletta, Rosella, Ska, Umberto, and all the amazing volunteers who have made the Festival No Dal Molin possible. Thanks also to the following groups: Assemblea Permanente We Want Sex, Casa per la Pace, Presidio Perma-nente No Dal Molin, Gruppo Donne No Dal Molin, and the public affairs offices at U.S. Army Garrison Vicenza and Aviano Air Base. A very special *grazie* to Guido Lanaro, Giulia Rampon, Chiara Spadaro, Francesca Marin, and Marco Palma for their help with interpretation, translation, analysis, and so much more in Vicenza. *Grazie mille* to Luca Rigon and Martina Copiello and to everyone who always welcomed me so warmly at Ca' Fornaci and made my research possible in so many ways. To Enzo Ciscato, Annetta Reams, and Emily Ciscato, I am listening to "Thank You" as I write this and will be forever grateful for all that we have shared.

In Japan, I am deeply thankful to Kozue Akibayashi, Lawrence Ber-lin, Daniel Broudy, Mitzi Uehara Carter, Robert Eldridge, Daniel Garrett, Eiichiro Ishiyama, Masami Mel Kawamura, Chie Miyagi, Christopher Nelson, Masahide Ota, Junko Otsuki, Michael and Gretchen Robbins, Makiko Sato, Peter Simpson, Chiyomi Sumida, Suzuyo Takazato, Yuki Tanaka, Miyume Tanji, Sunao Tobaru, Jessica Torres, Travis Tritten, Rose Welsch, Ginowan City Hall, the public affairs office at Kadena Air Base, Camp Smedley Butler, and many more friends and hosts in Tokyo, Iwakuni, Fukuoka, Naha, Takae, and Henoko. Special thanks for the help and always thoughtful engagement of Sayo, Jessica, Erin, Philemon, Elise, Anthony, Claire, Cydni, Daniel, Bethany, Tori, Huong, Vijaya, Chandler, and Charmaine.

For my research in South Korea, thank you to Christine Ahn, Wooksik Cheong, Sung-Hee Choi, Youngsil Kang, YouKyoung Ko, Mayor Dong-Kyun Kang, Seungsook Moon, Alpha Newberry, Hye-Ran Oh, Jung-Eun Park, Yunae Park, Regina Pyon, So-Hee Lee, Emily Wang, Yu Youngnim, the staff at Durebang, and all the wonderful and inspiring friends that I met on Jeju and elsewhere in Korea.

In the United States and elsewhere, thank you to Holly Barker, Gen. B. B. Bell, Rob Borofsky, Michael Cernea, Ted Conover, Kelvin Crow, CUNY's Graduate Center, Dave Davis, Peggy Madden Davitt, Ray DuBois, Lacy Dwyer, Daniel Else, Mieke Eoyang, Hermon Farahi, Paul Farmer, Bruce Gagnon, Lesley Gill, Dayne Goodwin, Zoltan Grossman, Matt Gutmann, Dud Hendrick, Andrew Hoehn, Amy Holmes, Raed Jarrar, Barbara Rose Johnston, Kyle Kajihiro, Rev. Deborah Lee, Louise Lennihan, Edward Luttwak, Tom Maloney, Barbara Miller, Leith Mullings, Network of Concerned Anthropologists, John Pike, Walter Pincus, Estefania Ponti, Barry Pavel, Henry Precht, Stephen Rossetti, Deb Sawyer, Lenny Siegel, Kent Slowinski, Sarah Stillman, SWAN, Nick Turse, Wilbert van der Zeijden, Andrew Yeo, Lesley Sharp, Nancy Chen, the School of Advanced Research and our Biosecurity and Vulnerability conference, and all the Pentagon officials and public affairs officers who assisted with my work, among many others. Thank you very much to Conrad Martin and the Stewart R. Mott Foundation's Fund for Constitutional Government for a grant to support some of my research travel in 2011–2012.

Among my many teachers, several base experts deserve special thanks for teaching me so generously, for their pathbreaking work, and for their friendship. They include Cynthia Enloe, John Feffer, Joseph Gerson, Hugh Gusterson, John Lindsay-Poland, Catherine Lutz, Kate McCaffrey, Miriam Pemberton, and Emira Woods.

In the writing of *Base Nation*, I am deeply thankful for the careful reading that many people gave to the book's chapters and for their thoughtful feedback. Others provided timely and much-needed advice about the book cover, title, and maps. They include Julian Aguon, Dan Aibel, Leevin Camacho, Natalie Chwalisz, Enzo Ciscato, Annie Claus, Bill Cummings, Cynthia Enloe, John Feffer, Dana Frank, Beth Geglia, Joseph Gerson, Sam Goodstein, Joan Greenbaum, Lindsay Harris, Dan Hirsch, Maria Höhn, Amy Holmes, Kate Horner, Ben King, Gwyn Kirk, Josh Kletzkin, Brooke Kroeger, Guido Lanaro, Willow Lawson, John Lindsay-Poland, Jana Lipman, Kate McCaffrey, Siobhán McGuirk, Anna Mecagni, Trisha Miller, Satoko Norimatsu, James Oelke, Alix Olson, Marco Palma, Joowon Park, Miriam Pemberton, Adrienne Pine, Marsha Pinson, Rachel Pinson, Max Pinson, Estefania Ponti, Elsa Rassbach, Annetta Reams, Joeva Rock, Chiara Spadaro, Elly Truitt, Kalfani Ture', Adam Vine, Joanne Vine, John Vine, Katherine Wilson, and Laura Zanardi.

Thank you to my wonderful Writers' Group friends, Hilary Galland, Kate Horner, Sarah Hughes, Andrea Johnson, Radha Kuppalli, and Adrienne Pine, not just for their brilliant feedback but also for enriching my life. I am incredibly grateful to Anna Stein for helping me craft my book proposal and improve my writing over many years. Thanks to Fred Appel for his long-standing support and friendship. Thank you to Chuck Lewis for taking an interest in my work and encouraging me with such enthusiasm. Thanks to Arnie and Susan Lutzker for generously helping with the book contract.

I will always be profoundly indebted to Shirley Lindenbaum and Michael Tigar for giving me the opportunity to work with the Chagossians and thus setting me on this path. Thank you, Brooke Kroeger, for your never-ending support, advice, and mentorship as a writer and in life. You are always there for me, and I am so grateful. Thanks to Rob Rosenthal for always being there no matter how much time has passed since the last visit.

At Metropolitan Books and Henry Holt, thank you to everyone who made the production of this book possible. Without exception, the entire team has been incredibly helpful and a pleasure to work with. I will be always grateful that you embraced this book and helped it into the world. Thank you especially to Sara Bershtel and Grigory Tovbis for your incredible editing work and for all you have done to guide the book and me through the publication process. Grigory, thank you for your remarkably hard work. You helped me clarify my writing and my thinking, and you improved the book in innumerable ways. I can't thank you enough for all your patience and willingness to forge the book together in such a collaborative fashion.

Thanks also to Kelly Too for your beautiful design work; to David Shoemaker and the other designers who created such a powerful cover and listened so carefully to my feedback; to Connor Guy and Christopher O'Connell for all of your terrific and hard work in the production process; and to Emily DeHuff for your careful copyediting and the many ways you improved the book, in both style and substance.

I will always be grateful to Tom Engelhardt and Steve Fraser for allowing me to join the "American Empire" series. I long harbored a dream that I might publish *Base Nation* in your important collection of books. Thank you for making it possible and for all your guidance, advice, and support. Thanks, too, to Tom for supporting my writing at TomDispatch .com. You made another of my wishes come true when you published my first article. I can't thank you enough for your help, your patience, and your understanding, when I know I've given you more than a few headaches!

Special appreciation also goes to Kelly Martin, the book's cartographer. Thank you, Kelly, for your incredibly hard work over such a long time. You produced gorgeous maps that are an incredibly important addition to the book. I can't thank you enough for putting up with my frequent changes and for working together to bring to life my vision for the maps. Thanks also to Johnny Harris and John Emerson for your equally hard work, and patience, on the Guam, Okinawa, and "Native Lands" maps. Thank you to all the wonderful photographers whose work is found in these pages and to everyone who granted permission to use an image.

At American University, thank you to so many colleagues and friends for your help and support through all the years that I worked on this book. Thank you to everyone in the Department of Anthropology community— undergraduates, graduates, faculty, and staff—for assisting me in so many ways. I wish I could name everyone here, but please know that I feel incredibly lucky to share a home with all of you. A special thanks goes to several remarkable research assistants who provided critical help: Mohammed Ali Lutfy, Andrea Elganzoury, Laura Jung, Menna Khalil, Sayo Saruta, and Michel Tinguiri. Thanks to Siobhán McGuirk for your always thoughtful work, often with tight deadlines, and for continually pushing my thinking (on bases, football, and otherwise). Thanks also to many tremendous colleagues who have taught me so much: Mysara Abu-Hashem, Sammi Aryani, Hope Bastian Martinez, Sarah Block, Abby Conrad, Robert Craycraft, Kaelyn Forde, Sean Furmage, Allie Gardner, Sabrina Gavigan, Beth Geglia, Harjant Gill, Rebecca Stone Gordon, Tony Gualtieri, Jeanne Hanna, Nell Haynes, Patrick Irelan, Dylan Kerrigan, Ben King, Anoosh Khan, Kelly Kundrat, Adomas Lapinskas, Emily Lelandais, Karen Lindsey, Julie Maldonado, Tam Mihailovic, Devin Molina, Ana Rebecca Mora, Deborah Murphy, Michelle Nelson, Kara Newhouse, Alexandra Papagno, Joowon Park, Chris Partridge, Becca Peixotto, Joeva Rock, Alyssa Rohricht, Serafima Rombe-Shulman, Carolina Sandoval, Rebecca Simpson, Michael Slater, Micah Trapp, Rodolfo Tello Abanto, Matt Thomann, Kalfani Ture', John Villecco, and Matt Wickens among many others. (Sorry not to be able to include everyone!)

Thank you to everyone in my "Understanding War, Building Peace" and "Writing Ethnography" classes, the Anthropology of Militarism Clinic, and the Thesis and Dissertation Seminar, as well as my other classes, for allowing me to share some of my thinking about the book and works in progress. Your feedback and encouragement have been incredibly helpful. Thank you to Juana Castro, Marta Portillo, Jacki Daddona, Jennifer Miranda, Stacy Terrell, and Jeanie Wogaman, and all our great work-study students for your terrific support.

Thank you to my other great colleagues who have supported me as friends and academics: Geoff Burkhart, Annie Claus, Audrey Cooper, Joe Dent, Nell Gabiam, Joan Gero, Dolores Koenig, Chap Kusimba, Sibel Kusimba, Bill Leap, David Lowry, Bryan McNeil, Adrienne Pine, Sabiyha Prince, Dan Sayers, Gretchen Schafft, Nina Shapiro-Perl, Judith Singleton, Ed Smith, Emily Steinmetz, Ayako Takamori, Sue Taylor, Brett Williams, Rachel Watkins, and Joshua Woodfork. A special thanks goes to Bill and Brett for being remarkable mentors, scholarly models, and friends; to Annie for reading and commenting on my writing, not to mention the baking; and to Adrienne for all your bighearted help in making my Honduras research possible.

Many others at American University have also been incredibly supportive. Thank you to Dean Peter Starr and Provost Scott Bass and the College of Arts and Sciences for providing research funds and critical time away from teaching, without which I could not have completed this book. Thanks also to many other wonderful supporters and friends, including Gordon Adams, Jennifer Arnold, Kim Blankenship, Daniel Esser, Mimi Fittig, Peggy Eskow, Max Paul Friedman, Nikhat Ghouse, Louis Goodman, Hadar Harris, Peter Kuznick, Carl LeVan, Charles Lewis, Jordan Maidman, Celine Marie-Pascale, Lynne Perri, Gwendolyn Reece, Cathy Schneider, Courtney Schrader, Susan Shepler, U. J. Sofia, Shoshana Sumka, Lauren Tabbara, Salvador Vidal-Ortiz, Barbara Wien, Sharon Weiner, Elizabeth Worden, and Matt Zembrzuski and the IRB.

There are many other beloved friends and family who have supported, sustained, and assisted me through this long process. Although I will surely forget some (sorry!), they include Roberto Abadie, Tick Ahearn, Max and Sonja Aibel, Sarah Kowal Alden, Blumenthals, Lisa Braun, Natalie Chwalisz, CAJ, Patricia Cogley, Jon and Gabriel Cook and Caroline Simmonds, Lindsay Davison, Dworkins, Andrew Epstein, FCB, Eric Frater, French's Dry Cleaners, Fritz, the Gan, the Goobs, Theo Goodstein, Alex Goren, Shaun and Adelaide Greenbaum and Antonia Stout, Josep Guardiola, Mamadou Gueye, Claire and Sue and Rudy Hirsch, Joanne Hirsch and A. T. Stephens, Megan Isaacson, Kiki Jenkins, Elizabeth Kanter, Lynn and Morris and David Kletzkin, Amy and Ken and Lydia and Rachel Krupsky, Linda Kuzmack, Nicole Laborde and Dylan Turner, Randi and Steve and Brenna Lavelle, Brian and Todd Levin, Kanhong Lin, Rae Linefsky, Kristen Lionetti, Lori Lovell and Shaun and Khyrell and Kiara McNeil, Leo M., Carola Mandelbaum and Roee and Olivia and Amalia Raz, Anna Mecagni, Enio and Concha and Leticia Molina, Derek Musgrove, Elli Nagai-Rothe, Kellye Nakahara, Jaime and Zinn Olson-Masick, Gary Olson, Laura Olson, Sascha Paladino, Park Monroe,

Quincy Street, Reyes family, Alison and Matt and Vivian and Veronica Rodgers, Rosenthals, Cliff Rosky, TaRita Scott, Mara Silver, Ed and Ellen and Jeremy and David and Jonathan Singer-Vine, Mitzi Sinnott, Roy Skeen, Mary Stephens, everyone at Stevens Plumbing, Karen Storey and Pam Dickinson and all the friends I met on Amtrak as I finished the book, Cathy Sulzberger and Joe Perpich, Maria Tonguino, Jancy Tonken, Mauricio Tscherny, Ellis Turner, Hugh and Lydia Vine, Lee Ving, David Vise, Katie Wiedmann, Vanessa White, and Deb Yurow.

Finally, thank you Mom, Dad, Joanne, Adam, Rachel, and Max for your love and never-ending support every day. I love you.

In addition to those named at the start of the book, *Base Nation* is dedicated to the memory of several of the most important and inspiring teachers and guides I will ever have. They will always be with us: Doere Bernhard, Vera Isenberg, Marty Pinson, Neil Smith, Lisette Aurélie Talate, and Neal Tonken.

INDEX

Page numbers in *italics* refer to maps and illustrations.

ABOUT THE AUTHOR

David Vine, an associate professor of anthropology at American University in Washington, D.C., is the author of *Island of Shame: The Secret History of the U.S. Military Base on Diego Garcia*. His writing has appeared in *The New York Times*, *The Washington Post*, *The Guardian*, *Mother Jones*, and *The Chronicle of Higher Education*, among other publications.

THE AMERICAN EMPIRE PROJECT

In an era of unprecedented military strength, leaders of the United States, the global hyperpower, have increasingly embraced imperial ambitions. How did this significant shift in purpose and policy come about? And what lies down the road?

The American Empire Project is a response to the changes that have occurred in America's strategic thinking as well as in its military and economic posture. Empire, long considered an offense against America's democratic heritage, now threatens to define the relationship between our country and the rest of the world. The American Empire Project publishes books that question this development, examine the origins of U.S. imperial aspirations, analyze their ramifications at home and abroad, and discuss alternatives to this dangerous trend.

The project was conceived by Tom Engelhardt and Steve Fraser, editors who are themselves historians and writers. Published by Metropolitan Books, an imprint of Henry Holt and Company, its titles include *Hegemony or Survival* and *Failed States* by Noam Chomsky, *The Limits of Power* and *Washington Rules* by Andrew J. Bacevich, *Blood and Oil* by Michael T. Klare, *Kill Anything That Moves* by Nick Turse, *A People's History of American Empire* by Howard Zinn, and *Empire's Workshop* by Greg Grandin.

For more information about the American Empire Project and for a list of forthcoming titles, please visit americanempireproject.com.